Energy Policy Advancement

Dmitry Kurochkin · Martha J. Crawford · Elena V. Shabliy

Editors

Energy Policy Advancement

Climate Change Mitigation and International Environmental Justice

 Springer

Editors
Dmitry Kurochkin
Harvard University
Cambridge, MA, USA

Martha J. Crawford
Jack Welch College of Business
Sacred Heart University
Fairfield, CT, USA

Elena V. Shabliy
New York University (NYU)
New York, NY, USA

ISBN 978-3-030-84992-4   ISBN 978-3-030-84993-1   (eBook)
https://doi.org/10.1007/978-3-030-84993-1

This Springer imprint is published by the registered company Springer Nature Switzerland AG
The registered company address is: Gewerbestrasse 11, 6330 Cham, Switzerland

Foreword

The current global COVID-19 pandemic and panic have revealed just how unprepared many nations are for massive widespread health crises and how their populations, especially those communities already living in precarity, are even more vulnerable than had been widely recognized or acknowledged. It is one thing to be quarantined not to mention become ill in a comfortable home with employment and/or finances relatively intact and a stockpile of necessities, and quite another to be laid off after one's place of employment has been shut down, after already working multiple jobs yet living paycheck to paycheck without the resources to prepare. But as frightening and disruptive COVID-19 has been to the lives of billions worldwide, we are even less prepared for the increasingly severe upheavals that human-induced climate change is certain to cause, upheavals that—given our knowledge of COVID-19 as of March 2020—will dwarf even the nearly unprecedented impacts of this disease. Long after researchers develop a vaccine and/or treatment for COVID-19 and long after this devastating illness has run its course, climate disruption will continue to plague the planet.

It is too early to predict with any certainty the fallout from COVID-19, the origins of which are not unrelated to increased human encroachment into a broader range of ecosystems. But what was obvious long before this disease became a pandemic was that the earlier cities, regions, and nations took action to contain the virus, the less severe their losses. And what rapidly became apparent as this disease accelerated and began impacting communities exponentially was that so much could have been done before the outbreak to prepare for such a pandemic and by so doing mitigate loss. These cautions are equally applicable to combatting not only future pandemics but also climate change and injustice/inequality. The sooner we start doing what we know needs to be done, the less severe the fallout for both human communities and the planet.

Cambridge, MA, USA
March 2020

Karen Thornber
thornber@fas.harvard.edu

Contents

Editors and Contributors

About the Editors

Dr. Dmitry Kurochkin is a Senior Research Analyst at Harvard University, where he teaches Data Science, Time Series Analysis, and Econometrics. Dmitry graduated *magna cum laude* from Lomonosov Moscow State University where he majored in Physics and earned his Ph.D. in Mathematics at Tulane University. Kurochkin is an interdisciplinary scholar and holds Master's Degrees in Applied Mathematics, Statistics, Chemistry, and Economic Analysis and Policy. He is a co-editor of *Renewable Energy: International Perspectives on Sustainability* (Palgrave Macmillan, 2019), *Global Perspectives on Women's Leadership and Gender (In)Equality* (Palgrave Macmillan, 2020), and *Discourses on Sustainability: Climate Change, Clean Energy, and Justice* (Palgrave Macmillan, 2020).

Dr. Martha J. Crawford is Dean of the Jack Welch College of Business & Technology at Sacred Heart University. She has both business and academic experience. She has served as senior vice president of Research & Development for several companies based in France such as L'Oreal and Air Liquide, where she has worked to foster technological innovation. Her academic background includes having taught MBA core-curriculum courses at the Harvard Business School on leadership and corporate responsibility in addition to developing a course on energy that was nominated for a national prize. Crawford earned her master's degree in business administration from the Collège des Ingénieurs in Paris and MS and doctorate degrees in environmental and chemical engineering from Harvard University. She has also served as a board member in both academic and professional settings for Sevres International School, French National Labs for Scientific Research and French National Energy Labs and board director for Altran, Suez and Ipsen all in France. Crawford also has several publications focusing on environmental management and quality.

Dr. Elena V. Shabliy is a Visiting Scholar at Columbia University and NYU; she was a Visiting Scholar at Harvard University in 2015–2017, NYU in 2020, and Boston University in 2020–2021. She is the editor of *Representations of the Blessed Virgin Mary in World Literature and Art* (Lexington, Rowman and Littlefield, 2017) and co-editor of *Emancipation Women's Writing at Fin de Siècle* (Routledge, 2018), *Renewable Energy: International Perspectives* (Palgrave Macmillan, 2019), *Global Perspectives on Women's Leadership and Gender (In)Equality* (Palgrave Macmillan, 2020), *Discourses on Sustainability: Climate Change, Clean Energy, and Justice* (Palgrave Macmillan, 2020), and *Women's Human Rights in Nineteenth-Century Literature and Culture* (Lexington, Rowman and Littlefield, 2020). She studied at Lomonosov Moscow State University; in 2018, Dr. Shabliy was a Postdoctoral Fellow at Harvard University.

Contributors

Edidiong Samuel Akpabio Department of Political Science, Trinity University, Lagos, Nigeria

Sedat Alataş Department of Economics, Faculty of Economics and Administrative Sciences, Aydın Adnan Menderes University, Nazilli, Aydin, Turkey

Mathias N. Bimir Hong Kong University of Science and Technology, Hong Kong, China

Mohomodou Boncana Department of Social Sciences, University of the Virgin Islands, Charlotte Amalie, U.S.A.

Correen Celestine Creative Leadership for Innovation and Change, University of the Virgin Islands, Charlotte Amalie, U.S.A.

Martha J. Crawford Jack Welch College of Business, Sacred Heart University, Fairfield, CT, USA

Christophe Dongmo Leiden University African Studies Centre, Leiden, Netherlands

Marcin Gabryś Department of Canadian Studies, Jagiellonian University, Kraków, Poland

Dmitry Kurochkin Cambridge, USA

Miriam Matejova Department of Political Science, Masaryk University, Brno, Czech Republic

Ilive Peltier Creative Leadership for Innovation and Change, University of the Virgin Islands, Charlotte Amalie, U.S.A.

Elena V. Shabliy Cambridge, USA

Gz. MeeNilankco Theiventhran Department of Computer Science, Electrical Engineering and Mathematical Science, Western Norway University of Applied Science, Bergen, Norway

Erginbay Uğurlu Faculty of Economics and Administrative Sciences, Istanbul Aydın University, Istanbul, Turkey

Małgorzata Zachara-Szymańska Faculty of International Topolowa 6/13 and Political Studies, Jagiellonian University, Krakow, Poland

Chapter 1
Climate Policy Advancement and International Environmental Justice

Elena V. Shabliy and Dmitry Kurochkin

Abstract Sustainability and environmental policies are complex and multidimensional problems, requiring political, economic, business, scientific, legal, and philosophical approaches (Cohen, Understanding environmental policy. Columbia University Press, 2006). Most countries, competent policymakers, and other stakeholders recognize the importance and urgency of climate change mitigation and adaptation, as well as the need for dynamic energy policies advancement and environment-oriented course of principle and immediate climate action. The quality of the environment depends on all stakeholders, and this quality could be also interpreted as a public good consumed by all members of society. At local and international levels, country Parties develop and adopt new best-practice climate policies seeking new solutions in meaningful and constructive climate change dialogue and promotion of environmental justice principles. Plato, Aristotle, Adam Smith, Karl Marx, John Rawls, John Mill, Amartya Sen, and many other influential thinkers contemplated on the theme of justice.

Introduction

Max Weber (1864–1920), in his essay "Politics as Vocation" (1919), defines the concept of *policy*, speaking of the currency policy of the banks, the strike policy of a traded union, the educational policy of a municipality or a township, the policy of the president of a voluntary association, etc.[1] The *Concise Oxford Dictionary* provides the following definition of *policy*: "[A] course of principle or action adopted or

---

[1] Weber (1965).

E. V. Shabliy (✉) · D. Kurochkin
Cambridge, USA
e-mail: eshabliy@g.harvard.edu

D. Kurochkin
e-mail: dkurochkin@fas.harvard.edu

D. Kurochkin et al. (eds.), *Energy Policy Advancement*,
https://doi.org/10.1007/978-3-030-84993-1_1

proposed by an organization or individual."[2] The second meaning of *policy* that the *Dictionary* suggests is "a contract of insurance."[3] Public policy scientists developed multiple frameworks, models, and theories to grasp the policy-making process (Weible et al., 2012; Birkland, 2010). Some scholars understand the policy design process as a failure to produce a single unifying theory.[4] (Larimer and Smith 2017; Weible et al. 2012). Sustainability and environmental policies are complex and multi-dimensional problems, requiring political, economic, business, scientific, legal, and philosophical approaches (Cohen, 2006). Most countries, competent policymakers, and stakeholders recognize the importance and urgency of climate change mitigation and adaptation strategies, as well as the need for dynamic energy policies advancement and environment-oriented course of principle and immediate climate action. The quality of the environment depends on all stakeholders, and this quality could be also interpreted as a public good consumed by all members of society.[5] At local and international levels, country Parties develop and adopt new best-practice climate policies seeking new solutions in meaningful and constructive climate change dialogue and promotion of environmental justice principles. Plato, Aristotle, Adam Smith, John Rawls, John Mill, Amartya Sen, and many other influential thinkers contemplated on the theme of justice. The theoretical underpinning of international environmental justice is still developing. When one discusses energy justice, for example, an important triumvirate occurs: distributive, procedural, and recognition justice. Distributive and procedural justice are closely related to the environmental justice movement.[6, 7]

In the U.S., federal agencies consider environmental justice in their activities under the National Environmental Policy Act (NEPA).[8] NEPA was enacted in 1969

---

[2] Pearsall (1999), 1106. The online Oxford dictionary provides a more detailed definition: "A principle or course of action adopted or proposed as desirable, advantageous, or expedient; esp. one formally advocated by a government, political party, etc." https://www.oed.com/view/Entry/146 842?rskey=Ob6eQC&result=1#eid (Last accessed 09/28/2020). This word has an archaic meaning as well: "prudent or expedient conduct of action."

[3] Ibid.

[4] Christopher M. Weible et al. "Understanding and Influencing the Policy Process." *Policy Sciences* 45, 1–21 (2012).

[5] Baumol and Oates (1975), 2.

[6] Salter et al. (2018), 3.

[7] See also Shabliy et al. (2020).

[8] "Environmental Justice Considerations in the NEPA Process," https://www.epa.gov/environmenta ljustice/environmental-justice-and-national-environmental-policy-act (Last accessed 10/05/2020). The environmental justice movement was started in the U.S in the 1960s, mostly by individuals, primarily people of color, who wished to address the inequality of environmental protection in the communities. WE ACT was one of the first New York's environmental justice organizations. In 1992, the Office of Environmental Justice (in the beginning—the Environmental Equity Group) was established. In 2010, the White House Forum on Environmental Justice invited Cabinet members and senior-level officials from various agencies, including the Department of Labor, the Department of Energy, and the Department of Justice, as well as other officials to support environmental justice dialogue. Please see: "A Promise of Environmental Justice for All Americans," https://oba mawhitehouse.archives.gov/blog/2010/12/20/a-promise-environmental-justice-all-americans (Last

and President Nixon signed it into law on January 1, 1970,[9] which is one of the first major environmental laws in the U.S. and often referred to as the "Magna Carta" of environmental laws.[10] The United States Environmental Agency (EPA) was established on July 9, 1970, and began to operate after Nixon signed an Executive Order, Reorganization Plan No. 3 of 1970. One of the EPA's principal roles is strengthening environmental protection programs and recommending policy changes.[11] NEPA is also responsible for establishing the U.S. national environmental policies.[12] In 2020, there was the 50th Anniversary of the Clean Air Act that was signed by President Nixon to foster the growth of a strong economy and industry while also improving human health conditions and the environment.[13]

Michael B. Gerrard writes that Environmental Justice (EJ) "arose in the context of siting of polluting facilities, such as landfills and incinerators, in low-income and minority communities."[14] In the U.S., environmental law and environmental justice developed around the notion that they are aimed at mitigating the adverse influence of discrete facilities.[15] The White House Council on Environmental Quality (CEQ) issued *Environment Justice; Guidance Under the National Environmental Policy Act* (in light of Executive Order 12,898 signed by President Clinton in 1994).[16] EJ Interagency Working Group (IWG) and NEPA Committee advance environmental justice principles through NEPA implementation and promote a more consistent and effective consideration of environmental justice during NEPA reviews.[17] Federal Guidance on Environmental Justice has six principles for environmental justice to

---

accessed 10/05/2020); "Environmental Justice," https://www.epa.gov/environmentaljustice/enviro nmental-justice-timeline (Last accessed 10/05/2020).

[9] "A Citizen's Guide to the NEPA. Having Your Voice Heard," December 2007: https://ceq.doe. gov/docs/get-involved/Citizens_Guide_Dec07.pdf (Last accessed 10/05/2020).

[10] Ibid.

[11] "Reorganization Plan No. 3 of 1970," https://archive.epa.gov/epa/aboutepa/reorganization-plan-no-3-1970.html (Last accessed 10/05/2020). EPA plays an important role in other agencies' NEPA processes; it is required to review and analyze the impact to the environment. Please see: "A Citizen's Guide to the NEPA. Having Your Voice Heard," December 2007: https://ceq.doe.gov/docs/get-inv olved/Citizens_Guide_Dec07.pdf (Last accessed 10/05/2020).

[12] "A Citizen's Guide to the NEPA. Having Your Voice Heard," December 2007: https://ceq.doe. gov/docs/get-involved/Citizens_Guide_Dec07.pdf (Last accessed 10/05/2020).

[13] "Clean Air Act Overview" https://www.epa.gov/clean-air-act-overview/40th-anniversary-clean-air-act#:~:text=The%20Clean%20Air%20Act%20was,human%20health%20and%20the%20envi ronment (Last accessed 5/25/2021); See also https://www.epa.gov/clean-air-act-overview/50th-anniversary-clean-air-act (Last accessed 5/26/2021).

[14] Michael B. Gerrard, "What Does Environmental Justice Mean in an Era of Global Climate Change?" *Journal of Environmental and Sustainability Law* Volume 19 Issue 2 Spring 2013: 282.

[15] Ibid., 282–283.

[16] "A Citizen's Guide to the NEPA. Having Your Voice Heard," December 2007: https://ceq.doe. gov/docs/get-involved/Citizens_Guide_Dec07.pdf (Last accessed 10/05/2020).

[17] "Promising Practices for EJ Methodologies in NEPA Reviews Report of the Federal Interagency Working Group on Environmental Justice & NEPA Committee" https://www.epa.gov/sites/pro duction/files/2016-08/documents/nepa_promising_practices_document_2016.pdf (Last accessed 10/05/2020).

"determine any disproportionately high and adverse human health or environmental effects to low-income, minority, and tribal populations."[18] Congress directed that all environmental policies, regulations, and public laws of the U.S. should be administered and interpreted in accordance with the NEPA policies; the NEPA policy implementation presupposes the environmental effect assessment process.[19]

Executive Order 12,898 has to ensure that "each Federal agency shall make achieving environmental justice part of its mission by identifying and addressing, as appropriate, disproportionately high and adverse human health or environmental effects of its programs, policies, and activities on minority populations and low-income populations in the United States and its territories and possessions, the District of Columbia, the Commonwealth of Puerto Rico, and the Commonwealth of the Mariana Islands."[20] The Order specified that each agency should develop an agency-wide environmental justice strategy.[21] EPA's Office of Environmental Justice gives the following definition of EJ: "The fair treatment and meaningful involvement of all people regardless of race, color, national origin, or income with respect to the development, implementation, and enforcement of environmental laws, regulations, and policies. Fair treatment means that no group of people, including racial, ethnic, or socioeconomic group should bear a disproportionate share of the negative environmental consequences resulting from industrial, municipal, and commercial operations or the execution of federal, state, local, and tribal programs and policies."[22] The EPA and the State Department collaborate to improve the environment not only in the U.S. but also internationally. The EPA discusses its programs with foreign countries on a regular basis, providing financial assistance to other countries when it is needed for environmental and public health protection program realization.[23] In 2016, the EPA Office of Environmental Justice participated, for example, in the Organisation for Economic Co-operation and Development (OECD) Environmental Review of Korea; the Korean Ministry of the Environment sought EPA's expertise in environmental justice.[24]

---

[18] "Environmental Justice Considerations 1n the NEPA Process," https://www.epa.gov/environmentaljustice/environmental-justice-and-national-environmental-policy-act (Last accessed 10/05/2020).

[19] "A Citizen's Guide to the NEPA. Having Your Voice Heard," December 2007: https://ceq.doe.gov/docs/get-involved/Citizens_Guide_Dec07.pdf (Last accessed 10/05/2020).

[20] "Presidential Documents," https://www.archives.gov/files/federal-register/executive-orders/pdf/12898.pdf (Last accessed 10/04/2020).

[21] Ibid.

[22] "Final Guidance for Incorporating Environmental Justice Concerns in EPA's NEPA Compliance Analyses," https://www.epa.gov/sites/production/files/2014-08/documents/ej_guidance_nepa_epa0498.pdf (Last accessed 10/04/2020).

[23] "EPA's Role in Promoting International Human Rights, Rights of Indigenous Peoples, and Environmental Justice," https://www.epa.gov/environmentaljustice/epas-role-promoting-international-human-rights-rights-indigenous-peoples-and#:~:text=Issues%20of%20environmental%20justice%20%E2%80%93%20meaning,in%20the%20context%20of%20human (Last accessed 10/05/2020).

[24] Ibid.

There is strong scientific evidence that human-caused climate change is harmful; many U.S. cities and states adopt and advance climate change policies, programs, and initiatives.[25] The Clean Water Act, the Safe Drinking Water Act, the National Environmental Policy Act, the Resource Conservation and Recovery Act (RCRA), the Emergency Planning and Community Right-to-Know Act, the Toxic Substances Control Act, the EPA's tribal programs, and the EPA's grants, the Comprehensive Environmental Response, as well as Compensation and Liability Act are very important legal frameworks in the promotion of environmental justice goals.[26]

The global environmental justice movement presupposes the development, evolution, and advancement of international environmental law. The EU's objective is to be climate-neutral by 2050; the development of the legal energy policy framework of the EU is a process that will enable the changes in environmental markets. The flagship initiative "A resource-efficient Europe" has recently been introduced as part of the European Commission strategy.[27] This initiative outlines the structural changes and technological innovations by 2050, including objectives that define all-important goals and targets set by the EU and aimed to be achieved by 2020. The Member States aim at reducing greenhouse gases (GHGs), to reach a 20% share of renewable energy sources (RES), and to get a 20% increase in energy efficiency.[28] The European Commission proposed in September 2020 to "raise the 2030 greenhouse gas emission reduction target, including emissions and removals, to at least 55% compared to 1990."[29] The process of making detailed legislative proposals is planned to be initiated by June 2021 to achieve this increased ambition.[30] The energy policy advancement has been challenged by many factors, including climate change, market reform, and energy security. This "energy triangle" is one of the main obstacles to optimal energy advancement on a global scale and one of the persisting problems of the twentieth-first century. The basic policy objectives of the "energy triangle" as described by Zillman et al. in *Innovation in Energy Law and Technology: Dynamic Solutions for Energy Transitions* are:

(1) Affordability or competitiveness;
(2) Climate change mitigation and adaptation;
(3) Security and energy supply.[31]

---

[25] Fiack and Kamieniecki (2017).

[26] Salter et al. (2018), 19–20. See also: Michael B. Gerrard, "What Does Environmental Justice Mean in an Era of Global Climate Change?" *Journal of Environmental and Sustainability Law* Volume 19 Issue 2 Spring 2013: 281.

[27] Simona Bigerna et al. *The Sustainability of Renewable Energy in Europe.* Springer International Publishing AG, 2015, 1.

[28] Ibid., 1.

[29] "2030 Climate & Energy Framework" https://ec.europa.eu/clima/policies/strategies/2030_en#tab-0-0 (Last accessed 10/04/2020).

[30] Ibid.

[31] Zillman et al. (2018).

The energy justice concept is also closely related to eight core principles as afford-ability, availability, transparency, accountability, sustainability, due-process, intra-generational equity, and responsibility. According to Salter et al., affordability, intra-generational equity, and availability also require the eradication of energy poverty and the availability of high-quality energy services.[32] These eight principles could provide practical guidance to policymakers.[33] The global transition to renewable energy sources as one of the climate change mitigation means requires effective energy policy development and advancement, allowing nations to take advantage of emerging economic opportunities and facilitating new forms of energy growth, energy distribution as well as governance (Zillman et al., 2018). Renewables are expected to be the future competitive source for energy generation; solar energy keeps getting more affordable. Solar energy is getting cheaper than coal, for example, and the cost of solar power continues to decrease rapidly.[34] Coal use in the U.S. and Europe has decreased.[35] However, developing nations continue to use coal that "imposes very large externalities in addition to its contribution to climate change."[36] In 2017 alone, global investment in solar technology exceeded $180 billion (Fig. 1.1), and clean energy investment attracted approximately $300 billion in 2018.[37] The Intergovernmental Panel on Climate Change (IPPC) advised investing US $2.4 tril-lion in clean energy yearly through 2035 to prevent global temperature rise. However, the COVID-19 pandemic may significantly impact the trajectory of the future global clean energy investment, as it has impacted the other sectors. In an Open Letter to EU Leaders from Investors on a Sustainable Recovery from COVID-19, the participating stakeholders stated:

> The COVID-19 pandemic is pushing Europe into an economic crisis, but it is also an opportu-nity for a green and sustainable recovery. Investors understand that accelerating the net zero emissions transition can create significant new employment and economic growth, along with other cobenefits such as energy security and clean air. With effective recovery poli-cies in place, private investment could be channeled to accelerate the development of new sustainable climate change mitigation and climate adaptation assets.[38]

---

[32] Salter et al. (2018), 3.

[33] Ibid.

[34] In the UK, one of the largest flat roof solar installations has been successfully installed at Cambridge University Press's office. CUP shows its commitment to reducing their impact on climate change and carbon footprint in the UK. Please see "Cambridge University Press Cuts its Carbon Emissions through One of the UK's Largest Flat Roof Solar," installa-tions http://services.cambridge.org/about-us/news/cambridge-university-press-cuts-its-carbon-emi ssions-through-one-uks-largest-flat-roof-solar-installations/ (Last accessed 09/28/2020).

[35] Michael B. Gerrard, "What Does Environmental Justice Mean in an Era of Global Climate Change?" *Journal of Environmental and Sustainability Law* Volume 19 Issue 2 Spring 2013: 293.

[36] Ibid., 294.

[37] "Global Trends in Renewable Energy Investment 2020," https://www.fs-unep-centre.org/wp-con tent/uploads/2020/06/GTR_2020.pdf. (Last accessed 09/28/2020).

[38] "An Open Letter to EU Leaders from Investors on a Sustainable Recovery from COVID-19" https://theinvestoragenda.org/wp-content/uploads/2020/06/Open-letter-to-EU-leaders-from-invest ors-on-a-sustainable-recovery-from-COVID-19.pdf (Last accessed 10/04/2010).

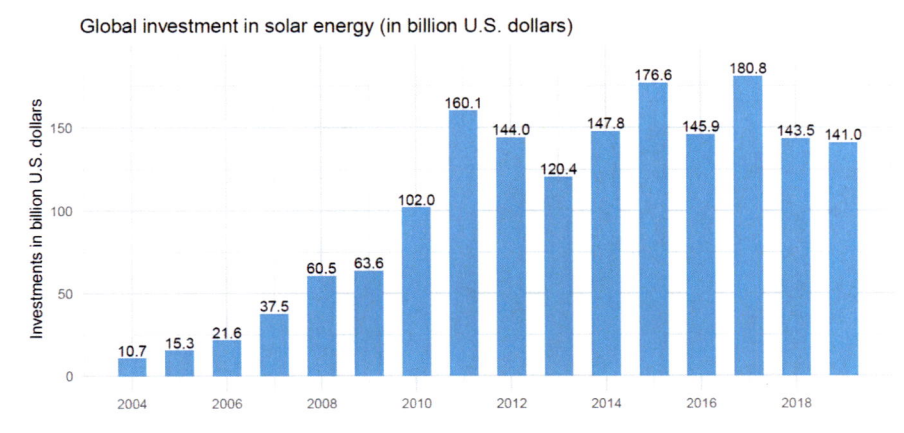

Fig. 1.1 Renewable energy—investment in solar energy technology 2004–2019. *Source* Bloomberg, UNEP, FS-UNEP

In this letter, investors highlighted that they face physical and transitional climate-related risks and encouraged the Member States to "factor in the foreseeable, acute, systematic and compounding climate-related economic and financial risks."[39] In addition to relaunching the global economy, investors underline that recovery plans should include sustainability and equity efforts, and "accelerate the transition to a net zero emissions economy to mitigate climate risk, create jobs and catalyse the sustainable development of private capital."[40] The IPCC admonished that limiting global warming to 1.5 °C (above pre-industrial levels) compared to 2 °C could facilitate a smoother transition to a more sustainable and equitable society.[41]

The Global Goals for Sustainable Development (the former SDGs) continue to prioritize 17 goals, among which is Goal 7 "Affordable and Clean Energy," Goal 11 "Sustainable Cities and Communities," and Goal 11 "Climate Action." Among 5 targets of Goal 11 is integrating climate change measures into national policies, strategies, and planning.[42] Goal 7 has 5 important targets: (1) universal access to modern energy; (2) improvement in energy efficiency; (3) expanding and upgrading energy services for developing countries; (4) increasing global percentage of renewable energy; (5) "enhancing international cooperation to facilitate access to clean energy research and technology" and promoting investment in clean energy technology.[43]

The affordability of clean energy—as one of the basic policy objectives—continues to positively change, and the renewables already compete in the Renewable

---

[39] Ibid.

[40] Ibid.

[41] "Summary for Policymakers of IPCC Special Report on Global Warming of 1.5 °C Approved by Governments" https://www.ipcc.ch/2018/10/08/summary-for-policymakers-of-ipcc-special-report-on-global-warming-of-1-5c-approved-by-governments/ (Last accessed 10/04/2020).

[42] The Global Goals for Sustainable Development, https://www.globalgoals.org/13-climate-action (Last accessed 09/28/2020).

[43] Ibid.

Global 2019 investment in renewable energy
by sector (in billion U.S. dollars)

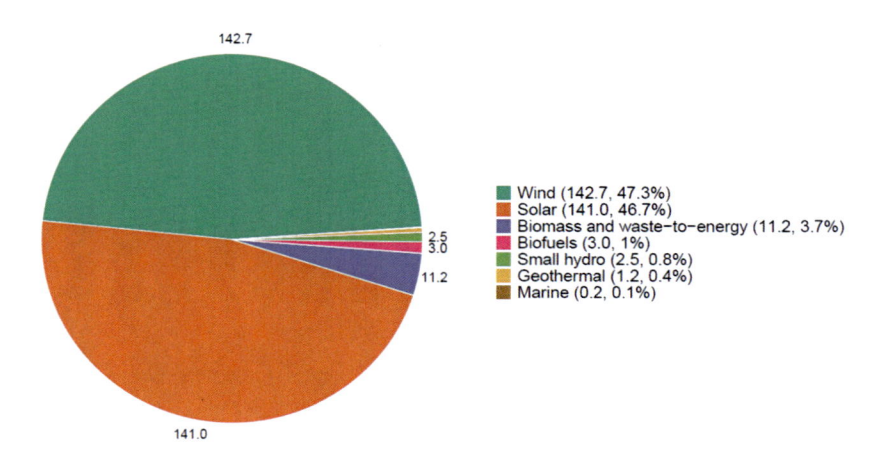

Fig. 1.2 Global 2019 renewable energy investment by sector. *Source* Bloomberg, UNEP, FS-UNEP

Energy Sector (RES) markets; wind energy development for example, competes with the solar energy sector. In 2019, wind energy investment exceeded investment in solar energy technology (Fig. 1.2). One of the largest wind farms with over 7,000 turbines is located in China—Gansu Wind Farm, capable of generating electricity to power a small country.[44] More than 90,000 wind turbines have been built in China. The cost of wind projects declines with the advances in technology and innovation and more efficient construction, making them even more competitive with plants powered fossil fuels like, for example, coal and natural gas.[45]

Security and energy supply are also among the basic policy objectives of the "energy triangle." Raphael J. Heffron et al. point out that "[e]nergy security and environmental goals are far more important to the long-term future of a society than economic competition."[46] The International Energy Agency (IEA) provides the following definition of energy security: "[T]he uninterrupted availability of energy sources at an affordable price." Energy security, according to the IEA, has many aspects, such as long-term energy security that deals with timely investments to supply energy in line with environmental needs and economic developments.[47] The IEA also speaks of short-term energy security, focusing on the "[a]bility of the

---

[44] "It Can Power a Small Nation. But This Wind Farm in China Is Mostly Idle." *The New York Times* January 15, 2017 by Javier C. Hernández; https://www.nytimes.com/2017/01/15/world/asia/china-gansu-wind-farm.html (Last accessed 09/28/2020).

[45] Ibid.

[46] Heffron et al. (2015).

[47] The IEA, "Energy Security Ensuring the Uninterrupted Availability of Energy Sources at an Affordable Price" https://www.iea.org/areas-of-work/ensuring-energy-security (Last accessed 09/28/2020).

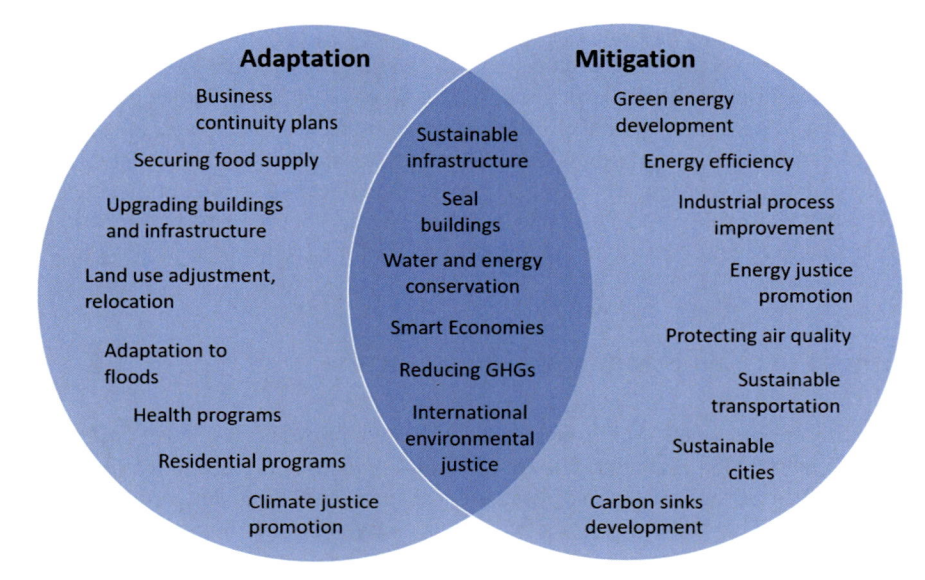

Fig. 1.3 Data. *Source* MAPC https://www.massaudubon.org/content/download/9197/154347/file/julie-conroy.pdf, p. 18

energy system to react promptly to sudden changes in the supply–demand balance."[48] The IEA assesses the energy security of its country members and promotion of emergency policy development, conducting peer reviews regularly.[49] Energy and electricity security have been challenged by the COVID-19 crisis.[50] All efforts and policies aimed at the GHGs emission reduction are part of climate change mitigation program; and efforts to cope with climate change—adaptation strategies (Fig. 1.3). The environmental justice problems in climate change mitigation, such as GHGs emissions reduction, are different in developed and developing countries.[51] Policies that would be most effective in climate change mitigation and adaptation strategies could be roughly divided into three categories: (1) implementing a price on the GHGs, "most likely either through a cap-and-trade program or a carbon tax;" (2) regulation of the carbon-emitting technologies use; (3) renewable energy development.[52]

Energy law and policy advancement are at the center of the energy triangle—and on the three vertices of the triangle are economics (e.g. energy finance), politics (e.g.

---

[48] Ibid.

[49] Ibid.

[50] Global Energy Review 2020: The Impact of the Covid-19 Crisis on Global Energy Demand and CO_2 Emissions, The IEA 2020: https://webstore.iea.org/download/direct/2995, 43.

[51] Michael B. Gerrard, "What Does Environmental Justice Mean in an Era of Global Climate Change?" *Journal of Environmental and Sustainability Law* Volume 19 Issue 2 Spring 2013: 287.

[52] Ibid., 288.

energy security), and environment (e.g. climate change mitigation).[53] Achieving a balance between economics, politics, and the environment of the energy law and policy is the so-called energy trilemma.[54] Overall, environmental justice that traces back to the 1970s and 1980s and climate justice since the 1990s are broad concepts.[55] Both climate justice and environmental justice have some positive effects on reducing GHGs and climate change prevention. However, the effectiveness of energy justice is believed to lead to policy advances.[56] Thus, this relatively new energy justice concept is believed to have success in a direct impact on policy advancement worldwide.

Support for New Sustainable Infrastructure

There are multiple well-established public policy theories and frameworks (Clark, 2002; Gerston, 2008; Sabatier, 2007). This volume focuses on recent best-practice energy policy advancements and discussion of climate change mitigation as well as adaptation. This book provides a better understanding of developing climate and energy policies on a global scale, bringing together scholars from various regions and contributing to the international climate change and environmental justice dialogue. Climate change policy advancements are of great importance in the current political opportunity structure worldwide; this dynamic advancement inevitably promotes energy justice facilitating energy democracy. At the international level, climate policies have been codified, for example, in the UNFCCC and the Kyoto Protocol.[57] The latter was adopted in 1997 and entered in force in 2005.[58] Currently, there are 192 Parties that participate in the Kyoto Protocol.[59] This international treaty requires these Parties to adopt best-practice policies and appropriate measures on mitigation and to report on all efforts regularly.[60] Moreover, the Kyoto Protocol places a heavier burden on developed countries, because it recognizes that these countries are largely responsible for the high levels of GHG emissions in the atmosphere.[61] One of the important targets of the Kyoto Protocol is the establishment of flexible markets, "which are based on the trade of emissions permits."[62] Furthermore, the Paris Agreement is one of the most important bridges "between today's policies and climate-neutrality

---

[53] Heffron et al. (2015).

[54] Ibid.

[55] Ibid., 175.

[56] Ibid.

[57] "Designing, Implementing, and Evaluating Climate Policies." National Research Council. 2010. Advancing the Science of Climate Change. Washington, DC: The National Academies Press. 402 https://www.nap.edu/read/12782/chapter/21 (Last accessed 09/28/2020).

[58] "What is the Kyoto Protocol?" https://unfccc.int/kyoto_protocol (Last accessed 09/28/2020).

[59] Ibid.

[60] Ibid.

[61] Ibid.

[62] Ibid.

before the end of the century."[63] The Agreement was signed in 2015 within the United Nations Framework Conventions on Climate Change (UNFCCC), "committed signatories to maintaining global warming to well below 2.0 °C above pre-industrial levels and pursuing efforts to limit this increase to 1.5 °C."[64] The IPCC identifies six forms of policy instruments intended to directly reduce GHGs.[65] There are many obstacles and challenges related to effective policy advancement. These are just a few aspects that were presented in Chapter 17 entitled "Designing, Implementing, and Evaluating Climate Policies" of *Advancing the Science of Climate Change*: (1) cross-scale integration of decision making; (2) removal of legal barriers; (3) lack of mechanisms; (4) effective linking of science and the decision making process; (5) "identification of efficiencies, co-benefits and potential negative feedback among adaptation options and between mitigation and adaptation efforts in various sectors and across levels;" (6) "the monitoring and evaluation of implementation of policies occurring (and depending on actions) at multiple levels."[66]

Not only policymakers change their decision-making patterns due to the climate change problems; Andrew Winston writes in the *Harvard Business Review* that a growing number of companies are declaring support of climate policy advancement—Apple just signed onto the Climate Declaration, also joining Nike and other companies.[67] According to Winston, all of the large company CEOs agree that sustainability problems are important to the future success of the business strategy.[68] He writes in "What 1000 CEOs Really Think About Climate Change and Inequality"

> On the biggest challenge of our times, climate change, the denial level in the c-suite has shrunk dramatically (in my anecdotal experience and in the data in this report). Companies no longer see climate change as an issue for future leaders to manage. The chairman of BASF, Martin Brudermüller, says, "We are already experiencing the impact of climate change today, and virtually every day." The report also notes that CEOs are understanding the need for system-level change to tackle issues as big as climate.

Companies and universities will make a significant change in tackling climate change problems and creating a platform for successful and efficient policies. Chapter 2 of this book emphasizes that universities and higher education institutions may become and often are the leaders in discussing climate change challenges because universities are committed to bringing about positive change in both individuals and society while incorporating policy advancement through theory and practice that enables such change to begin with (Sterling, 2001). Caribbean universities take

---

[63] "Paris Agreement," https://ec.europa.eu/clima/policies/international/negotiations/paris_en (Last accessed 10/04/2020).

[64] "Summary for Urban Policy Makers," What the IPCC Special Report on Global Warming of 1.5 °C Means for Cities," December 2018: https://www.ipcc.ch/site/assets/uploads/sites/2/2018/12/SPM-for-cities.pdf (Last accessed 10/05/2020).

[65] "Designing, Implementing, and Evaluating Climate Policies."

[66] Ibid. National Research Council. 2010. Advancing the Science of Climate Change. Washington, DC: The National Academies Press. 401 https://www.nap.edu/read/12782/chapter/21(Last accessed 09/28/2020). See also Adger et al., 2009b.

[67] Winston (2014).

[68] Winston (2019), pp. 2–5.

the issue of climate change seriously: the Caribbean is one of the at-risk tourist destinations. In Chap. 2, Boncana et al. gain deep insight into the function of Caribbean universities that deal with ethical dimension of sustainability and climate change mitigation. The ideas of this study can be utilized by stakeholders in higher education for an ecological justice realization in ensuring sustainability for the Caribbean region as well as policymakers. It is crucial for Caribbean institutions to develop and advance educational policies that aim at climate change mitigation and adaptation. Universities take a lead in climate change discussion and dialogue. There seems to be a pressing need for a new kind of education that takes into account all the aspects of sustainability. This chapter well demonstrates that climate change is impacting the Caribbean. In Chap. 3, Matejova examines the issues of social and international environmental justice. This chapter analyzes sudden and structural grievances in environmental protest mobilization; the latter type of grievances is related to social and international environmental justice. In Chap. 4, Uğurlu concentrates on renewable energy sources for climate change mitigation—an important aspect of basic policy objectives of the "energy triangle." Renewable energy, Uğurlu argues, is one of the mitigation ways of climate change. Chapter 4 considers as part of climate change mitigation strategy the development of bioenergy, solar energy, geothermal energy, hydropower, and wind energy. Chapter 5 concentrates on income inequality and the environment and explores the interconnectedness of these phenomena from the environmental policy perspective. Chapter 6 explores energy justice, security, and transformation towards modern energy sources in Canada's northern territories and analyzes current energy strategies of three territories: Nunavut, Northwest Territories, and Yukon. Canada has introduced changing programs to support renewable projects in the North. Further, Chap. 7 of this book discusses the Republic of Kenya and demonstrates the intersection of several climate-related existing issues; Dongmo explains that Kenya's economy and ecological system are fragile and vulnerable to climate change. The country's key poverty-environment challenges are related to soil degradation, deforestation, loss of biodiversity and ecosystem services, land, air and water pollution, environmental health concerns due to malnutrition, pollution, environmental migrations, vulnerability to natural disasters, lack of secured land and unreliable access to food and water. In the recent past, Kenya has developed a number of laws, strategies, and policies frameworks to support sustainability and green economy. Referring to prospective policy and strategy measures, the chapter reveals the prevailing gaps between the environmental commitments made and the actual implementation to improve development outcomes. Dongmo concludes that weak capacity in environmental management, insufficient law enforcement and monitoring are shortcomings that need to be addressed in order to meet Millennium Development Goals (MDGs) targets (especially MDG 7 on environmental sustainability) to move the country towards green growth. It is important to note that the loss of forest is the "second largest source of anthropogenic GHG emissions, after fossil fuel combustion."[69] Next, Chap. 8 focuses on Ethiopia's climate change policies: the

---

[69] Michael B. Gerrard, "What Does Environmental Justice Mean in an Era of Global Climate Change?" *Journal of Environmental and Sustainability Law* Volume 19 Issue 2 Spring 2013: 295.

government of Ethiopia acknowledged the alarming climate change problems. This chapter provides an overview of the evolution of climate discourses, actions, and strategies demonstrating climate policy shift. Bimir also considers climate change as an opportunity. Further, Chap. 9 examines the relation of energy transitions and climate change mitigation from an environmental justice perspective in Sri Lanka; this chapter investigates how the climate commitment paradigm has influenced the energy justice framework in Sri Lanka. Chapter 10 offers an insight into environmental policy development in Nigeria. In conclusion, Chap. 11 of this book uses the concept of sustainability not only as a signifier of the direction of economic development, but also a factor of resilience understood as the capacity of socio-ecological systems to withstand and respond to changes. It considers COVID-19 as the moment of this major global crisis, revealing profound, longstanding vulnerabilities in the global system; it can either open policy windows for a more effective transformation, Zachara-Szymańska argues, or signify a major shock that fragile systems may be not able to absorb.

International energy policy framework also interacts and impacts national laws and agreements: "Processes at the global and national levels will influence local adaptation decisions and vice versa; in the United States and around the world, a great variety of actors and institutions including local, regional, state, federal. And tribal authorities will influence those decisions."[70] Global GHG emission level, climate change, rising average temperature, renewable energy implementation as a climate change mitigation strategy—all these and many other aspects require new policy development internationally. Developing and advancing policies may be also challenging because of interaction with other climate and nonclimate policies.[71] On the other hand, however, these interactions may be beneficial for policy implementation and advancement.

Conclusion

Human-induced climate change is one of the first environmental problems that is global in character (Cohen, 2006). There is strong scientific evidence that human-caused climate change is harmful to all social strata. Human activities continue to negatively impact Earth's climate that also changes its radiative balance.[72] In the decision-making arena, "there is now tremendous momentum towards building smarter and cleaner energy infrastructure."[73] Political, business and economic dimensions are crucial for climate strategies and effective energy policies development; however, these dimensions are not always supportive for the best-practice policy

---

[70] "Designing, Implementing, and Evaluating Climate Policies."

[71] Ibid.

[72] "Physical Drivers of Climate Change," https://science2017.globalchange.gov/downloads/CSSR_Ch2_Physical_Drivers.pdf (Last accessed 10/05/2020).

[73] Salter et al. (2018), 1.

advancement. Salter et al. emphasize the link between climate change, energy, and international environmental justice: "the energy sector contributes to climate change more than any other industry; climate change is predicted to affect environmental justice communities most; and the energy has a long history with environmental injustice."[74] Especially, at this time of high uncertainty that the world faced due to the global crises—COVID-19, the urgency of climate policy advancement is evident. EPA has recently announced grant opportunities for the discussion of the impact of COVID-19 on environmental justice practices. The business-as-usual scenario would not be acceptable in the circumstances that prevail. Policy advancement serves as the incentive that also directs the flow of capital across the global economy.[75] Urban and other policymakers should familiarize themselves with climate science, because, without their decision-making, there will be no limiting global warming to 1.5 °C.[76] Policymakers should concentrate their efforts on creating an appropriate policy framework supporting investment in low-carbon assets, enabling investment in climate adaptation and mitigation, and enacting a just transition for global communities.[77] Policy actors, in their decision-making process, should also consider all posed risks and opportunity structures presented by climate change and climate-related problems.[78] Investors usually directly influence policymakers and policy engagement.[79] Leading investors are ready to work closely with national policymakers and help them to invest in a better future.[80] The group of 631 investors from around the world signed a letter in 2019 agitating governments to concentrate their efforts on climate change and achieve the goals of the Paris Agreement.[81] In an open letter to the Governments of World the CEOs of the seven partner organizations of the Investor Agenda supported the IPPC special report on 1.5 °C and restated to world

---

[74] Ibid., 5of.

[75] "Policy Advocacy" https://theinvestoragenda.org/focus-areas/policy-advocacy/ (Last accessed 10/04/2020).

[76] "Summary for Urban Policy Makers," What the IPCC Special Report on Global Warming of 1.5 °C Means for Cities," December 2018: https://www.ipcc.ch/site/assets/uploads/sites/2/2018/12/SPM-for-cities.pdf (Last accessed 10/05/2020).

[77] Ibid.

[78] Ibid.

[79] Ibid.

[80] "Open Letter to EU Leaders from Investors on a Sustainable Recovery from COVID-19," https://theinvestoragenda.org/wp-content/uploads/2020/06/Open-letter-to-EU-leaders-from-investors-on-a-sustainable-recovery-from-COVID-19.pdf (Last accessed 10/04/2020).

[81] "Record 631 Institutional Investors Managing More than $37 Trillion in Assets Urge Governments to Step up Ambition to Tackle Global Climate Crisis" https://www.ceres.org/news-center/press-releases/record-631-institutional-investors-managing-more-37-trillion-assets-urge (Last accessed 10/04/2020). See also "Global Investment Statement to Governments on Climate Change," https://theinvestoragenda.org/wp-content/uploads/2019/12/191201-GISGCC-FINAL-for-COP25.pdf (Last accessed 10/04/2020). The Investor Agenda has been established for the global investor community to accelerate the actions that are important for climate change issues and achieving the goals set by the Paris Agreement. The Investor Agenda seeks to speed up the transition to a net-zero emissions economy by 2050. Please see https://theinvestoragenda.org/ (Last accessed 10/04/2020).

governments the urgency of achieving the goals set by the Paris Agreement.[82] In the recent past, many investors and companies changed their strategies and focused their efforts on sustainable trends.[83] Among these companies is, for example, Black-Rock that also moved towards sustainability and climate change awareness making the environmental impacts the central investment business strategy.[84] More companies become engaged and interested in research related to the economic dimensions of climate change. The energy consumption reduction and cutting GHGs are those leading ways that could contribute to the objectives and targets set by the IPCC.[85] The GHGs cutting through the advancement of climate change policy can be seen as a valuable component of the broader sustainability movement. The GHGs spread globally and remain in the atmosphere for a long time—decades or centuries.[86] Furthermore, there are many examples of climate policy advancement. One of these is the cap-and-trade policy that was developed in California as part of the California Global Warming Solutions Act A.B. 32; it aims at limiting GHGs in the atmosphere.[87] However, some environmental justice advocates argued that cap-and-trade policy tool does not address the "co-pollutants."[88] Moreover, in 2012, there was a complaint with the EPA "alleging the cap-an-trade program violates the Civil Rights Act of 1964 by allowing emitters to purchase offsets that let them avoid reducing their emissions."[89] As a result, there was tension between the environmental community and the environmental justice community.[90]

It is also crucial to understand how, for example, science can contribute to policy design advancement as well as its implementation and evaluation.[91] Technological development and innovations in the field of energy could lead to significant energy savings.[92] According to Res Rutter, good energy behavior and culture create platforms for senior management decision-making, standards, policies, plans, and optimizing the technology used.[93] A program cultivating a good energy culture includes,

---

[82] "Open Letter to the Governments of World," https://theinvestoragenda.org/wp-content/uploads/2019/06/190611-FINAL-Cover-letter-for-GISGCC-corrected.pdf (Last accessed 10/04/2020).

[83] The New York Times, Andrew Ross Sorkin, "BlackRock CEO. Larry Fink: Climate Crisis Will Reshape Finance" https://www.nytimes.com/2020/01/14/business/dealbook/larry-fink-blackrock-climate-change.html.

[84] Ibid.

[85] Res Rutter, "Behaviour Change not Climate Change" https://www.jrpsolutions.com/client/assets/media/Property_Journal_January-February_2020_pp54-55.pdf (Last accessed 10/04/2020).

[86] Michael B. Gerrard, "What Does Environmental Justice Mean in an Era of Global Climate Change?" *Journal of Environmental and Sustainability Law* Volume 19 Issue 2 Spring 2013: 283.

[87] Ibid., 290–291.

[88] Ibid., 291.

[89] Ibid., 292.

[90] Ibid.

[91] "Designing, Implementing, and Evaluating Climate Policies." 2.

[92] Res Rutter, "Behaviour Change not Climate Change" https://www.jrpsolutions.com/client/assets/media/Property_Journal_January-February_2020_pp54-55.pdf (Last accessed 10/04/2020).

[93] Ibid.

for example, developing a best-practice energy policy and an energy action plan.[94] It is necessary to invest in low-carbon technologies and innovations as well as energy efficiency and to significantly reduce capital flows in high-emitting activities.[95] The current decision-making model is characterized by uncertainty and complexity caused by the COVID-19 crisis what undoubtedly may impact the policy-making process and agenda-setting; the policymaking process in a crisis may be different from policymaking in a business-as-usual situation.[96] The trilemma of energy policy can be resolved through energy justice.[97]

References

2030 Climate & Energy Framework. https://ec.europa.eu/clima/policies/strategies/2030_en#tab-0-0

Baumol, W. J., & Oates, W. E. (1975). *The theory of environmental policy: Externalities, public outlays, and the quality of life*. Prentice-Hall.

Bigerna, S., et al. (2015). *The sustainability of renewable energy in Europe*. Springer International Publishing AG.

Birkland, T. A. (2010). *An introduction to the policy process* (3rd ed.). M.E. Sharpe.

Clark, T. W. (2002). *The policy process: A practical guide for natural resource professionals*. Yale University Press.

Cohen, S. (2006). *Understanding environmental policy*. Columbia University Press.

Designing, Implementing, and Evaluating Climate Policies. National Research Council. (2010). Advancing the Science of Climate Change. Washington, DC: The National Academies Press. 402 https://www.nap.edu/read/12782/chapter/21. Last accessed September 28, 2020.

Fiack, D., & Kamieniecki, S. (2017). Stakeholder engagement in climate change policymaking in American cities. *Journal of Environmental Studies and Sciences, 7*, 127–140.

Gerston, L. N. (2008). *Public policymaking in a democratic society: A guide to civic engagement* (2nd ed.). M.E. Sharpe.

Global Trends in Renewable Energy Investment 2020. https://www.fs-unep-centre.org/wp-content/uploads/2020/06/GTR_2020.pdf. Last accessed September 04, 2020.

Heffron, R. J., McCauley, D., & Sovacool, B. K. (2015). Resolving society's energy Trilemma through the energy justice metric. *Energy Policy, 87*, 168–176.

It Can Power a Small Nation. But This Wind Farm in China Is Mostly Idle. The New York Times January 15, 2017 by Javier C. Hernández; https://www.nytimes.com/2017/01/15/world/asia/china-gansu-wind-farm.html. Last accessed September 28, 2020.

Kurochkin, D., Shabliy, E. V., & Shittu, E. (2019). *Renewable energy: International perspectives on sustainability*. Springer International Publishing.

Larimer, C. & Smith, K. (2017). The Public Policy Theory Primer (Third ed.). Boulder, Colorado: Westview Press.

Paris Agreement. https://ec.europa.eu/clima/policies/international/negotiations/paris_en. Last accessed October 04, 2020.

Pearsall, J. (1999). *The concise Oxford dictionary*, 10th ed. In J. Pearsall (Ed.) Oxford University Press.

Record 631 Institutional Investors Managing More than $37 Trillion in Assets Urge Governments to Step up Ambition to Tackle Global Climate Crisis. https://www.ceres.org/news-center/press-releases/record-631-institutional-investors-managing-more-37-trillion-assets-urge. Last accessed October 04, 2020.

---

[94] Ibid.

[95] "Investment" The Investor Agenda—Accelerating Action for a Net-Zero Emissions Economy https://theinvestoragenda.org/focus-areas/investment/ (Last accessed 10/04/2020).

[96] Wenzelburger et al. (2019).

[97] Heffron et al. (2015).

Res Rutter, Behaviour Change not Climate Change. https://www.jrpsolutions.com/client/assets/media/Property_Journal_January-February_2020_pp54-55.pdf. Last accessed October 04, 2020.

Sabatier, P. A. (2007). *Theories of the policy process.* Westview Press.

Salter, R., et al. (2018). *Energy justice.* Edward Elgar Publishing Limited.

Shabliy, E. V., Crawford, M. J., & Kurochkin, D. (2020). *Discourses on sustainability: Climate change, clean energy, and justice.* Springer International Publishing AG.

The Global Goals for Sustainable Development. https://www.globalgoals.org/13-climate-action. Last accessed October 04, 2020.

The IEA. Energy Security Ensuring the Uninterrupted Availability of Energy Sources at an Affordable Price. https://www.iea.org/areas-of-work/ensuring-energy-security. Last accessed September 09, 2020.

Weber, M. (1965). *Politics as a vocation.* Fortress Press.

Weible, C., Heikkila, T., DeLeon, P., & Sabatier, P. (2012). "Understanding and Influencing the Policy Process." Policy Sciences, *45*(1), 1–21.

Wenzelburger, G., König, P. D., & Wolf, F. (2019). Policy theories in hard times? Assessing the explanatory power of policy theories in the context of crisis. *Public Organization Review, 19,* 97–118.

What is the Kyoto Protocol? https://unfccc.int/kyoto_protocol. Last accessed September 28, 2020.

Winston, A. (2014, March). How much do companies really worry about climate change? *Harvard Business Review* Digital Articles, pp. 2–5.

Winston, A. (2019, September). What 1000 CEOs really think about climate change and inequality. *Harvard Business Review* Digital Articles.

Zillman, D. M., Roggenkamp, L. P., & Godden, L. (2018). *Innovation in energy law and technology: Dynamic solutions for energy transitions.* Oxford University Press.

Elena V. Shabliy is a Visiting Scholar at Columbia University; she was a Visiting Scholar at Harvard University in 2015–2017, NYU in 2020, and Boston University in 2020–2021. She is the editor of *Representations of the Blessed Virgin Mary in World Literature and Art* (Lexington, Rowman and Littlefield, 2017) and co-editor of *Emancipation Women's Writing at Fin de Siècle* (Routledge, 2018), *Renewable Energy: International Perspectives* (Palgrave Macmillan, 2019), *Global Perspectives on Women's Leadership and Gender (In)Equality* (Palgrave Macmillan, 2020), *Discourses on Sustainability: Climate Change, Clean Energy, and Justice* (Palgrave Macmillan, 2020), and *Women's Human Rights in Nineteenth-Century Literature and Culture* (Lexington, Rowman and Littlefield, 2020). She studied at Lomonosov Moscow State University; in 2018, Dr. Shabliy was a Postdoctoral Fellow at Harvard University.

Dmitry Kurochkin is a Senior Research Analyst at Harvard University, where he teaches Data Science, Time Series Analysis, and Econometrics. Dmitry graduated *magna cum laude* from Lomonosov Moscow State University where he majored in Physics and earned his Ph.D. in Mathematics at Tulane University. Kurochkin is an interdisciplinary scholar and holds Master's Degrees in Applied Mathematics, Statistics, Chemistry, and Economic Analysis and Policy. He is a co-editor of *Renewable Energy: International Perspectives on Sustainability* (Palgrave Macmillan, 2019), *Global Perspectives on Women's Leadership and Gender (In)Equality* (Palgrave Macmillan, 2020), and *Discourses on Sustainability: Climate Change, Clean Energy, and Justice* (Palgrave Macmillan, 2020).

Chapter 2
A Changing Paradigm for Caribbean Universities: Climate Change Mitigation, Sustainability, and Policy

Ilive Peltier, Correen Celestine, and Mohomodou Boncana

Abstract The purpose of this chapter is to gain deep insight into the function of the Caribbean universities as it pertains to ethical practices of sustainability with reference to climate change mitigation. A clarification of such ethical practices will provide the institutions of higher education in the region with different ideas on how to educate communities for their present and future survival with respect to the economy, environment, and equity. This chapter will also serve as a valuable guide in changing the paradigm in education. Research suggests that human beings often tend to view things within categories rather than seeing them as a system. In these times where climate change impacts are at the forefront of the issues facing the Caribbean, there seems to be a pressing need for a new kind of education that takes into account all the aspects of sustainability. This new education can be seen as the cornerstone in the change of minds on which sustainable initiatives can be accomplished. Furthermore, the ideas generated through this research can be utilized by stakeholders (e.g., leaders, staff, professors, and students) in higher education for a new ecological design in education sustainability for the Caribbean region. The ecological design, in this context, is perceived as the process that makes things (e.g., environmental, social, and cultural) fit well together over long periods of time.

Introduction

The Caribbean described in this chapter does not denote a single country or a body of water. Instead, it is an immense watery area that embraces the Caribbean Sea, the Gulf of Mexico, and a section of the northeastern Atlantic Ocean. This region is diverse in its elevated cultural and political make-up that, in turn, is influenced by its colorful history. Both its political and geographical layout assumes significance in

I. Peltier (✉) · C. Celestine
Creative Leadership for Innovation and Change, University of the Virgin Islands, Charlotte Amalie, U.S.A.

M. Boncana
Department of Social Sciences, University of the Virgin Islands, Charlotte Amalie, U.S.A.
e-mail: mohomodou.boncana@uvi.edu

© The Author(s), under exclusive license to Springer Nature Switzerland AG 2022
D. Kurochkin et al. (eds.), *Energy Policy Advancement*,
https://doi.org/10.1007/978-3-030-84993-1_2

the context of sustainability and climate change mitigation. The region is comprised of twenty-four independent nations (fourteen of those are island nations) and eleven territories of distant countries (The United States, Holland, France, and the United Kingdom). It is pertinent to mention that eight million kilometers of land (e.g., from the Upper Mississippi Basin in Southern Canada to the Orinoco Basin of Columbia and Venezuela) drain into the Caribbean region (Walker & Salt, 2015).

Even a minute alteration in the make-up of any one system can result in large, even catastrophic change in the performance of the entire system (Sachs, 2015). Sachs posits that just as death is the result of a small change in the chemical make-up of a cell, a tiny disruption in the environment can result in far-reaching and cascading changes to living organisms within that environment. Hence, a good society will require taking precautions when dealing with environmental issues. In their 2011 Annual Report, the *United Nations Economic Commission for Latin America and the Caribbean (UNECLAC)* pointed out that climate change poses a crucial danger to supportable human expansion in the Caribbean Region, inflicting harm upon livelihoods, ecosystems, infrastructure, health, and the industrial sectors.

Over the past few decades, climate change and mitigation have become common household terms. Climate change is a gradual process that can be seen globally. History is replete with examples that the earth's surface has undergone many cycles of climate change that are palpably affecting some countries more than others and people's way of living. These impacts can be felt across all aspects of the Caribbean way of life—economics, environment, education, etc. Changes are being made within communities, especially the way institutions of higher learning are developing their students to preserve and sustain the future of their countries. Throughout the Caribbean, extreme change can be seen manifesting in the form of heightened intensity of hurricanes, bleaching of coral reefs, increasing salt levels in the ocean, growing incidents of droughts, and rising sea levels (Watts, 2018; Salt and Walker, 2015). Notwithstanding the resilience of the Caribbean, seeking ways to sustain each island's cultural uniqueness and sustainable survivability is also an important factor of mitigation.

The Oxford Dictionary (2003) defines mitigation as the accomplishing reduction of the harshness, significance, or misery of a phenomenon. Meanwhile, FEMA referred to migration as a method of lessening loss of life and property by shrinking the impression of catastrophe. Since 1988, reports from *the Intergovernmental Panel on Climate Change (IPCC)* have outlined two main findings: (1) global temperatures have been rising; and (2) a considerable expanse of such increase is credited to human activities, in particular, the release of carbon dioxide and other chemicals into the atmosphere by burning fossil fuels (Portney, 2015). As such, the questions being asked of higher learning institutions are as follows: Why does a changing paradigm for Caribbean universities seem to be critical at this time with reference to sustainability? What role do ethics play in climate change mitigation? How does culture assist in shaping climate change mitigation?

Caribbean Universities Becoming the Centers of the Sustainable Revolution

Caribbean universities must not only join the Sustainable Revolution, but also become active change agents and knowledge providers of this revolution themselves. The Caribbean needs a dynamic new approach to tackling climate change, and Caribbean universities can make provision to accomplish that objective. Secondly, owing to their transformative capabilities, these institutions are also imbued by the influence of designing a developmental, innovative social ethos that accentuates the very fiber of relationships which establishes a linkage with current trials faced by individuals. Finally, Caribbean universities can become the means of better equipping individuals for tackling complex problems that involve open-minded and cooperative tactics. The Sustainability Revolution espouses a different ideology from that which is provided by the Industrial Revolution for supporting economic capability and vigorous ecosystems by adjusting consumption patterns and applying a more impartial social framework (Edwards, 2005). According to Edward, such attractions assume significance and have a global influence that extends over a variety of interests with mutual essential values. When the Sustainable Revolution is compared to the Industrial Revolution, Edwards asserted of its ability to have comprehensive and philosophical impacts, thereby fashioning the way individuals live and eat, as well as, their pursuits and development of their communities.

However, Edwards commented that the Sustainability Revolution continues to be subversive and misinterpreted by many individuals, businesses, and organizations, although it strengthens thoughtful impressions on the economy, ecology, and social factors of global societies. Along with the rest of the world, discussions are being held on ensuring sustainability in the region (*ECLAC*, 2011). However, within the Caribbean, there is a need for change in both human activity and education by way of a shift in the habits of thinking and act. For this reason, a call for sustainable literacy in Caribbean universities is necessary as part of the agenda of climate change mitigation. Sterling (2001) posited that the role of any education system is to ensure that an effort is made to house the rigidity between preserving society and replicating or reassuring change. Universities simply speaking of "going green" is not enough; it involves so much more comprehensive and sustainable action. It is essential and pragmatic for institutions getting involved in climate change mitigation in order to understand the difference between: (1) *education for change,* and (2) *education in change.* Education for this new generation, therefore, is required to be participative, systemic, connective, adaptive, integrative, transformative, and purposeful (Sterling, 2001).

As asserted by Huckle and Sterling (1996), real sustainability is growing in significance and increasingly becoming the norm, instead of being debased, marginalized, and regulated. Therefore, it is necessary to embed the eclectic tapestry of this phenomenon. However, such shift and transformative critical thinking with action inexorably require an essential change, and such educational views and perspectives need to be holistic (e.g., extended, invigorated, and purposeful), with the individual embracing level capacities both as a learner and as a leader. In practicality, according to Huckle and Sterling, Caribbean society and its universities are faced with a "holistic reality and dual challenge"; acquiring understanding cannot transpire without change, and change will not transpire without acquiring understanding. Therefore, *Education for change* and *education in change* will pave the way towards an ecological paradigm that will assist Caribbean universities in becoming the revolution for adaptation and accommodation to climate change impacts. The universities in the Caribbean region are supposed to develop the understanding that the sustainable revolution is now in its third stage, that of diffusion (thus implying that distribution to other developing nations has occurred from its geneses in the United States and European Union countries) (Edwards, 2005). The region is currently fraught with several restrictions: limited natural resources, small geographical areas, unique political make-up, sporadic innovative renewable energy ideas, small agriculture production sectors, and struggling local finances. The preceding factors are exacerbated by the serious complexities of climate change. In essence, it will take nothing less than a concerted effort of all nations and territories in the region to resolve these issues. Towards that end, universities may be the leaders in tackling such a challenge because universities are committed to bringing about change in both individuals and society while incorporating policy changes through theory and practice that enables such change to begin with (Sterling, 2001). Select questions that remain include: How can this be done? How urgent is climate change? and Where can the region begin?

The Importance of Climate Change Mitigation

According to Romm (2018), climate change will influence humanity far greater than the Internet. This implies that information about climate change will revolutionize individuals' thoughts and practices, and that knowledge about climate change will be valuable to all those living on the planet. Romm claimed that climate change is crucial in shaping human destiny because its impact will influence a great number of decisions to be made by humans in decades to come. Climate change impact will affect how individuals purchase property, where they choose to dwell, their retirement decisions, as well as their occupations and career paths. Additionally, it will also affect students' study decisions and whether or not they should invest in their future. These decisions may seem basic, and for a few even foolish; however, this new reality reinforces the urgency with which institutions within the Caribbean should shift their paradigms towards preparation. People living in the region will need to develop their abilities in deciphering many of these visceral complexities affecting them. The insights gained from various disasters of the past decade are reasons enough to change the thoughts and actions with reference to climate change.

According to the *United Nations Educational, Social and Cultural Organization* (UNESCO) report (2015), the Caribbean is the most tourist-concentrated region in the world, and Caribbean economies are susceptible to natural disasters. As an example, the majority of *Caribbean Community (CARICOM)* countries are reported to have a percent chance of being hit by a storm on an annual basis (International Monetary Fund (IMF), 2013). The document added that even temperate storms can affect the Gross Domestic Product (GDP) growth by 0.5 percent. A prediction by the *World Travel and Tourism Council* placed the Caribbean in the ranks of being the most at-risk tourist destination between 2025 and 2050, calling for the region to take climate change adaptation seriously given that the region will be hard-pressed in tackling major meteorological disasters in the future (UNESCO Science Report, 2015).

Basically, the Caribbean needs to be apprehensive and more discerning in proactivity when addressing long-term political, economic, and social consequences of climate disruption. Since the region is bearing the brunt of climate change, it requires sustainable and revolutionary preparations for such disruptions. In 2016, accurate research and studies determined that the concentration of carbon dioxide (CO_2) was increasing and had crossed the 402 parts per million (ppm) threshold (Orr, 2016). At present, the world has gained cognizance of the fact that the climate system is multi-layered and nonlinear. Most individuals are aware of the complexities accompanied by the phenomenon of climate change. However, Orr explicated that it ignored that humans have contributed to vast changes, not always in the best interest of human survivability and sustainability, in Earth's atmosphere with the duration measured in ages. As a case in point, the Caribbean spent $14,000,000,000 (Fourteen Billion Dollars) USD on importing fossil fuels in 2008 to support a ninety percent consumption dependency in CARICOM countries alone (UNESCO Science Report, 2015). Despite the growing awareness of the climatic changes, institutions, organizations, systems of governance, and economies tend to direct their focus on short-term issues and solutions. Nevertheless, owing to the intensity and frequency of natural disasters such as hurricanes and earthquakes, efficient and effective solutions are to be found that provide expeditious and long-term survivability outcomes.

The world recognizes the urgency of climate change mitigation. Presently, many individuals in the Caribbean, on account of their experiences during the past few years with frequent and near-apocalyptic disasters manifesting within this region, may be preoccupied by the idea that the future is at stake and therefore, recognize the urgent need to identify solutions. In that context, it is notable that experiences that have been gained during and after natural disasters tend to create opportunities for individuals to utilize their skills and science in trying to find solutions for careless actions. However, this endeavor to seek viable solutions entails an honest acknowledgment and understanding that some of humanity's previous actions may have provided complications that influence present-day living in ways that are incomprehensive, and that such complex changes may endure well into the distant future. Orr (2016) mentioned that many leaders in society (corporate CEOs, bankers, university presidents, heads of state, mayors, and foundation presidents) pledge initiatives that are sustainable without the adage of what the very idea means, thus underscoring the importance of education in the field of sustainability.

According to Taylor (2017), the Caribbean is facing climate change issues that are unfamiliar, unprecedented, and urgent. He described the climate of the Caribbean region as recognizing the appearance of new climatic intricacies in wake of the magnitude of two Category 5 hurricanes occurring in the same year in the region, something that has never transpired before. With Taylor's reference to climate change being unprecedented, he suggested that if the world continues on its existing path, the Caribbean region will witness an increase in warmth by 2–3 °C, and a decrease in rainfall of about 40%. There will also be an anticipated upsurge in sea level to about 1–2 m. All issues will inevitably have a detrimental impact on islands where most are already strained for water and are small in landmass.

At the time of writing this study, Taylor predicted many more dangerous storms for the region. His grim forecasts turned out to be with Hurricane Dorian in 2019, as storm surges up to twenty-three feet claimed the lives of thousands on Great Bahama and Abaco Islands in the Bahamas (National Hurricane Center, 2019). Such storms not only affect the economies of the islands (e.g. Dominica and Barbuda with Hurricane Maria had their economies destroyed), but also result in widespread devastation of social life, healthcare, loss of culture and cultural assets, lives, and biodiversity (Taylor, 2017). One of the serious challenges that the Caribbean region is fraught with is that small islands, such as Barbuda, had to be completely evacuated after Irma in 2017. As climate change assumes more alarming proportions in size, scale, and impact, will the region be able to keep pace with accommodating such change? This is the solution finding effort that institutions of higher learning may be required to focus on.

The lessons of the recent storms are now sending an unambiguous message to the rest of the world about the sheer gravity of climate change impact. The Caribbean region and other small developing states have been debating with the United Nations about the margin of global warming at 1.5 °C. To their credit, the islands have made courageous pledges regarding greenhouse gas emissions (Taylor, 2017). According to a report by the UNECLAC (2011), there is evidence of an increase in both maximum and minimum annual temperatures. Additionally, changes have also been reported in rainfall extremes. In that very report, it was predicted that under the Intergovernment Panel on Climate Change's (IPCC's) models A2 and B2 sourced from the Regional Climate Modeling (RCM) system, temperatures will rise above the base period average to about 1.52 and 2.64 °C by 2050, with a mean escalation of 1.78 °C in Scenario A1 in the sub-region. The predictions included in that report portended that future storms affecting the northern tropical Atlantic may become more intense with greater ultimate winds and denser storm rainfall. Also, this report pointed out that the frequency of Category 3–5 storms and the likelihood of such storms reaching Category 5 capacity within twenty-four hours will increase. The hurricanes of 2017 and 2019 proved those predictions. Consequently, the institutions of higher learning in the Caribbean may need to redefine their ways of educating the communities that they serve.

The possibility of gaining both local and global attention is impelling local institutions to participate in changing the manner in which the people of the Caribbean think and live. If education is to serve its true purpose, it must be used to ascertain the survival of a region that has been in existence for the past 300 years. Lessons from Hurricane Irma, Maria, Dorian, and at this moment, the earthquakes in Puerto Rico, provide opportunities to exemplify a new way of thinking and doing. The region's educational institutions may need to become fully involved in the sustainability efforts in order to help the region recognize the sheer urgency of solution finding when it refers to climate change impacts.

Sustainability Defined

The term "sustainability," which is used by many educators, may be perceived by some as being contrary to unsustainability or obliteration of the ecology. Others may focus on the term with reference to uncontrolled free-market entrepreneurship, consumerism, consumption, and exploitation. Against this backdrop, Jickling and Sterling (2017) contended that sustainability can serve as a position that provides hidden space for insensitively evaluating the status quo. They went on to add that educators do not feel uneasy about what the term sustainability really entails because for many, it implies moving on interminably with slight or no essential direction about what should be sustained. Others feel that there is value in flexibility, and sustainability contains just that leaving room for debate.

Caribbean Culture and How It Shapes the Climate Change Debate

Hoffman (2015) postulated that social scientists' interpretation of the public's understanding of climate change is not an absence of enough information, but the intended or unintended avoidance of that information. Hoffman added that such evasion is deeply embedded in culture and psychology and can be summed up into four major themes: *(1) all individuals have cognitive filters, (2) cognitive filters replicate individuals' identity, (3) cultural identity can suppress scientific perception, and (4) political economy produces inertia for change.*

Hoffman (2015) concurred that *all individuals have cognitive filters*, and in this regard, social scientists have discovered that it is not the physical scientist who has the last say when it comes to shaping public debate on climate change. Instead, the final opinions lay in the hands of the general public, who subtract and authenticate conclusions made by the scientific community by sifting their declarations through the world opinions of individuals. Humans relate to climate change through their previous inclinations, personal experiences, and knowledge. According to Hoffman (2015), humans are inclined to seek information and reach conclusions about multifaceted, transcultural, and politically disputed issues in ways that lead them to discover helpful indications of their current views, a concept referred to as *motivated reasoning*. Undoubtedly, it is the cultural debate as it pertains to climate change that shapes the discourse of mitigation and may even be the strongest force as to whether individuals in the Caribbean region support or disregard its overarching impact.

Lewis and Conaty (2012) explicated that deep cultural change may be disquieting. They contended that as one begins to gain understanding, this newly-acquired awareness may have severely detrimental psychological effects. The unsettling experiences of recent natural disasters have primarily focused Caribbean region planning and discussions on climate change impacts with reference to resilience (McField, 2017; UNESCO, 2015; Fromovic et al., 2013; UNECLAC, 2011). Considering the possibility that these ideas may become overpowering for native indigenous Caribbean persons, ways may have to be sought to gain their endorsement. A method of teaching that resilience is an evolving asset of a self-organizing system is necessary, and all stakeholders may do well to acknowledge the fact that it is about adaptive cycles. It must be clearly understood that resilience is not about systems staying the same. Rather, it is about a system's capability to take in disturbance and identify it in order to fundamentally maintain the same purpose, configuration, and feedback to retain similar uniqueness. Resilience encompasses changing inside the parameters or even penetrating those (Walker and Salt, 2015). Therefore, as far as climate change mitigation is concerned, it is essential for Caribbean institutions to develop educational policies that cultivate the idea that resilience implicates adaptive alternations, connected measures, and fields, which, in turn, comprise of both adaptation and transformation approaches accompanying each other (Walker and Salt, 2015). This reinforces the need for a radical cultural shift in the Caribbean mindset.

Hoffman's idea of *cognitive filters replicates individuals' identity* implicates that worldwide views are typically in consonance with the values espoused by those within the group that individuals identify themselves as asserted and devised as cultural cognition by psychology professor Dan Khan at Yale University. Humans are influenced by group norms and will customarily support what the group holds to be valuable. This may not necessarily imply that scientific opinions do not matter, but such opinions will be weighted and valued differently in accordance with how they are perceived by friends, colleagues, trusted sources, and/or respected leaders. Individuals are commonly regarded and embraced as being the products of their environments. As such, they will move towards views that are in alignment with those they identify and associate cultural norms, behaviors, and attitudes with.

Consequently, Caribbean institutions may have to develop a more comprehensive and equitable tapestry into the fabric of their systems that maximize ways of making individuals more mindful, tenacious, and structured while kindling the authenticity of climate change impacts in a manner that stimulates reconsideration of how they live and act, both independently and communally (Lewis & Conaty, 2012). In assisting individuals' learning, they will become better prepared to emotionally and psychologically manage unexpected encounters.

Thirdly, Hoffman (2015) posited that *cultural identity can suppress scientific perception*, and as such, the certainty or uncertainty of climate change tends to become rooted in one's cultural uniqueness. This means that challenging scientific suggestions can legitimately make a person become more unrelenting in countering assumptions that modify his or her cultural beliefs. He went on to explicate that higher levels of education and a self-reported understanding of climate science parallels heightened both among those who formerly believe in climate change, but lower among those who do not. He also argued that individuals, who are more knowledgeable in science and technical reasoning, are the ones who are most culturally opposed to climate change. He concluded that more knowledge may strengthen one's position on climate change, regardless of one's position on the matter. However, this does not imply that a shared notion that more scientific information will help convince Caribbean people to be prepared for tackling climate change that has manifested or become inclusive in the framework of sustainability or cultural competence that supports human survivability. Instead, engaging individuals in climate change discourse will have to speak towards in-depth philosophical, cultural, and social filters examined by this concern.

Finally, Hoffman (2015) suggested that *political economy fashions inertia for change.* He could not have made the point any clearer when he opined that the political economy generates inaction for change. He further elaborated that the social events directing human thoughts are not well-defined if economic, political, and technological authenticities are the predictability of their values and the foundation of inactivity to changing such values. This is attributed to two reasons: (1) the large physical infrastructure around fossil fuels and the lifestyle they create, and (2) the strong economic and political interests jeopardized by the issue of climate change. Most of the aforementioned infrastructures are in control of the economic and political interests. Research suggests that many higher learning institutions form part of such infrastructural paradigms (Hoffman, 2015). Yet, the world, including the Caribbean, has reached a point where even if economic and political interests feel threatened by climate change issues, it is no longer possible to ignore the fact that there is an urgency for change. History has predicted that the responses to most environmental problems, both successful and unsuccessful, have advanced through a process of experimental, miscalculation, and societal learning. Hence, in order to make sense of present-day occurrences while getting ahead, it is vital to understand this evolution (Mazmanian & Kraft, 2009).

According to Bishop (2013), expansion in the English-speaking Caribbean has been habituated by two key factors: vulnerability and dependence. The first issue remains that the territories, especially the Eastern Caribbean, has been disadvantaged with reference to layout, population, and natural resources. As a result, the region has conventionally exceedingly been reliant on the global economy for distribution of main agricultural goods, products and agri-business services. The second issue is that the previous notion has rendered them defenseless to extraneous and uncontrollable pressures (i.e., political, economic, or natural). Such outside influences have manifested in the Caribbean region in the form of natural disasters, currency crises, environmental degradation, and political interferences. Therefore, operating within the restrained space of the region while maximizing the limited resources is a matter that needs to be deeply calibrated.

Therefore, instead of looking outward for solutions to these complex situations, the region must seek innovative ways to protect its economy and growth within the space and layout that constitutes the best solutions for the Caribbean. The concept of the commons, where "paradigms combine a specific community with a set of social practices, values, and norms that are used to manage resources,"[1] is one form of moving forward with sustainability in mind, but the institutions of higher learning in the Caribbean may be the ones to lead the intellectual discourses. This is because education acts as a catalyst that helps initiate and maintain social change (Sterling 2017). However, as Hoffman (2015) implicated, determinations to alter cultural views on climate change will be required to embrace changes in the larger institutions and infrastructure of the Caribbean economy. In doing so, however, they will need to devise methods of safeguarding themselves from the confrontation by all those who stand to profit from these giant infrastructural establishments.

The Importance of Ethical Practices of Sustainability for Caribbean Universities

The Caribbean Region, along with the rest of the world, has seen an end to the United Nations Decade of Education for Sustainable Development (2005–2014)— a ten year projected plan from 2005 to 2014 aimed at incorporating the necessary values and practices of sustainable development into every part of education and learning, to inspire changes in knowledge, values, and attitudes for empowering a more sustainable and just society for all—the next decade would witness an innovative prospect to reassess forthcoming educational intentions that will encompass both environmental and ecological ideals across the field of education (e.g., this will include curriculum and philosophical research) (Jickling & Sterling, 2017). Nonetheless, this prospect for change is timely and crucial. According to Sterling (2001), the world is living in paradoxical times that is replete with both threat and prospect, prompt change, and a pursuit for grounding and identity. He suggested that there is an urgency in refurbishing the image and perception of education. This is particularly true for the Caribbean Region. In the past decade, there have been many compelling reasons for seeking new ways of living and outlining new ideas for preparation where climate change impacts are concerned. The catastrophic destruction caused by the 2010 earthquake in Haiti, Hurricanes Irma and Maria (IrMaria) from Dominica, Barbuda, Virgin Islands (US and British), Puerto Rico and beyond of 2017, the floods of 2018, Hurricane Dorian of 2019, the most recent earthquakes in Puerto Rico of 2020, and other disasters relating to climate change impacting the Caribbean region, present situations and opportunities for institutions of higher learning to become vigilant and proactively involved in the ideas, behaviors, and research action of implementing sustainability solutions for the islands-nations as well as the living spaces they represent. Educators and students at these institutions must demand involvement in projects that are focused on finding solutions. Instructors will be required to develop courses that allow students to become curious

---

[1] David Bollier. *Think Like a Commoner: A Short Introduction to the Life of the Commons* (Canada: New Society Publishers, 2014), 15.

while finding collaborative ways of advancing a consciousness that is conducive for a mindset change towards the sustainability revolution.

It is not that conversations on the impacts of climate change and sustainability efforts are taking place in universities; rather, it is the urgency or lack thereof regarding what actions are being taken to ensure that students and local communities are more proactive on the concerns affecting what is happening to offset the impending devastation of immediate environments. According to Boring and Forbes (2013), more than 650 college presidents have placed signatures on the American College and University President's Climate Commitment (ACUPCC), whereas the Association for the Advancement of Sustainability in Higher Education (AASHE) has a membership of about 1000. On a related note, the University of the West Indies (UWI) was awarded a grant of US six hundred thousand United States dollars ($600,000.00 USD) approved by the Inter-American Development Bank (IADB) in order to cultivate capability in sustainable energy technologies across the Caribbean (United Nation Educational and Cultural Organization Report, 2011). All these efforts may look great on paper; however, how much have the cultural beliefs of their students, staff, and communities changed as a result?

There is a call for a far-reaching trans-cultural global view of learning and educating with reference to the new complexities being confronted by the region. As Sterling (2001) suggested, higher learning institutions may need to become involved in the type of education that takes shape from humanistic educational methods of the past while considering new improvements that relate to complexity, systems, learning theories, and the concept of sustainability. This new form of educating will focus on valuing and sustaining both humans and nature by highlighting their entrenched interdependence.

The duty of Caribbean higher learning institutions will be to present a form of education that is holistic, participatory, and practical. As corroborated by Sterling, Caribbean universities should leave behind the tapered instrumental view that is presently dominating education and begin to cultivate a new paradigm that will positively affect educational beliefs, policies, and practices. No longer should education be concerned with sustainability while practicing a form of education that "sustains unsustainability."[2] The Caribbean educational establishments may have to contend on nurturing the vivid development of mindfulness of the environment over the last forty years. They need to search through each decade, bringing into focus the interconnection between humans and natural systems, as well as the restriction of the Caribbean region's aptitude to withstand for the foreseeable future, its growing human population and intensities of reckonable depletion (Mazmanian & Kraft, 2009).

---

[2] Steven Sterling. *Sustainable Education: Re-visioning Learning and Change*. (Cambridge, England: Green Books, 2001), 14.

Cultural Literacy: A Significant Skill for Climate Mitigation

Sterling (2001) stated that "a key to more sustainable and peaceful world is learning. It is the change of mind on which change towards sustainability depends; the difference of thinking that stands between a sustainable or chaotic future."[3] If education is the key to any kind of change, then it is important for universities to lead that change through ethical practices. Caribbean universities, therefore, are required to make proactive adjustments in the comprehensive strategic planning process in order to accommodate the complex changes and opportunities that have been and continue to be presented by climate change. Thus, there is a need for revolutionary actions since climate change creates an issue that is not only complex but also urgent.

Sterling (2001) also proposed that re-envisioning education calls for one to gaze further than the often-barred world of education. According to him, sustainable education is only expected to develop as it can be connected with and fortified by an optimistic cultural change from a larger perspective. The need for systematic thinking arises considering the complexities of climate change. Universities will be obliged to seek answers for three questions that focus on the very nature and ultimate roles of education. (1) What is education for?; (2) What is education?; and (3) Whose education? Subsequently, institutions will need to incorporate into the curriculum a new type of literacy that brings the ideology of sustainability into the forefront.

Sustainability literacy is needed to evaluate self and society when discussing culture. Stibbe (2009) used the term *sustainability literacy* to indicate the skills, attitudes, competencies, dispositions, and values that are necessary for surviving and thriving in the declining conditions of the world in ways that provide cessation to such deterioration as far as possible. Therefore, going forward, students would do well to acquire new skills for both climate change mitigation and the multidimensional issues that correspond with the concomitant multidimensional impact of the various effects, behaviors, and attitudes associated with climate. Additionally, when discussing sustainability literacy, the skill of cultural literacy assumes great significance. Following environment, economy, and education, the adaptation of sustainability literacy presents cultural literacy as the fourth section. It is a noteworthy skill for dealing with cultural diversity and/or *cultural competence*. Cultural literacy includes, but is not limited to, cultural competence, which imparts the ability to critically reflect on and, if necessary, bring about change in one's own culture. A significant factor includes the ability to examine customary behaviors within primary cultures in relation to both complementary and external secondary cultures.

According to Stibbe (2014), cultural competence refers to any policy practice or behavior that uses the essential elements of cultural proficiency as the standards for interaction on a consistent basis. With the West having a dominant culture, it is necessary to consider all Caribbean cultural traditions in order to maintain local cultural values, traditions, and infrastructure. At the same time, culturally competent educators should incorporate culturally appropriate behavior in performance appraisals and advocate for changes in policies, practices, as well as procedures

---

[3] Ibid., 12.

throughout the institutions of higher and the community. Lindsey (2009) defined cultural competence from an education's point of interest as viewing one's personal and organizational work as an interactive arrangement wherein the educator enters diverse settings in a manner that is respectfully inclusive to cultures that are different from that of the educator. However, as global education develops, both views incorporate the essential elements for culturally competent values, behaviors, policies, and practices that allow one to value, manage, assess, and adapt cultural knowledge to a sustainable environment.

An institution of higher learning's philosophy affects every aspect of learning within the environment. Most notably, in reference to sustainable and cultural literacy, an environment is cultivated with an inclusive approach that allows for the success of cultural competence. Given that global education promotes cultural diversity, there are cultures that are able to fulfill human needs from the local environment in ways which are sustainable, or at least, more sustainable than consumerism-based cultures (Stibbe, 2014). Within a sustainability framework, cultural competence allows institutions of higher learning to examine Caribbean cultures holistically while gaining ideas about climate change from them. With the West having a dominant culture, all Caribbean cultural traditions must be taken into consideration in order to maintain local (indigenous and/or native) cultural values, traditions, and infrastructure.

One may ask, why cultural literacy? If the mindset of individuals is to be changed rapidly, then the focus must be on how they operate within the group. According to Stibbe (2014), hyper-culture and indifference are opposing to a culture of specificity and difference, as a result of which they inflict damage on sustainable literacy because they quiet the requisite for self-critiquing, self-reflecting, or reflecting on the course adopted by society. However, the culture of specificity and difference proposes critical reflective thinking as a form of a dialogue between learners and educators on aspects of cultural and social discourse such as climate change impacts. This skill also brings into fruition whole group experiences with provision for answerability to oneself (Stibbe, 2014).

Designing for Change

As stated in the UNESCO (2015) report, there are many complex issues related to climate change in the Caribbean; however, mitigation and alternative approaches can lessen the multiple impacts. Although there seem to be several ideas for mitigation and adaptation, most of them tend to focus on sustainable development with significant interest in economic wealth. These research projects and strategic plans that are being developed appear to grant attention to economic advancement. Planning essentially emphasizes sustainability as a holistic paradigm (i.e., economy, environment, and equity), and as such, universities are obligated to provide innovative, collaborative, and explorative pathways to sustainability. Sterling and Jickling (2017) argued that there is a communal precipitousness to the globally pervasively systematic issues that are influencing individual and environmental prospects. This communal reck-lessness is evidently eroding both the broader civilization and educational systems, which is why it can subsequently be considered as maladaptive to this actuality. A profound learning reaction within educational thinking, policymaking, and prac-tice should be increasingly mounting in a society that is diverse in its behaviors and actions. An idea of this type of education will allow attention to be brought to generating resolves and assumptions in education (Jickling & Sterling, 2017).

As a result, Bartels and Parker (2012) called for faculty members in higher educa-tion to comprehend and come to terms with the nominative consequences of sustain-ability. They need to ask themselves why this is so significant currently. The study of sustainability can lead faculty members and students not only to rethink what is viable for their economies, but also to develop ways of utilizing their imagination for developing novel situations to mitigate this challenging situation. Universities in the Caribbean must inculcate the mindset that all is subject to change, which is often unexpected and unconceivable at the inception of the shift. Therefore, welcoming the idea of change will transform the lives of those who educate complementary to those being educated. However, if educators are skeptical of such transformative alterations, future adaptation will inexorably be rendered much more problematic. Considering this viewpoint, it is essential for those higher learning to see sustain-ability as (1) a boundless practice of continuous applications, assessments, and modi-fications, and (2) every choice concerning sustainable life claims is a compromise, as opposed to a solution because solution-finding involves change, and change is continuous.

Another factor to be considered is whether or not all the areas of academia will be able to integrate sustainability into specific course disciplines. Such integration will require moral rectitude and pragmatic knowledge of appreciative inquiry manage-ment styles on behalf of the instructor in developing courses that are aimed at finding an answer to what can be done in the specific disciplines with regard to the unparal-leled challenge facing the region due to climate change. Secondly, the idea of whether some disciplines will stand the test of time may arise. Consequently, universities may have to concentrate not only on teaching sustainability, but also on teaching sustain-ability where programs of study within schools foster their survivability. The ideal for survival, however, will be contingent on whether or not the said disciplines possess the ability to transform in the emerging age of sustainability. It is then a matter of the level of understanding demonstrated by those in the discipline of looking at ascer-taining whether integrating sustainability into specific courses and whether some disciplines will stand the test of time as being a symbiotic and fully encompassing ideal (Bartels & Parker, 2012).

It is then imperative for the Caribbean institutions to begin developing courses that are integral to sustainability which breakthrough disciplinary restrictions, not simply for the reason that there should be transitional and interdisciplinary methods to teaching such courses, but that they will be required for careers in the future. Caribbean universities, like their counterparts all over the globe, need to comprehend that institutions are student-driven. To that end, any institution that refuses to prepare students with the intellectual dexterity to segue between disciplines will have aborted their accountabilities of meeting these students' needs for achievement (Bartels & Parker, 2012).

Presently, sustainability may be seen as the all-encompassing philosophy that will rule the lives of present and future individuals; it appears to be the only progressive idea that both educators and students are currently experiencing (Bartels & Parker, 2012). Therefore, both instructors and students in the Caribbean higher learning institutions need to involve themselves in prioritizing sustainable practices, with reference to climate change. Consequently, sustainable practices outperform all ideas (i.e., geographical, political, economic, societal, and cultural) and classify them as being human. Bartels and Parker (2012) further explained that this presents sustainability, not only as an issue for deliberation, but also as a means of life that surpasses all further arrangements in the extent and intensity of its possibilities. Sustainability, therefore, if fully understood, will become transformative for Caribbean universities.

Consequently, universities must pave the way for interdisciplinary dialogue. This is the only way for bridging transformational knowledge (Bartel & Parker, 2012). According to Bilodieau et al. (2014), in the absence of a prepared or fixed formula to embed sustainability into higher education, the onus is on each institution to apply practices that are best suited to its existence. With creative and innovative developments taking place within Caribbean institutions, it is notable that the learner is instructed to become an agent of change. Guerra (2017) stated that educators must better understand these concepts to upgrade their disciplines, develop effective educational projects, and act as authentically engaged agents of change in order to promote these principles within society.

Correspondingly, Nolet (2017) encouraged students to investigate their communities, families, and cultures to create conditions that enable them to see that their own situations and ways of knowing are just as pertinent as those occurring in other communities and/or around the world. Institutions of higher learning will be required to find ways of applying culturally-based knowledge to real-world challenges so that students in the Caribbean can explore aspects of their own culture, and identity. In this context, Bandar et al. (2019) affirmed that the role of higher education institutions extends far beyond sustainable education and sustainable practices. They concluded that their essential role is necessary for the journey of learning and cultural literacy knowledge that endures over the years within institutions' intergenerational chronology. Institutions, then, ought to be available to the community in order to foster meaningful discussions about central, local, regional, and global issues such as climate change impacts. As stated by Orr (2002), an approach must be sorted out where the predicaments attributed to climate change are similar to ideas defined in the consumer culture. Therefore, designing for change should take into consideration a "culture permeated with old and solid knowledge."[4] He added that this task must be accomplished in three ways: (1) the public imagination has to be captured through a dramatization of all the aspects of the current situation, (2) a strategy for altering how humans view the world through the creation of more precise and expressive

---

[4] David W. Orr. *The Nature of Design: Ecology, Culture, and Human Intention* (New York. Oxford University Press, 2002), 72.

descriptions, and (3) political change. The efficacy of these strategies will depend on whether the public is cultured and prepared to understand these ideas. Orr called on institutions of higher learning (e.g., Caribbean universities included) to cease their ambitions to become "the research and development wing of high modernism."[5] Rather, they would do well to keep changing the paradigm of higher education by eradicating all impediments (i.e., both institutional and disciplinary) that hinder the fluid exchange of ideas upon which a long-lasting and decent Caribbean region may be developed.

Conclusion

To summarize, it is indeed a fact that climate change is impacting the Caribbean. The waters of the Caribbean continue to be beleaguered by bleaching of coral reefs, ocean acidification, and physical damage attributed to stronger hurricanes (McField, 2017). According to multiple regional and international news networks, such as NBC, ABC, and United Nations Reports, the loss of life, property, infrastructure, and setbacks to the economy from the floods and storms of 2015, 2017, 2018, and 2019 were devastating and cost Caribbean islands millions of dollars. Climate change mitigation is imperative in the Caribbean region because there is already evidence of complex issues being presented by the earthquakes in Puerto Rico in addition to the rest of the region in 2020.

However, disasters are also accompanied by opportunities for change. With change comes transformational learning. As Lewis and Conaty (2012) stated, humans need to brace themselves for intense trials over the next one hundred years. Climate change will be at the forefront of these challenges, but short-term solutions will be unable to ensure human survival. They suggested that there needs to be a radical shift in action, foresight, and thought in order to move each other as well as the planet to sustainable survivability. While humans have demonstrated their adaptive and resilient skills in the past, it remains to be seen whether or not it can be done on the measure and at the speed that is essential to change the existing dysfunctional and catastrophic course.

Lewis and Conaty (2012) made three suggestions that may be vital for universities embracing transformational engagement and taking comprehensive action with climate change mitigation: (1) sociological, ecological, and economical changes require the planet and humans to be viewed differently by redefining the vision, expanding knowledge, and displaying a fertile imagination in discovering new ways of providing for basic needs; (2) strategic pathways must be sought as an avenue to foster more balanced relationships between individual behavior and the earth. The pernicious imbalance that humans are faced with currently can be overwhelming, difficult, and even hopeless. Therefore, there is a need for creative action; (3) knowledge must be shared. Put succinctly, it is imperative for humans, who

[5] Ibid., 74.

possess the understanding and know-how for possibilities, to pass that knowledge and understanding onto others (Table 2.1).

Table 2.1 Framework of select skills needed when moving towards sustainability (Adopted from Stibbe, 2014)

Sustainability literacy skills	Abilities
The way of the commons thinking	The ability to visualize and permit a feasible future through joint action
Permaculture design	The ability to design life with nature as the model
Community gardening	The ability for building community and working within environmental limits
Ecological intelligence	The ability to develop the view that all systems in the world are interconnected
Futures thinking	The ability to envision scenarios of a more desirable future
New media literacy	The ability to develop communication skills for sustainability
Cultural literacy	The ability to develop an understanding of and respect for the cultural aspects of sustainability
Carbon capability	Developing an understanding of climate change and reducing carbon emissions
Greening business	The ability to drive environmental and sustainability improvements in the workplace
Materials awareness	The ability to expose the hidden impact of materials on sustainability
Appropriate technology and appropriate design	The ability to design systems, technologies and equipment in an appropriate way
Technological appraisal	The ability to evaluate technological innovations and decide whether they are valuable for our environment or situation at a particular time
Complexity, systems thinking and practice	The ability to develop skills and techniques for managing complex systems
Advertisement Awareness	The ability to expose advertisement discourse that undermines sustainability
Gaia awareness	Develop an awareness of the animate qualities of the earth

(continued)

Table 2.1 (continued)

Sustainability literacy skills	Abilities
Grounded economic awareness	The ability to develop an economic awareness that is based on ecological and ethical value
Transition skill	The ability to transition from the post-fossil fuel age
Effortless action	The ability to fulfill human needs effortlessly through working with nature
Values reflection and the earth charter	The ability to critique the values of an unsustainable society and consider alternatives
Social conscience	The ability to reflect on the deeply held opinions about social justice and sustainability
Coping with complexities	The ability to manage complex sustainable problems that we encounter, whether they are sudden, or they occur over time
Emotional and Well-being	The ability to research and reflect on the roots of emotional well-being and its valuable place in any given environment
Finding meaning in consuming	The ability to experience meaning, purpose, and satisfaction through non-material wealth
Being-in-the-world	The ability to think about self in interconnection and interdependence with the surrounding world

References

Bandar, A., Wafa, L., Talal, A., & Abdelhakim, A. (2019). Analyzing sustainability awareness among higher education faculty members: A case study in Saudi Arabia. Retrieved on March 07, 2020, from https://doi.org/10.3390/su11236837

Bilodeau, L., Podger, J., & Abd-El-Aziz, A. (2014). Advancing campus and community sustainability: Strategic alliances in action. *International Journal of Sustainability in Higher Education., 15*, 157–168.

Dictionary, O. (2003). *New York*. Oxford University Press.

Edwards, A. R. (2005). *The sustainability revolution: A portrait of a paradigm shift*. New Society Publishers.

Federal Emergency Management Agency, FEMA (2016). Federal insurance and mitigation: resilience and climate change adaptation. www.fema.gov.

Guerra, A. (2017). Integration of sustainability in engineering. Education. *International Journal of Sustainability in Higher Education., 18*, 436–454.

Hoffman, A. J. (2015). *How culture shapes the climate change debate*. Stanford University Press.

Huckle, J., & Sterling, S. (1996). *Education for sustainability*. Routledge Press.

Jickling, B., & Sterling, S. (2017). *Post-sustainability and environmental education: Remaking education for the future*. Switzerland: Palgrave McMillan.

Lewis, M., & Conaty, P. (2012). *The resilience imperative: Cooperative transitions to a steady-state economy*. New Society Publishers.

Lindsey, D. B., Jungwirth, L. D., Pahl, J. V. N. C., Lindsey, R. B. (2009). Culturally proficient leaning communities, confronting inequities through collaborative curiosity. California. Sage.

Mazaniaan, D. A., & Kraft, M. E. (2009). *Towards sustainable communities: Transition and transformations in environmental policy.* Institute of Technology Press.

McField, M. (2017). Impacts of climate change on coral in the coastal and marine environments of Caribbean Small Island Developing States (SIDS). Caribbean marine climate change report card: Science Review, P. 52.

National Hurricane Center. (2019). National hurricane center report.

Nolet, V. (2017). Quality education: Cultural competence and a sustainability worldview. *Kappa Delta Psi Record, 53,* 162–167. Retrieved on March 07, 2020, from https://doi.org/10.1080/002 28958.2017.1369276

Orr, D. W. (2002). *The nature of design: Ecology, culture, and human intention.* Oxford University Press.

Orr, D. W. (2016). Climate change, the long emergency, and a way forward. United States. Yale.

Portney, K. E. (2015). *Sustainability.* MIT Press.

Romm, J. (2018) Climate Change: What Everyone Needs to Know. Second edition. New York: Oxford University Press.

Sachs, J. D. (2015). *The age of sustainable development.* Columbia University Press.

Sterling, S. (2001). *Sustainable education: Re-visioning learning and change.* Green Books.

Stibbe, A. (2009). *The handbook of sustainability literacy.* Totnes, England: Green Books.

Stibbe, A. (Ed.). (2014). *The handbook of sustainable literacy: Skills for a changing world.* Green Books.

Taylor, M. (2017) *Climate change in the Caribbean—Learning lessons from Irma and Maria.* The Guardian. Retrieved on March 07, 2020, from www.thegardian.com

United Nations Economic Commissions for Latin America and the Caribbean UNECLAC. (2011). The economics of climate change in the Caribbean—Summary report.

United Nations Educational, Social and Cultural Organization, UNESCO. (2014). Shaping the Future We Want—UN Decade of Education for Sustainable Development (Final report).

UNESCO Science Report: Towards 2030. (2015). http://uis.unesco.org/sites/default/files/docume nts/unescoscience-report-towards-2030-part1.pdf.

Walker, B., & Salt, D. (2015). Resilience Thinking. Washington, DC: Island Press.

Watts, J. (2018). We have 12 years to limit climate change catastrophe, Warns UN. *The Guardian.* Retrieved on March 07, 2020, from www.theguardian.com/environment

What is Mitigation? (n.d.). Department of Homeland Security. Retrieved on March 08, 2020, from https://www.fema.gov/what-mitigation

Stibbe, A, ed. (2009) The Handbook of Sustainable Literacy: Skills for a Changing World. Cambridge, United Kingdom. Green Books.

Ilive R. Peltier is a Ph.D. student of Creative Leadership for Innovation and Change at the University of the Virgin Islands, where she is completing a dissertation on the Role of education, creativity and innovation in sustainability efforts. Her research focuses on the effects of climate change in the Caribbean region and what can be done to prepare not just Caribbean region leaders, but all who inhabit those islands with reference to unexpected, present and unforeseen changes that they face. As part of her public scholarship, she has presented parts of her research on sustainability at the 7th International Conference on Sustainable Development, 2019 in Rome, Italy, and has also co-written chapters for *A Companion to: Beyond the Long* Lines, The Caribbean Writer Press, The College of Liberal Arts and Social Sciences, University of the Virgin Islands.

Correen J. Celestine is a Ph.D. student at the University of the Virgin Islands, where she is majoring in Educational/Academic Leadership. Her research interests have been influenced by her M.A. in Teaching of English as a Second Language, which consists of cultural education, cultural sustainability, and equity in the teaching of English as a second language. In pursuit of her educational endeavors, she has also co-written chapters for *A Companion to: Beyond the Long Lines,*

The Caribbean Writer Press, The College of Liberal Arts and Social Sciences, University of the Virgin Islands, along with Ilive R. Peltier.

Dr. Mohomodou Boncana is an Associate Professor in the Department of Social Sciences at the University of the Virgin Islands where he teaches research methods (i.e., Quantitative Research, Qualitative Research, Participatory Action Research) and leadership theories. His teaching and scholarship have been informed by his Ph.D. Educational Leadership and Policy, his master's degree in educational research and statistical data analysis, and minor in qualitative research methods. In his scholarship, he has focused on topics related to educational leadership (e.g., parental involvement, mentoring, and organizational change) as well as issues associated with climate change. On September 20, 2019, Dr. Boncana and his students published a book at the UVI: Caribbean Writer Press titled: A companion to: Beyond the long lines. The book was a participatory action research on the impact of Hurricanes Irma and Maria on the population of the Virgin Islands.

Chapter 3
What Can Environmental Disasters Teach us About Grievances? A GIS Analysis

Miriam Matejova

Abstract Grievances are a crucial factor in social and protest movements, but there is disagreement over the exact ways in which they matter. This study re-examines the concept of grievance through the lens of environmental crises and in particular industrial environmental disasters. Such events have a potential to generate sudden grievances. These, unlike structural grievances, potentially affect non-deprived groups, which may then be mobilized for protest. I theorize that sudden grievances are rooted in objective losses of environmental values and associated reactionary emotions due to damage to the natural and built environment and human health. I use a geospatial analysis to examine the relationship between large industrial disasters, their proximity to locations that people value, and post-disaster protest. I find that while the loss of environmental value likely matters in protest mobilization, it is not sufficient for protest to develop or grow. This is in line with the theoretical expectation that grievances alone are not enough to mobilize people for protest. Whether sudden grievances serve as a prominent mobilizing factor or not depends on their meaning, rooted in the values that individuals attach to the affected environment. This suggests that more theoretical fine-tuning of the concept of grievance in protest mobilization may be able to answer the question of whether grievances are relevant—or explain why there is such mixed empirical evidence when it comes to their effects.

Grievances are among the most prominent reasons behind people's willingness to participate in collective action (Opp & Kittel, 2010; Van Stekelenburg & Klandermans, 2013). Scholars have established that grievances are a crucial factor in social movements; yet, despite volumes of research, there is still disagreement over the exact ways in which they matter (Grasso & Giugni, 2016; Pinard, 2011, 36–51; Walsh, 1981). In this chapter, I revisit the concept of grievances, examining them through the lens of environmental crises. Sudden environmental crises, such as

M. Matejova (✉)
Department of Political Science, Masaryk University, Joštova 218/10, 602 00 Brno, Czech Republic
e-mail: matejova@fss.muni.cz

industrial disasters, harm the environment valued by humans and therefore generate grievances that motivate protest. Recently, such protests have been on the rise in Europe, North America, and elsewhere, signaling public discontent with environmental degradation and related natural resource projects, including fracking, mining, and pipeline constructions (CBC, 2018; Halliday, 2017; Visser, 2017). What is the role of grievances in environmental protest? Why do environmental disasters generate grievances?

In this study, I discuss two types of grievances linked to environmental crises: structural and sudden. While structural environmental grievances are related to the issues of social and environmental justice, sudden grievances potentially affect (and lead to mobilization of) non-deprived groups. I focus on sudden grievances, theorizing that they are rooted in objective losses of environmental values (and associated reactionary emotions) due to damage to the natural environment, human health, and built environment. I then use geospatial analysis to examine the relationship between large industrial environmental disasters, their proximity to locations that people value, and post-disaster protest. I find that while the loss of environmental value likely matters in protest mobilization, it is not sufficient for a protest to develop or grow. This is in line with the theoretical expectation that grievances alone are not enough to mobilize people for protest (McCarthy & Zald, 1973; Oberschall, 1978). Whether sudden grievances serve as a prominent mobilizing factor or not likely depends on their meaning, rooted in the values that individuals attach to the affected environment. More theoretical fine-tuning of the concept of grievances in protest mobilization may be able to answer not only *whether* but *how* they are relevant.

This chapter is divided into two main parts. The first discusses the concepts of structural and sudden grievances, several grievance-generating factors linked to industrial environmental disasters, and hypotheses derived from those factors. The second part consists of a geographic information system (GIS) analysis as a preliminary evaluation of the proposed hypotheses based on the available geospatial evidence. It contains a discussion of the significance of using GIS in social science research, means of data collection and visualization, as well as analysis and discussion of the findings. The chapter concludes with a summary and implications of the findings as well as suggestions for future work.

Environmental Disasters and Grievances

Along with resources, political opportunity structures, and framing, grievances are some of the most fundamental building blocks of social (and protest) movements (della Porta & Diani, 2006; Eckstein, 2001; McAdam et al., 2001; Tarrow, 1994; Tilly, 1978). A grievance is "the feeling of having been wronged, as distinguished from the actual or supposed circumstance, acts, or events that are believed responsible for that feeling" (Giuliano, 2011, 13). Various deprivation scholars have argued that discontent and collective grievances that give rise to particular social movements are a product of some specific set of structural conditions as well as the perceived gap between expectations and reality (Gurney & Tierney, 1982; Gurr, 1970; Morrison, 1971). Environmental justice scholars have examined ways in which grievances interact with elite responses and state mechanisms of control, environmental justice frames, or environmental networks (Cable & Shriver, 1995; Čapek, 1993; Rootes, 2013; Sanchez et al., 2017; Shriver et al., 2014; Walker, 2009). Generally, these studies have focused on structural grievances that arise from slow-moving social processes and structural conditions related to economic and social variables. Through the lens of industrial environmental disasters, however, grievances may also be abrupt, suddenly imposed conditions.

Industrial environmental disasters generally arise from human exploitation of natural resources; frequently, they are events that damage ecosystems or ecological complexes valued by humans (Birkland, 1998; Gephart, 1984; Sindermann, 2006). They tend to be "acts of corporations" rather than "acts of God." Acute (also known as sudden-onset) disasters cause sudden harm (e.g., loss of life, illness) shortly after a single exposure, while chronic (or slow-onset) disasters take a longer time to manifest and are often viewed as social problems involving complex agents (see Table 3.1) (Hannigan, 2012, 13). Grievances can be linked to industrial disasters because such events frequently have clear perpetrators and occur in the context of existing (or lacking) government regulations. In other words, if a destructive disaster is preventable, it is likely to lead to public feelings of being wronged—either by the polluter, the government, or both. Three types of grievances are relevant in the context of environmental disasters: issues of social justice, issues of environmental justice, and sudden grievances.

Environmental disasters are likely to channel (rather than generate) grievances rooted in issues of social and environmental justice. The former may encourage mobilization by economically and socially marginalized communities protesting a variety of issues, including inequality, poverty, crime, or political exclusion (Pelling & Dill, 2008). For example, the larger and more widespread the income inequality, the larger the related grievance and therefore potential for protest. However, in such cases, disasters and their impacts likely serve as a trigger (given the underlying conditions) rather than a true reason for protesting.

Similarly, grievances related to environmental justice concern the issue of an inequitable share of environmental ills with which poor communities, indigenous communities, and communities of colour live (Carruthers & Rodriguez, 2009; Kuehn, 2000; Martinez-Alier, 2016; Schlosberg, 2004). Inequitable share of environmental ills often mirrors the inequity in socio-economic and cultural status. Therefore,

Table 3.1 Typology of environmental disasters according to source and onset

	Acute	Chronic
"Natural"	e.g., Hurricanes, typhoons, earthquakes, volcanic eruptions	e.g., Desertification, droughts, extreme winter conditions
Industrial	e.g., Marine blowouts, oil tanker accidents, nuclear accidents	e.g., Leaking pipelines, hazardous waste contamination, long-term mine leaks, oil seepage, nuclear testing sites

a disaster may disproportionally affect certain groups relative to others (Adeola, 2011; Drury & Olson, 1998), thus exacerbating existing environmental and socio-economic problems. In such cases, a disaster serves as a catalyst to public demands for potentially broader societal changes, but these demands are more directly linked to environmental concerns than to grievances rooted in issues of social justice.

There is a third, less traditional type of grievances—sudden rather than structural. Environmental disasters generate (as opposed to channel) sudden grievances because such grievances stem from certain characteristics of disasters like the speed of onset and extent of the damage. These grievances potentially affect (and lead to mobilization of) non-deprived groups; they can be "suddenly realized" (in cases of chronic industrial disasters) or "suddenly imposed" (in cases of acute industrial disasters) (Walsh, 1981). Sudden environmental grievances are crosscutting; they can affect a lot of people irrespective of wealth, education, or class as long as those people value the affected area. Whether sudden grievances motivate environmental protest rests on both objective conditions and felt sentiments (Pinard, 2011, 5). There are many ways in which environmental disasters can create such objective conditions. In the following paragraphs, I discuss two: loss of environmental values from damage to the natural environment and impacts on human health, life, and economies due to disaster proximity.

Grievances and Environmental Values

A disaster that damages the environment will likely generate anger and frustration because of affected people's perceptions that the environment's value has been diminished. Two types of values are likely to be most affected: (1) market values (related to economic concerns for livelihood) and non-market values (linked to the values inherent in nature that are not traded in the markets). Market values of ecosystem services are "prices" for natural capital as they are traded on commodity markets. If disasters diminish nature's "ecological yields," the resulting loss can be expressed in monetary terms. For example, the Deepwater Horizon spill resulted in large revenue losses to the Gulf of Mexico's commercial fishing industry, estimated at $94.7 million to $1.6 billion in the first eight months (Schleifstein, 2016). Non-market values include, among other things, existence value (derived from knowing that nature exists) and consumptive and non-consumptive use values such as resources and recreational activities that do not enter the market (Greenley et al., 1981; Haab & McConnell, 2002). Environmental disasters diminish any of these values—some are provided as examples in Table 3.2.

Although the valuation of natural capital has been criticized for putting a price tag on nature (Monbiot, 2011), it is necessary for policymaking that involves monetary trade-offs in resource allocation. "Pricing" nature also allows for comparing environmental values over time and across societies. Valuation is therefore useful in understanding and measuring the values that the public holds for the environment. Valuation studies, of course, do not show whether the willingness to pay

Table 3.2 Environmental values and pollution from industrial disasters

	Type of value	Area	Species	Disaster (example)
Market		Forest harvested for timber; access to parks; ecotourism	Commercial fish and seafood; commercial livestock	Chernobyl—impacts on the reindeer industry in Sweden (Soderqvist, 2000)
Non-market	Consumptive	Resources (e.g., firewood for personal use)	Recreational hunting and fishing	Deepwater Horizon—recreational fishing (Alvarez et al., 2014)
	Non-consumptive	Recreational activities (hiking, boating)	Birdwatching	Exxon Valdez—nature viewing (Hausman et al., 1995)
	Option	Water quality for recreational purposes; groundwater quality	Yet undiscovered medicinal plants available in the future	Loss of option value due to water contamination from mining (Greenley et al., 1981)
	Existence	Protected areas	Protected/at risk species	Prestige—oiled habitats and fauna (Loureiro et al., 2009)
	Bequest	Protected areas	Protected/at risk species	Prestige—avoid future oiled species and habitats (Loureiro & Loomis, 2013)

for oil spill prevention programs or habitat restoration equates to the willingness to protest. However, some studies have linked the diminishment of environmental values to emotions (Kahneman & Knetsch, 1992; Leon et al., 2014), which are at the core of social movements (Goodwin & Polletta, 2001). Emotions, and particularly fear and anger as they relate to risk perception, are also central to understanding grievance-generating effects of disasters that occur in proximity to human populations (Rasmussen, 1992).

Grievances and Disaster Proximity

Aside from generating sudden grievances due to loss of environmental values, industrial disasters concern the public when they occur in people's "backyards." There are several likely reasons why: the NIMBY syndrome, impacts on human health, human life toll, and property damage and other economic losses.[1]

Public resistance to industrial development and its negative consequences has been well-examined in studies of the so-called NIMBY syndrome.[2] The NIMBY phenomenon involves the public protesting different types of land use—from sites to store hazardous chemical or nuclear waste to low-income housing and airports to wind power generation stations—because such developments are considered undesirable (Armour, 1984; Guo et al., 2015; Rabe, 1994; Weisberg, 1993; Wolsink, 1994).[3] NIMBY is usually discussed in the context of unwanted land use, but the underlying contention is also applicable to industrial disasters that occur in close proximity to human populations—the public does not want to be disproportionally affected by negative consequences of technological processes that, in general, benefit a wider population. For example, oil is needed for people's daily lives, and a fraction of the population usually suffers the consequences of an oil spill. A variety of reasons for NIMBY syndrome have been proposed—from embracing new environmental values (Thomashaw, 1995) to fear of new technological risks (Slovic, 1987) to public distrust of authorities (Kraft & Clary, 1991).

When it comes to industrial disasters, much of the dissatisfaction is likely due to perceptions of high risk due to the toll on human health and life. Nuclear accidents, for example, produce both short and long-term health effects that may reach well beyond disaster origin. Exposure from inhalation and both ground-level and atmospheric external pathways as well as due to ingestion of contaminated water and food is likely to lead to a spike in illnesses and cancer-related mortalities (Anspaugh et al., 1988). Long-term psychological effects such as fear, anxiety, and depression have been linked to large nuclear disasters such as Chernobyl and Fukushima (Bromet, 2012; Hoeve & Jacobson, 2012). In cases of oil spills and mine leaks, inhalation and touching of oil products (e.g., during clean-up) and ingestion of contaminated food can lead to adverse health effects (Lyons et al., 1999; Solomon & Janssen, 2010).

Although less frequently than disasters from natural hazards, industrial environmental disasters also claim lives. For example, the 1972 Buffalo Creek mining disaster resulted in at least 118 fatalities, destroyed 500 homes, and displaced 4,000 people (Davies et al., 1972, 1). The event was a massive flood caused by a collapsed coal slurry dam in West Virginia. Other similar disasters have resulted in human casualties: a burst dam at the Ajka alumina plant in Hungary killed ten and injured 120 people (Taylor, 2011), and a dam failure at the Tashan iron ore mine in China claimed 254 lives (BBC, 2008).

Industrial disasters also result in property damage and economic losses not necessarily or solely linked to nature. The ten most damaging industrial accidents between

---

[1] These may include losses in the non-market values of ecological goods and services.

[2] The syndrome is defined as "intense, often emotional and usually organized opposition to siting proposals that residents of a local community believe will result in adverse impacts" (Wexler, 1996).

[3] The central problem of these developments, as seen by the affected residents, is the distribution of costs and benefits such as effects on human health vs. economic benefits—while the costs may be geographically concentrated, the benefits are usually enjoyed by a wider, more dispersed population.

1900 and 2017 caused economic losses[4] between \$541 million[5] (\$1.4 billion in 2019 dollars) and US\$20 billion (\$23 billion in 2019 dollars).[6] For example, the Prestige oil spill resulted in US\$10 billion (\$14 billion in 2019 dollars) worth of damages, and the Chernobyl nuclear disaster caused US\$2.8 billion (\$6.5 billion in 2019 dollars) in economic losses.

Industrial Disasters and Protest: Variables and Hypotheses

Over the past hundred years, at least 38 large[7] oil spills, mine leaks, and nuclear accidents[8] occurred in OECD countries. Varying sizes of non-violent protest followed these disasters, from none to small-sized demonstrations to mass protest movements. For example, Canada's 2014 Mount Polley mining disaster, one of the largest in Canadian history, led to only a small localized protest even though the responsible corporation suffered no charges or fines (Linnitt, 2016). Japan's 2011 Fukushima Daiichi nuclear disaster generated almost immediate anti-nuclear protests in Germany, but it took much longer for the Japanese people to take to the streets, and the movement was less organized and had far less political traction (The Economist, 2014). Many large industrial disasters have gone without notice or have been quickly forgotten (see Tables 3.3, 3.4 and 3.5). The variation in the public response to these events allows for an examination of the relationship between sudden grievances and their potential role in public protest.

   This study is an analytical probe to establish whether there are any patterns between disaster location, nonviolent protest, and several geospatial variables linked to the values that people hold for the environment. My hypotheses are derived from the theoretical insights discussed in the previous two sub-sections; they rely on five independent variables (IVs) and two dependent variables (DVs). The IVs relate to disaster damage in terms of the location of pollution. Pollution is defined as a volume

---

[4] The economic losses include damage to property, crops, and livestock.

[5] This was the San Juanico disaster—a series of explosions at a liquid petroleum gas tank farm in San Juanico, Mexico on November 19, 1984.

[6] The Deepwater Horizon disaster. See CRED, "The Emergency Events Database (EM-DAT)," http://www.emdat.be/ (last accessed in 2020).

[7] In terms of the size and scale of their ecological damage.

[8] Chemical spills are not included in the dataset, since large, environmentally damaging chemical spills are uncommon, and most of the spills that have occurred in the past decades are small, especially compared to large oil spills. Data on chemical spills are available from NOAA's incident database (https://incidentnews.noaa.gov—last accessed in 2020) and CEDRE's database on spills (http://wwz.cedre.fr/en/Our-resources/Spills/—last accessed in 2020).

[11] The 2000 Baia Mare mine cyanide spill is included in the dataset, because, at the time, it was Europe's worst environmental disaster since Chernobyl (BBC, 2000).

[12] There is no INES level linked to this uranium mine spill; although, the radiation was reportedly comparable to that of the Three Mile Island disaster (Graf, 1990).

[13] Arnold (1995).

Table 3.3 Large oil spills in advanced industrial democracies, 1900—present[a]

Name	Location	Date	Size (tonnes, thousand)	Protest[9]	
				Size (participants)	Scope
Kalamazoo river	USA, MI	July 10	3	N/A[10]	
Deepwater Horizon	USA, Gulf of Mexico	Apr–July 10	645	Up to 849,000 (USA) Small (UK)	Transnational
Prestige	Spain, Galicia	Nov 02	77	Up to 200,000	National
Sea Empress	UK, Wales	Feb 96	72	Up to 100,000	National
MV Braer	UK, Scotland	Jan 93	85	N/A	
Aegean Sea	Spain, A Coruña	Dec 92	74	10,000	Local
MT Haven	Italy	Apr 91	144	N/A	
Exxon Valdez	USA, AK	Mar 89	34	Up to 10,000	National
Odyssey	Canada, NS	Nov 88	132	N/A	
Irenes Serenade	Greece	Feb 80	100	N/A	
Independenta	Turkey	Nov 79	94	N/A	
Atlantic Empress/Aaegean Ccaptain	Trinidad and Tobago	July 79	287	N/A	
Betelgeuse	Ireland	Jan 79	40	N/A	
Andros Patria	Spain, A Coruña	Dec 78	60	N/A	
Amoco Cadiz	France, Brittany	Mar 78	223	Up to 15,000	Local
Hawaiian Patriot	USA, HI	Feb 77	95	N/A	
Urquiola	Spain, A Coruña	May 76	100	N/A	
Jakob Maersk	Portugal	Jan 75	88	N/A	
Othello	Sweden	Mar 70	60–100	N/A	
Torrey Canyon	UK, England	Mar 67	119	N/A	
Lakeview Gusher	USA, CA	Mar 1910–Sept 1911	1230	N/A	

[a]Data are from NOAA's incident database (https://incidentnews.noaa.gov/raw/index—last accessed in 2020), cross-referenced with ITOPF's oil spill statistics ("Oil Tanker Spill Statistics 2019," http://www.itopf.com/knowledge-resources/data-statistics/statistics—last accessed in 2020) and CEDRE's database of oil and chemical spills (http://wwz.cedre.fr/en/Our-resources/Spills/—last accessed in 2020)

---

[9] Data on post-disaster protests were gathered from a systematic search of LexisNexis Academic (and Hasegawa 2014).

[10] N/A stands for "data not available" due to lack of available information on protests that could be linked to these disasters.

Table 3.4 Large mine leaks in advanced industrial democracies, 1900—present[a]

Name	Location	Date	Size (m^3, thousand)	Protest	
				Size	Scope
Mount Polley	Canada, BC	Aug 14	4500	Small	Local
Talvivaara	Finland	Nov 12	1200	Up to 20,000	National
Kingston Fossil Plant	USA, TN	Dec 08	4200	N/A	
Martin County	USA, KY	Oct 00	1200	N/A	
Aitik	Sweden	Sept 00	2500	N/A	
Baia Mare[11]	Romania and the region	Jan 00	100	N/A	
Los Frailes	Spain	Apr 98	5000	N/A	
Tyrone	USA, NM	Oct 80	2000	N/A	

[a]Data are from the US CDC database (https://www.cdc.gov/niosh/mining/statistics/content/allminingdisasters.html; last accesses in 2020), Canadian Disaster Database (https://www.publicsafety.gc.ca/cnt/rsrcs/cndn-dsstr-dtbs/index-elastn.aspx; accesses in 2020) and other sources (EPA, 1997; European Commission, 2010; European Environmental Agency, 2010; Mudder & Botz, 2004; WISE, 2017)

Table 3.5 Large nuclear disasters in advanced industrial democracies, 1900—present[a]

Name	Location	Date	INES scale	Protest	
				Size	Scope
Fukushima	Japan	Mar 11	7	Up to 110,000 (Germany) Up to 64,000 (Tokyo)	Transnational
Tokaimura	Japan	Sept 99	4	2170	National
Saint Laurent des Eaux	France	Mar 80	4	N/A	
Church Rock	USA, NM	Jul 79	N/A[12]	N/A	
Three Mile Island	USA, PA	Mar 79	5	Over 75,000	National
Lucens reactor	Switzerland	Jan 69	5	N/A	
SL-1	USA, ID	Jan 61	4	N/A	
Windscale fire	UK, England	Oct 57	5	NO[13]	
Chalk River	Canada, ON	Dec 52	5	N/A	

[a]Data are from The Guardian (2011), Sovacool (2008, 2010, 2011)

of contaminants (i.e., chemical substances from industrial processes) that enter the environment and change it adversely. In the context of industrial disasters, pollution is understood in two ways: type (i.e., oil, mine, and nuclear pollution) and volume (i.e., the spilled substance measured in tonnes or cubic meters).[14] The specific IVs then follow:

---

[14] An additional way to think about pollution is in terms of its scope (i.e., the size and type of affected area). The scope of pollution differs for each disaster in the database. Therefore, it is not feasible to create consistent categorization of scope of damage. Instead, this type of impact can be mapped to allow for a more accurate analysis of disaster damage than simply using points of origin for disaster locations.

- Presence/absence of pollution in protected areas such as designated parks or otherwise areas of conservation value;
- Presence/absence of pollution that affects designated species at risk or charismatic species;
- Presence/absence of pollution of major waterways and/or groundwater;
- Presence/absence of pollution in densely populated areas;
- Presence/absence of pollution in recreational areas near human dwellings such as public beaches and parks.

The dependent variables are protest occurrence and protest size. The former is a binary variable, either present or absent. The latter is an ordinal variable with three categories: small (1–999 participants), medium (1,000–99,999), and large (100,000–1,000,000).[15] Measuring this DV entails counting the estimated maximum number of individuals that participated in relevant protest events.

It is likely that all the IVs are positively correlated with post-disaster protest. Since other factors than grievances are likely needed for protest movements to develop, we may see no protests even if the IVs are present, but we should see no protest if they are absent (e.g., in cases of disasters far away from population centers and away from protected areas). Furthermore, protest size is unlikely to be linked to disaster characteristics. Large protests require a large initial pool of sympathizers who are mobilized through framing (Cooper, 2002; Opp, 2009, p. 216; Van Stekelenburg & Klandermans, 2013). Disaster damage may provide fuel for framing efforts but by itself is unlikely to determine protest size. Therefore, there may or may not be a relationship between protest size and the IVs.

Human proximity to a disaster is likely to generate public concerns over health impacts, property damage, and/or concerns over losses of some environmental values—for example, aesthetic or recreational. The more densely populated the impact zone, the larger the potential pool of affected (and concerned) individuals, which increases the likelihood of protest. This leads to my first hypothesis:

> **H1:** The closer the disaster to dense population centers such as cities, the more likely are protests to occur. Therefore, given their common locations, nuclear accidents are likely to be linked to large protests, mine leaks to small protests, and oil spills to small, medium, or large protests, depending on the spill remoteness.

Concerns over environmental losses may be linked but not necessarily limited to human proximity to a disaster. For example, individuals have been shown to value charismatic species such as whales and bald eagles even if they live nowhere close to those species' habitats (Richardson & Loomis, 2009). Similarly, protected areas such as national parks may be valuable to some due to an opportunity to visit (if one lives nearby) but also for other reasons—as national heritage, for example, which may be important to individuals who have never visited. Therefore, even damage

---

[15] According to Chenoweth and Stephan (2011, 32), an average nonviolent campaign has about 200,000 participants. This is, however, with respect to political resistance and campaigns aimed at overthrowing the established regimes. Environmental campaigns in democracies tend to be smaller, depending on the country (see Rootes, 2003).

to remote protected areas may generate sudden grievances and public protests. This leads to my second hypothesis:

H2: The greater the loss of environmental values (understood in terms of market and non-market values of the affected environment), the more likely are protests to occur.

Lastly, if the disaster impact zone is away from dense population centers and protected areas, the damage is unlikely to generate sudden grievances. Therefore, in such cases, there is no immediate reason to expect post-disasters protests to develop. The third hypothesis therefore states:

H3: There should be no protests if a disaster occurs in remote areas with low environmental value.

The above hypotheses are rooted in two different understandings of the human relationship with the natural environment. The first is the instrumental view. From this perspective, the environment only has value when perceived in relation to human societies. As such, environmental losses only translate into grievances if those losses directly affect humans and human activities. The second, opposing belief holds that the environment has intrinsic (or inherent) value regardless of humans and human needs. Research shows that a lot of people believe in intrinsic value of nature, but it is unclear whether such beliefs are more powerful in motivating actions like protest (Nelson et al., 2015). While the analysis presented in this chapter cannot provide a definite answer, an evaluation of the above hypotheses might offer some evidence one way or another. Hypothesis 1, for example, is rooted in the instrumental logic, while Hypotheses 2 and 3 rely in part on the recognition of the intrinsic value of nature. The rest of the chapter discusses an evaluation of these hypotheses through a GIS method, along with an explanation of the significance of this approach, and the process of data collection, coding, and mapping.

GIS Analysis

A geographic information system is a computer-based database system and mapping technology used for capturing, storing, analyzing, and displaying geographically referenced data (Batty, 2003). Through GIS one can display multiple layers of different data on a single map, which allows for analyzing patterns and relationships. For example, GIS can calculate distances and area sizes and layer thematic maps vertically (e.g., layer population density over a city map), or display data for one area over time (e.g., fluctuations in air quality) (Batty, 2003; Maantay & Ziegler, 2006; Mitchell, 1999).

In academic research, the use of GIS and spatial analysis has been prevalent in earth sciences, geography, and regional science, but few studies have attempted to integrate spatial analysis into social science (Goodchild et al., 2000). Despite its obvious utility in environmental studies at both local and global levels, the use of GIS has been limited to analyzing relationships between human activities and local

Table 3.6 Coding post-disaster protest data

Protest population range	Label	Code
0	None	0
1–999	Small	1
1000–99,999	Medium	2
100,000–1,000,000	Large	3

environmental changes (e.g., deforestation, land use patterns, or spatial dimensions of sustainability) (Bockstael, 1996; Chomitz & Gray, 1995; Nelson & Hellerstein, 1997; Stonich, 1998). The relationship between human activities and global environmental changes has not been fully articulated, with a disconnect between earth system science research and human effects such as migration, urbanization, and others (see O'Neil et al., 2017). Similar disconnect is evident in disaster studies, as well. GIS has been used for disaster response and planning purposes as well as to map and analyze the impacts of some disasters (Ivanov & Zatyagalova, 2008; Joyce et al., 2009; Turner, 2003). My study utilizes GIS to evaluate the linkages between large-scale ecological damage from disasters within countries and disasters' social impacts both within and across states.

Data, Analysis, and Mapping

The database used for the analysis contains 21 oil spills, eight mine leaks, and nine nuclear accidents (see Tables 3.3, 3.4 and 3.5). The information on the disaster occurrence and location was collected from several databases, including NOAA's Incident News, ITOPF's oil spill statistics, and CEDRE data on oil and chemical spills as well as various governmental, scholarly, and media publications.

The initial GIS data collection and classification was completed in three steps. First, all disasters were located through their coordinates[16] through ArcMap, part of the ArcGIS software. The different disaster types were labelled in ArcMap, using simple graphics. Second, protest was coded as an ordinal variable and ranked from zero (none occurred) to three (large protest). The categories, as shown in Table 3.6, are based on protest population ranges (i.e., counts of protest participants). Overall, the protest data include the locations of protest occurrence, the counts of participants as well as several types of nonviolent protest: demonstration, petition, boycott, and activist stunts.[17] The data were collected through a systematic search of LexisNexis Academic and, in some cases, supplemented by scholarly literature. Protest points were then located on the ArcMap and presented as graduated symbols based on their assigned codes (i.e., size).

---

[16] Most coordinates are available in NOAA's Incident News database, but some were obtained from GeoHack and GoogleMaps. Consequently, some of these coordinates may be less accurate.

[17] These were counted as separate protest events if different types occurred concurrently.

Third, data from national statistical agencies and other sources were used to create several layers on ArcMap, to correspond with the independent variables identified in the previous section. Specifically, the protest data were overlaid with those on disaster origin as well as the data on population density and protected areas. The latter has been published by the United Nations Environment World Conservation Monitoring Centre and is available as part of the World Database on Protected Areas (WDPA).[18] The database contains global data on marine and terrestrial protected areas as defined by the International Union for Conservation of Nature (IUCN) and the Convention on Biological Diversity (CBD).[19] These include national parks, wildlife protection areas, ecosystem reserves, conservation areas, green corridors, and protected water surfaces (and the common fishery area in Japan) and are available for download as shapefiles.[20]

The population density data were more difficult to acquire since each country collects and publishes this information in their own way. The data for Asia are from Harvard University's JapanMap and ChinaMap online platforms.[21] The European census data are available from the European Commission's Eurostat database.[22] However, since it was difficult to work with this dataset in ArcGIS (due to its large size), an alternative dataset was acquired from ESRI's ArcGIS online platform, which offers the same data at a lower resolution. For North America, the data sources were Statistics Canada and the US Census Bureau.[23] The census population data for Mexico, used in this analysis, have been assembled by an independent researcher and made publicly available online.[24] Since the timeline for the disasters as a whole spans a century, displaying the census data for each disaster year in a single map along with other variables was not feasible. Therefore, the maps display the latest available population density data: 2010 for Japan and the United States, 2016 for Europe, and 2017 for Canada and Mexico.[25]

Due to difficulties with data collection, three independent variables have not been mapped: species at risk/charismatic species, important waterways/groundwater, and recreational areas near population centers (e.g., public beaches and city parks). These,

---

[18] Available at https://protectedplanet.net (last accessed in 2020).

[19] See http://www.biodiversitya-z.org/content/protected-area (last accessed in 2020). Proposed protected areas are excluded from this dataset.

[20] The data used for this analysis were published in November 2017. For information on data collection, see https://protectedplanet.net/c/calculating-protected-area-coverage (last accessed in 2020).

[21] See http://worldmap.harvard.edu/japanmap/ and http://worldmap.harvard.edu/chinamap/.

[22] See http://ec.europa.eu/eurostat (last accessed in 2020).

[23] For the US Census data, see https://www.census.gov. The Statistics Canada data are available through Simply Analytics from www.simplyanalytics.com (last accessed in 2020).

[24] See https://blog.diegovalle.net/2013/06/shapefiles-of-mexico-agebs-manzanas-etc.html (last accessed in 2020).

[25] Using the most recent data for disasters that occurred much further in the past is, of course, problematic. Some disaster impact zones may have been more sparsely populated at the time of the disaster occurrence than they are now. Therefore, the likelihood of protest mobilization in such cases may have been lower.

however, are to some extent captured in the data on protected areas and densely populated areas. A variety of tools, including TextMate, Sublime Text, and Microsoft Excel, were used to consolidate and input the different data formats into the ArcMap. Finished maps were then fine-tuned in Adobe Illustrator. Figs. 3.1, 3.2 and 3.3 present the results of these data collection and mapping efforts. To reduce visual clutter, the data were divided regionally and presented as three maps: Europe, North America, and Asia. In each map, the respective disaster symbols mark the geographic origin of the particular disaster. Each is then linked, through solid lines, to its associated protest. As the primary independent variables, both the population density and protected area layers are also displayed.

Discussion

Upon examining the maps, one can see slight regional differences in post-disaster protest patterns. Europe has experienced most large-scale disasters and most post-disaster protests with the highest number of participants. Of all disaster types, mine leaks have generated the fewest public protests in both North America and Europe.[26] This is not surprising, given that mining accidents are generally viewed as less threatening (Perrow, 1984). In contrast, oil spills have resulted in the highest number and variety of protests—some of them transnational. With respect to nuclear disasters, only those originating in North America and Japan led to protests, with the Fukushima disaster having the largest social impact in Japan and Europe. The proximity of disasters to population centers and protected areas does not seem to consistently affect post-disaster protest mobilization. I discuss these findings in detail below.

As seen from the maps in Figs. 3.1, 3.2 and 3.3, mining disasters with large environmental impacts are often followed by minimal public response. Of the four large North American mine leaks, small public protests erupted only in the aftermath of the Mount Polley disaster in Canada. Similarly, in Europe, out of four large mining disasters, only one—Talvivaara in Finland—led to protests. The population density in disaster zones did not seem to affect the protest occurrence in the expected direction, since mine leaks that occurred close to more densely populated areas (such as Los Frailes in Spain and Kingston in the USA) generated no public protests. Both Mount Polley and Talvivaara mines are located in remote and largely unpopulated areas, with Talvivaara being much further from population centers than Mount Polley. In both cases, protests occurred in cities (Vancouver for Mount Polley and Helsinki for Talvivaara); although, in Finland, there were also protests in smaller towns. The sizes of protests after these two disasters differed—in Vancouver, the protest was small, with only a handful of people, while in Finland, it ranged from ten to 20,000

---

[26] There were no large-scale mine leaks and oil spills in Japan and South Korea (i.e., the only Asian OECD members).

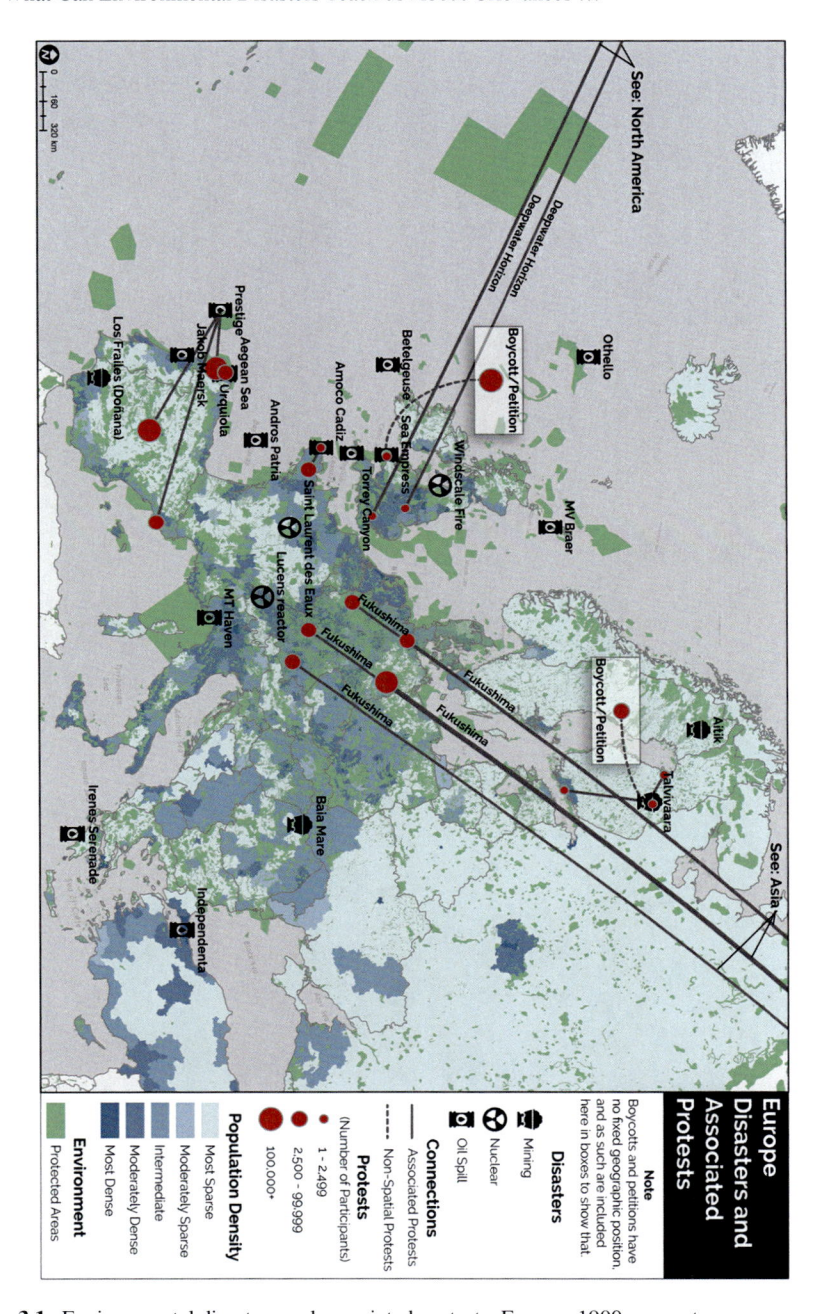

Fig. 3.1 Environmental disasters and associated protests: Europe, 1900–present

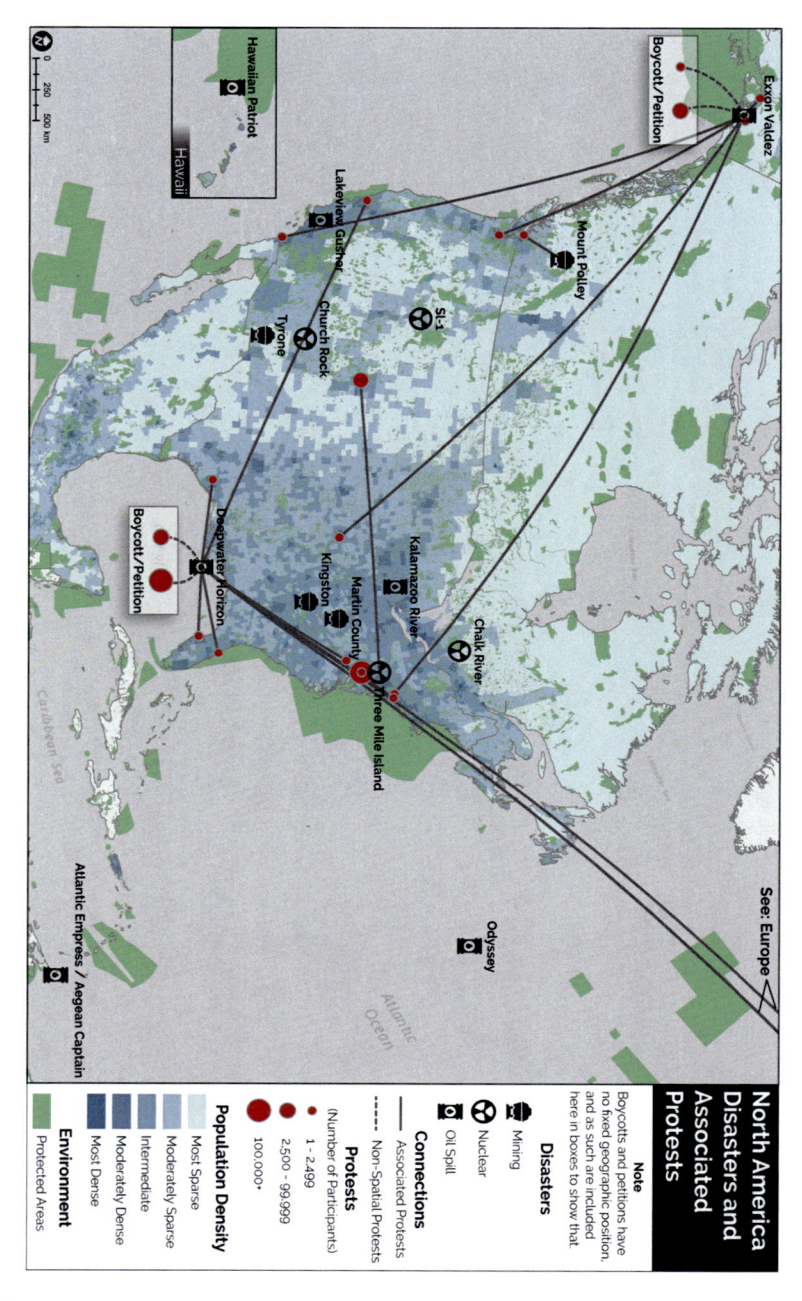

Fig. 3.2 Environmental disasters and associated protests: North America, 1900–present

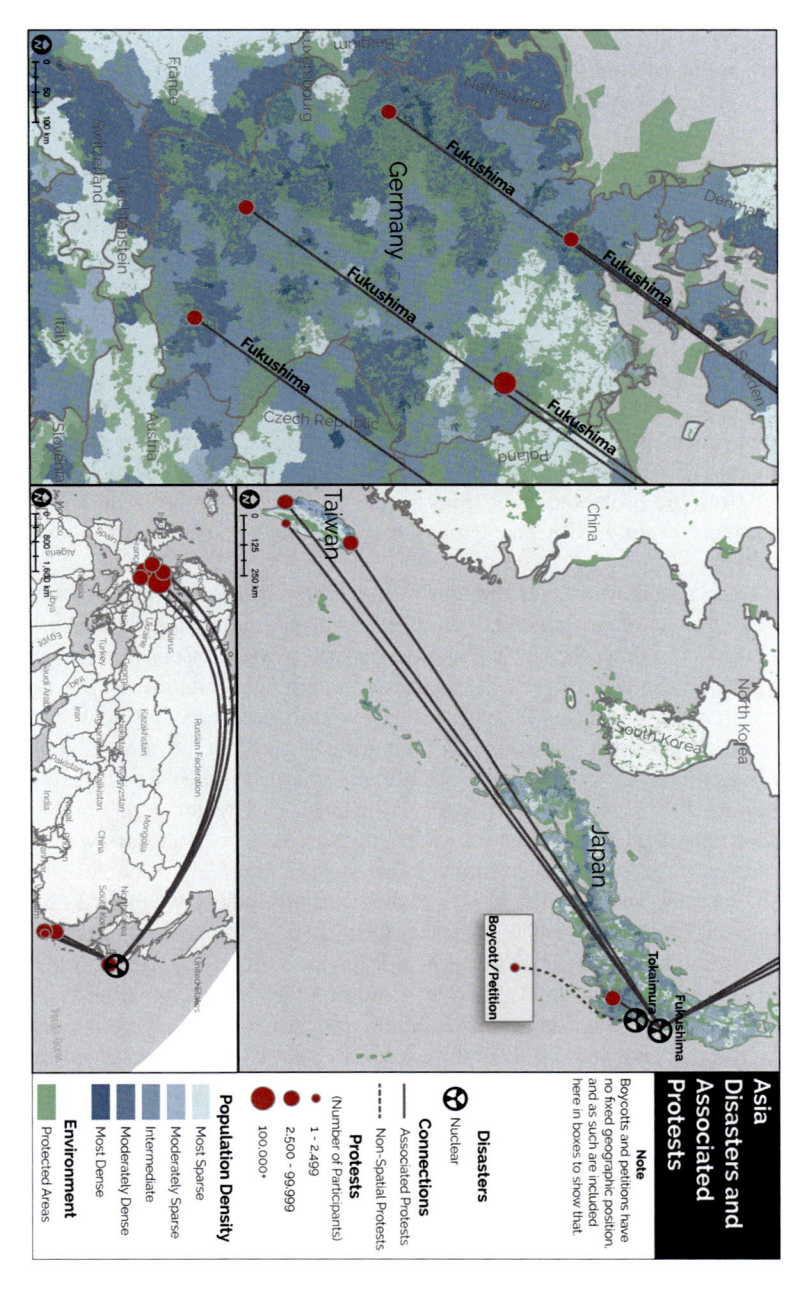

Fig. 3.3   Environmental disasters and associated protests: Asia, 1900–present

protesters (Yle, 2012).[27] This suggests that the population density of the impact zone may not be a deciding factor in the post-disaster protest size. A similar pattern emerges when mapping the proximity of these disasters to protected areas.

Unlike in the USA, the European and Canadian mines can be found close to protected areas. Curiously, the two Nordic mines—Aitik and Talvivaara—are surrounded by national parks, but these are much larger and much less scattered in Sweden than in Finland. Yet, while the Finnish protesters demanded the mine's closure (Yle, 2012), no public protests followed the Swedish disaster. In comparison, Mount Polley is located near large stretches of protected areas—the Tweedsmuir Provincial Park, Bowron Lake Provincial Park, Wells Gray Provincial Park, and several others. The associated protest occurred in Vancouver where the participants were primarily Vancouver-based indigenous activists. Calling the water their "lifeblood" and the salmon "the backbone of [their] communities," these activists drew attention to the disaster's impacts on the subsistence value of the damaged environment (Richmond, 2014). Therefore, although the impact zone, as it relates to the proximity to protected areas, may be less important in mobilizing individuals directly affected by the disaster, it may have mobilizing potential in more distant communities.

With respect to North American and European nuclear disasters, only the Three Mile Island (TMI) event generated protests (in the United States). These, again, occurred not within the disaster's impact zone but in two densely populated areas: Washington, DC, and Rocky Flats, a nuclear weapons production facility north of Denver, Colorado. It is more likely that these two locations are significant for political rather than geospatial reasons (DC being the seat of the US government and a nuclear weapons plant symbolizing a politically charged issue of nuclear weapons proliferation). TMI is relatively close to a large marine protected area, but the newspaper coverage of the post-disaster protests reveals that the protesters were part of an anti-nuclear movement—their main concerns were the safety of nuclear facilities across the country and the ethical issues surrounding nuclear weapons rather than environmental damage from the TMI disaster (Allen, 1979; Lynton, 1979; Martin, 1979). The remaining nuclear disasters in North America and Europe, although close to densely populated zones and similarly sized protected areas, generated no public protests. Again, this suggests that geospatial characteristics of large environmental industrial disasters may not be a deciding factor in post-disaster protest mobilization. The nuclear disasters in Japan support this conclusion.

Two major nuclear disasters occurred in Japan within a decade—one at the Tokaimura plant in Tokai, Ibaraki in 1999, and the other at the Fukushima Daiichi plant in 2011. Both facilities are located close to densely populated zones and protected areas, but protests erupted only after Fukushima and only in Tokyo (although, there was a petition in Japan after the Tokaimura disaster). Fukushima, however, inspired protests in other countries across the world—the most notable due

---

[27] See also Nuclear Heritage, "Talvivaara Mine: Environmental Disaster in Finland," http://www.nuclear-heritage.net/index.php/Talvivaara_mine:_environmental_disaster_in_Finland#cite_note-1 (last accessed in 2020).

to their size were those in Germany. These were, of course, outside of the Fukushima impact zone and occurred in densely populated areas, specifically in Berlin, Hamburg, Munich, and Cologne (see Table 3.7).

Lastly, oil spills have lined the coastlines of North America and Europe. Protests linked to these disasters vary the most out of all disaster types, in both location and size. The Deepwater Horizon and Exxon Valdez spills generated the largest number of protest events—across the United States and, in the case of Deepwater Horizon, beyond the US borders. Yet, it was the Prestige oil spill that was followed by the largest demonstrations (see Table 3.7). The Prestige disaster occurred far away from population centers, with related protests taking place in densely populated areas of Spain. In contrast, the Independenta spill in Turkey, which led to no public protests, occurred in an area with a very high population density. Likewise, both the MT Haven and Amoco Cadiz spills were close to populated areas, but the latter was followed by protests while the former was not. A similar pattern is evident for other oil spills in Europe and North America. Being close to the disaster does not seem to motivate protests consistently, but once protests occur, they are likely to be in densely populated areas.

A similar conclusion arises from the mapping of protected areas in both North America and Europe. The Exxon Valdez disaster is the only oil spill clearly linked to concerns over environmental damages. In Europe, even though most of the spills occurred near marine protected areas, only the Sea Empress, Amoco Cadiz, Aegean Sea, and Prestige disasters generated protests. Therefore, the findings from this preliminary GIS analysis fully support neither Hypothesis 1 nor Hypothesis 2.[28] Hypothesis 3, however, seems to stand. Arguably, more cases are needed to make this claim convincingly. The only truly remote disaster in this dataset is the oil spills from Odyssey—no protests are linked to this event. The Andros Patria and Betelgeuse disasters, followed by no protests, also occurred in remote locations (although these were relatively closer to protected areas). Overall, this suggests that sudden grievances, motivated by the disaster damage of areas that people value, may be a necessary but not sufficient driver of post-disaster protest.

More specific theoretical propositions arise from this analysis, and particularly from examining Figs. 3.1, 3.2 and 3.3. Population density, for example, may matter in post-disaster protests in at least two ways. First, if the disaster impact zone is sparsely populated, protests may not develop simply because the pool of potential protesters is not large enough. In the immediate disaster aftermath, directly affected individuals may be more concerned with disaster response and recovery than with mobilizing for protest. Second, outside of the disaster impact zone, protests tend to occur in densely populated areas. Aside from widening the pool of potential protesters, such places may house individuals who not only hold strong environmental values but, by not having to participate in clean-up, are also available for protest. A disaster is likely to encourage protest mobilization of directly unaffected groups if the risk of occurrence of a similar event is either sufficiently high or perceived as such (Birkland, 1998; Bishop, 2014). Since this risk threshold is rather subjective, framing is likely to play

---

[28] Although, the sizes of protests that did occur align with expectations of Hypothesis 1.

Table 3.7 Post-disaster protest events

Event	Protest type	Date	Location	Size	Size accuracy	Source
Deepwater Horizon	Demonstration	May 24, 2010	Houston	50	Sourced	Christian Science Monitor, June 12, 2010; Houston Chronicle, May 24, 2010
Deepwater Horizon	Petition	June 1, 2010	USA	21,000	Sourced	Christian Science Monitor, June 12, 2011
Deepwater Horizon	Demonstration	May 1, 2010	Clearwater, FL	50	Sourced	St. Petersburg Times, June 1, 2010
Deepwater Horizon	Sabbotage/activist stunt	July 27, 2010	London, UK	10	Estimate (small)	Business World, July 27, 2010
Deepwater Horizon	Demonstration	May 1, 2010	New York, NY	200	Sourced	The Daily Telegraph, June 5, 2010
Deepwater Horizon	Sabbotage/activist stunt	July 13, 2010	London, UK	10	Estimate (small)	The Daily Telegraph, July 14, 2010
Deepwater Horizon	Activist stunt	June 1, 2010	London, UK	10	Estimate (small)	The Guardian, June 24, 2010
Deepwater Horizon	Activist stunt	July 1, 2010	Nottingham, UK	10	Estimate (small)	Nottingham Evening Post, July 13, 2010
Deepwater Horizon	Activist stunt	May 1, 2010	London, UK	10	Estimate (small)	The Gold Coast Bulletin, May 21, 2010
Deepwater Horizon	Demonstration	May 30, 2010	Pantops, VA	15	Sourced	The Clover Herald, June 1, 2010
Deepwater Horizon	Demonstration	May 1, 2010	Daytona Beach Shores, FL	100	Sourced	News-Journal (Daytona Beach, Florida), June 17, 2010

(continued)

Table 3.7 (continued)

Event	Protest type	Date	Location	Size	Size accuracy	Source
Deepwater Horizon	Online petition/campaign	Aug 1, 2010	USA	849,000	Sourced	The Washington Post, August 21, 2010
Deepwater Horizon	Activist stunt	July 30, 2010	UC Berkeley	10	Estimate (small)	Morning Star, August 2, 2010
Prestige	Demonstration	Dec 15, 2002	Barcelona, Spain	50,000	Sourced (range)	The Guardian, December 16, 2002
Prestige	Demonstration	Dec 1, 2002	Santiago de Compostela, Spain	200,000	Sourced	The Times, December 2, 2002
Prestige	Demonstration	Feb 1, 2003	Madrid, Spain	100,000	Sourced	Daily Post (North Wales), February 24, 2003
Sea Empress	Petition	Apr 1, 1996	UK	100,000	Sourced	The Independent (London), April 25, 1996
Sea Empress	Sabotage/activist stunt	Apr 1, 1996	Milford Haven, Wales	10	Estimate (small)	The Independent (London), April 25, 1996
Aegean Sea	Demonstration	Jan 10, 1993	La Coruna, Spain	10,000	Sourced	The Herald (Glasgow), January 11, 1993
Exxon Valdez	Sabotage	Apr 1, 1989	St. Loius, MO	1	Sourced	St. Louis Post-Dispatch, April 16, 1989
Exxon Valdez	Demonstration	Apr 1, 1989	Alki Beach, Seattle, WA	2000	Sourced	St. Louis Post-Dispatch, April 16, 1989
Exxon Valdez	Demonstration	July 1, 1989	Tidelands Park, Coronado, CA	100	Sourced	St. Louis Post-Dispatch, April 16, 1989
Exxon Valdez	Boycott	May 1, 1989	USA	10,000	Sourced	The New York Times, July 12, 1989
Exxon Valdez	Activist stunt	Apr 1, 1989	Anchorage, Alaska	1	Sourced	St. Louis Post-Dispatch, May 3, 1989

(continued)

Table 3.7 (continued)

Event	Protest type	Date	Location	Size	Size accuracy	Source
Exxon Valdez	Demonstration	May 1, 1989	Parsippany, NJ	250	Sourced	St. Louis Post-Dispatch, April 30, 1989
Exxon Valdez	Activist stunt	Sept 1, 1989	Valdez harbor, Alaska	50	Sourced	The New York Times, May 19, 1989
Exxon Valdez	Demonstration	May 1, 1989	Anchorage, Alaska	400	Sourced	The New York Times, September 10, 1989
Exxon Valdez	Boycott	Apr 1, 1989	USA	1000	Sourced	St. Louis Post-Dispatch, May 3, 1989
Amoco Cadiz	Demonstration	Mar 1, 1978	France	15,000	Sourced	The New York Times, April 17, 1989
Amoco Cadiz	Demonstration	Mar 27, 1978	Portsall, France	2000	Sourced	The New York Times, March 31, 1978
Fukushima	Demonstration	Mar 12, 2011	Germany: 45 km between Stuttgart and the Neckarwestheim nuclear power plant	60,000	Sourced	The Globe and Mail, March 29, 1978
Fukushima	Demonstration	Mar 26, 2011	Berlin, Germany	110,000	Sourced	Hasegawa (2014)
Fukushima	Demonstration	Mar 26, 2011	Hamburg, Germany	45,000	Sourced	San Jose Mercury News, March 26, 2011
Fukushima	Demonstration	Mar 26, 2011	Munich, Germany	35,000	Sourced	San Jose Mercury News, March 26, 2011
Fukushima	Demonstration	Mar 26, 2011	Cologne, Germany	40,000	Sourced	San Jose Mercury News, March 26, 2011
Fukushima	Demonstration	Apr 10, 2011	Tokyo, Japan	15,000	Sourced	San Jose Mercury News, March 26, 2011

(continued)

Table 3.7 (continued)

Event	Protest type	Date	Location	Size	Size accuracy	Source
Fukushima	Demonstration	June 11, 2011	Tokyo, Japan	20,000	Sourced	Hasegawa (2014)
Fukushima	Demonstration	Sept 19, 2011	Tokyo, Japan	64,000	Sourced	Hasegawa (2014)
Fukushima	Demonstration	Apr 30, 2011	Taipei, Taiwan	10,000	Sourced	Hasegawa (2014); Elliott (2013)
Fukushima	Demonstration	Apr 30, 2011	Kaohsiung, Taiwan	5000	Sourced	BBC Monitoring Asia Pacific, April 30, 2011
Fukushima	Demonstration	Apr 30, 2011	Taitung, Taiwan	1000	Sourced	BBC Monitoring Asia Pacific, April 30, 2011
Tokaimura	Petition	Oct 1, 1999	Japan	2170	Sourced	BBC Monitoring Asia Pacific, April 30, 2011
Three Mile Island	Demonstration	May 6, 1979	Washington, DC	75,000	Estimate	World News Digest, May 11, 1979
Three Mile Island	Demonstration	Apr 28, 1979	Rocky Flats nuclear weapons plant, CO	7700	Sourced	The Washington Post, May 7, 1979
Three mile Island	Demonstration	Apr 8, 1979	Washington, DC	500	Sourced	The Washington Post, April 29, 1979
Mount Polley	Demonstration	Aug 11, 2014	Vancouver, BC	10	Estimate (small)	The Washington Post, April 29, 1979
Talvivaara	Demonstration	Nov 14, 2012	Helsinki, Finland	1000	Sourced	US Official News, August 16, 2014
Talvivaara	Petition	Nov 18, 2012	Finland	20,000	Sourced	Yle, November 14, 2012
Talvivaara	Demonstration	Nov 18, 2012	Oulu, Finland	10	Estimate (small)	Nuclear Heritage 2016
Talvivaara	Demonstration	Apr 1, 2012	Sotkamo, Finland	100	Sourced	Nuclear Heritage 2016

a crucial role in shaping disaster risk perception as well as public reaction to disaster impacts.

Furthermore, this mapping of disasters and protests suggests that intrinsic values of nature are unlikely to motivate people to take action since no protests have been linked to natural areas with no clear value to humans. The analysis does not offer clear support for the motivating role of instrumental value. It does, however, suggest that, at the minimum, we should re-visit the concept of grievance. Psychological studies claim that we are more risk-taking in face of losses (e.g., Tversky & Kahneman, 1981), but some losses seem more important than others. Sudden grievances may not be simply about a perception of loss but a perception of a specific type of loss, some perhaps based on instrumental values, while others on something else.

Conclusion

The aim of this chapter was to assess how ecological damage from large industrial disasters may be linked to post-disaster protests. Since industrial disasters harm the environment valued by humans, they generate sudden grievances that motivate protest. I, therefore, used geospatial analysis to assess the relationship between industrial disasters, their proximity to locations that people value, and post-disaster protests. The findings reveal that disaster damage is likely to be important in generating sudden grievances but is not sufficient for post-disaster protest mobilization. Perhaps not surprisingly, protests are more likely to spring up in densely populated areas and less likely after mining disasters. Oil spills also tend to motivate people more than nuclear disasters. Disaster proximity to protected and populated areas seems to serve as a motivational factor and no protests have been linked to areas that are of little instrumental value to humans. This gives some support to the motivational effect of instrumental rather than the intrinsic value of nature and poses a further research question: While people have been found to value nature intrinsically, why do such attitudes fail to motivate political action (Vucetich et al., 2015)?

To answer such a question, we might have to move away from the traditional understanding of grievance (i.e., based on severity) and instead focus on the meaning of grievances through consideration of both material and ideational factors (Simmons, 2014). For example, an environmental disaster may represent ideas of technology, progress, or broader forces of environmental destruction, depending on place and time. An examination of how and why individuals value certain parts of nature might shed more light on the relevance of grievances in protest mobilization and explain why there is such mixed empirical evidence when it comes to their effects.

This study was not meant to test hypotheses but instead search for patterns between disaster damage and protest in geospatial terms. Further work is needed to build on the preliminary findings. There are two common ways of testing hypotheses through GIS: comparing observed patterns to those generated by an independent random process (IRP) and the Monte Carlo technique, which involves formulating competing hypotheses, simulating many realizations of the hypothesized process, and comparing observed data to the simulated patterns (see Gimond, 2018). The preliminary findings from this analysis offer two additional ideas for further GIS work: an examination of the role of disaster recurrence and cumulative impacts and an analysis of the relationship between post-disaster protests and local dependence on the responsible industry.

First, certain geographic regions or industrial zones (e.g., oil tanker routes or mining towns) have a higher chance of disaster occurrence than others.[29] Theoretically, in such areas, there are two potential opposing effects of disaster recurrence on protest. Frequent recurrence may inspire better disaster preparedness or may come with a lower "shock value." Over time, this may lead to desensitization and therefore less public outrage and a lower likelihood of post-disaster protests. Conversely, frequent disaster recurrence is likely to result in cumulative destructive impacts on the environment, which may compound sudden grievances and eventually prompt the public to demand better environmental protection and better disaster preparedness. Aside from GIS, a process-tracing study could shed light on the validity of these theoretical propositions.

The second area of further study involves mapping local dependence on the industry that caused the disaster. In a disaster impact area, individuals affected by pollution may demonstrate greater support for environmental protection—because of the direct impact that pollution has on their lives. Alternatively, even when faced with environmental costs, they may maintain their support for the local industry in fear of losing employment or other benefits the industry provides.[30] Such individuals and groups would be therefore less likely to act on a sudden grievance and not participate in a protest aimed against that industry. They may, however, engage in a post-disaster protest against other actors, including various levels of government. By allowing for someone to be blamed, industrial disasters open different pathways to potential social clashes. "Acts of God" may bring people together to endure their faith, but "acts of corporations" may bring them together to demand change.

Acknowledgements I am grateful to Devin Lussier for his invaluable help with data collection and for creating the maps used in this analysis.

References

Adeola, F. (2011). *Hazardous wastes, industrial disasters, and environmental health risks.* Palgrave Macmillan.

---

[29] For example, there were three large oil tanker disasters in Spain along the same stretch of coastline between 1976 and 2002, with the Prestige oil spill being the last of them (and the only one followed by large-sized protests).

[30] Such support would likely be stronger in communities affected by nuclear and mining disasters (because of the "stationary" nature of the industry). Oil tanker disasters are less likely to see local support for the oil industry in the impact zone unless the industry happens to be particularly well established there.

Allen, H. (1979). May days for the no-nukers: A new march, another cause—and echoes from the past. *The Washington Post*, May 3.

Alvarez, S., Larkin, S., Whitehead, J., & Haab, T. (2014). A revealed preference approach to valuing non-market recreational fishing losses from the deepwater horizon oil spill. *Journal of Environmental Management, 145*, 199–209.

Anspaugh, L., Robert, C., & Marvin, G. (1988). The global impact of the chernobyl reactor accident. *Science, New Series, 242*(4885) (December), 1513–1519.

Armour, A. (Ed.). (1984). *The not-in-my-backyard syndrome*. York University Press.

Arnold, L. (1995). *Windscale 1957: Anatomy of a nuclear accident*. Macmillan.

Batty, M. (2003). Using geographical information systems. In N. J. Clifford & G. Valentine (Eds.), *Key methods in geography* (pp. 409–423). SAGE Publications.

BBC. (2000). Death of a river. *BBC News,* February 15. http://news.bbc.co.uk/2/hi/europe/642 880.stm.

BBC. (2008). Chinese landslide toll passes 250. *BBC News*, September 13. http://news.bbc.co.uk/2/hi/asia-pacific/7614653.stm.

Birkland, T. (1998). Focusing events, mobilization, and agenda setting. *Journal of Public Policy, 18*(1), 53–74.

Bishop, B. (2014). Focusing events and public opinion: evidence the deepwater horizon disaster. *Political Behaviour, 36*, 1–22.

Bockstael, N. (1996). Modeling economics and ecology: The importance of a spatial perspective. *American Journal of Agricultural Economics, 78*, 1168–1180.

Bromet, E. (2012). Mental health consequences of the chernobyl disaster. *Journal of Radiological Protection, 32*, N71–N75.

Cable, S., & Shriver, T. (1995). Production and extrapolation of meaning in the environmental justice movement. *Sociological Spectrum, 15*, 419–442.

Čapek, S. (1993). The 'environmental justice' frame: A conceptual discussion and an application. *Social Problems, 40*, 5–21.

Carruthers, D., & Rodriguez, P. (2009). Mapuche potest, environmental conflict and social movement linkage in chile. *Third World Quarterly, 30*(4), 743–760.

CBC. (2018). Protesters rally across canada over trans mountain pipeline decision. *CBC News*, June 4. https://www.cbc.ca/news/canada/british-columbia/protesters-rally-across-canada-over-trans-mountain-pipeline-decision-1.4691338.

Chenoweth, E., & Stephan, M. (2011). *Why civil resistance works: The strategic logic of nonviolent conflict*. Columbia University Press.

Chomitz, K., & Gray, D. (1995). Roads, land use, and deforestation: A spatial model applied to belize. *The World Bank Economic Review, 10*, 487–512.

Cooper, A. (2002). Media framing and social movement mobilization: German peace protest against INF missiles, the gulf war, and NATO peace enforcement in Bosnia. *European Journal of Political Research, 41*, 37–80.

Davies, W., Bailey, J., & Kelly, D. (1972). *West Virginia's buffalo creek flood: A study of the hydrology and engineering geology*. United States Geological Survey.

della Porta, D., & Diani, M. (2006). *Social movements: An introduction*. Blackwell Publishing.

Drury, C., & Olson, R. S. (1998). Disasters and political unrest: An empirical investigation. *Journal of Contingencies and Crisis Management, 6*(3), 153–161.

Eckstein, S. (2001). *Power and popular protest. Latin American social movements*. University of California Press.

Elliott, D. (2013). *Fukushima: impacts and implications*. Palgrave Macmillan.

EPA. (1997). *Damage cases and environmental releases from mines and mineral processing Sites, U.S. Environmental protection agency*. EPA.

European Commission. (2010). Impacts of gold extraction in the EU. European Commission—EUROSTAT," April 2. http://ec.europa.eu/environment/waste/mining/pdf/IH_2010-001.pdf.

European Environmental Agency. (2010) Mapping the impacts of natural hazards and technological accidents in Europe. *EEA Technical Report*, no. 13/2010. https://www.eea.europa.eu/publicati ons/mapping-the-impacts-of-natural.

Gephart, R. P., Jr. (1984). Making sense of organizationally based environmental disasters. *Journal of Management, 10*(2), 205–225.

Gimond, M. (2018). Intro to GIS and spatial analysis. https://mgimond.github.io/Spatial/.

Giuliano, E. (2011). *Constructing grievance. Ethnic nationalism in Russia's Republics.* Cornell University Press.

Goodchild, M., Anselin, L., Appelbaum, R., & Harthorn, B. H. (2000). Toward spatially integrated social science. *International Regional Science Review, 23*(2), 139–159.

Goodwin, J., & Polletta, F. (2001). *Passionate politics: Emotions and social movements.* University of Chicago Press.

Graf, W. (1990). Fluvial dynamics of thorium-230 in the church rock event, Puerco River, New Mexico. *Annals of the Association of American Geographers, 80*(3), 327–342.

Grasso, M., & Giugni, M. (2016). Protest participation and economic crisis: The conditioning role of political opportunities. *European Journal of Political Research, 55*(4), 663–680.

Greenley, D., Richard, W., & Robert, Y. (1981). Option value: Empirical evidence from a case study of recreation and water quality. *The Quarterly Journal of Economics, 96*(4), 657–667.

Gurney, J. N., & Tierney, K. (1982). Relative deprivation and social movements: A critical look at twenty years of theory and research. *The Sociological Quarterly, 23*(1), 33–47.

Gurr, T. (1970). *Why men rebel.* Princeton University Press.

Haab, T., & McConnell, K. (2002). *Valuing environmental and natural resources. The econometrics of non-market valuation.* Edward Elgar.

Halliday, J. (2017). Fracking protesters vow to 'put their lives on line' after scaling rig. *The Guardian*, October 22. https://www.theguardian.com/environment/2017/oct/22/fracking-protesters-vow-to-put-their-lives-on-line-after-scaling-rig.

Hannigan, J. (2012). *Disasters without borders. The international politics of natural disasters.* Polity.

Hasegawa, K. (2014). The Fukushima nuclear accident and Japan's civil society: context, reactions, and policy impacts. *International Sociology, 29*(4), 283–301.

Hausman, J., Leonard, G., & McFadden, D. (1995). A utility-consistent, combined discrete choice and count data model: Assessing recreational use losses due to natural resource damage. *Journal of Public Economics, 56*(1), 1–30.

Hoeve, J., & Jacobson, M. (2012). Worldwide health effects of the fukushima daiichi nuclear accident. *Energy and Environmental Science, 5*, 8743–8757.

Ivanov, A. Y., & Zatyagalova, V. (2008). A GIS approach to mapping oil spills in a marine environment. *Journal International Journal of Remote Sensing, 29*(21), 6297–6313.

Joyce, K., Belliss, S., Samsonov, S., McNeill, S., & Glassey, P. (2009). A review of the status of satellite remote sensing and image processing techniques for mapping natural Hazards and disasters. *Progress in Physical Geography, 33*(2), 183–207.

Kahneman, D., & Knetsch, J. (1992). Valuing public goods: The purchase of moral satisfaction. *Journal of Environmental Economics and Management, 22*(1), 57–70.

Kraft, M. E., & Clafy, B. B. (1991). Citizen participation and the NIMBY syndrome: Public response to radioactive waste disposal. *The Western Political Quarterly, 44*, 299–328.

Kuehn, R. (2000). A taxonomy of environmental justice. *Environmental Law Report, 30*, 10681–10703.

Leon, C., Araña, J., Hanemann, W., & Riera, P. (2014). Heterogeneity and emotions in the valuation of non-use damages caused by oil spills. *Ecological Economics, 97*, 129–139.

Linnitt. C. (2016). No fines, no charges laid for mount polley mine disaster. *Desmog Canada*, January 6. https://regulatorwatch.com/reported_elsewhere/no-fines-no-charges-laid-for-mount-polley-mine-disaster/.

Loureiro, M., Loomis, J., Vázquez, M. X. (2009). Economic valuation of environmental damages due to the prestige oil spill in Spain. *Environmental Resource Economics, 44*, 537–553.

Loureiro, M., & Loomis, J. (2013). International public preferences and provision of public goods: Assessment of passive use values in large oil spills. *Environmental and Resource Economics, 56*(4), 521–534.

Lynton, S. (1979). Antinuclear protesters call for construction ban. *The Washington Post*, April 9: A13. https://www.washingtonpost.com/archive/politics/1979/04/09/antinuclearprotest ers-call-for-construction-ban/813ec42d-160e-41a8-bf9c-d369a7e71968/.

Lyons, R., Mark Temple, J., Evans, D., Fone, D., & Palmer, S. (1999). Acute health effects of the sea empress oil spill. *Journal of Epidemiology and Community Health, 53*, 306–310.

Maantay, J., & Ziegler, J. (2006). *GIS for the urban environment*. ESRI Press.

Martin, L. (1979). U.S. Rally turns anti-nuclear protest into national movement. *The Globe and Mail*, May 8.

Martinez-Alier, J. (2016). Global environmental justice and the environmentalism of the poor. In T. Gabrielson, C. Hall, J. Meyer, & D. Schlosberg (Eds.), *The Oxford handbook of environmental political theory*. Oxford University Press.

McAdam, D., Tarrow, S., & Tilly, C. (2001). *Dynamics of contention*. Cambridge University Press.

McCarthy, J., & Zald, M. (1973). *The trend of social movements in America: professionalization and resource mobilization*. General Learning Corporation.

Mitchell, A. (1999). *The ESRI guide to GIS analysis. Volume 1: Geographic patterns and relationships*. Environmental Systems Research Institute, Inc.

Monbiot, G. (2011). The true value of nature is not a number with a pound sign in front. *The Guardian*, June 6. https://www.theguardian.com/commentisfree/2011/jun/06/monetisation-nat ural-world-definitive-neoliberal-triumph.

Morrison, D. (1971). Some notes toward theory on relative deprivation, social movements, and social change. *The American Behavioral Scientist, 14*(5), 675–690.

Mudder, T., & Botz, M. (2004). Cyanide and society: A critical review. *The European Journal of Mineral Processing and Environmental Protection, 4*(1), 62–74.

Nelson, M., J., Bruskotter, J., & Vucetich, J. (2015). Does nature have value beyond what it provides humans? *The Conversation,* October 2. https://theconversation.com/does-nature-have-value-bey ond-what-it-provides-humans-47825.

Nelson, G., & Hellerstein, D. (1997). Do roads cause deforestation? Using satellite images in econometric analysis of land use. *American Journal of Agricultural Economics, 79*, 80–88.

O'Neill, K., Weinthal, E., & Hunnicutt, P. (2017). Seeing complexity: Visualization tools in global environmental politics and governance. *Journal of Environmental Studies and Sciences, 7*(4), 490–506.

Oberschall, A. (1978). Theories of social conflict. *Annual Review of Sociology, 4*, 291–315.

Opp, K.-D. (2009). *Theories of political protest and social movements*. Routledge.

Opp, K.-D., & Kittel, B. (2010). The dynamics of political protest: Feedback effects and inter-dependence in the explanation of protest participation. *European Sociological Review, 26*(1), 97–109.

Pelling, M., & Dill, K. (2008). Disaster politics: From social control to human security. *Environment, Politics and Development Working Paper Series*, 1–24.

Perrow. (1984). *Normal accidents: Living with high risk technologies*. Basic Books.

Pinard, M. (2011). *Motivational dimensions in social movements and contentious collective action*. McGill-Queen's University Press.

Rabe, B. (1994). *Beyond NIMBY: Hazardous siting in Canada and the United States*. The Brookings Institute.

Rasmussen, T. (1992). Not in my backyard: The politics of siting prisons, landfills, and incinerators. *State & Local Government Review, 24*(3), 128–134.

Richardson, L., & Loomis, J. (2009). The total economic value of threatened, endangered and rare species: An updated meta-analysis. *Ecological Economics, 68*, 1535–1548.

Richmond, J. (2014). *Protesters slam Imperial Metals over Mount Polley*. Mining.com, August 12. http://www.mining.com/protesters-slam-imperial-metals-over-mount-polley/

Rootes, C. (2003). *Environmental protest in Western Europe*. Oxford University Press.

Rootes. (2013). From local conflict to national issue: When and how environmental campaigns succeed in transcending the local. *Environmental Politics, 22*(1), 95–114.

Sanchez, H., Adams, A., & Shriver, T. (2017). Confronting power and environmental injustice: legacy pollution and the timber industry in southern mississippi. *Society & Natural Resources, 30*(3), 347–361.

Schleifstein, M. (2016). BP oil spill cost fishing industry at least $94.7 million in 2010. *The Times-Picayune,* June 27. https://www.nola.com/news/environment/article_462806af-c1e5-5712-9608-31b125c43c8c.html#:~:text=The%20BP%20oil%20disaster%20cost,Bureau%20of%20Ocean%20Energy%20Management.

Schlosberg, D. (2004). Reconceiving environmental justice: Global movements and political theories. *Environmental Politics, 13*(3), 517–540.

Shriver, T., Adams, A., & Messer, C. (2014). Power, quiescence, and pollution: The suppression of environmental grievances. *Social Currents, 1*(3), 275–292.

Simmons, E. (2014). Grievances do matter in mobilization. *Theory and Society, 43*, 513–546.

Sindermann, C. (2006). *Coastal pollution. Effects on Living Resources and Humans.* Taylor and Francis.

Slovic, P. (1987). Perception of risk. *Sciences, 236*, 80–85.

Soderqvist, T. (2000). Natural resources damage from chernobyl: Further results. *Environmental and Resource Economics, 16*, 343–346.

Solomon, G, & Janssen, S. (2010). Health effects of the gulf oil spill. *Journal of American Medical Association, 304*(10) (September), 1118–1119.

Sovacool, B. (2008). The costs of failure: A preliminary assessment of major energy accidents, 1907–2007. *Energy Policy, 36*(5), 1802–1820.

Sovacool, B. (2010). A critical evaluation of nuclear power and renewable electricity in Asia. *Journal of Contemporary Asia, 40*(3), 369–400.

Sovacool, B. (2011). *Contesting the future of nuclear power: A critical global assessment of atomic energy.* World Scientific.

Stonich, S. (1998). The political ecology of tourism. *Annals of Tourism Research, 25*, 25–54.

Tarrow, S. (1994). *Power in movement: Social movements and contentious politics.* Cambridge University Press.

Taylor, A. (2011). A flood of red sludge, one year later. *The Atlantic,* September 28. https://www.theatlantic.com/photo/2011/09/a-flood-of-red-sludge-one-year-later/100158/.

The Economist. (2014). Japan's anti-nuclear movement. where's the protest? *The Economist,* August 3. http://www.economist.com/blogs/banyan/2014/08/japan-s-anti-nuclear-movement.

The Guardian. (2011). Nuclear power plant accidents: Listed and ranked since 1952. *The Guardian,* March 14. https://www.theguardian.com/news/datablog/2011/mar/14/nuclear-power-plant-accidents-list-rank.

Thomashaw, M. (1995). *Ecological identity: Becoming a reflective environmentalist.* MIT Press.

Tilly, C. (1978). *From mobilization to revolution.* Random House.

Turner, M. (2003). Methodological reflections on the use of remote sensing and geographic information science in human ecological research. *Human Ecology, 31*(2), 255–279.

Tversky, A., & Kahneman, D. (1981). The framing of decisions and the psychology of choice. *Science, 211*(4481), 453–458.

Van Stekelenburg, J., & Klandermans, B. (2013). The social psychology of protest. *Current Sociology Review, 61*(5-6), 886–905.

Visser, N. (2017). Thousands fought against the dakota access pipeline. Now It's set to flow oil. *Huffington Post,* January 6. https://www.huffingtonpost.ca/entry/dakota-access-pipeline-protest-photos_us_592faa01e4b0540ffc847a58.

Vucetich, J., Bruskotter, J., & Nelson, M. (2015). Evaluating whether nature's intrinsic value is an axiom of or anathema to conservation. *Conservation Biology, 29*(2), 321–332.

Walker, G. (2009). Globalizing environmental justice: The geography and politics of frame contextualization and evolution. *Global Social Policy, 9*, 355–382.

Walsh, E. J. (1981). Resource mobilization and citizen protest in communities around three mile Island. *Social Problems, 29*(1), 1–21.

Weisberg, B. (1993). One city's approach to NIMBY: How new york city developed a fair share siting process. *Journal of the American Planning Association, 59*, 93–97.

Wexler, M. N. (1996). A sociological framing of the NIMBY (Not-In-My-Backyard) syndrome. *International Review of Modern Sociology, 26*(1), 91–110.

WISE. (2017). *Chronology of major tailings dam failures.* WISE Uranium Project, April 3. http://www.wise-uranium.org/mdaf.html.

Wolsink, M. (1994). Entanglement of interests and motives: Assumptions behind the NIMBY theory on facility siting. *Urban Studies, 31*, 851–866.

Yle, N. (2012). *Stop talvivaara' protest brings carnival mood to helsinki.* November 14. https://yle.fi/uutiset/osasto/news/stop_talvivaara_protest_brings_carnival_mood_to_helsinki/6376956.

Yue, G., Peng, R., Jun, S., & Anadon, L. D. (2015). Not in my backyard, but not far away from me: Local acceptance of wind power in China. *Energy, 82*, 722–733.

Miriam Matejova is an Assistant Professor at the Department of Political Science, Masaryk University and a Fellow at the Norman Paterson School of International Affairs, Carleton University. She is formerly a lecturer at the University of British Columbia and visiting researcher at the University of Oxford. Her research focuses on energy security, environmental disasters, protest movements, and foreign intelligence liaison. Matejova has previously worked as an advisor, analyst, and project assistant for national and international organizations, including the Government of Canada, the United Nations, and the United Nations Association in Canada. She holds a Ph.D. in Political Science from the University of British Columbia.

Chapter 4
Renewale Energy Sources and Climate Change Mitigation

Erginbay Uğurlu

Abstract In this chapter, we focus on renewable energy sources for climate change mitigation. Whereas the cost of mitigating climate change is increasing by the time, the cost of producing renewable energy is decreasing (Uğurlu, in Understanding complex systems climate change and energy dynamics in the Middle East, pp 259–291, 2019a). Renewable energy sources are one of the mitigation ways of climate change. Therefore, the chapter will investigate renewable energy sources. The sources are bioenergy, solar energy, geothermal energy, hydropower, and wind energy. There are many comprehensive reports of the cost of mitigating climate change; (IPCC in Contribution of working group III to the fourth assessment report, Cambridge University Press, 2007; IPCC in Renewable energy sources and climate change mitigation special policymakers and technical summary, 2012; IPCC in Contribution of working groups I, II and III to the fifth assessment report of the intergovernmental panel on climate change. IPCC, Geneva, Switzerland, 151 pp, 2014). Similar way with these reports, I will investigate climate change and argue ways of mitigation of climate change and renewable energy strategies of climate change mitigation and its cost. I will demonstrate that renewable sources have different features, and some of them can be performed based on the conditions of a region's geography. The rest of the chapter is organized as follows: Sect. "Climate Change Mitigation" gives information about climate change mitigation. Section "Renewable Energy for Climate Change Mitigation" overviews renewable energy sources and their potential to mitigate climate change. Section "Conclusion" presents some concluding remarks.

Introduction

Since the first conference about environmental degradation in Stockholm in 1972, which was held by the United Nations Conference on the Human Environment, climate change, and environmental degradation have been very vital issues for the

E. Uğurlu (✉)
Faculty of Economics and Administrative Sciences, Istanbul Aydın University, Istanbul, Turkey
e-mail: erginbayugurlu@aydin.edu.tr

world (Schirndin et al., 2001). The first steps on the issue were taken at the Conference of the Parties (COP) that took place in Berlin in 1995. The most important milestone is the Kyoto Protocol, voted by 165 nations in 1997, whose aim was to reduce greenhouse gases (GHGs) to the 1990 level during the period from 2008 to 2012 (Chichilnisky, 2006). This protocol was in the Third Conference of the Parties (COP-3) to the UNFCCC. Another milestone came during the thirteenth session (COP 13). In COP13, it was decided that developing countries should be compensated for adaptation costs to climate change by financing from the Adaptation Fund. Adaptation Fund is an essential and complementary response to climate change mitigation (Hof et al., 2009). In the past decades, many studies have considered the cost of mitigating climate change and, they argue that if mitigation is delayed, its cost tends to increase (Rosen & Guenther, 2015).

Different kinds of solutions can be selected to mitigate climate change. Reducing fossil fuel consumption is one of them, and using renewable energy sources instead of primary energy sources is a well-known and widespread method.

In this chapter, we focus on renewable energy sources for climate change mitigation. Whereas the cost of mitigating climate change is increasing over time, the cost of producing renewable energy is decreasing (Uğurlu, 2019a). Renewable energy sources are one of the mitigation ways of climate change. Therefore the chapter will investigate renewable energy sources. The sources are bioenergy, solar energy, geothermal energy, hydropower, and wind energy.

There are many comprehensive reports of the cost of mitigating climate change; IPCC (2007, 2012, 2014). In a similar way with these reports, I will investigate climate change and argue ways of mitigation of climate change and renewable energy strategies of climate change mitigation and its cost. I will demonstrate that renewable sources have different features, and some of them can be performed based on the conditions of a region's geography. The rest of the chapter is organized as follows: Sect. "Climate Change Mitigation" gives information about climate change mitigation. Section "Renewable Energy for Climate Change Mitigation" overviews renewable energy sources and their potential to mitigate climate change. Section "Conclusion" presents some concluding remarks.

Climate Change Mitigation

Around the world, some strategies are used to mitigate climate change. Moreover, Sustainable Development Goal 13 of the United Nations is mainly focused on climate change and mitigation of climate change (Uğurlu, 2019b). Renewable energy use and increasing the share of renewable energy is one of the strategies. Since we have many renewable energy sources, we have many questions such as which is the most used one, which is a more convenient one, what are their advantages and disadvantages?

Climate Change Process

The climate change process, caused by human activities such as land-use changes, fossil fuel burning, is summarized in Fig. 4.1. Land-use changes are defined as a change in the use or management of land, which may result from various human activities (IPCC, 2012). Fossil fuel burning rises because of transportation, agricultural activities, heating, and industrial activities that release quantities of greenhouse gases into the Earth's atmosphere. In other words, we can call these activities as economic activities; also economic growth is one of the reasons for carbon dioxide emission and there is extensive literature about economic growth and CO_2 emissions relationship (Muratoğlu and Uğurlu, 2014). This process, namely economic growth, continues and leads to the greenhouse effect, resulting in climate change.

In the figure, we can see some of these observations and major threats, and main climate change characteristics. Average temperature rise triggers natural disasters, and disaster causes biodiversity losses, famines, economic loses, etc. Primary energy

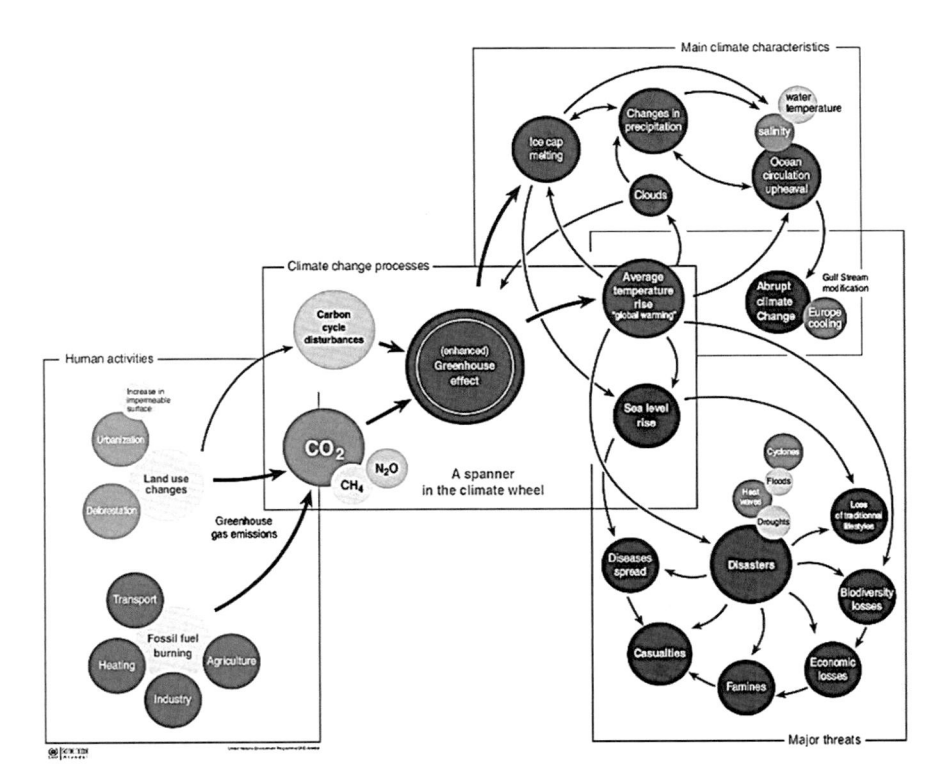

Fig. 4.1 Climate change: processes, characteristics and threats. *Source* Vital Climate Change Graphics Update Philippe Rekacewicz, Emmanuelle Bournay, UNEP/GRID-Arendal https://www.grida.no/resources/6889

sources are used in many sectors, such as agriculture, industry, heating, and transportation. Because of primary energy use, these sectors cause CO_2, CH_4, and N_2O emissions. CO_2 emissions cause the greenhouse gases effect, and more primary energy use causes more fossil fuel burning, then fossil fuel burning enhances the greenhouse effect. The greenhouse effect directly causes the average temperature rise and ice cap melting. Also, they have effects indirectly; for example, the average temperature rise creates clouds, and clouds increase the greenhouse effect.

Average temperature rise causes to ice cap melting, changes in precipitation, clouds, ocean circulation upheaval, and the consequences have bivariate causalities among themselves. Another result of the average temperature rise is sea level rises, and it triggers diseases spread and loss of traditional lifestyles. These consequences of average temperature rise are global problems to solve; there should be a global effort. On the other hand, local mitigation policies can have effects globally.

The IPCC's Fourth Assessment Report declares the observations, which are below as pieces of evidence for rapid climate change (Vijayavenkataraman et al., 2012):

- Sea-level rise;
- Global temperature rise;
- Warming oceans;
- Shrinking ice sheets;
- Declining Arctic sea ice;
- Glacial retreat;
- Ocean acidification.

We will review sea-level rise, global temperature rise, warming oceans, shrinking ice sheets, and declining Arctic sea ice by the following graphs.

Figure 4.2 shows sea-level rise around the world for the period of 1000–2019. If we focus on the time after the nineteenth century, there is a structural break around 1890

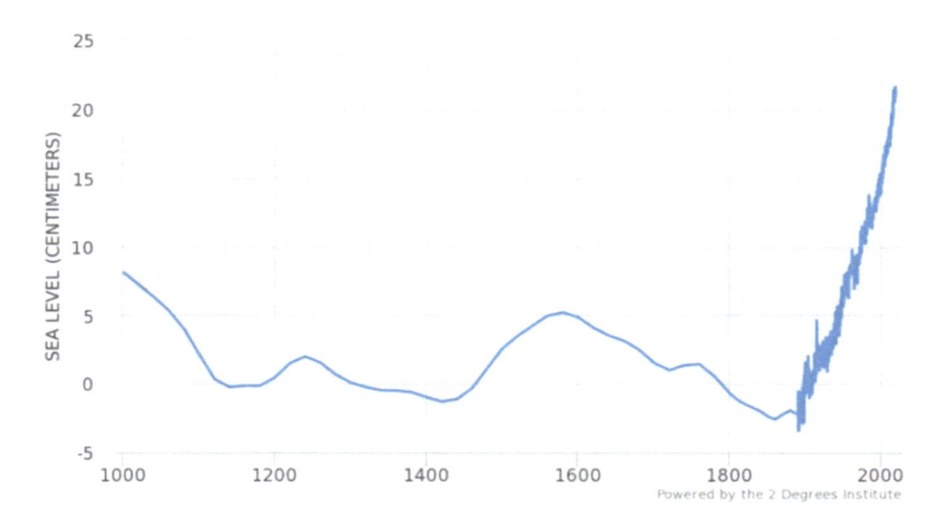

Fig. 4.2 Sea levels and temperature

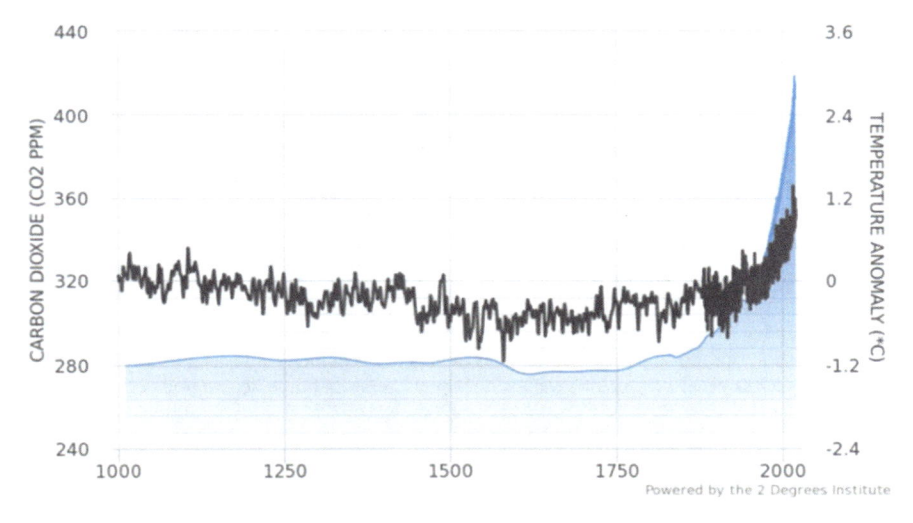

Fig. 4.3 Global CO_2 levels and temperature. *Source* h2degreesinstitute.org, https://www.co2lev els.org/

in the graph. After the break, the increasing trend starts and never stops. Although there are small fluctuations in the short-term, data shows an increasing trend in the long-term with a very steep trend. Moreover, the graph has no sign of slowing down or decrease.

Figure 4.3 shows global temperature rise and CO_2 levels for the period of 1000–2019. The left axis of the graph shows CO_2 levels (ppm), and the right axis shows temperature anomaly (°C). Until 1910 CO_2 levels are under 300 parts per million (ppm), and after 1910 CO_2 levels never decrease under 300 ppm. After 2013, CO_2 levels reach approximately 400 ppm. We can see that the structural changes start around the 1950s. In both—Figs. 4.2 and 4.3, the nineteenth century is the turning point for the data, and this means that the nineteenth century is a turning point of climate change.

Figure 4.4 shows the global ocean temperature for the last 100 years. Until 1977 there are some negative values in the graph. After the end of the 1900s, we cannot see any negative values. While there are some decreases in some years; in the long term, it is continuously increasing. The temperature has increased by approximately 0.13 °C per decade over the past 100 years.

Another observation is shrinking ice sheets. We can see the declining area of ice sheets from Figs. 4.5 and 4.6 in gigatonnes per year. Figure 4.5 presents Antarctica mass variation, and Fig. 4.6 presents Greenland mass variation. There are variations of values, graphs are volatile, but the general trend of the values show a declining trend. Moreover, we can see from the figures that the shrink of Greenland is higher than Antarctica.

Figure 4.7 shows the decline of the arctic sea level from 1979 to 2018. The figure shows that the level was above 7 million square km in 1979, there are decreases and

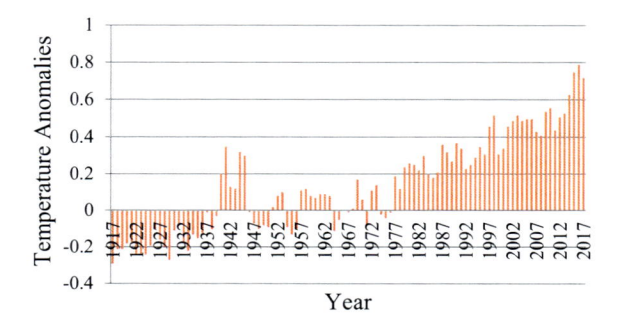

Fig. 4.4 Global Ocean temperature anomalies January–December Units: Degrees Celsius base period: 1901–2000. *Source* https://www.ncdc.noaa.gov/cag/global/time-series/globe/ocean/ytd/12/1880-2017

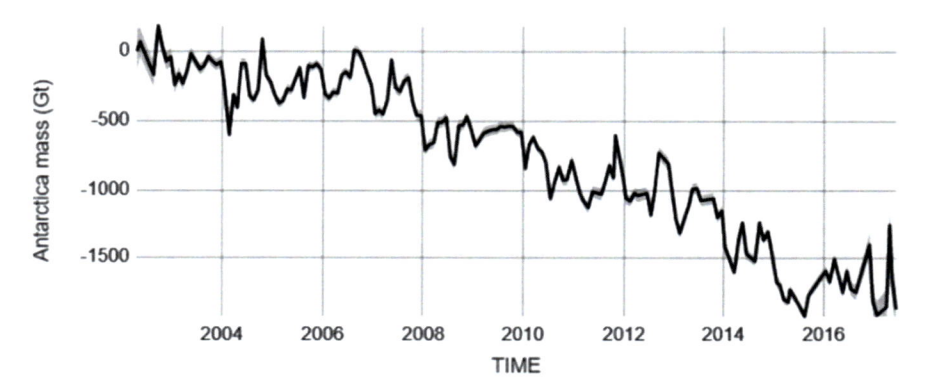

Fig. 4.5 Antarctica mass variation since 2002. *Source* Ice mass measurement by NASA's grace satellites. https://climate.nasa.gov/vital-signs/ice-sheets/

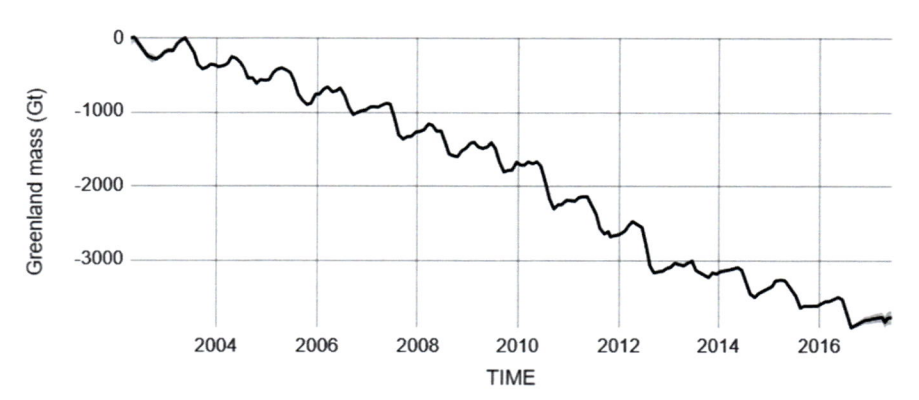

Fig. 4.6 Greenland mass variation since 2002. *Source* ice mass measurement by NASA's grace satellites. https://climate.nasa.gov/vital-signs/ice-sheets/

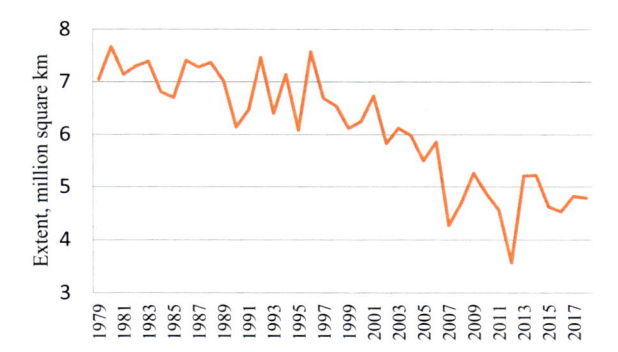

Fig. 4.7 Arctic sea extent. *Source* Satellite observations. *Credit* NSIDC/NASA, https://climate.nasa.gov/system/internal_resources/details/original/1929_Arctic_data_1979-2019.txt

increases until 2000. After 2000 the increasing trend starts. In 2012, the lowest sea ice extent was observed in the satellite record.

All these figures above show that the adverse effects of climate change are observed and measured in nature. It is measured by increasing sea-level rise, increasing global temperature rise, warming oceans, shrinking ice sheets, declining Arctic sea ice. It is an increasing problem around the world. Moreover, climate change has numerous effects on social life, health, and economic factors. That is why climate change is a very vital issue for the environment, economy, and social life.

Effects and Costs of Climate Change

Climate change has many impacts, and the mitigation of climate change has many costs. Hunt and Watkiss (2010) argue various potential impacts of climate change on cities and present the most important effects based on findings of previous researches. The effects are below:

- Effects of sea-level rise on coastal cities;
- Effects of extreme events on built infrastructure;
- Effects on health arising from higher average temperatures and/or extreme events;
- Effects on energy use;
- Effects on water availability and resources.

Hunt and Watkiss (2010) characterize these effects as direct effects; moreover, they mentioned tourism and cultural heritage, urban biodiversity, and the ancillary effects of air pollution as less critical effects.

IPCC (2014) mentions natural forcing and anthropogenic radiative forcing, and human activities as drivers of climate change. The data in IPCC (2014) shows that radiative forcing has shown substantial increases since 1750, which consist of carbon dioxide (CO_2), methane (CH_4), and nitrous oxide (N_2O), aerosols, cloud adjustments. About half of the cumulative anthropogenic CO_2 emissions between 1750 and 2011 have occurred in the last 40 years (high confidence). The IPCC (2001) states that in the second report (IPCC, 1996) "there is new and stronger evidence that most of the observed warming observed over the last 50 years is attributable to human activities." The atmospheric concentration of carbon dioxide (CO_2) has increased by 31% since 1750 (IPCC, 2001), and since 1970, cumulative CO_2 emissions from fossil fuel combustion, cement production, and flaring have tripled (IPCC, 2014).

Another research by Vijayavenkataraman et al. (2011) splits the impact of climate change into four groups. The first group is air, water, plants, and animals; the second group is the economy, the third group is agriculture, and the fourth group is health.

Two kinds of approaches are used to estimate the impacts of climate change: the top-down approach and the bottom-up approach. The top-down approach assumes that climate change damage functions as reduced-form formulations linking climate variables to economic impacts. In the bottom-up approach, a range of emission scenarios is used to provide insights into the effects of climate change policy (Ciscar, 2009). Because top-down agreements need a centralized institution to distribute and enforce rights authoritatively, all international agreements are theoretically bottom-up agreements. Then there are no top-down agreements in the world. Also, the Kyoto Protocol encourages the top-down approach (Andresen, 2015).

Different kinds of approaches, different variety of renewable energy sources can be selected, and they have different costs by means of economy, environment, social life, etc. Winchester et al. (2010) listed the cost of climate policies as an emissions price, welfare change, consumption change, GDP change per-capita, per-family costs, discounted costs, and marginal abatement cost. In addition to this information, major mitigation cost concepts can be broadly divided into two categories, which are energy system (or sectoral) and economy-wide (or macroeconomic) (Paltsev & Capros, 2013). Also, these categories have sub-categories. In terms of sub-categories, the energy system category can be divided into capital costs, fuel and electricity costs, payments for GHG emissions, and disutility costs. Economy-wide category can be divided into a change in GDP, or a change in consumption, or a change in welfare. The authors state that these categories are formed based on the assessment of GHG emissions mitigation. These two categories are modeled by using energy system models and macroeconomic models, respectively. If we consider the energy system models, costs include capital costs, fuel and electricity costs, payments for GHG emissions, and disutility costs. If we consider macroeconomic models, costs include a change in GDP, or a change in consumption, or a change in welfare.

Table 4.1 summarizes the definition of costs and benefits of mitigation and adoption. Hof et al. (2014) state that there are two factors of mitigation costs in underlying studies. The first factor in these studies assumes a perfect world with complete information, rational actors, and one global decision-maker; the second factor is the negative side effects of mitigation measures that are not taken into account. The Paris Agreement accepts the target to keep the increase in global average temperature to well below 2 °C (Gao et al., 2017), but some studies have different targets. For example, Stanford University's Energy Modeling Forum (EMF27), which is focused on the development and cross model comparison, has two different long

Table 4.1 Definitions of mitigation and adaptation of the costs and benefits

	Mitigation	Adaptation
Costs	Definition: Costs of reducing greenhouse gas emissions	Definition: Costs of adapting society to climate change
Benefits	Definition: Avoided climate change damage because of less climate change as a result of mitigation measures	Definition: Avoided climate change damage because of adaptation to climate change

Source Hof et al. (2014, p: 9)

term targets; the first is to achieve a 2 °C target with medium probability and the second is to achieve a 2 °C target with low probability (Kriegler et al., 2014).

Moreover, the cost of the first target is estimated to be approximately 1% of GDP for the first half of this century. The cost of the second target is estimated to be approximately 2% of GDP for the whole century (Hof et al., 2014). These costs can be seen as very low mathematically, but it is an essential cost for world economies. That is the most crucial reason for the governments, whether to be part of the Paris Agreement. Governments have to give the decision to spend their income on climate change mitigation or not. The decision shows the priority of the governments to spend on the income of the country.

EMF is not the only study on climate change; many other studies have investigated climate change mitigation. Although these studies are not in the focus of this chapter, I would like to mention them, which are used models to investigate climate change. Three types of studies can be considered based on the geographical context. The first type is global level studies, the second type is European Union level studies, and the last type is USA level studies.

At the global level, the study is "The Innovation Modeling Comparison Project (IMCP)." At the EU level, the studies are "The Economics of Low Stabilization Project" (Edenhofer et al., 2010) and "Assessment of Climate Change Mitigation Pathways and Evaluation of the Robustness of Mitigation Cost Estimates (AMPERE)." At the USA level, the studies are "Program on Integrated Assessment Modeling Development, Diagnostic and Inter-Comparisons (PIAMDDI)" and "Climate Change Science Program (CCSP)" are USA models (Weyant & Kriegler, 2014).

In the literature, many authors have compared the cost of mitigation and adaptation costs or benefits. They have aimed to see which has more cost or more benefits, and which will emerge first? Some of them are Kriegler et al. (2014), Nordhaus and Sztorc (2013), and Weitzman (2012).

Weitzman (2012) uses a cost–benefit analysis (CBA) or an integrated assessment model (IAM) and focuses on the uncertainty of "equilibrium climate sensitivity," which is defined as "the global average surface warming that follows a sustained doubling of atmospheric carbon dioxide (CO_2) after the climate system has reached a new equilibrium."[1] Nordhaus and Sztorc (2013) use IAM analysis under the DICE model (Dynamic Integrated model of Climate and the Economy) and the RICE model (Regional Integrated model of Climate and the Economy). The models represent the economic aspect, policy aspect, and scientific aspect of climate change. The RICE model is the regional version of the DICE model. These two models were used around 1990 at first and revised several times; at last, the DICE-2013R model and the RICE-2010 model are the last versions of the models. If we do not take into consideration errors in the software and structure of these kinds of models; the results show that the optimal carbon price will be rose $18 per ton of CO_2 in 2015 to $18 per ton of CO_2 in 2100. Also, results show that the real interest rate is critical for policy estimations. Moreover, some major variables for the environment are determined in these models. These major variables are industrial CO_2 emissions, atmospheric CO_2 concentrations, and global mean temperature.

These two papers conclude that cost and benefits can be evaluated in the short term and long term. While mitigation cost will be higher than avoided damage in the short term, it will be smaller than avoided damage in the long term. Kriegler et al. (2013) use the Stanford Energy Modeling Forum Study 27 (EMF27) for two key dimensions of mitigation pathways: technology availability and climate policy regime. They used five policy dimensions and nine technology dimensions to design the scenarios. Different emissions reductions are needed to reach different GHG concentration levels based on the authors' calculations.

Renewable Energy for Climate Change Mitigation

The energy sector is a tool for mitigation of climate change by using renewable energy sources. While the sector is solving climate change problems, at the same time, it copes with climate change problems, such as aging and damages (Davis & Clemmer, 2014,[2] Auld & MacIver, 2006). Moreover, Auld and MacIver (2006) focuses on the effect of changing weather patterns on infrastructure risks and summarized projected changes in climate extremes due to climate change. These changes are more intense precipitation events, increased summer drying, and associated risk of drought, mean and peak precipitation intensities, and increased intensity of mid-latitude storms; which are taken from IPCC (2001). These weather events are extreme sometimes and cause a big amount of costs. Data shows that while the cost of weather events

---

[1] Also, the Intergovernmental Panel on Climate Change in its IPCC-AR4 (2007) Executive Summary explains S this way: "The equilibrium climate sensitivity is a measure of the climate system response to sustained radiative forcing. It is not a projection but is defined as the global average surface warming following a doubling of carbon dioxide concentrations. It is *likely* to be in the range 2–4.5 °C with a best estimate of 3 °C, and is *very unlikely* to be less than 1.5 °C. Values substantially higher than 4.5 °C cannot be excluded, but agreement of models with observations is not as good for those values." (Weitzman, 2012).

[2] Davis & Clemmer (2014).

was $20 billion per year in the 1980s, it was reached $85 billion in the 2010s in the USA (Weiss & Weidman, 2013).

Morand et al. (2015) state that there are two actions for climate change: mitigation with GHG emissions and help to adaptation to climate change. The suggestion of the authors is to use both mitigation and help to adapt successfully. Since it is estimated that the majority of global anthropogenic GHG emissions are generated by fossil fuel consumption (IPCC, 2012), reducing fossil fuel consumption is the first way to mitigate climate change. Therefore, GHG emissions generated in the process of the energy consumption of primary energy sources, the solution turns to reduce energy consumption or to reduce the amount of primary energy sources production in energy generation and to use renewable energy sources instead of them. Several options can be used to reduce GHG emissions by using primary energy sources. These options are energy conservation, energy efficiency, fossil fuel switching, and carbon capture and storage (CCS).

In this chapter, we discuss bioenergy, direct solar energy, geothermal energy, hydropower energy, and wind energy. All of these energies have different amounts of potential stock and a different number of technologies to generate and also different technical maturity. The decision to generate energy from these sources based on potential stock, technologies, and technical maturity, also accessibility and availability based on the place have an effect on this decision. In this section, we will read how these renewable energy sources are used in climate change mitigation.

Figure 4.8 shows global renewable energy consumption, measured in terawatt-hours (TWh) per year. In the figure, because of the big differences between two groups of variables, natural gas and traditional biofuel consumption values are shown on the

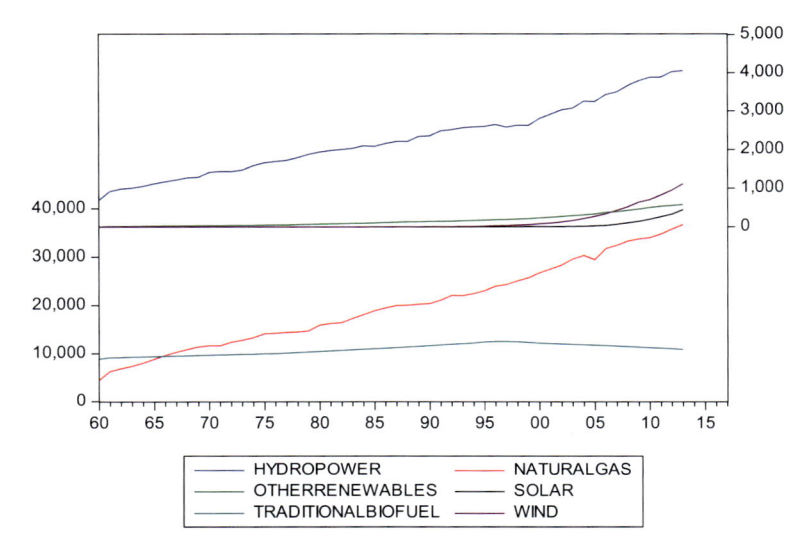

Fig. 4.8 Global renewable energy consumption. *Source* https://ourworldindata.org/energy: Smil (2017) & BP Statistical Review of World Energy

left axis, then the rest of the variables are shown on the right axis. However, it is crucial to remember that the using areas of these sources are different. For example, natural gas is mostly used for heating, but the wind is mostly used to generate electricity. From the figure, we can see that natural gas and traditional biofuel consumption are very high compared to other sources, and the wind has the least amount of consumption. The renewable energy sources which are used in the graph were chosen based on data availability. We take into consideration not only an increase in renewable energy sources but also a decrease in fossil fuel consumption. It is very clear from the data there is an increasing trend in all renewable energy sources. At the same time, if they provide a decrease in fossil fuel sources or a decrease in their ratio of increase, an increase in renewable energy consumption is more meaningful. Therefore, we investigate the consumption rate of these energy sources for 2000, 2005, 2010, and 2017. To calculate the shares, we summed all the values of energy sources in Fig. 4.4 and divided by each source's amount.

Figure 4.9 shows the share of energy sources for the years mentioned above. The values of shares of the energy sources in Fig. 4.9 have some round-up and round-down.[3] Because of these rounded numbers, we cannot talk about changes in decimal numbers. However, if we look overall at the period between 2000 and 2017, there have not been significant changes among energy sources. Wind energy could not reach even 1% among other energy sources, and coal has never been under 24%, and crude oil has never been under 35%. This figure shows us while there has been an increase in renewable energy use, their share generally at the same levels among all renewable energy sources. If there is a decrease in fossil fuel use at the same time as renewable energy increases, the share of renewable energy sources must be significantly differentiated by years. However, we cannot see these increases in the share of renewable energy sources. The shares can be interpreted that renewable energy use and fossil fuel use increasing together. Nevertheless, if this comparison starts from the 1980s or previous years, there will be significant changes in values. There were big changes before the 1980s maybe the 1990s, but after 2000 we cannot see significant differences among the shares of the investigated energy sources.

These energy sources are produced from various resources, and they produce a different kind of energy. Table 4.2 summarizes the sources of renewable energy and what they produce.

Bioenergy

Bioenergy is an essential renewable energy source for climate change mitigation. However, it has some risks for climate change such as net increases in GHG emissions, increases N_2O, negative environmental or socio-economic impacts and detrimental climate effects (Creutzig, 2014) and air pollution, biodiversity loss, as well

---

[3] For example crude oil 34,7% in 2010 and 35% in 2017 but because of round up, it is written as 35% both—in 2010 and 2017.

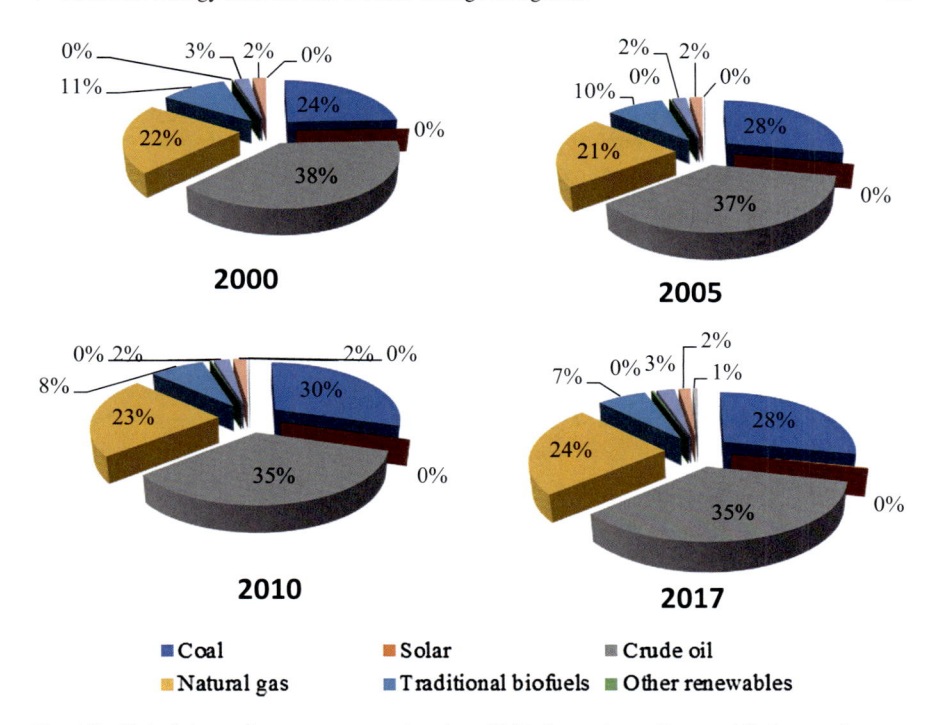

Fig. 4.9 Global share of energy consumption since 2017. *Source* https://ourworldindata.org/energy: Smil (2017). Energy Transitions: Global and National Perspectives & BP Statistical Review of World Energy, Author Calculations

Table 4.2 Renewable energy sources and features

Source	Resource	Produced energy
Bioenergy	Biomass feedstocks, short-rotation forest plantations; energy crops; the organic component of municipal solid waste; and other organic waste streams	Electricity or heat
Direct solar energy	Photovoltaics (PV) and concentrating solar power (CSP)	Electricity, thermal energy
Geothermal energy	Geothermal reservoirs	Electricity, district heating
Hydropower	Reservoirs	Electricity
Wind energy	Kinetic energy of moving air	Electricity

Source The IPCC (2012), 8. Table constructed by the author as risks to food security (Scharleman & Laurence, 2008). Bioenergy is needed to hold some conditions to increase its production. These conditions are competition with rival products (food and fibre), land-use changes, and agriculture and forestry yields. An increase in competing for food and fibre demand must be moderate, land use changes must be manageable, and agricultural and forestry yields must be sustainable.

One of the results of bioenergy is land use; it is considered as an undermining effect of climate change mitigation benefits. However, Berndes et al. (2010) present that only 1% of global agricultural land is used for cultivating biofuel crops; therefore, it has no significant effect of contributing to global emissions of GHG. On the contrary, land use caused by deforestation and expansion of agricultural food production causes 15% of global emissions of GHG. One of the main features of the bioenergy use is bioenergy systems are replaceable with primary energy sources. Based on this feature, when the effect on the mitigation of climate change of bioenergy is measuring, the effect of climate change of the system they replaced by must be considered too (Berndes et al., 2010). Based on the EU bioenergy targets, in 2020, it is aimed to reach 10% biomass use in primary energy requirements (Röder and Thornley, 2016).

The deployment of renewable power technologies is essential to understand the development of renewable energy use. I will use electricity capacity and electricity generation of the renewables as a proxy of the development. Figure 4.10 presents world electricity capacity and generation of bioenergy for selected years. Both the capacity and the generation are nearly tripled in the last 17 years. The increasing capacity is a sign that investors invest in bioenergy. The growing generation value of electricity production can be interpreted as a reason for the growing interest of consumers.

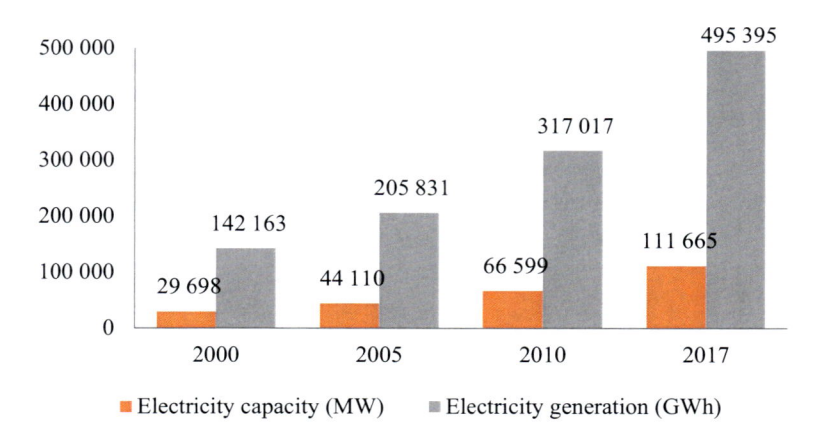

Fig. 4.10 Bioenergy electricity capacity and electricity generation. *Source* https://www.irena.org/Statistics/View-Data-by-Topic/Capacity-and-Generation/Statistics-Time-Series IRENA (2019), Renewable Energy Statistics 2019, The International Renewable Energy Agency, Abu Dhabi

Souza et al. (2015, 2017) provide comprehensive overviews on sustainable bioenergy approaches. Precisely, Souza et al. (2015) is an in-depth investigation of bioenergy by the contribution of 137 researchers from 82 institutions in 24 countries. The project is initiated by the Scientific Committee on Problems of the Environment (SCOPE) with a collaboration of the FAPESP (São Paulo Research Foundation) on Bioenergy (BIOEN), Global Climate Change (RPGCC), Research Program on Global Climate Change—(RPGCC). It is stated in Souza et al. (2015) traditional ways of bioenergy production, which is derived from wood and crop residues, are inefficient and traditional productions primarily used for household. While biofuel consumption has a big share of fuel consumption in many countries, it has a small share globally.

Bioenergy can be widely used based on the biodiversity of the countries. But it has not only production cost but also the opportunity cost because of land use. Moreover, because of the agricultural area use, it will have an effect on food prices. There will be an opportunity cost of using land for bioenergy production instead of food production. These topics have to be considered before allocating resources for bioenergy. For this reason, in the last decade, not only bioenergy but also sustainable bioenergy is recognized by governments. Some researchers are worried about land use, and their arguments are: existing sizable areas of land can be made a small contribution to food production, and it is forecasted that in 2050 only 5% of the amount of land that can be converted to cropland. It will be vital to land use: "In terms of land-use change, the issue is not how much land we use but how we use the land." (Souza et al., 2017).

Solar Energy

In nature, solar energy is converted into chemical energy and stored in as biomass by plants through the process of photosynthesis. Global installed capacity for solar-powered electricity reached around 290 GW at the end of 2016 and major solar energy produces are China, Japan, Germany, and the United States (Nwaigwe et al., 2019).

To see the development of the solar energy use electricity capacity of solar energy and electricity generation of solar energy presented in Fig. 4.11. If we compare the amounts in 2000 and 2017 very huge gap can be seen. It is nearly 300 times higher in 2017, comparing to 2000. The interest in solar energy starts in the 2010s in the figure. Technological developments contribute to this increase.

Moreover, technology allows residential solar panel use. The number of residential "prosumers" is rapidly increasing in many countries (Palm & Eriksson, 2018). Also, new technologies such as smart grids and blockchain can be used in solar energy systems (Andoi et al., 2019). Solar energy is straightforward to develop and integrate with new technologies. More than that, it allows installation by individuals. Also, residential user can sell their surplus energy. That is why they are called a "prosumer."

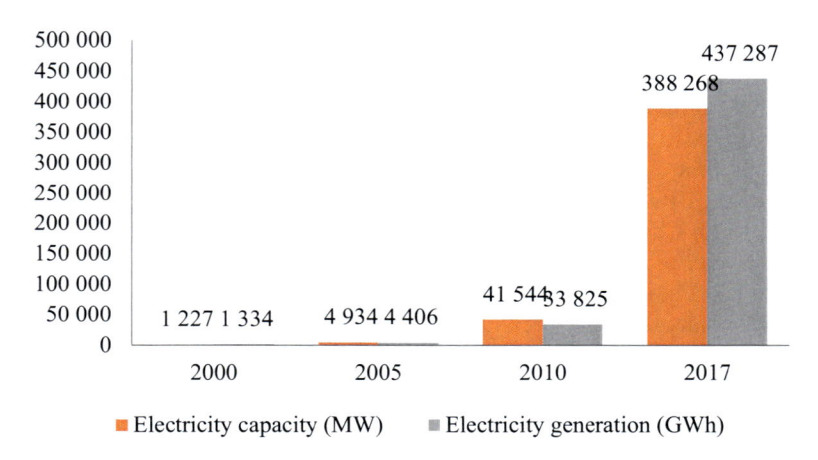

Fig. 4.11 Solar energy electricity capacity and electricity generation. *Source* https://www.irena.org/Statistics/View-Data-by-Topic/Capacity-and-Generation/Statistics-Time-Series IRENA (2019), Renewable Energy Statistics 2019, The International Renewable Energy Agency, Abu Dhabi

After all renewable energy sources, electricity capacity, and electricity generation are reviewed, it will be seen that solar energy has not the greatest value among the sources selected in this chapter, but it is the fastest and highest growing source.

The cost and productivity of solar energy depend on the geographic situation of the regions. Different regions have different levels of radiation. If in any region total radiation level is higher than 10,000 MJ/m^2.a—a region has a stronger level of radiation if it is between 8000 and 10,000 MJ/m^2.a—a region has a strong level of radiation, if it is between 5000 and 7000 MJ/m^2.a—a region has a moderate level of radiation. If it is under and equal to 2500 MJ/m^2 a—a region has a poor level of radiation (Sun et al., 2019). Therefore, the regions classified as follows:

Stronger: North Africa, Sahara, Australia, Southern Europe, Southwest United States, Southwest China, etc.

Strong: Southern Africa, Central Europe, Southern South America etc.

Moderate: Southeast Asia, Central America, Central Asia, Northern South America, East Asia, etc.

Poor: North and South Bipolar Region are poor.

However, the IPCC (2012) report uses solar energy, referring to the use of Sun's energy. To use direct solar energy there are various ways such as solar thermal, photovoltaic, concentrating solar power (CSP), and solar fuels. To capture the Sun's energy using solar thermal a flat-plate collectors are used. Various PV technologies are used such as wafer-based crystalline silicon PV, the thin-film technologies of copper, etc. CSP is another way to generate solar energy by concentrating the Sun's rays to heat a medium. The last way mentioned is solar fuel production; it is produced by an electrolysis process driven by solar-derived electrical power. Solar energy cannot be used in all targets. In actual technologies, it is adapted in two targets heating and cooling networks and end-use sectors. In the integration of direct solar energy into heating and cooling networks, solar thermal sources are used. To integrate direct solar energy into end-use sectors, solar thermal water, and space heating, and solar sorption cooling systems are used.

Geothermal Energy

Geothermal energy is produced from the Earth's interior stores. It is continuously restored by natural heat production, conduction, and convection from surrounding hotter regions. It is a very old energy source since ancient times of civilization; steaming grounds were utilized for a variety of purposes such as bathing and cooking etc. The direct use of geothermal energy thus has a long history over the last few millenniums. The direct use of geothermal energy is currently extended to the hot-water.

Geothermal energy can be integrated into heating and cooling networks by using heat from geothermal. Also, it can be integrated into end-use sectors by using geothermal resources for heat and steam demands.

Like solar energy depends on the level of radiation of the region, geothermal energy depends on geographic structure or, in other words, the geothermal potential of a region. But it can be found in all parts of the world. One of the advantages of geothermal energy is that it is reachable independently from the time of the day, night, weather, or season. Also, it has geophysical exploration costs. When we talk about geothermal energy, we have to think about its peculiar challenges. Mainly these challenges are high start-up cost, complicated and expensive technologies, and long production time (Ómarsdóttir, 2016).

Although in the earlier times, geothermal energy was mostly used in volcanic countries, nowadays its usage is not related to the volcanic history of the countries (Muraoka, 2017). Figure 4.12 gives us a tool to understand the development of geothermal energy use by using electricity capacity and electricity generation from it.

Compared with the other renewable energy sources increase of geothermal energy use is moving a smooth and stable way. Averagely every five years it increases between 5 and 10%. The percentages are valid for both capacity and generation. We can say that there is a smooth and constant increase in geothermal energy in the context of electrical energy.

Hydropower

Hydropower is derived from the energy of water moving from higher to lower elevations. One of the distinctive features of hydropower is its interaction with climate change. Hydropower is a mitigation way of climate change. On the other hand, both hydropower resources and hydropower generation have to cope with climate

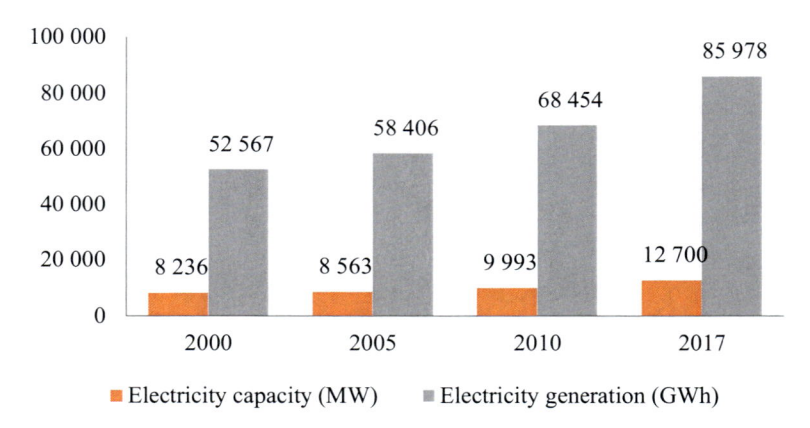

Fig. 4.12 Geothermal energy electricity capacity and electricity generation. *Source* https://www.
irena.org/Statistics/View-Data-by-Topic/Capacity-and-Generation/Statistics-Time-Series   IRENA
(2019), Renewable Energy Statistics 2019, The International Renewable Energy Agency, Abu Dhabi

change because climate change has adverse effects on hydropower. Therefore climate
change characteristics decrease the likelihood of using hydropower. For example, the
Himalayan glaciers will gradually melt as a result of global warming; it will cause
to reduce river flow (Shu et al., 2018).

Hydropower can be used to integrate renewable energy into water management
systems, electrical power systems, and industry sectors. Hydropower plants come in
three main project types: run-of-river (RoR), storage, and pumped storage. According
to the 2015 data, approximately 1200 large dams were under construction in mainly
Asia in 49 countries, and 347 of them are major dams, which means that their height
is over 60 m; also, hydropower is one of the main objectives of these dams (Berga,
2016). Furthermore, over the past few decades, instream (kinetic) turbines have been
directly installed to rivers without dam (Jia et al., 2017).

Like other renewable energy sources, we investigate electricity capacity and electricity production from hydropower is presented in Fig. 4.13. The greatness of the
values is paid attention to at first glance. While other energy sources have very low
values in 2000 compared to their values in 2010, geothermal energy only doubled in
17 years. There is a constant moderate increase according to the electricity sector.
The values are the underline the high rate of use of hydropower.

Berga (2016) presents that hydropower energy use depends on the countries' technological level; the countries which have tapped more than 50% of their feasible
technical potential have been extensively used hydropower energy. The author
states that "In general, developed countries have already exploited much of their
hydropower potential, while emergent and developing." WEC (2016) represents the
top hydropower capacity of the world and countries with the highest capacity are
China, the USA, Brazil, Canada, India, and Russia, respectively. The values show
that China has three times higher capacity than the USA; other countries respectively
have approximately 10% difference from a country behind them. On the other hand,

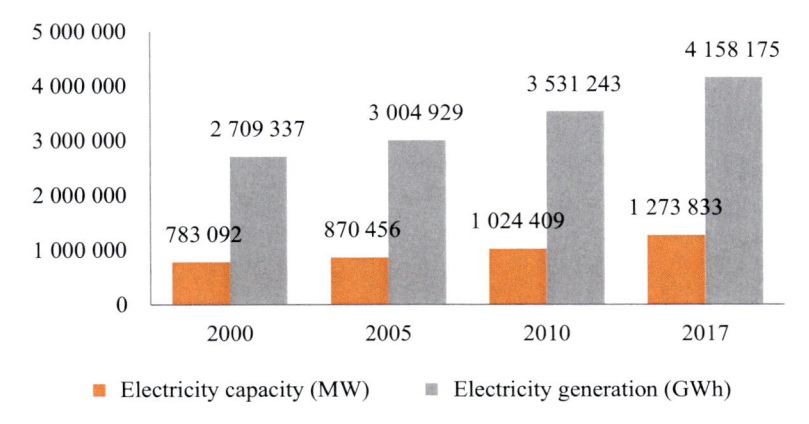

Fig. 4.13 Hydropower electricity capacity and electricity generation. *Source* https://www. irena.org/Statistics/View-Data-by-Topic/Capacity-and-Generation/Statistics-Time-Series IRENA (2019), Renewable Energy Statistics 2019, The International Renewable Energy Agency, Abu Dhabi

an order of the production capacity of the countries are China, Brazil, Canada, the USA, Russia, and India also according to production China has a great difference from other countries.

Wind Energy

Generating electricity from the wind requires that the kinetic energy of moving air be converted to electrical energy. The potential of wind energy depends on the wind surface of the regions. However, the potential of installed capacity is the decision of the people or government of a region. Most of the installed capacity was in the USA, EU, China, and India respectively based on the 2008 data and wind energy deployment growth rate was 30% from 1999 to 2008 (Lenzen & Baboulet, 2017).

One of the advantages of wind energy is plant outages are problematic like fossil energy, nuclear energy, or hydropower (Archer & Jacobson, 2007). Although plant outages are not problematic, the penetration rate of wind is one of the challenges (Fig. 4.14).

To understand the increase in wind energy, electricity capacity and wind electricity generation values are used. Every time period we used the amount of capacity and the generation increase nearly three times than the previous time. The reason for the increase can be decreasing of the cost of wind energy. After 1980 the cost of wind energy has declined significantly (IPCC, 2012).

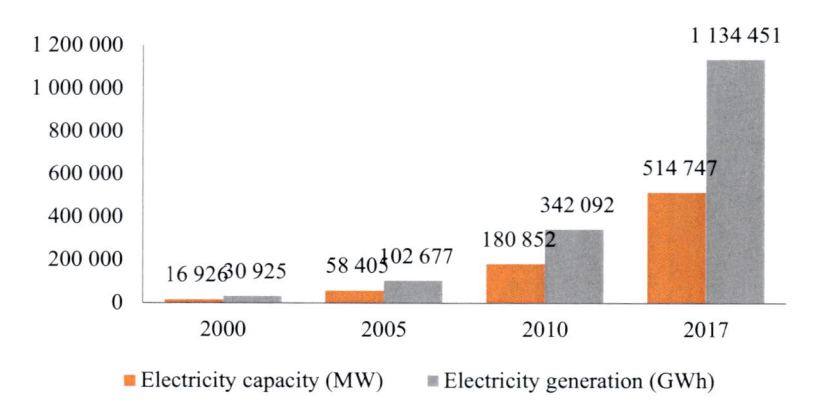

Fig. 4.14 Wind energy electricity capacity and electricity generation. *Source* https://www.irena.org/Statistics/View-Data-by-Topic/Capacity-and-Generation/Statistics-Time-Series   IRENA (2019), Renewable Energy Statistics 2019, The International Renewable Energy Agency, Abu Dhabi

Conclusion

Environmental degradation, global warming, and climate change have interaction among themselves. Since the 1997 Kyoto Protocol, we can see growing attention on climate change and initiatives from governments and non-governmental organizations. Individuals, institutions, or organizations can take numerous actions for climate change to decrease their carbon footprint. Nevertheless, mainly in the global approach, we can divide actions into two groups: mitigation with climate change and adaptation to climate change.

In this chapter, we focused on the first action, climate change mitigation in terms of renewable energy use. At first, we tried to explain the process of climate change. In the second chapter, we investigated the climate change process and its reasons and its consequences briefly, then we focus on the effect of climate change on the world. Some observations such as sea-level rise, global temperature rise, warming oceans, shrinking ice sheets, and declining Arctic sea ice were examined. The data showed us that the effects of climate change are observable and undeniable. We suggest that climate change has many detrimental effects on the world and renewable mostly used way to mitigate climate change. Also, I presented their shares and usage to show their developments for the 2000–2017 period. We investigated their potential stock, technologies, and maturity of the technologies of them.

In the world, we have different kinds of renewable energy sources and we investigate bioenergy, solar energy, geothermal energy, hydropower, and wind energy. Each of them has costs and benefits. Governments try to replace their primary energy sources with renewable energy sources to decrease the adverse effects of climate change. The decision to choose one of the renewable energy sources depends on not only its cost but also its existence in a region or the amount of it in a region. The decreasing cost of some of the renewable energy sources and have established a growing demand for renewables. In the third section of the chapter, we saw that some of the renewables can be produced in every country, but some of the renewables can be produced depending on geographical factors. Therefore their production is changeable based on the region. Moreover, some renewables specialize to produce some kind of energy, for example, natural gas is in heating, the wind energy is in electricity.

As a final remark, the world has remarkable opportunities to increase its renewable energy use to decrease climate change effects. If these opportunities can be used with the knowledge of the features of the renewables, it will be an accelerator to reach Paris Agreement global climate objectives.

References

Andoni, M., Robu, V., Flynn, D., Abram, S., Geach, D., Jenkins, D., et al. (2019). Blockchain technology in the energy sector: A systematic review of challenges and opportunities. *Renewable and Sustainable Energy Reviews. 100*, 143–174. https://doi.org/10.1016/j.rser.2018.10.014

Andresen, S. (2015). International climate negotiations: Top-down, bottom-up or a combination of both? *The International Spectator, 50*(1), 15–30. https://doi.org/10.1080/03932729.2014.997992

Archer, C. L., & Jacobson, M. Z. (2007). Supplying baseload power and reducing transmission requirements by interconnecting wind farms. *Journal of Applied Meteorology and Climatology, 46*(11), 1701–1717. https://doi.org/10.1175/2007jamc1538.1

Auld, H., & Maclver, D. (2006). Changing weather patterns, uncertainty and infrastructure risks emerging adaptation requirements. In *Proceedings of the IEEE EIC Climate Change Conference* (pp. 1–10), Ottawa, ON, Canada, May 10–12, 2006.

Berga, L. (2016). The role of hydropower in climate change mitigation and adaptation: A review. *Engineering, 2*(3), 313–318. https://doi.org/10.1016/j.eng.2016.03.004

Berndes, G., Bird, N., & Cowie, A. (2010). *Bioenergy, land use change and climate change mitigation*. Report for Policy Advisors and Policy Makers. Chalmers University of Technology. https://www.ieabioenergy.com/wp-content/uploads/2013/10/Bioenergy-Land-Use-Change-and-Climate-Change-Mitigation-Background-Technical-Report.pdf

Chichilnisky, G. (2006). Global property rights: The Kyoto protocol and the knowledge revolution. *SSRN Electronic Journal.* https://doi.org/10.2139/ssrn.1377902

Ciscar, J. C. (Ed.) (2009). *Climate Change Impacts in Europe: Final Report of the PESETA Research Project, JRC, IPTS and IES.*

Creutzig, F. (2014). Economic and ecological views on climate change mitigation with bioenergy and negative emissions. *GCB Bioenergy, 8*(1).

Davis, M., & Clemmer. S. (2014). *Power failure: How climate change puts our electricity at risk and what we can do?*. Union of Concerned Scientists. Accessed from https://www.ucsusa.org/resources/power-failure

Edenhofer, O., Knopf, B., Barker, T., Baumstark, L., Bellevrat, E., Chateau, B., Patrick, C., et al. (2010). The economics of low stabilization: Model comparison of mitigation strategies and costs. *The Energy Journal, 31*(01), 11–48. https://doi.org/10.5547/issn0195-6574-ej-vol31-nosi-2

Gao, Y., Gao, X., Zhang, X. (2017). The 2 °C global temperature target and the evolution of the long-term goal of addressing climate change—From the United Nations framework convention on climate change to the Paris agreement. *Engineering, 3*(2), 272–278. https://doi.org/10.1016/j.eng.2017.01.022. Accessed November 20, 2019.

Hof, A. F., de Bruin, K. C., Dellink, R. B., den Elzen, M. G., & van Vuuren, D. P. (2009). The effect of different mitigation strategies on international financing of adaptation. *Environmental Science & Policy, 12*(7), 832–43. https://doi.org/10.1016/j.envsci.2009.08.007

Hof, A., Boot, P., van Vuuren, D., & van Minnen, J. (2014).*Costs and benefits of climate change adaptation and mitigation: An assessment on different regional scales*. PBL Netherlands Environmental Assessment Agency, The Hague.

Hunt, A., & Watkiss, P. (2010). Climate change impacts and adaptation in cities: A review of the literature. *Climatic Change, 104*(1), 13–49. https://doi.org/10.1007/s10584-010-9975-6

IPCC. (1996). Climate change 1995: The science of climate change. In J. T. Houghton, L. G. Meira Filho, B. A. Callander, N. Harris, A. Kattenberg, K. Maskell (Eds.), *Contribution of working group I to the second assessment report of the intergovernmental panel on climate change.* Cambridge University Press. Accessed November 10, 2019.

IPCC. (2001). Climate Change 2001: The Scientific Basis. Available at https://www.ipcc.ch/site/assets/uploads/2018/07/WG1_TAR_FM.pdf. Accessed November 10, 2019.

IPCC. (2007). *Contribution of working group III to the fourth assessment report* (p. 2007). Cambridge University Press.

IPCC. (2012). *Renewable Energy Sources and Climate Change Mitigation Special Policymakers and Technical Summary.* In O. Edenhofer, et al. (Eds.). Available at https://www.ipcc.ch/site/assets/uploads/2018/03/SRREN_FD_SPM_final-1.pdf. Accessed November 10, 2019.

IPCC. (2014). Climate change 2014: Synthesis report. In Core Writing Team, Pachauri, R. K. & Meyer, L. A. (Eds.), *Contribution of working groups I, II and III to the fifth assessment report of the intergovernmental panel on climate change* (151 pp.). IPCC, Geneva, Switzerland. Accessed November 10, 2019.

IRENA. (2019). Renewable Energy Statistics 2019. Available at https://www.irena.org/Statistics/View-Data-by-Topic/Capacity-and-Generation/Statistics-Time-Series. Accessed September 20, 2019.

Jia, J., Punys, P., & Ma, J. (2017). Hydropower. In W.-Y. Chen, T. Suzuki, & M. Lackner (Eds.), *Handbook of climate change mitigation and adaptation* (pp. 2085–2132). Springer International Publishing Switzerland.

Kriegler, E., et al. (2014). The role of technology for achieving climate policy objectives: Overview of the EMF 27 study on global technology and climate policy strategies. *Climatic Change, 123*(3–4), 353–367.

Lenzen, M., & Baboulet, O. (2017). Wind energy. In *Handbook of climate change mitigation and adaptation* (pp. 1975–2007). Springer International Publishing Switzerland.

Morand, A., Hennessey, R., Pittman, J., & Douglas, A. (2015). *Linking mitigation and adaptation goals in the energy sector: A case study synthesis report* (122 p.). Report submitted to the Climate Change Impacts and Adaptation Division, Natural Resources Canada.

Muraoka, H. (2017). Geothermal energy. In *Handbook of climate change mitigation and adaptation* (pp. 2057–2084). Springer International Publishing Switzerland.

Muratoğlu, Y., & Uğurlu, E. (2014). An empirical test of the environmental kuznets curve for CO_2 in G7: A panel cointegration approach. *Proceedings of the New York State Economics Association, 7*, 148–154.

Nordhaus, W., & Sztorc, P. (2013). *DICE 2013R: Introduction and user's manual* (2nd Ed.). 0Cowles Found.

Nwaigwe, K. N., Mutabilwa, P., & Dintwa, E. (2019). An overview of solar power (PV systems) integration into electricity grids. *Materials Science for Energy Technologies, 2*(3), 629–33. https://doi.org/10.1016/j.mset.2019.07.002

Ómarsdóttir, M. (2016). The role of geothermal in combating climate change. In *Short Course I on Sustainability and Environmental Management of Geothermal Resource Utilization and the Role of Geothermal in Combating Climate Change* (pp. 1–11), El Salvador, September 4–10, 2016.

Palm, J., & Eriksson, E. (2018). Residential solar electricity adoption: How households in Sweden search for and use information. *Energy, Sustainability and Society, 8*(1), 8–14. https://doi.org/10.1186/s13705-018-0156-1

Paltsev, S., & Pantelis, C. (2013). Cost concepts for climate change mitigation. *Climate Change Economics, 4*(1), 1340003. https://doi.org/10.1142/s2010007813400034.

Roder, M., & Thornley, P. (2016). Bioenergy as climate change mitigation option within a 2 °C target—uncertainties and temporal challenges of bioenergy systems. *Energy, Sustainability and Society, 6*. https://doi.org/10.1186/s13705-016-0070-3

Rosen, R. A., & Guenther, E. (2015). The economics of mitigating climate change: What can we know? *Technological Forecasting and Social Change, 91*, 93–106. https://doi.org/10.1016/j.techfore.2014.01.013

Scharlemann, J. P. W., & Laurance, W. F. (2008). How Green are biofuels? *Science, 319*(5859), 43–44. https://doi.org/10.1126/science.1153103

Schirnding, Y., Bruce, N., Smith, K., Ballard-Treemer, G., Ezzati, M., & Lvovsky, K. (2001). *Addressing the impact of household energy and indoor air pollution on the health of the poor—implications for policy action and intervention measures* (52 pp.). WHO/HDE/HID/02.9, Commission on Macroeconomics and Health, World Health Organization, Geneva, Switzerland.

Shu, J., Qu, J., Motha, R., Xu, J., Dong, D. (2018). Impacts of climate change on hydropower development and sustainability: A review. *IOP Conference Series: Earth and Environmental Science, 163*, 012126.

Smil, V. (2017). *Energy transitions: Global and national perspectives* (2nd ed.). Praeger.

Souza, G. M., Victoria, R., Joly, C., & Verdade, L. (Eds). (2015). *Bioenergy & sustainability: Bridging the gap.* SCOPE Paris. ISBN978-2-9545557-0-6. http://bioenfapesp.org/scopebioenergy/index.php

Souza, G. M., Ballester, M. V. R., de Brito Cruz, C. H., Chum, H., Dale, B., Dale, V. H., Fernandes, E. C. M., Foust, T., Karp, A., Lynd, L., Maciel Filho, R., Milanez, A., Nigro, F., Osseweijer, P., Verdade, L. M., Victoria, R. L., & Van der Wielen, L. (2017). The role of bioenergy in a climate-changing world. *Environmental Development, 23*, 57–64.

Sun, T. Q., Cheng, D. L., Xu, L., & Qian, B. L. (2019). Status and trend analysis of solar energy utilization technology. *IOP Conference Series: Earth and Environmental Science, 354*, 12010. https://doi.org/10.1088/1755-1315/354/1/012010

Uğurlu, E. (2019b). Renewable energy strategies for sustainable development in the European Union. In *Renewable energy: International perspectives on sustainability.* Springer International Publishing, Cham.

Uğurlu, E. (2019a). Greenhouse gases emissions and alternative energy in the Middle East. In Qudrat-Ullah, H., & Kayal, A. A. (Eds.), *Understanding complex systems climate change and energy dynamics in the Middle East* (pp. 259–291). https://doi.org/10.1007/978-3-030-11202-8_9

VijayaVenkataRaman, S., Iniyan, S., & Goic, R. (2012). A review of climate change, mitigation and adaptation. *Renewable and Sustainable Energy Reviews, 16*(1), 878–897.

WEC. (2016). Wec-France.Org, World Energy Resources 2016. http://www.wec-france.org/DocumentsPDF/Etudes_CME/World-Energy-Resources_SummaryReport_2016.pdf. Accessed November 8, 2019.

Weiss, D., & Weidman, J. (2013a). *Pound foolish: Federal community resilience investments swamped by disaster damages.* https://www.americanprogress.org/wp-content/uploads/2013/06/FedResilienceSpending.pdf

Weitzman, M. (2012). GHG targets as insurance against catastrophic climate damages. *Journal of Public Economic Theory, 14*, 221–244.

Weyant, J., & Kriegler, E. (2014). Preface and introduction to EMF 27. *Climatic Change, 123*(3–4), 345–352. https://doi.org/10.1007/s10584-014-1102-7

Winchester, N., Paltsev, S., Morris, J., & Reilly, J. (2010). Costs of mitigating climate change in the United States. *Annual Review of Resource Economics, 2*(1), 257–273. https://doi.org/10.1146/annurev.resource.012809.104234

Erginbay Uğurlu is a Professor in the Faculty of Economics and Administrative Sciences at Istanbul Aydın University. He is head of the Department of International Trade and Finance. Uğurlu received his B.A. in Econometrics from Marmara University in 2004. He has attended to İstanbul Technical University in 2004 and received M.Sc. in Economics in 2006. He had a

Ph.D. degree in the field of Econometrics in 2011 at Gazi University. He was a Visiting Scholar at Columbia University Department of Economics and Post-Doctoral Academic Researcher at the Columbia Consortium for Risk Management in 2013. He got an Associate Professor degree in 2014 in Econometrics. He became a Professor in 2020.

Chapter 5
Income Inequality and the Environment: Mechanisms, Empirics and Policy

Sedat Alataş

Abstract Income inequality and environmental degradation are two growing threats that received significant attention from the international community at the onset of the twenty-first century. While growing concerns about income inequality have become dominant in science, policy, and society since the 1980s, environmental deterioration has been significantly accelerating since the 1950s in most countries worldwide. In this regard, the question of whether these two crises are linked becomes highly important from the environmental policy perspective as the balance of power between the poor and the rich determines the level of environmental degradation. However, despite many different theoretical and empirical studies, a clear consensus regarding the relationship between these two challenges has not yet been reached. The main objective of this chapter is to review and discuss the theoretical and empirical explanations linking income inequality and environmental deterioration by addressing some key issues. To this end, we seek to answer the following questions: how does the distribution of income affect the environment? Does environmental quality have an impact on income inequality? How should environmental policies be designed to tackle both of these challenges?

Introduction

We have been witnessing several global environmental problems since the beginning of the industrial era. Among these problems, climate change emerges as the most critical one. The excessive use of fossil fuels results notably in widespread impacts on human and natural systems by increasing greenhouse gases (GHGs) in the atmosphere. According to the Fifth Assessment Report of the Intergovernmental Panel on Climate Change (Intergovernmental Panel on Climate Change, 2014, 2015), carbon dioxide (CO_2) emissions are responsible for 78% of the total GHG emissions. More importantly, about half of the cumulative anthropogenic CO_2 emissions have

S. Alataş (✉)
Department of Economics, Faculty of Economics and Administrative Sciences, Aydın Adnan Menderes University, Nazilli, Aydın, Turkey
e-mail: sedat.alatas@adu.edu.tr

© The Author(s), under exclusive license to Springer Nature Switzerland AG 2022
D. Kurochkin et al. (eds.), *Energy Policy Advancement*,
https://doi.org/10.1007/978-3-030-84993-1_5

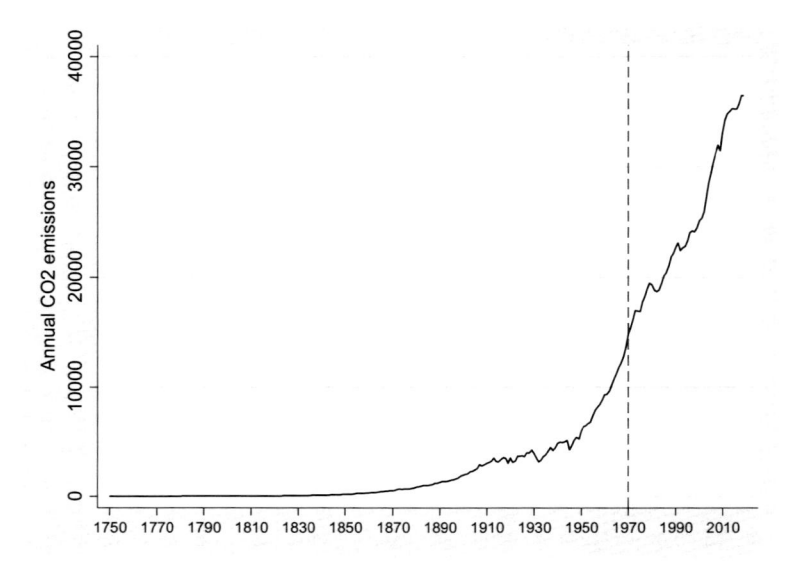

Fig. 5.1 Annual production-based CO_2 emissions (1750–2019). *Source* Global Carbon Project (Friedlingstein et al., 2020)

occurred between 1970 and 2010. Figure 5.1 depicts this considerable increase by showing the global anthropogenic CO_2 emissions for the period between 1750 and 2019.

The second problem faced by humankind in the twenty-first century is how income is distributed between countries. Like the worrying trend observed in the environment, income disparity between countries widens (Acemoğlu et al., 2004; Hall & Jones, 1998; Rodrik et al., 2002). According to the Penn World Table (PWT) version 9.1 (Feenstra et al., 2015), while the gap in income per capita between the rich and the poor nations was 48 in 1960, this gap has risen to 136 in 2017, meaning that the world's most prosperous country is more than 136 times as rich as the country at the bottom. Figure 5.2 shows the distribution of income per capita in 1960 and 2019. As seen, the vast majority of countries have experienced an increase in their income per capita over the years. However, this increase is not equally distributed among nations, implying a widening income inequality. While some countries have a considerable increase in their income per capita, this does not hold for some other nations (Acemoğlu, 2009; Dowrick, 2010; Durlauf et al., 2005).

Considering these trends depicted in Figs. 5.1 and 5.2 regarding the environment and income distribution, it is quite evident that these issues are two growing global threats faced by humankind in the contemporary period. This simultaneous worsening trend for both of them motivates many researchers and policymakers in the field to ask the following questions: Does there exist a relationship between income

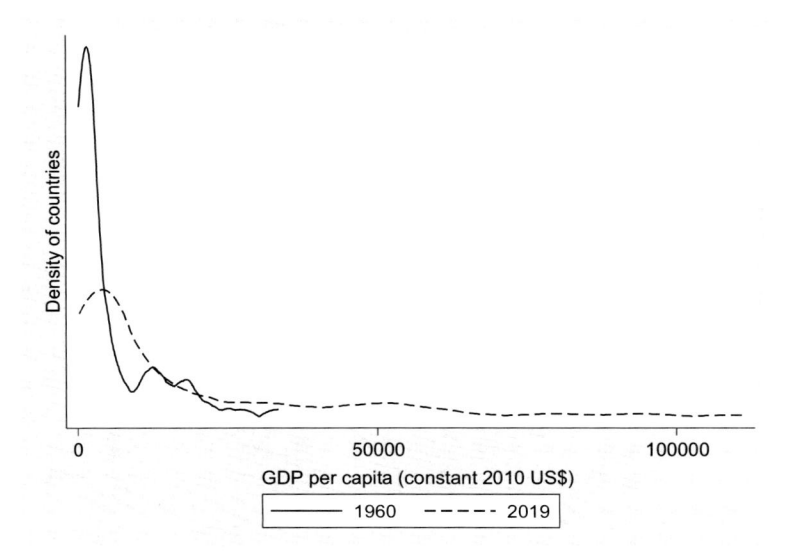

Fig. 5.2 The distribution of countries in 1960 and 2019. *Source* World Bank (2021)

inequality and environmental quality? Does the widening income gap between countries have important implications for the environmental outcome? (Berthe & Elie, 2015; Grunewald et al., 2017).

The studies conducted so far to answer these questions generally confirm the link between income distribution and environmental quality (Chen et al., 2020; Huang & Duan, 2020; Knight et al., 2017; Yang et al., 2020). For example, the Oxfam report states that more than half of the cumulative carbon emissions (52%) come from the richest 10% of the world's population from 1990 to 2015. However, this figure is only 7% for the poorest 50% (Gore et al., 2020). Moreover, this strong correlation is valid not only for carbon emissions but also for other dimensions of the environment, such as biodiversity loss. As shown in Fig. 5.3, there is a positive linkage between the number of threatened species and the Gini index. In other words, the number of threatened species increases in countries where income is not equally distributed.

Despite many attempts to identify the link between environmental degradation and income inequality, scholars have not reached a clear theoretical and empirical consensus regarding the direction of the relationship between these two crises (Boyce, 1994). While some studies confirm the positive effect of income inequality on carbon emissions (Chen et al., 2020; Grunewald et al., 2017; Marsiliani & Renstroem, 2000; Torras & Boyce, 1998), others highlight the trade-off between them (Hailemariam et al., 2020; Heerink et al., 2001; Ravallion et al., 2000; Scruggs, 1998; Wolde-Rufael & Idowu, 2017). In other words, the studies yield an unclear picture by reporting conflicting results (Berthe & Elie, 2015; Grunewald et al., 2017).

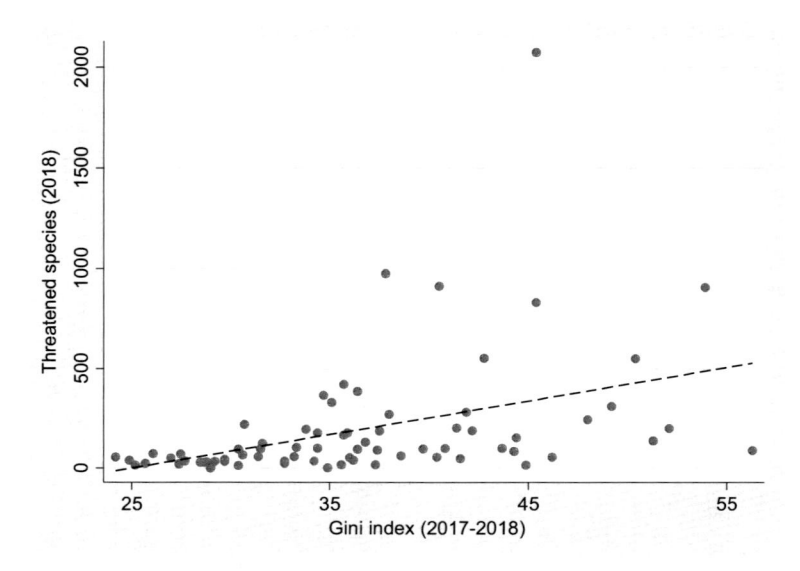

Fig. 5.3 Income inequality and threatened species (Threatened species are the number of species (bird, fish, mammal, plant) classified by the International Union for Conservation Nature (IUCN) as endangered, vulnerable, rare, indeterminate, out of danger, or insufficiently known (World Bank, 2021)). *Source* World Bank (2021)

   This study intends to contribute to this growing literature on income distribution and environmental sustainability. To this end, we first introduce theoretical mechanisms explaining the channels running from income distribution to environmental quality. After briefly reviewing the existing empirical literature, we secondly conduct an empirical investigation for a panel of 120 countries over the period between 1980 and 2019 using the system generalized method of moments (GMM). Lastly, we discuss the importance of the inequality-environment nexus for designing appropriate economic and environmental policies to reduce CO_2 emissions and improve environmental quality. The study results reveal that income distribution is an important source of carbon emissions.

   The chapter proceeds in five sections. In the next section, we discuss the theoretical background. While we introduce our empirical investigation and results in Sect. 3, we show the policy relevance of the subject in Sect. 4. In Sect. 5, we conclude.

Theoretical Mechanisms

A substantial body of literature investigates the nexus between income and the environment since the pioneering work of Grossman and Krueger (1991, 1995). The vast majority of these studies building on the empirical testing of the environmental

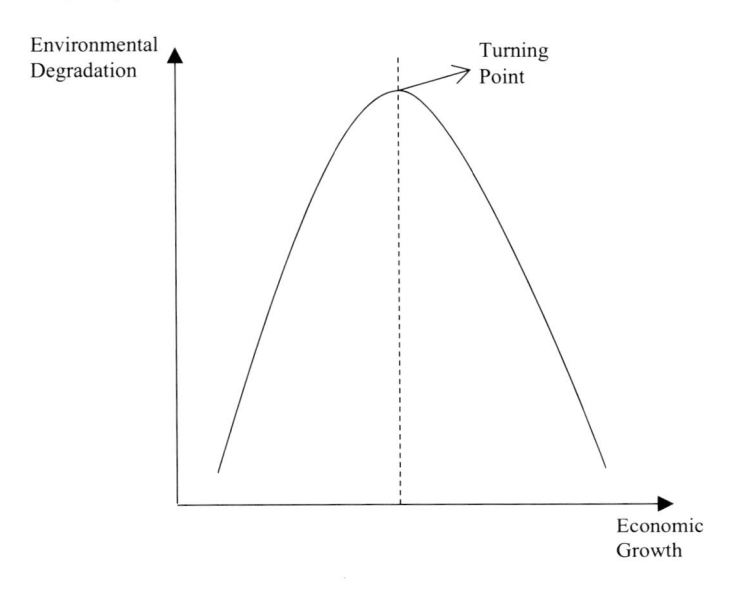

Fig. 5.4 Environmental Kuznets curve. *Source* Author, adapted from Sinha et al. (2019)

Kuznets curve (EKC) (Cole et al., 1997; Holtz-Eakin & Selden, 1995; Panayotou, 1993; Richmond & Kaufmann, 2006; Shafik & Bandyopadhyay, 1992; Shahbaz & Sinha, 2019) mainly suggests that the effect of economic growth on CO_2 emissions is two-sided. As depicted in Fig. 5.4, while an increase in income harms the environment in the first stage, this effect turns out to be negative and improves the environmental quality after reaching a turning point in income level (Ozcan & Ozturk, 2019; Sinha et al., 2019).[1]

One of the main limitations of the EKC hypothesis is the exclusion of other explanatory variables from the model specification that might potentially affect CO_2 emissions. In other words, as the EKC framework solely considers economic growth as a determinant of CO_2 emissions, it might not be appropriate for analyzing other driving factors of environmental degradation (Lantz & Feng, 2006). To overcome this problem, some researchers started to modify this model with some other variables in the earlier 1990s (Borghesi, 2000; Torras & Boyce, 1998). Income distribution is one of these variables, which is seen as a potential determinant of environmental degradation (Boyce, 1994; Marsiliani & Renstroem, 2000; Ravallion et al., 2000; Scruggs, 1998).

Boyce (1994) is the first author to highlight the environmental role of income distribution. The main argument behind the hypothesis of Boyce (1994) (known as the political economy approach) is that if the political power of the rich (winner) group in a society is more than the poor (loser) ones, this unequal distribution of

---

[1] The EKC hypothesis is based on the work of Kuznets (1955), which suggests a similar link between inequality and income.

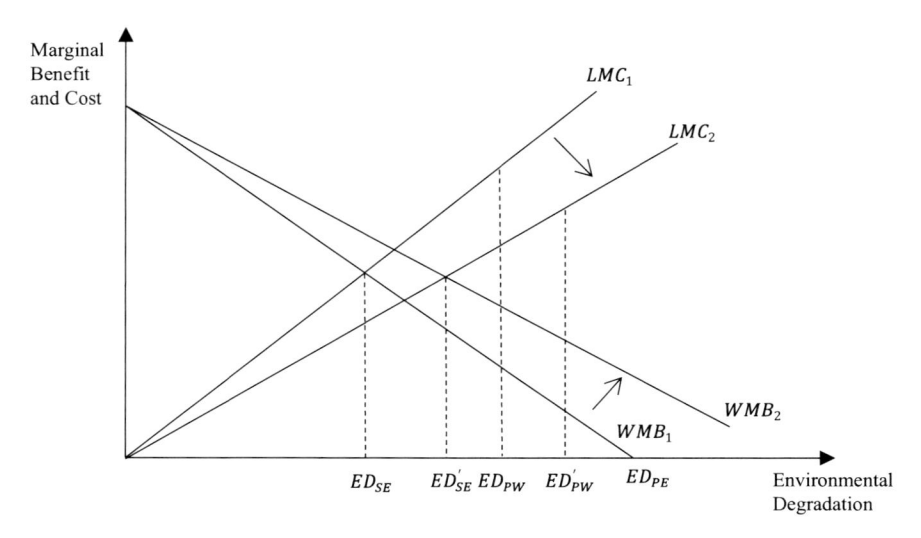

Fig. 5.5 The level of environmental degradation under the political economy approach. *Source* Author, adapted from Boyce (1994)

power leads to environmental degradation more, compared to the reverse case. This effect occurs in three ways: (i) via the cost–benefit analysis; (ii) via asymmetries in the political power; (iii) via impacts on the rate of time preference. While the cost–benefit analysis mainly refers to the purchasing power differences across individuals, groups, and classes in willingness to pay to avoid pollution, asymmetries in the political power are related to the political power differences across individuals, groups, and classes in determining environmental policies. On the other hand, the rate of time preference emphasizes the willingness to trade present benefits for future costs (Borghesi, 2000; Boyce, 2007).

Figure 5.5 shows how the level of environmental degradation is determined under the political economy approach. We have two lines in Fig. 5.5: the negatively-sloped marginal benefit of the winners (WMB_1) and the positively-sloped marginal cost of losers (LMC_1). Based on the cost–benefit analysis, the intersection of these curves gives us the socially efficient environmental degradation level (ED_{SE}). However, this equilibrium might not occur at this level in some cases and vary depending on the relative political power of two (winners and losers) groups. For example, if the power of the losers constraint the winners to some extent, the environmental degradation level might be limited to a level below privately efficient level (ED_{PE}). Similarly, when the power of losers is less than the winners, the environmental degradation level might exceed ED_{SE}, or vice versa. According to Fig. 5.5, the actual environmental degradation level determined based on the political power of groups is ED_{PW}, which is between ED_{SE} and ED_{PE}. If we assume that there exists a regressive income redistribution from losers to winners, both WMB_1 and LMC_1 lines shift to the right (WMB_2 and LMC_2). As clearly seen, socially efficient and actual environmental degradation levels increase from ED_{SE} to ED'_{SE} and from ED_{PW} to ED'_{PW}. In sum, an increase in income inequality leads to environmental degradation more (Boyce, 1994).

The hypothesis advanced by Boyce (1994) mainly states that the environmental benefits and costs will not be equally distributed across the population. Therefore, it is highly consistent with the environmental justice literature. While unequal societies tend to harm the environment more, societies with relatively less economic and political inequality produce an opposite outcome (Boyce, 2007; Bullard & Johnson, 2000; Bullard et al., 2008; Laurent, 2011; Pastor, 2001).

Another mechanism establishing a positive association between inequality and environmental degradation has been proposed by Marsiliani and Renstroem (2000). This hypothesis highlights the role of income inequality within a country in explaining the stringency of environmental policy using the overlapping generations models. It suggests that countries with relatively less economic inequality tend to implement stricter environmental policies than unequal nations. Therefore, according to this approach, income inequality is expected to be positively correlated with environmental degradation as it results in less stringent environmental policies (Borghesi, 2000).

Scruggs (1998) challenges the political economy approach from theoretical and empirical perspectives. According to Scruggs (1998), unlike Boyce (1994) and Torras and Boyce (1998), greater income equality might not reduce environmental degradation under some conditions. The main argument behind this criticism is the differences in preferences for environmental degradation across income groups. Scruggs (1998) states that the wealthy class with increasing income does not always prefer environmental degradation more. It is because the environment is considered a normal or superior good. Therefore, rich people might tend to promote environmental regulations and increase their demand for a cleaner environment as their income rises. In this regard, environmental deterioration might rise with inequality, but only at lower levels of wealth.

Figure 5.6 compares three different cases at the individual level to show how differences in individuals' preferences towards the environment are more likely to change the sign of the relationship between inequality and the environment. For all

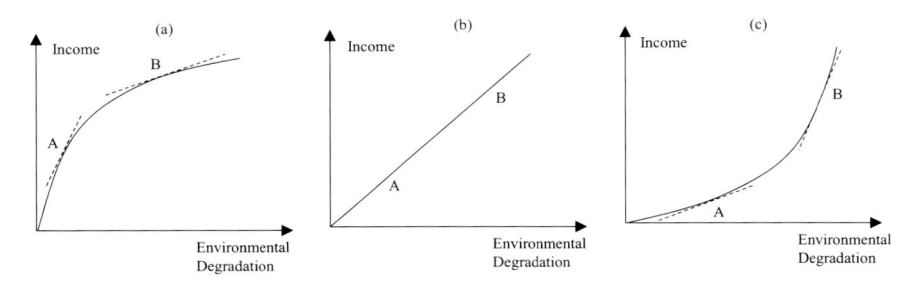

Fig. 5.6 The level of environmental degradation under three different cases. *Source* Author, adapted from Scruggs (1998)

panels (a–c) in Fig. 5.6, it is assumed that there exist two individuals: A (poorer and powerless) and B (richer and powerful). If the assumption of Boyce (1994) regarding the individuals' preferences towards the environment is valid, we observe a convex relationship between income and environmental degradation. As shown in panel (a), the negative impact of a slight increase in A's income on the environment is smaller than that of B. In this case, economic equality is expected to minimize environmental degradation. However, as suggested by Scruggs (1998), if the environment is considered a normal (panel b) or superior good (panel c), B prefers less environmental degradation at the margin than A due to the income effect. For example, as shown in panel (c), a slight increase in B's income might harm the environment less than does A. Scruggs (1998) considers that panel (c) better represents reality than the other two cases.

The hypothesis proposed by Ravallion et al. (2000) supports the findings of Scruggs (1998). However, Ravallion et al. (2000) use the marginal propensity to emit (MPE) to explain the channel between inequality and the environment. The concept of MPE mainly measures the change in emissions with respect to the change in income, as used in the Keynesian framework for the marginal propensity to consume (MPC). The authors claim that as the MPE of poor people is higher than those of rich ones, any improvements in income equality harms the environment more by increasing the income of poor ones. Consequently, narrowing the income gap in society negatively contributes to the environment (Hailemariam et al., 2020).

Empirical Analysis

Literature

As discussed in the previous section, there is no clear consensus among scholars regarding the environmental effect of income inequality in the existing literature. Therefore, as an expected consequence of the theoretical disagreement, many researchers in the field now empirically investigate this relationship using different econometric techniques, datasets, country samples, and indicators.[2]

In the empirical literature, CO_2 emissions and the Gini coefficient are the most commonly used indicators as a proxy for environmental quality and income distribution, respectively (Baek & Gweisah, 2013; Bai et al., 2020; Chen et al., 2020; Grunewald et al., 2017; Hao et al., 2016; Huang & Duan, 2020; Liu et al., 2019b, 2020; Mittmann & de Mattos, 2020; Mushtaq et al., 2020; Uddin et al., 2020; Uzar & Eyuboglu, 2019; Yang et al., 2020; You et al., 2020; Zhang & Zhao, 2014; Zhu et al., 2018). However, the empirical findings do not produce a uniform outcome regarding the inequality-emissions nexus. While some studies obtain empirical results that are consistent with the political economy approach proposed by Boyce (1994), some

---

[2] For further information about the survey of the literature, please see Berthe & Elie (2015).

others support the arguments of Scruggs (1998) and Ravallion et al. (2000). Based on the autoregressive distributed lag (ARDL) model, Baek and Gweisah (2013) and Uzar and Eyuboglu (2019) find that an equal income distribution leads to better environmental outcomes in the USA and Turkey, confirming the political economy approach. The GMM estimates of Hao et al. (2016) indicate that the income gap is positively correlated with emissions at the national and regional level in China. Three other studies conducted by Zhang and Zhao (2014), Liu et al. (2019b), and Mushtaq et al. (2020) for China at the regional and province-level also emphasize the regional and provincial differences in China. Based on the stochastic impacts by regression on population affluence and technology (STIRPAT) model, Yang et al. (2020) obtain a statistically significant relationship between income inequality and environmental degradation for 47 developing countries over the period from 1980 to 2016. You et al. (2020) conduct a panel data analysis for 41 Belt and Road Initiative countries and suggest that the widening income gap harms the environment through poor institutional quality. Zhu et al. (2018) and Mittmann and de Mattos (2020) show that the direction of effect between inequality and the environment depends on income and emissions levels in Latin American and BRICS countries. For the developing countries of G20, Chen et al. (2020) obtain that narrowing the income gap positively contributes to the environmental quality. Uddin et al. (2020) investigate the inequality-emissions nexus by using historical data (1870–2014) for the G7 nations. The results obtained from the non-parametric panel estimates reveal that the environmental effect of inequality varies over the period covered. While this effect is positive from 1870 to 1880, it is found to be negative for the period between 1950 and 2000. On the other hand, Huang and Duan (2020) report negative estimates for the relationship between inequality and emissions for 92 countries over the period between 1991 and 2015.

The conflicting results are also valid for different income inequality (Guo, 2014; Hailemariam et al., 2020; Jorgenson et al., 2015; Jorgenson et al., 2017; Liu 2019a, b) and environmental quality measures (Brännlund & Ghalwash, 2008; Clement & Meunie, 2010; Drabo, 2011; Holland et al., 2009; Kashwan, 2017; Kasuga & Takaya, 2017; Knight et al., 2017; Morse, 2018; Pattison et al., 2014; Qu & Zhang, 2011; Ridzuan, 2019). For example, Boyce et al. (1999) investigate the relationship between environmental stress index and Gini coefficient for the US states. The results support the political economy approach. Magnani (2000) reach a similar result for the 19 OECD countries for the period between 1980 and 1991 by using the R&D expenditures for the environment data. Brännlund and Ghalwash (2008) use three different emissions indicators as a proxy for environmental quality: CO_2, nitrogen oxides (NOX), and sulphur dioxide (SO_2). In addition to these environmental quality measures, Kasuga and Takaya (2017) use the following pollutants: suspended particulate matter (SPM), biological oxygen demand (BOD), and fecal coliform for river water quality. Pattison et al. (2014) and Knight et al. (2017) highlight the consumption-based CO_2 emissions. While Jorgenson et al. (2015) measure income inequality with the Theil index, Kashwan (2017) and Hailemariam et al. (2020) use the income share of the richest 10% of the population.

A wide range of econometric techniques has been used in the empirical literature. Based on the decomposition and cointegration analyses, Padilla and Serrano (2006) and Coondoo and Dinda (2008) reveal that income distribution is one of the most important driving forces of emissions. On the other hand, Heerink et al. (2001) argue that the empirical investigation of the income-emissions nexus at the household level might significantly change the environmental effect of inequality in terms of sign and magnitude. The empirical results confirm this argument and reveal a trade-off between inequality and the environment, which contradicts the political economy argument. The simultaneous quantile regression results of Hübler (2017) also support the findings of Heerink et al. (2001). Wolde-Rufael and Idowu (2017) obtain statistically insignificant coefficient estimates for the nexus between inequality and CO_2 emissions for China and India by using the ARDL model.

Data and Method

To empirically test the relationship between income inequality and the environment, we work on a panel of 120 countries for the period between 1980 and 2019. We present the countries included in the empirical investigation in Table 5.6 in the appendix. We use the following variables in the empirical analysis. The dependent variable is the per capita territorial CO_2 emissions. We retrieve this data from the Global Carbon Budget (Friedlingstein et al., 2020). To proxy for income inequality, we use three different inequality measures: the Gini coefficient, the income share of the richest 10% of the population, and the income share of the richest 1% of the population. All these inequality indicators are measured based on the pre-tax national income (World Inequality Database, 2021).

We include income per capita and the square of income per capita in our model specifications in line with the EKC framework. Data for income per capita come from the World Bank Development Indicators (World Bank, 2021). As indicated in previous sections, the environment is not only affected by income and income inequality. Therefore, we extend the empirical specification of the EKC framework with some commonly used control variables in order to avoid the potential for misspecification and biased estimation (Inglesi-Lotz, 2019; Li et al., 2016; Shahbaz & Sinha, 2019; Sinha et al., 2019). These control variables are urbanization (the share of urban population (%) in the total population) and globalization (KOF globalization index). While we retrieve data for urbanization from the World Bank Development Indicators (World Bank, 2021), the source of the globalization index is the Swiss Economic Institute (Gygli et al., 2019). Unlike single indicators of openness, such as trade openness or capital flows, the KOF index measures globalization by considering the economic, social, and political dimensions of it together. Therefore, it is one of the widely used indicators of globalization in the academic literature (Gygli et al., 2019). Table 5.1 provides a detailed explanation for variables used in the study. We present the summary statistics in Table 5.2.

Table 5.1 Data description and sources

Variable	Definition	Source
CO2	Territorial emissions in tCO2 per person	Friedlingstein et al. (2020)
GINI	Gini coefficient (pre-tax national income)	World Inequality Database (2021)
TOP10	The income share of the top 10% (pre-tax national income)	World Inequality Database (2021)
TOP1	The income share of the top 1% (pre-tax national income)	World Inequality Database (2021)
GDP	Gross domestic product (GDP) per capita (constant 2010 US$)	World Bank (2021)
URB	Urban population (% of the total population)	World Bank (2021)
KOF	The KOF Globalization Index	Gygli et al. (2019)

Table 5.2 Summary statistics

Variable	Observation	Mean	Std. Dev	Min	Max
lnCO2	4800	0.3378	1.7392	−5.3711	3.6338
lnGINI	4800	4.0108	0.1837	3.1565	4.4221
lnTOP10	4800	3.8111	0.2212	2.8154	4.3804
lnTOP1	4800	2.7541	0.3758	0.6627	4.1551
lnGDP	4785	8.3062	1.5855	5.1019	11.6634
lnURB	4800	3.8542	0.5725	1.4676	4.6052
lnKOF	4675	3.9131	0.3443	2.8286	4.5107

Note ln denotes the natural logarithm

Following many studies using the dynamic panel data setting in the academic literature (Bond & Caselli et al., 1996; Hoeffler, 2001; Islam, 1995; Wesley Burnett & Madariaga, 2017), we use 5-year span data to avoid business cycle fluctuations and serial correlation problem. In other words, we divide our sample into eight periods for each country (1980–1984, 1985–1989, 1990–1994, 1995–1999, 2000–2004, 2005–2009, 2010–2014, and 2015–2019). Besides, we add the lagged term of the dependent variable to capture the dynamic nature of environmental quality (Hao et al., 2016; Li et al., 2016; Mittmann & de Mattos, 2020). Accordingly, we specify our dynamic model to be estimated as follows

$$\ln \mathrm{CO}_{2it} = \beta_0 + \beta_1 \ln \mathrm{CO}_{2i,t-1} + \beta_2 \ln \mathrm{GDP}_{it} + \beta_3 \ln(\mathrm{GDP}_{it})^2$$
$$+ \beta_4 \ln \mathrm{INQ}_{it} + \beta_5 \ln \mathrm{URB}_{it} + \beta_6 \ln \mathrm{KOF}_{it} + \varepsilon_{it} \tag{5.1}$$

where ln denotes the natural logarithm, INQ is the variable used as a proxy for income inequality (lnGINI, lnTOP10, lnTOP1), and u_{it} is the error term. While $lnCO2_{i,t-1}$

denotes the first-order lag of the per capita CO_2 emissions, the subscripts i and t represent country and period, respectively.

Using the first-order lag of the dependent variable as an independent variable on the right-hand side of Eq. (5.1) leads to an endogeneity problem due to the correlation between $lnCO2_{i,t-1}$ and the fixed effects in ε_{it}. Therefore, the estimation of Eq. (5.1) by using the standard estimation techniques, such as pooled ordinary least-squares (OLS), fixed effects (FE), or random effects (RE), violates the necessary assumption for the consistent estimates and produces biased estimates. To overcome the weaknesses of the traditional estimators, we employ the system generalized method-of-moments (GMM) approach (Arellano & Bover, 1995; Blundell & Bond, 1998). System GMM designed for dynamic models with small T and large N panels solves the endogeneity problem with the instrumental variables. Besides, some regressors might be endogenous in this estimator (Roodman, 2009). Due to these advantages of system GMM over other standard estimators, it is one of the widely-used estimators in the literature (Apergis & Ozturk, 2015; Du et al., 2012; Lee et al., 2009; Ozturk & Al-Mulali, 2015; Sinha & Sen, 2016; Sinha et al., 2017; Tamazian & Bhaskara Rao, 2010; Zoundi, 2017).

According to Eq. (5.1), if the estimated β_2 and β_3 parameters are found to statistically significant and $\beta_2 > 0$ and $\beta_3 < 0$, it suggests that there exists an inverted U-shaped relationship between emissions and income, as indicated by the EKC hypothesis (Shahbaz & Sinha, 2019). Besides, the political economy approach is supported if β_4 is found to be statistically significant and positive (Boyce, 1994; Marsiliani & Renstroem, 2000). On the other hand, negative estimates of β_4 imply the trade-off between inequality and environmental quality (Ravallion et al., 2000; Scruggs, 1998).

Results

Before turning our attention to the estimation results, we first plot the relationship between CO_2 emissions per capita and income inequality for 120 countries in Fig. 5.7. While we use the Gini coefficient as a proxy for income inequality in panel (a), income inequality measures are the income share of the top 10% and 1% in panels (b) and (c), respectively. For all panels (a-c), environmental quality is proxied by the per capita CO_2 emissions. As can be seen, there is a negative relationship between carbon emissions and inequality, implying that reducing income inequality harms the environment. However, it is worth noting that this graphical representation does not enable us to check whether this relationship is statistically significant and accurate. Therefore, in the second step, we estimate Eq. (5.1) with 5-year span data of 120 countries.

Tables 5.3, 5.4, and 5.5 report the system GMM estimation results. For all tables, we have two panels, i.e., panel (a) (columns 1–6) and panel (b) (columns 7–12). While panel (a) presents the two-step robust system GMM estimation results, panel (b) uses the one-step approach to estimate the same model specifications. It is widely accepted

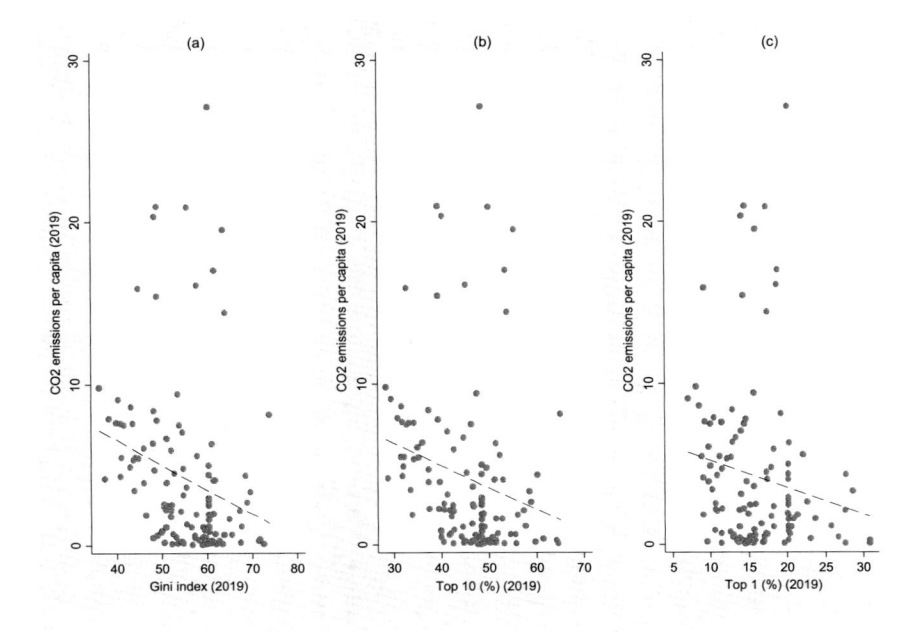

Fig. 5.7 Income inequality and CO_2 emissions per capita (2019). *Source* Friedlingstein et al. (2020) and World Inequality Database (2021)

that two-step GMM produces more efficient estimates than one-step GMM. However, the efficiency gain is rather small in finite samples (Roodman, 2009). Although the country sample used in the study is large enough, as our two-step estimates are quite similar to those obtained from the one-step estimations, we report both results. In Table 5.3, we employ the Gini coefficient (lnGINI) as a proxy for income inequality. The estimates using the income share of the top 10% (lnTOP10) and the income share of the top 1% (lnTOP1) are reported in Tables 5.4 and 5.5, respectively. For all estimates, time dummies are included, and all variables are treated as endogenous.

The consistency of the system GMM estimates depends on three conditions to be satisfied: the number of instruments, serial correlation, and the validity of instruments (Roodman, 2009). As reported at the bottom of the tables, the number of instruments does not outnumber the number of cross-sections in any estimates. Besides, the p-values of the Hansen and difference-in-Hansen tests show that the null hypothesis can not be rejected at the 1% significance level for almost any model specifications. It means that the instruments used in the regressions are valid. However, the Arellano-Bond test (AR(2)) does not strongly accept the null hypothesis of no serial correlation. Therefore, we extend our model specification with the second-order lag of the dependent variable. We report these estimation results in the even-numbered columns of the Tables. The results of the extended model specification with $lnCO2_{t-2}$ provide convincing evidence for no serial correlation problem in the error terms.

Table 5.3 The system GMM estimates with the Gini coefficient (lnGINI)

	Two-step robust estimation (a)						One-step robust estimation (b)					
	(1)	(2)	(3)	(4)	(5)	(6)	(7)	(8)	(9)	(10)	(11)	(12)
$lnCO2_{t-1}$	0.726***	0.719***	0.665***	0.723***	0.733***	0.755***	0.702***	0.724***	0.653***	0.747***	0.734***	0.763***
	(0.116)	(0.110)	(0.111)	(0.123)	(0.127)	(0.108)	(0.112)	(0.097)	(0.122)	(0.114)	(0.131)	(0.112)
$lnCO2_{t-2}$		−0.133***		−0.194***		−0.144***		−0.125**		−0.195***		−0.135**
		(0.051)		(0.048)		(0.052)		(0.052)		(0.054)		(0.056)
lnGDP	2.241***	2.489***	2.067***	2.120***	2.011***	2.084***	2.392***	2.490***	2.050***	2.081***	2.166***	2.238***
	(0.515)	(0.545)	(0.655)	(0.740)	(0.751)	(0.655)	(0.574)	(0.543)	(0.663)	(0.667)	(0.758)	(0.728)
$lnGDP^2$	−0.116***	−0.123***	−0.111***	−0.108***	−0.106***	−0.104***	−0.123***	−0.123***	−0.109***	−0.106***	−0.115***	−0.114***
	(0.024)	(0.026)	(0.031)	(0.035)	(0.035)	(0.030)	(0.028)	(0.026)	(0.031)	(0.031)	(0.035)	(0.033)
lnGINI	−1.052***	−1.203***	−1.012***	−0.979**	−0.994***	−0.961***	−1.236***	−1.258***	−1.262***	−1.278***	−1.114***	−1.154**
	(0.311)	(0.392)	(0.296)	(0.404)	(0.295)	(0.335)	(0.354)	(0.486)	(0.378)	(0.475)	(0.398)	(0.481)
lnURB	−0.394***	−0.368**			−0.470***	−0.562***	−0.448**	−0.378**			−0.542***	−0.480**
	(0.147)	(0.182)			(0.155)	(0.218)	(0.175)	(0.177)			(0.192)	(0.205)
lnKOF			0.111	0.364	0.489	0.781*			0.105	0.318	0.514	0.596
			(0.323)	(0.416)	(0.353)	(0.401)			(0.324)	(0.373)	(0.349)	(0.414)
Constant	−4.505**	−5.447**	−5.517**	−7.320***	−5.085**	−6.834***	−4.297*	−5.185**	−4.448**	−5.713**	−5.105**	−6.217**
	(2.230)	(2.615)	(2.419)	(2.838)	(2.525)	(2.389)	(2.352)	(2.681)	(2.267)	(2.797)	(2.515)	(2.773)
Observations	840	720	840	720	840	720	840	720	840	720	840	720
Cross-section	120	120	120	120	120	120	120	120	120	120	120	120
Instruments	65	64	66	64	74	72	66	64	66	64	74	72
AR(2) test	−1.759	−0.0492	−1.810	0.143	−1.746	−0.367	−1.892	−0.144	−1.950	0.0766	−1.883	−0.412
p-value	0.0785	0.961	0.0703	0.886	0.0808	0.714	0.0585	0.885	0.0511	0.939	0.0597	0.681

(continued)

Table 5.3 (continued)

	Two-step robust estimation (a)						One-step robust estimation (b)					
	(1)	(2)	(3)	(4)	(5)	(6)	(7)	(8)	(9)	(10)	(11)	(12)
Hansen	75.60	76.82	73.76	75.26	76.89	80.02	70.83	76.82	73.76	75.26	76.89	80.02
p-value	0.0278	0.0142	0.0382	0.0191	0.0825	0.0357	0.0619	0.0142	0.0382	0.0191	0.0825	0.0357
Diff-in-Hansen	13.98	15.44	6.35	15.25	7.77	19.34	9.36	15.44	6.35	15.25	7.77	19.34
p-value	0.174	0.117	0.785	0.123	0.734	0.055	0.498	0.117	0.785	0.123	0.734	0.055

Note The dependent variable is $lnCO_2$ for all estimates. The superscripts ***, **, and * denote the significance at 1%, 5%, and 10% level, respectively. Heteroscedasticity-consistent standard errors are in parentheses

Table 5.4 The system GMM estimates with the income share of the top 10% (lnTOP10)

	Two-step robust estimation (a)						One-step robust estimation (b)					
	(1)	(2)	(3)	(4)	(5)	(6)	(7)	(8)	(9)	(10)	(11)	(12)
lnCO2$_{t-1}$	0.741***	0.729***	0.689***	0.752***	0.752***	0.761***	0.724***	0.751***	0.682***	0.781***	0.754***	0.786***
	(0.122)	(0.111)	(0.117)	(0.135)	(0.136)	(0.120)	(0.114)	(0.098)	(0.124)	(0.114)	(0.131)	(0.111)
lnCO2$_{t-2}$		-0.130***		-0.191***		-0.144***		-0.121**		-0.193***		-0.135**
		(0.049)		(0.048)		(0.051)		(0.051)		(0.054)		(0.056)
lnGDP	2.267***	2.547***	2.053***	2.085***	2.040**	2.172***	2.391***	2.463***	2.018***	2.036***	2.159***	2.213***
	(0.550)	(0.559)	(0.670)	(0.769)	(0.823)	(0.736)	(0.583)	(0.548)	(0.664)	(0.660)	(0.767)	(0.736)
lnGDP^2	-0.118***	-0.126***	-0.111***	-0.107***	-0.108***	-0.109***	-0.124***	-0.123***	-0.109***	-0.105***	-0.115***	-0.113***
	(0.025)	(0.027)	(0.032)	(0.036)	(0.039)	(0.034)	(0.028)	(0.026)	(0.031)	(0.031)	(0.036)	(0.034)
lnTOP10	-0.850***	-0.955***	-0.790***	-0.730*	-0.819***	-0.765**	-1.018***	-0.984**	-0.961***	-0.935**	-0.901**	-0.922**
	(0.269)	(0.352)	(0.271)	(0.379)	(0.267)	(0.311)	(0.324)	(0.427)	(0.341)	(0.423)	(0.365)	(0.437)
lnURB	-0.439***	-0.433**			-0.512***	-0.590***	-0.496***	-0.430**			-0.583***	-0.528**
	(0.160)	(0.190)			(0.160)	(0.212)	(0.179)	(0.175)			(0.197)	(0.207)
lnKOF			0.110	0.390	0.472	0.755*			0.123	0.337	0.530	0.615
			(0.339)	(0.428)	(0.374)	(0.416)			(0.325)	(0.363)	(0.351)	(0.410)
Constant	-5.396**	-6.638***	-6.425***	-8.301***	-5.827**	-7.950***	-5.145**	-6.094**	-5.670**	-7.035***	-5.968***	-7.062***
	(2.377)	(2.543)	(2.487)	(2.888)	(2.703)	(2.472)	(2.330)	(2.600)	(2.238)	(2.666)	(2.478)	(2.693)
Observations	840	720	840	720	840	720	840	720	840	720	840	720
Cross-section	120	120	120	120	120	120	120	120	120	120	120	120
Instruments	65	64	66	64	74	72	66	64	66	64	74	72
AR(2) test	-1.780	-0.108	-1.808	-0.0259	-1.764	-0.396	-1.913	-0.304	-1.947	-0.104	-1.898	-0.548
p-value	0.0750	0.914	0.0706	0.979	0.0778	0.692	0.0558	0.761	0.0516	0.917	0.0576	0.584

(continued)

Table 5.4 (continued)

	Two-step robust estimation (a)						One-step robust estimation (b)					
	(1)	(2)	(3)	(4)	(5)	(6)	(7)	(8)	(9)	(10)	(11)	(12)
Hansen	77.06	77.58	76.13	80.37	78.32	79.85	71.80	77.58	76.13	80.37	78.32	79.85
p-value	0.0214	0.0123	0.0253	0.00701	0.0669	0.0367	0.0530	0.0123	0.0253	0.00701	0.0669	0.0367
Diff-in-Hansen	14.95	16.58	7.68	19.97	8.16	20.14	9.88	16.58	7.68	19.97	8.16	20.14
p-value	0.134	0.084	0.660	0.030	0.699	0.043	0.451	0.084	0.660	0.030	0.699	0.043

Note The dependent variable is $lnCO2$ for all estimates. The superscripts ***, **, and * denote the significance at 1%, 5%, and 10% level, respectively. Heteroscedasticity-consistent standard errors are in parentheses

Table 5.5 The system GMM estimates with the income share of the top 1% (lnTOP1)

	Two-step robust estimation (a)						One-step robust estimation (b)					
	(1)	(2)	(3)	(4)	(5)	(6)	(7)	(8)	(9)	(10)	(11)	(12)
$lnCO2_{t-1}$	0.720***	0.719***	0.677***	0.755***	0.756***	0.756***	0.730***	0.750***	0.696***	0.787***	0.773***	0.793***
	(0.128)	(0.104)	(0.116)	(0.138)	(0.140)	(0.120)	(0.109)	(0.099)	(0.121)	(0.116)	(0.127)	(0.114)
$lnCO2_{t-2}$		−0.118***		−0.168***		−0.136***		−0.110**		−0.174***		−0.127**
		(0.045)		(0.045)		(0.049)		(0.045)		(0.050)		(0.053)
lnGDP	2.421***	2.668***	2.195***	2.193***	2.104***	2.300***	2.496***	2.569***	2.068***	2.145***	2.168***	2.269***
	(0.538)	(0.548)	(0.653)	(0.743)	(0.816)	(0.716)	(0.523)	(0.507)	(0.614)	(0.619)	(0.756)	(0.725)
$lnGDP^2$	−0.122***	−0.131***	−0.116***	−0.113***	−0.109***	−0.115***	−0.127***	−0.127***	−0.111***	−0.111***	−0.114***	−0.115***
	(0.024)	(0.026)	(0.031)	(0.035)	(0.038)	(0.033)	(0.025)	(0.024)	(0.029)	(0.029)	(0.035)	(0.033)
lnTOP1	−0.299**	−0.338*	−0.272**	−0.239	−0.345**	−0.318*	−0.361**	−0.325*	−0.288**	−0.257	−0.352**	−0.355*
	(0.131)	(0.191)	(0.116)	(0.160)	(0.146)	(0.168)	(0.149)	(0.191)	(0.136)	(0.172)	(0.163)	(0.195)
lnURB	−0.453***	−0.447**			−0.602***	−0.620***	−0.552***	−0.460***			−0.685***	−0.605***
	(0.173)	(0.206)			(0.176)	(0.221)	(0.168)	(0.160)			(0.210)	(0.213)
lnKOF			0.199	0.502	0.564	0.805**			0.221	0.387	0.689**	0.717*
			(0.302)	(0.353)	(0.348)	(0.365)			(0.275)	(0.304)	(0.316)	(0.379)
Constant	−8.667***	−9.973***	−9.787***	−11.34***	−8.447***	−10.74***	−8.48***	−9.45***	−9.19***	−10.62***	−8.77***	−10.07***
	(2.574)	(2.560)	(2.556)	(2.905)	(3.024)	(2.571)	(2.234)	(2.355)	(2.326)	(2.393)	(2.613)	(2.538)
Observations	840	720	840	720	840	720	840	720	840	720	840	720
Cross-section	120	120	120	120	120	120	120	120	120	120	120	120
Instruments	65	64	66	64	74	72	66	64	66	64	74	72
AR(2) test	−1.744	−0.0243	−1.800	−0.157	−1.771	−0.345	−1.866	−0.227	−1.918	−0.150	−1.897	−0.541
p-value	0.0812	0.981	0.0719	0.875	0.0765	0.730	0.0620	0.821	0.0551	0.881	0.0578	0.589

(continued)

Table 5.5 (continued)

	Two-step robust estimation (a)						One-step robust estimation (b)					
	(1)	(2)	(3)	(4)	(5)	(6)	(7)	(8)	(9)	(10)	(11)	(12)
Hansen	76.35	80.08	79.96	89.58	80.39	84.28	72.01	80.08	79.96	89.58	80.39	84.28
p-value	0.0243	0.00744	0.0124	0.000930	0.0488	0.0171	0.0511	0.00744	0.0124	0.000930	0.0488	0.0171
Diff-in-Hansen	11.16	20.00	8.33	25.02	7.95	23.71	8.15	20.00	8.33	25.02	7.95	23.71
p-value	0.345	0.029	0.597	0.005	0.718	0.014	0.615	0.029	0.597	0.005	0.718	0.014

Note The dependent variable is $lnCO_2$ for all estimates. The superscripts ***, **, and * denote the significance at 1%, 5%, and 10% level, respectively. Heteroscedasticity-consistent standard errors are in parentheses

According to the system GMM estimation results, we obtain the following outcomes. First, the coefficients of the lagged dependent variable (both $lnCO2_{t-1}$ and $lnCO2_{t-2}$) are statistically significant in all regressions. For example, the results reported in Table 5.3 suggest that a 1% increase in the per capita emissions will lead to about a 0.7% (ranging between 0.653 and 0.763%) increase in the per capita emissions in the next period. The results illustrated in Tables 5.4 and 5.5 also support this finding and strongly justifies our dynamic model specification. The system GMM estimates of Du et al. (2012) and Li et al. (2016) produce similar results for the provincial data of China.

Second, both coefficients of per capita income ($lnGDP$ and $lnGDP^2$) are statistically significant in all estimations. While the coefficient of $lnGDP$ is positive, the effect of the square of per capita income ($lnGDP^2$) on emissions turns out to be negative. Therefore, we strongly confirm the inverted U-shaped EKC hypothesis. Our result regarding the EKC hypothesis is consistent with many studies in the literature. Apergis and Ozturk (2015) for the sample of 14 Asian countries, Sinha and Sen (2016) for the BRIC countries, Tamazian and Bhaskara Rao (2010) for 24 transition economies also support the presence of the inverted U-shaped associations between emissions and income per capita.

The validation of the EKC hypothesis produces three important results: (i) income level is a key determinant of carbon emissions; (ii) an increase in income harms the environment during the early stages of economic growth. However, after reaching a certain income threshold, it positively contributes to the environment; (iii) the positive effect of $lnGDP$ on emissions is greater than the negative effect of $lnGDP^2$ in terms of magnitude. Therefore, the rate at which income increases emissions is expected to be lower than the reduction rate.

Third, there exists a statistically significant relationship between per capita CO_2 emissions and all three income inequality measures ($lnGINI$ in Table 5.3, $lnTOP10$ in Table 5.4, and $lnTOP1$ in Table 5.5). This finding is valid for almost all model specifications and reveals that income distribution is a crucial source of carbon emissions. Therefore, when considered together with the coefficient estimates of income variables ($lnGDP$ and $lnGDP^2$), we can suggest that income distribution among individuals is as important as raising income to reduce emissions. The statistically significant estimates of $lnGINI$, $lnTOP10$, and $lnTOP1$ are compatible with many empirical studies in the literature. The decomposition analysis of Padilla and Serrano (2006) for 113 countries, Morse (2018) for the selected environmental performance indexes of 180 countries, and Baek and Gweisah (2013) for the US reveal similar outcomes to our study. However, our finding contradicts the statistically insignificant estimates found by Wolde-Rufael and Idowu (2017) for China and India and the Gini coefficient-based results of Jorgenson et al. (2017) for the US states.

Forth, turning to the sign of income inequality, the estimated parameters reported in Table 5.3 reveal that all statistically significant coefficients of $lnGINI$ are negative, indicating that an increase in the Gini coefficient (widening income gap) leads to a decrease in per capita carbon emissions. For example, the two-step robust estimation shown in the sixth column of Table 5.3 suggests that a 1% increase in the Gini coefficient decreases per capita CO_2 emissions by 0.96%. This result is robust to different alternative model specifications and income inequality measures (lnTOP10 and lnTOP1), as illustrated in Tables 5.4 and 5.5. In this regard, we can suggest that our findings are consistent with the arguments of Scruggs (1998) and Ravallion et al. (2000). Our negative estimates for all inequality measures are somewhat different from Hailemariam et al. (2020). In line with our study, Hailemariam et al. (2020) find a negative association between the Gini index and emissions in the OECD countries. However, this negative link does not hold for the income share of the top 10% and 1%.

From the policy perspective, we should approach the found negative relationship between inequality and emissions cautiously. As also stated by Scruggs (1998) and Mittmann and de Mattos (2020), this result does not necessarily imply that maintaining income inequality in society might significantly contribute to environmental quality. Our result, instead, signals a challenge from the sustainability perspective and points to the need for a balance and cooperation in many fields (in both production and consumption ideas) with countries' policymakers when formulating policies with regard to income inequality (Guo, 2014).[3]

Lastly, regarding the role of urbanization and globalization in environmental degradation, we found that urbanization has a statistically significant and negative effect on CO_2 emissions. It means that increased urbanization contributes to reducing per capita carbon emissions and improving environmental quality. This result is largely consistent with N. Zhang et al. (2017), but not with Sadorsky (2014) and Yazdi and Dariani (2019). On the other hand, the impact of globalization on emissions is generally found to be positive but statistically insignificant.

Policy

No doubt that one of the most important reasons for investigating the relationship between income inequality and the environment is to design appropriate economic and environmental policies to reduce CO_2 emissions and improve environmental quality. In this context, some transmission channels that help us explain the linkage between inequality and the environment are considered to be highly crucial from the economic and environmental policy perspectives.

One of the transmission channels explaining the nexus running from inequality to the environment occurs through social norms, which include individualism, short-termism, and consumerism. Individualism resulting from the rising income gap across individuals harms the social cohesion in the community. Due to the lack of collective action, people start to show less sensitivity toward the environment. By ignoring the long-term adverse effect of their current consumption, they have willing to prioritize their short-term benefits (short-termism). Besides, to maintain or further improve their social status, they increase their conspicuous consumption (consumerism) and tend to put more pressure on the environment. Therefore, in such

---

[3] The following section discusses the inequality-emissions nexus from the policy perspective.

communities, environmental degrading activities do not face social resistance, and demand for better environmental quality substantially decreases (Awaworyi et al., 2021; Berthe & Elie, 2015; Laurent, 2015; Uzar, 2020; Wilkinson & Pickett, 2010). In this regard, it is evident that narrowing income inequality plays an essential role for better environmental outcomes. For that purpose, it is considered that macro-level policies that reform the tax system, decrease the size of the shadow economy and unemployment rate by creating new employment opportunities might significantly contribute to environmental quality by reducing the income gap (Uzar & Eyuboglu, 2019). However, these policies alone are not sufficient. Therefore, they should be supported with other measures at the micro-level that raise public awareness of the population regarding the environment, such as the use of clean energy, social resistance against environmental degrading activities, and consumption style of individuals (Wolde-Rufael & Idowu, 2017). This outcome can be interpreted that the policies at the micro and macro-level (individuals, households) should be given considerable importance simultaneously for sustainable environmental quality.

Another critical issue to be taken into account in determining an environmental policy is related to the distribution of political power between different social groups. As previously discussed, Boyce (1994) states that if the political power is unequally distributed in favor of the wealthy (powerful) group, such a political power distribution is more likely to degrade the environment. As the powerful class can better protect themselves from environmental pollution than the poor ones, this group tends to use its power to support the environment polluting policies. Unlike Boyce (1994), Scruggs (1998) highlights that the powerful group is more sensitive to the environment than the poor. Therefore, such a distribution in favor of the wealthy class contributes to environmental quality. In this case, the rich group does not undermine environmental policies but supports strictness. These two different theoretical mechanisms proposed by Boyce (1994) and Scruggs (1998) produce conflicting channels and outcomes as they focus on different aspects of the inequality-environment nexus (Berthe & Elie, 2015). However, from the policy perspective, which mechanism will be more dominant largely depends on the quality of institutions and how strictly environmental policies are implemented in the society. In other words, as institutional quality is a vital determinant of energy use, environmental policy, and income inequality (Fredriksson & Svensson, 2003; Sequeira & Santos, 2018), it plays a crucial role in determining how the channel between inequality and emissions will be transmitted. In this context, it is considered that policies that improve institutional quality, encourage the public's desire for democratic regimes, limit corruption, promote political stability, and strengthen the stringency of environmental regulations might produce favorable outcomes.

Recent studies by Uzar (2020) and Awaworyi et al. (2021) reveal that income inequality is negatively correlated with renewable energy consumption. This result can be interpreted that higher economic equality increases renewable energy consumption. It is crucial because the negative correlation between renewable energy use and income inequality obviously broadens the scope of policymakers for implementing incentives and subsidies in renewable energy, such as wind, geothermal, and solar. Therefore, policymakers can reduce CO_2 emissions by promoting the use of renewable energy through policies narrow income inequality. This is a case where a win–win opportunity occurs as both fairer income distribution and deployment of renewable energy production can be acquired.

Conclusion

Climate change and income inequality are two growing global threats faced by humankind in the contemporary period. Therefore, whether there is a relationship between income inequality and environmental quality is one of the most studied topics in the academic literature, especially since the 1990s. This chapter seeks to contribute to this literature by discussing the relationship between these two crises from three perspectives: theory, empirics, and policy. To this end,

- First, we review the theoretical background of the issue and introduce the transmission channels linking economic inequality and environmental deterioration. This section shows that scholars have not reached a clear theoretical consensus regarding the direction of the relationship between these two issues. While some studies confirm the positive effect of income inequality on carbon emissions, others emphasize the trade-off between them.
- Second, we focus on the empirical investigation. To this end, after summarizing the related empirical literature, we perform an empirical analysis for a panel of 120 countries over the period between 1980 and 2019. We use the following key variables. The dependent variable is the per capita territorial CO_2 emissions. To proxy for income inequality, we use three different inequality measures: the Gini coefficient, the income share of the richest 10% of the population, and the income share of the richest 1% of the population. Our empirical investigation is based on the system GMM estimator. The empirical findings reveal that both income and income inequality are the crucial determinants of carbon emissions. While we strongly confirm the inverted U-shaped EKC hypothesis, the per capita CO_2 emissions are negatively correlated with all three income inequality measures.
- Third, we discuss the importance of the inequality-environment nexus for designing appropriate economic and environmental policies to reduce CO_2 emissions and improve environmental quality. We show that many factors, such as social norms, political power asymmetry, and institutional quality, play a key role in policy-making.

Appendix

See Table 5.6.

Table 5.6 List of countries

Albania	Cameroon	Ethiopia	Italy	Netherlands	South Africa
Algeria	Canada	Finland	Jamaica	New Zealand	Spain
Angola	C. Afr. Rep	France	Jordan	Nicaragua	Sri Lanka
Argentina	Chad	Gabon	Kenya	Niger	Sudan
Austria	Chile	Gambia	Lao PDR	Nigeria	Suriname
Bahamas	China	Germany	Luxembourg	Norway	Sweden
Bahrain	Colombia	Ghana	Macao SAR	Oman	Switzerland
Bangladesh	Comoros	Greece	Madagascar	Pakistan	Thailand
Belgium	Congo D. R	Guatemala	Malawi	Panama	Togo
Belize	Congo Rep	Guinea-Bissau	Malaysia	P. N. Guinea	Tri. and Tob
Benin	Costa Rica	Guyana	Mali	Paraguay	Tunisia
Bhutan	Cote d'Ivoire	Haiti	Malta	Peru	Turkey
Bolivia	Cuba	Honduras	Mauritania	Philippines	Uganda
Botswana	Cyprus	Iceland	Mauritius	Portugal	UAE
Brazil	Denmark	India	Mexico	Rwanda	UK
Brunei D	Dom. Rep	Indonesia	Mongolia	Saudi Arabia	USA
Bulgaria	Ecuador	Iran	Morocco	Senegal	Uruguay
Burkina Faso	Egypt	Iraq	Mozambique	Seychelles	Vietnam
Burundi	El Salvador	Ireland	Myanmar	Sierra Leone	Zambia
Cabo Verde	Eq. Guinea	Israel	Nepal	Singapore	Zimbabwe

References

Acemoğlu, D. (2009). *Introduction to modern economic growth.* New Jersey: Princeton University Press.

Acemoğlu, D., Johnson, S., & Robinson, J. (2004). *Institutions as the fundamental cause of long-run growth* (No. 10481). https://doi.org/10.3386/w10481

Apergis, N., & Ozturk, I. (2015). Testing environmental Kuznets curve hypothesis in Asian countries. *Ecological Indicators, 52,* 16–22. https://doi.org/10.1016/j.ecolind.2014.11.026

Arellano, M., & Bover, O. (1995). Another look at the instrumental variable estimation of error-components models. *Journal of Econometrics, 68*(1), 29–51. https://doi.org/10.1016/0304-4076(94)01642-D

Awaworyi, S., Ivanovski, K., & Ephraim, M. (2021). Income inequality and renewable energy consumption: Time-varying non-parametric evidence. *Journal of Cleaner Production, 296,* 126306.https://doi.org/10.1016/j.jclepro.2021.126306

Baek, J., & Gweisah, G. (2013). Does income inequality harm the environment?: Empirical evidence from the United States. *Energy Policy, 62,* 1434–1437. https://doi.org/10.1016/j.enpol.2013.07.097

Bai, C., Feng, C., Yan, H., Yi, X., Chen, Z., & Wei, W. (2020). Will income inequality influence the abatement effect of renewable energy technological innovation on carbon dioxide emissions? *Journal of Environmental Management, 264*,110482.https://doi.org/10.1016/j.jenvman.2020.110482

Berthe, A., & Elie, L. (2015). Mechanisms explaining the impact of economic inequality on environmental deterioration. *Ecological Economics, 116*, 191–200. https://doi.org/10.1016/j.ecolecon.2015.04.026

Blundell, R., & Bond, S. (1998). Initial conditions and moment restrictions in dynamic panel data models. *Journal of Econometrics, 87*(1), 115–143. https://doi.org/10.1016/S0304-4076(98)00009-8

Bond, S., & Hoeffler, A. (2001). GMM estimation of empirical growth models. *CEPR Discussion Papers/Centre for Economic Policy Research Discussion Papers.*

Borghesi, S. (2000). *Income inequality and the environmental Kuznets curve.* Milano. Retrieved from http://hdl.handle.net/

Boyce, J. K. (1994). Inequality as a cause of environmental degradation. *Ecological Economics, 11*(3), 169–178. https://doi.org/10.1016/0921-8009(94)90198-8

Boyce, J. K. (2007). Is inequality bad for the environment? *Research in Social Problems and Public Policy, 15*(15), 267–288. https://doi.org/10.1016/S0196-1152(07)15008-0

Boyce, J. K., Klemer, A. R., Templet, P. H., & Willis, C. E. (1999). Power distribution, the environment, and public health: A state-level analysis. *Ecological Economics, 29*(1), 127–140. https://doi.org/10.1016/S0921-8009(98)00056-1

Brännlund, R., & Ghalwash, T. (2008). The income-pollution relationship and the role of income distribution: An analysis of Swedish household data. *Resource and Energy Economics, 30*(3), 369–387. https://doi.org/10.1016/j.reseneeco.2007.11.002

Bullard, R., & Johnson, G. (2000). Environmental Justice: Grassroots activism and its impact on public policy decision making. *Journal of Social Issues, 56*(3), 555–578. https://doi.org/10.1111/0022-4537.00184

Bullard, R., Mohai, P., Saha, R., & Wright, B. (2008). Toxic wastes and race at twenty: Why race still matters after all of these years. *Environmental Law, 38*(2), 371.

Caselli, F., Esquivel, G., & Lefort, F. (1996). Reopening the convergence debate: A new look at cross-country growth empirics. *Journal of Economic Growth, 1*(3), 363–389. https://doi.org/10.1007/BF00141044

Chen, J., Xian, Q., Zhou, J., & Li, D. (2020). Impact of income inequality on CO_2 emissions in G20 countries. *Journal of Environmental Management, 271*(May). https://doi.org/10.1016/j.jenvman.2020.110987

Clement, M., & Meunie, A. (2010). Is inequality harmful for the environment? An empirical analysis applied to developing and transition countries. *Review of Social Economy, 68*(4), 413–445. https://doi.org/10.1080/00346760903480590

Cole, M. A., Rayner, A. J., & Bates, J. M. (1997). The environmental Kuznets curve: An empirical analysis. *Environment and Development Economics, 2*(4), 401–416. https://doi.org/10.1017/S1355770X97000211

Coondoo, D., & Dinda, S. (2008). Carbon dioxide emission and income: A temporal analysis of cross-country distributional patterns. *Ecological Economics, 65*(2), 375–385. https://doi.org/10.1016/j.ecolecon.2007.07.001

Dowrick, S. (2010). Inequality (Global). In S. Durlauf & L. Blume (Eds.), *Economic growth* (pp. 161–171). Palgrave Macmillan. https://doi.org/10.1057/9780230280823

Drabo, A. (2011). Impact of income inequality on health: Does environment quality matter? *Environment and Planning A, 43*(1), 146–165. https://doi.org/10.1068/a43307

Du, L., Wei, C., & Cai, S. (2012). Economic development and carbon dioxide emissions in China: Provincial panel data analysis. *China Economic Review, 23*(2), 371–384. https://doi.org/10.1016/j.chieco.2012.02.004

Durlauf, S. N., Johnson, P. A., & Temple, J. R. W. (2005, January 1). Chapter 8 growth econometrics. *Handbook of economic growth*, Vol. 1, (pp. 555–677). Elsevier. https://doi.org/10.1016/S1574-0684(05)01008-7

Feenstra, R. C., Inklaar, R., & Timmer, M. P. (2015). The next generation of the penn world table. *American Economic Review, 105*(10), 3150–3182. Retrieved from https://www.jstor.org/stable/43821370?seq=1#metadata_info_tab_contents

Fredriksson, P. G., & Svensson, J. (2003). *Political instability , corruption and policy formation : The case of environmental policy.* 87, 1383–1405. https://doi.org/10.1016/S0047-2727(02)00036-1

Friedlingstein, P., O'sullivan, M., Jones, M. W., Andrew, R. M., Hauck, J., Olsen, A., Peters, G. P., Peters, W., Pongratz, J., Sitch, S., & Le Quéré, C., (2020).Global carbon budget 2020. *Earth System Science Data, 12*(4), 3269–3340.https://doi.org/10.5194/essd-12-3269-2020

Gore, T., Alestig, M., & Ratcliff, A. (2020). *Confronting carbon inequality.* (September). Retrieved from https://oxfamilibrary.openrepository.com/bitstream/handle/10546/621052/mb-confronting-carbon-inequality-210920-en.pdf

Grossman, G., & Krueger, A. (1991). Environmental impacts of a north american free trade agreement. *National Bureau of Economic Research,* (3914). https://doi.org/10.3386/w3914

Grossman, G., & Krueger, A. (1995). Economic growth and the environment. *The Quarterly Journal of Economics, 110*(2), 353–377. https://doi.org/10.1016/B978-0-12-384719-5.00433-0

Grunewald, N., Klasen, S., Martínez-Zarzoso, I., & Muris, C. (2017). The trade-off between income inequality and carbon dioxide emissions. *Ecological Economics, 142*, 249–256. https://doi.org/10.1016/j.ecolecon.2017.06.034

Guo, L. (2014). CO_2 emissions and regional income disparity: Evidence from China. *Singapore Economic Review, 59*(1). https://doi.org/10.1142/S0217590814500076

Gygli, S., Haelg, F., Potrafke, N., & Sturm, J. E. (2019). The KOF Globalisation Index—revisited. *Review of International Organizations, 14*(3), 543–574. https://doi.org/10.1007/s11558-019-09344-2

Hailemariam, A., Dzhumashev, R., & Shahbaz, M. (2020). Carbon emissions, income inequality and economic development. *Empirical Economics, 59*(3), 1139–1159. https://doi.org/10.1007/s00181-019-01664-x

Hall, R. E., & Jones, C. I. (1998). *Why do some countries produce so much more output per worker than others?* (No. 6564). https://doi.org/10.3386/w6564

Hao, Y., Chen, H., & Zhang, Q. (2016). Will income inequality affect environmental quality? Analysis based on China's provincial panel data. *Ecological Indicators, 67*, 533–542. https://doi.org/10.1016/j.ecolind.2016.03.025

Heerink, N., Mulatu, A., & Bulte, E. (2001). Income inequality and the environment: Aggregation bias in environmental Kuznets curves. *Ecological Economics, 38*(3), 359–367. https://doi.org/10.1016/S0921-8009(01)00171-9

Holland, T. G., Peterson, G. D., & Gonzalez, A. (2009). A cross-national analysis of how economic inequality predicts biodiversity loss. *Conservation Biology, 23*(5), 1304–1313. https://doi.org/10.1111/j.1523-1739.2009.01207.x

Holtz-Eakin, D., & Selden, T. M. (1995). Stoking the fires? CO_2 emissions and economic growth. *Journal of Public Economics, 57*(1), 85–101. https://doi.org/10.1016/0047-2727(94)01449-X

Huang, Z., & Duan, H. (2020). Estimating the threshold interactions between income inequality and carbon emissions *Journal of Environmental Management, 263*,110393.https://doi.org/10.1016/j.jenvman.2020.110393

Hübler, M. (2017). The inequality-emissions nexus in the context of trade and development: A quantile regression approach. *Ecological Economics, 134*, 174–185. https://doi.org/10.1016/j.ecolecon.2016.12.015

Inglesi-Lotz, R. (2019). Recent studies (Extending basic environmental kuznets curve model by adding more variables). In *Environmental Kuznets Curve (EKC)* (pp. 15–23). Elsevier. https://doi.org/10.1016/b978-0-12-816797-7.00003-5

Intergovernmental Panel on Climate Change. (2014). *Climate change 2014 mitigation of climate change*. Cambridge University Press.https://doi.org/10.1017/cbo9781107415416

Intergovernmental Panel on Climate Change. (2015). *Climate change 2014 synthesis report*. Retrieved from https://www.ipcc.ch/site/assets/uploads/2018/05/SYR_AR5_FINAL_full_wcover.pdf

Islam, N. (1995). Growth empirics: A panel data approach. *The Quarterly Journal of Economics*, (November), 1127–1170.

Jorgenson, A., Schor, J. B., Huang, X., & Fitzgerald, J. (2015). Income inequality and residential carbon emissions in the United States: A preliminary analysis. *Human Ecology Review, 22*(1), 93–105. https://doi.org/10.22459/HER.22.01.2015.06

Jorgenson, A., Schor, J., & Huang, X. (2017). Income inequality and carbon emissions in the United States: A state-level analysis, 1997–2012. *Ecological Economics, 134*, 40–48. https://doi.org/10.1016/j.ecolecon.2016.12.016

Kashwan, P. (2017). Inequality, democracy, and the environment: A cross-national analysis. *Ecological Economics, 131*, 139–151. https://doi.org/10.1016/j.ecolecon.2016.08.018

Kasuga, H., & Takaya, M. (2017). Does inequality affect environmental quality? Evidence from major Japanese cities. *Journal of Cleaner Production, 142*, 3689–3701. https://doi.org/10.1016/j.jclepro.2016.10.099

Knight, K. W., Schor, J. B., & Jorgenson, A. K. (2017). Wealth inequality and carbon emissions in high-income countries. *Social Currents, 4*(5), 403–412. https://doi.org/10.1177/2329496517704872

Kuznets, S. (1955). Economic growth and income inequality. *The American Economic Review, 45*(1), 1–28.

Lantz, V., & Feng, Q. (2006). Assessing income, population, and technology impacts on CO_2 emissions in Canada: Where's the EKC? *Ecological Economics, 57*(2), 229–238. https://doi.org/10.1016/j.ecolecon.2005.04.006

Laurent, E. (2011). Issues in environmental justice within the European Union. *Ecological Economics, 70*(11), 1846–1853. https://doi.org/10.1016/j.ecolecon.2011.06.025

Laurent, E. (2015). *Social-ecology : Exploring the missing link in sustainable development*. OFCE. Retrieved from OFCE website: https://hal-sciencespo.archives-ouvertes.fr/hal-01136326

Lee, C. C., Chiu, Y. B., & Sun, C. H. (2009). Does one size fit all? A Reexamination of the environmental Kuznets curve using the dynamic panel data approach. *Review of Agricultural Economics, 31*(4), 751–778. https://doi.org/10.1111/j.1467-9353.2009.01465.x

Li, T., Wang, Y., & Zhao, D. (2016). Environmental Kuznets Curve in China: New evidence from dynamic panel analysis. *Energy Policy, 91*, 138–147. https://doi.org/10.1016/j.enpol.2016.01.002

Liu, C., Jiang, Y., & Xie, R. (2019a). Does income inequality facilitate carbon emission reduction in the US? *Journal of Cleaner Production, 217*, 380–387. https://doi.org/10.1016/j.jclepro.2019.01.242

Liu, Q., Wang, S., Zhang, W., Li, J., & Kong, Y. (2019b). Examining the effects of income inequality on CO_2 emissions: Evidence from non-spatial and spatial perspectives. *Applied Energy, 236*(November 2018), 163–171. https://doi.org/10.1016/j.apenergy.2018.11.082

Liu, Y., Zhang, M., & Liu, R. (2020). The impact of income inequality on carbon emissions in china: A household-level analysis. *Sustainability (switzerland), 12*(7), 1–22. https://doi.org/10.3390/su12072715

Magnani, E. (2000). The Environmental Kuznets Curve, environmental protection policy and income distribution. *Ecological Economics, 32*, 431–443.

Marsiliani, L., & Renstroem, T. I. (2000). Inequality, environmental protection and growth. *SSRN Electronic Journal*. https://doi.org/10.2139/ssrn.235083

Mittmann, Z., & de Mattos, E. J. (2020). Income inequality and carbon dioxide emissions: Evidence from Latin America. *Journal of International Development, 32*(3), 389–407. https://doi.org/10.1002/jid.3459

Morse, S. (2018). Relating environmental performance of Nation States to income and income inequality. *Sustainable Development, 26*(1), 99–115. https://doi.org/10.1002/sd.1693

Mushtaq, A., Chen, Z., Ud Din, N., Ahmad, B., & Zhang, X. (2020). Income inequality, innovation and carbon emission: Perspectives on sustainable growth. *Economic Research-Ekonomska Istrazivanja, 33*(1), 769–787. https://doi.org/10.1080/1331677X.2020.1734855

Ozcan, B., & Ozturk, I. (2019). Environmental Kuznets Curve (EKC): A manual. In B. Ozcan & I. Ozturk (Eds.), *Environmental Kuznets Curve (EKC): A manual*. Academic Press. https://doi.org/10.1016/c2018-0-00657-x

Ozturk, I., & Al-Mulali, U. (2015). Investigating the validity of the environmental Kuznets curve hypothesis in Cambodia. *Ecological Indicators, 57*, 324–330. https://doi.org/10.1016/j.ecolind.2015.05.018

Padilla, E., & Serrano, A. (2006). Inequality in CO_2 emissions across countries and its relationship with income inequality: A distributive approach. *Energy Policy, 34*(14), 1762–1772. https://doi.org/10.1016/j.enpol.2004.12.014

Panayotou, T. (1993). Empirical tests and policy analysis of environmental degradation at different stages of economic development. In *Technology and employment programme* (No. 238; Vol. 4). Geneva.

Pastor, M. (2001). *Building social capital to protect natural capital: The quest for environmental justice* (No. 11).

Pattison, A., Habans, R., & Clement, M. T. (2014). Ecological modernization or aristocratic conservation? Exploring the impact of affluence on carbon emissions at the local level. *Society and Natural Resources, 27*(8), 850–866. https://doi.org/10.1080/08941920.2014.911996

Qu, B., & Zhang, Y. (2011). Effect of income distribution on the environmental Kuznets curve. *Pacific Economic Review, 16*(3), 349–370. https://doi.org/10.1111/j.1468-0106.2011.00552.x

Ravallion, M., Heil, M., & Jalan, J. (2000). Carbon emissions and income inequality. *Oxford Economic Papers, 52*(4), 651–669. https://doi.org/10.1093/oep/52.4.651

Richmond, A. K., & Kaufmann, R. K. (2006). Is there a turning point in the relationship between income and energy use and/or carbon emissions? *Ecological Economics, 56*(2), 176–189. https://doi.org/10.1016/j.ecolecon.2005.01.011

Ridzuan, S. (2019). Inequality and the environmental Kuznets curve. *Journal of Cleaner Production, 228*, 1472–1481. https://doi.org/10.1016/j.jclepro.2019.04.284

Rodrik, D., Subramanian, A., & Trebbi, F. (2002). *Institutions rule: The primacy of institutions over integration and geography in economic development* (No. 9305). https://doi.org/10.3386/w9305

Roodman, D. (2009). How to do xtabond2: An introduction to difference and system GMM in Stata. *Stata Journal, 9*(1), 86–136. https://doi.org/10.1177/1536867x0900900106

Sadorsky, P. (2014). The effect of urbanization on CO_2 emissions in emerging economies. *Energy Economics, 41*, 147–153. https://doi.org/10.1016/j.eneco.2013.11.007

Scruggs, L. A. (1998). Political and economic inequality and the environment. *Ecological Economics, 26*(3), 259–275. https://doi.org/10.1016/S0921-8009(97)00118-3

Sequeira, T. N., & Santos, M. S. (2018). Renewable energy and politics: A systematic review and new evidence. *Journal of Cleaner Production, 192*, 553–568. https://doi.org/10.1016/j.jclepro.2018.04.190

Shafik, N., & Bandyopadhyay, S. (1992). *Economic growth and environmental quality: Time series and cross-country evidence*. Washington, DC.

Shahbaz, M., & Sinha, A. (2019). Environmental Kuznets curve for CO_2 emissions: A literature survey. *Journal of Economic Studies, 46*(1), 106–168. https://doi.org/10.1108/JES-09-2017-0249

Sinha, A., & Sen, S. (2016). Atmospheric consequences of trade and human development: A case of BRIC countries. *Atmospheric Pollution Research, 7*(6), 980–989. https://doi.org/10.1016/j.apr.2016.06.003

Sinha, A., Shahbaz, M., & Balsalobre, D. (2017). Exploring the relationship between energy usage segregation and environmental degradation in N-11 countries. *Journal of Cleaner Production, 168*, 1217–1229. https://doi.org/10.1016/j.jclepro.2017.09.071

Sinha, A., Shahbaz, M., & Balsalobre, D. (2019). Data selection and environmental kuznets curve models—environmental kuznets curve models, data choice, data sources, missing data, balanced and unbalanced panels. In *Environmental Kuznets Curve (EKC)* (pp. 65–83). Elsevier. https://doi.org/10.1016/b978-0-12-816797-7.00007-2

Tamazian, A., & Bhaskara Rao, B. (2010). Do economic, financial and institutional developments matter for environmental degradation? Evidence from transitional economies. *Energy Economics, 32*(1), 137–145. https://doi.org/10.1016/j.eneco.2009.04.004

Torras, M., & Boyce, J. K. (1998). Income, inequality, and pollution: A reassessment of the environmental Kuznets curve. *Ecological Economics, 25*(2), 147–160. https://doi.org/10.1016/S0921-8009(97)00177-8

Uddin, M. M., Mishra, V., & Smyth, R. (2020). Income inequality and CO2 emissions in the G7 1870–2014: Evidence from non-parametric modelling. *Energy Economics, 88*, 104780.https://doi.org/10.1016/j.eneco.2020.104780

Uzar, U. (2020). Is income inequality a driver for renewable energy consumption? *Journal of Cleaner Production, 255*, 12028.https://doi.org/10.1016/j.jclepro.2020.120287

Uzar, U., & Eyuboglu, K. (2019). The nexus between income inequality and CO_2 emissions in Turkey. *Journal of Cleaner Production, 227*, 149–157. https://doi.org/10.1016/j.jclepro.2019.04.169

Wesley Burnett, J., & Madariaga, J. (2017). The convergence of U.S. state-level energy intensity. *Energy Economics, 62*, 357–370. https://doi.org/10.1016/j.eneco.2016.03.029

Wilkinson, R., & Pickett, K. (2010). *The spirit level: Why equality is better for everyone.* Penguin Books.

Wolde-Rufael, Y., & Idowu, S. (2017). Income distribution and CO_2 emission: A comparative analysis for China and India. *Renewable and Sustainable Energy Reviews, 74*(November 2016), 1336–1345. https://doi.org/10.1016/j.rser.2016.11.149

World Bank. (2021). World Bank development indicators. Retrieved March 15, 2021, from https://databank.worldbank.org/reports.aspx?source=world-development-indicators

World Inequality Database. (2021). World inequality database. Retrieved March 15, 2021, from https://wid.world/

Yang, B., Ali, M., Hashmi, S. H., & Shabir, M. (2020). Income inequality and CO_2 emissions in developing countries: The moderating role of financial instability. *Sustainability (Switzerland), 12*(17). https://doi.org/10.3390/SU12176810

Yazdi, S. K., & Dariani, A. G. (2019). CO2 emissions , urbanisation and economic growth : Evidence from Asian countries. *Economic Research-Ekonomska Istraživanja, 32*(1), 510–530. https://doi.org/10.1080/1331677X.2018.1556107

You, W., Li, Y., Guo, P., & Guo, Y. (2020). Income inequality and CO_2 emissions in belt and road initiative countries: The role of democracy. *Environmental Science and Pollution Research, 27*(6), 6278–6299. https://doi.org/10.1007/s11356-019-07242-z

Zhang, C., & Zhao, W. (2014). Panel estimation for income inequality and CO_2 emissions: A regional analysis in China. *Applied Energy, 136*, 382–392. https://doi.org/10.1016/j.apenergy.2014.09.048

Zhang, N., Yu, K., & Chen, Z. (2017). How does urbanization affect carbon dioxide emissions? A cross-country panel data analysis. *Energy Policy, 107*(January), 678–687. https://doi.org/10.1016/j.enpol.2017.03.072

Zhu, H., Xia, H., Guo, Y., & Peng, C. (2018). The heterogeneous effects of urbanization and income inequality on CO_2 emissions in BRICS economies: evidence from panel quantile regression. *Environmental Science and Pollution Research, 25*(17), 17176–17193. https://doi.org/10.1007/s11356-018-1900-y

Zoundi, Z. (2017). CO_2 emissions, renewable energy and the Environmental Kuznets Curve, a panel cointegration approach. *Renewable and Sustainable Energy Reviews, 72*(July 2016), 1067–1075. https://doi.org/10.1016/j.rser.2016.10.018

Sedat Alataş has a B.A. degree from the Department of Economic at Eskişehir Anadolu University, Turkey, and M.A. and Ph.D. degrees in economics from Aydın Adnan Menderes University, Turkey. During his doctoral research, he has participated in the Advanced Studies Program organized by the Kiel Institute for the World Economy. He is currently working as a research assistant in the Department of Economics at Aydın Adnan Menderes University. Dr. Alataş's research mainly focuses on resource and energy economics, climate change, economic growth, convergence, and input substitution. He has published several articles in journals, such as *Resources Conservation & Recycling, Resources Policy, Energy Economics, Sustainable Production and Consumption, Energy Efficiency, Social Indicators Research, and Research in Transportation Economics*. At Aydın Menderes University, he teaches undergraduate courses on economics and econometrics.

Chapter 6
Energy Transformation in Canada's Northern Territories

Marcin Gabryś

Abstract The purpose of this article is to provide an overview of the ongoing energy transition in Nunavut, Yukon and the Northwest Territories towards modern energy sources. It begins briefly with Canada's climate policy and the Liberal Party's support for a clean energy transformation as a way of dealing with the impact of climate change on the environment and people of the North. The text then focuses on the energy and climate strategies of the three territories. The different ways all territorial governments have chosen to move towards renewable energy and reducing greenhouse gas emissions are also analyzed. Finally, the article examines how remote and Indigenous communities in the territories are involved in the transition from fossil fuels to clean energy sources.

Introduction

The three Canadian territories (Yukon, Northwest Territories, and Nunavut) cover over one-third of Canada (approximately 3.6 million km^2) and are located almost entirely above the 60th degree parallel north. The harsh Arctic and sub-Arctic climate with cold and long winters, as well as darkness above the Arctic Circle, make energy the key to survival for over 110,000 people living in Canada's territorial north. Three additional factors contribute to the region's specific situation. Firstly, the territories are not connected to Canada's energy grid.[1] The situation of the territories differs significantly though. Hydro-based electricity generation dominates in Yukon and the Northwest Territories and only a few communities are outside the territorial grids. In contrast, electricity in 25 communities and three commercial operations in Nunavut are almost entirely locally produced by diesel generators. (Canada Energy

M. Gabryś (✉)
Department of Canadian Studies, Jagiellonian University, Kraków, Poland
e-mail: marcin.gabrys@uj.edu.pl

[1] There are 87 communities in the territories: 21 in Yukon, 38 in NWT and 28 in Nunavut. The largest off-grid communities in Canada are Whitehorse, Yukon; Yellowknife, Northwest Territories (Natural Resources Canada, 2018b).

Regulator, 2020a) Most communities in three territories, however, rely only on fossil fuels, mostly diesel, for heating.[2]

Secondly, although diesel has many benefits, including being energy dense, widely available, and offering relative reliability, it also has many disadvantages. It must be transported from southern Canada (by a truck on icy roads in the winter or by a barge in the summer), resulting in high transportation costs and security of supply issues. In addition, volatility and high prices in international oil markets contribute to the excessive costs of energy generation in off-grid communities. Combined with high per capita energy consumption, energy affordability is a challenge and the second highest priority for territories, after energy security.

Thirdly, burning fossil fuels contributes to health problems of the population and negatively affects climate as diesel generators and furnaces release pollutants and particulate matter.[3] Additionally, fuel spills happen regularly (Canada Energy Regulator 2020a).[4] And finally, diesel installations emit large volumes of greenhouse gas (GHG).[5] While territories' emissions are only a fraction of Canada's total 723 megatons of carbon dioxide equivalent—all three territories combined produced 2.87 megatons (or 0.4%) in 2015—per capita rates are double the Canadian average and raise the region to one of the biggest emitters in the world (Government of Canada, 2021).[6] The region is also particularly vulnerable to global temperature increases. Experts have been warning for decades that due to the albedo effect of ice and melting permafrost the Arctic is warming faster than other areas of the globe (WWF International Arctic Programme, 2005). In tackling the effects of climate change in territories, a key issue has been how to bring together reduced fossil fuels use with affordability, security and sustainability, especially in off-grid communities. For decades, this dilemma seemed unsolvable. In recent years, the situation has started to change as the territories have begun a process of transformation towards clean energy as a way of dealing with the impact of climate change on the environment and people of the North. This change also affects remote Indigenous communities, bringing an opportunity to strengthen reconciliation.

Canada's Climate Change Policy

After years of political stalemate and inaction, climate change was elevated in 2015 by the Liberal Party as one of the top political issues in Canada. Newly elected Prime

---

[2] 60 communities in the three territories rely on diesel and only two (Inuvik and Norman Wells) use natural gas (Lovekin et al., 2020, 2).

[3] E.g., mercury, formaldehyde and sulfur dioxide (Thomson, 2019).

[4] Since the 1970s more than 9.1 million liters of diesel have been spilled in the Northwest Territories and Nunavut (Thomson, 2019). See also (Pollon, 2017).

[5] Diesel is only second to coal in terms of the amount of carbon dioxide when burned (McDiarmid, 2017).

[6] For example, the NWT produced about 37 tones of GHG per person annually, whereas Canada's average is about 19 tones per person (Government of Northwest Territories, 2018, 10).

Minister Justin Trudeau, declaring "Canada is back," presented himself as a climate champion (Prime Minister of Canada, 2016b). In a sudden transformation from an international climate laggard to a global leader in a low-carbon economy, Canada took part in 2015 meetings of the Conference of the Parties (COP21) in Paris, approved the Paris Agreement with the goal to limit global temperature rise to two degrees Celsius and committed to reducing its greenhouse gas emissions by 30% below 2005 levels by 2030 or to 523 megatons. In 2015 in Paris the parties also agreed that new energy policies were the key solutions to climate change (Poelzer et al., 2016). This view guided Trudeau's government as it began transforming Canada's climate policy.[7]

Announced on December 9, 2016, the federal government's climate change strategy—the Pan-Canadian Framework on Clean Growth and Climate Change—was built around consensus Ottawa reached with provinces and territories, and recognized "diversity of provincial and territorial economies" and the need to use "flexible approaches" ("Vancouver Declaration on Clean Growth and Climate Change", 2016). The Pan-Canadian Framework has four pillars: carbon taxation, measures to reduce emissions, adaptation to the effects of climate change, and innovation to support clean technology and job creation (Government of Canada, 2016, 2). In practice, the government proposed more than 50 actions that covered all sectors of the Canadian economy. The key mitigation measures were the price on carbon pollution (enacted in 2018[8]), a low-carbon fuel standard, as well as a national coal phase-out by 2030. At the same time, provinces and territories were given the option to independently design "their own policies to meet emission-reductions targets, including their own carbon pricing mechanisms" (Government of Canada, 2016, 3–4). Their strategies were to be supported by federal funds.

Moreover, in December 2020 Ottawa released its strengthened federal climate plan, "A Healthy Environment and a Healthy Economy," expected to exceed the 2030 emissions reduction target under the Paris Agreement (Environment and Climate Change Canada, 2020).[9] The measures contained in the new document included continued pricing carbon pollution, energy efficiency retrofits for buildings, efforts to ensure clean, affordable electricity (including work towards net-zero electricity generation by 2050), and further methane reduction. Additionally, the federal government committed to working towards connecting parts of Canada "that have abundant clean hydroelectricity with parts that are currently more dependent on fossil fuels for electricity generation." The new climate plan pledged an additional 15 billion CAD in investments to speed up the fight against climate change (Environment and

---

[7] In 2019 Canada's energy sector emitted 81% of Canada's total GHG emissions (Government of Canada, 2021).

[8] The Greenhouse Gas Pollution Pricing Act, enacted in 2018, put in place carbon pollution pricing systems in all Canada's provinces and territories, either as provincial/territorial systems or the federal system. In March 2021, the Supreme Court of Canada ruled that the Liberal government's carbon pricing plan is constitutional (*Reference Re Greenhouse Gas Pollution Pricing Act*, 2021 SCC 11).

[9] On April 22, 2021, Prime Minister Trudeau announced that Canada would increase the GHG emissions reduction target by 40–45% below 2005 levels, by 2030 (Prime Minister of Canada, 2021).

Climate Change Canada, 2020). Furthermore, Canada has also committed to reaching net-zero GHG emissions by 2050 (or "carbon neutrality") by 2050 (Government of Canada, 2021).[10]

Both climate change strategies took into account the particular circumstances of the North (including the disproportionate impacts of climate change and the high cost of living and energy) as well as the need for partnerships with Indigenous Peoples on "mitigation and adaptation actions." The federal government also recognized opportunities for communities in the transition which will result in "locally owned and sourced power generation" (Government of Canada, 2016, 8, 12, 14; Environment and Climate Change Canada, 2020). In terms of more specific measures, Ottawa identified the need to transition to non-carbon electricity systems by increasing the number of renewable and low-carbon sources, connecting off-grid locations to clean energy sources, upgrading electrical systems and reducing dependence on diesel in northern remote and Indigenous communities (Government of Canada, 2016, 11).[11]

A key decision for the territories was the federal government's commitment to eliminate diesel dependence in northern and remote communities by 2030. This was announced by Prime Minister Trudeau during the 2019 federal election campaign, along with a series of federal programs aimed at, among other things, retrofitting homes (McKay, 2019). At that time, no specific plan was presented on how to achieve these goals, and the 2030 deadline was not on the phase-out of heating diesel (Lovekin et al., 2020, 1).

Initially, the funds offered by the federal government were too small even for a single project—for example, the costs of construction of a small ("run-of-river") hydro plant can reach 100 million CAD and the old diesel generators in the northern territories need hundreds of millions of dollars in investment to remain operational (Pollon, 2017). However, in subsequent years, the funds contributed by Ottawa have grown.[12] In the 2017 budget, Ottawa committed 650 million CAD over four years to support the Pan-Canadian Framework on Clean Growth and Climate Change (Fitzgerald and Lovekin, 2018, 20). Among the funds was 400 million CAD over 10 years for the Arctic Energy Fund (AEF) intended only for the territories to replace or upgrade "aging fossil fuel energy infrastructure" (Infrastructure Canada, 2018). In 2018 Ottawa announced an additional 220 million CAD over six years through the Clean Energy for Rural and Remote Communities (CERRC) to support rural and remote communities in their "transition towards more secure, affordable, and cleaner sources of energy" (Natural Resources Canada 2018a). Of several programs directed

---

[10] The legislation establishing a legally binding process of interim targets, plans and reports (the proposed Canadian Net-Zero Emissions Accountability Act) has not yet progressed throughout parliament (Parliament of Canada, 2020).

[11] While Canada's electricity in about 80% came from non-emitting sources, electricity generation was still Canada's fourth-largest source of GHG emissions (Government of Canada, 2016, 11). Additionally, the use of energy to heat and cool buildings accounted for approximately 12% of Canada's GHG emissions in 2014, or 17% if emissions related to the generation of electricity used in buildings are also included (Government of Canada, 2016, 15).

[12] According to Ottawa, between 2015 and 2019 the federal government invested 60 billion CAD for all actions in the Pan-Canadian Framework (Government of Canada, 2021).

at remote diesel-dependent communities were also 53.5 million CAD over 10 years from Indigenous and Northern Affairs Canada to continue the Northern Responsible Energy Approach for Community Heat and Electricity Program (Northern REACHE) which funds clean energy, heating and energy efficiency programs in Yukon, the Northwest Territories, Nunavut, Nunavik and Nunatsiavut and 75 million CAD over four years for innovative challenge-based approaches for clean technologies (Fitzgerald and Lovekin, 2018, 20–21). An additional 20 million CAD over three years were offered to communities to transitioning off diesel consumption by developing community-led green energy projects under the Indigenous Off-Diesel Initiative (Natural Resources Canada, 2019; Heerema and Lovekin, 2019, 42). Further funding opportunities brought the new 2020 federal climate plan with a pledge to invest 964 million CAD over four years to advance smart renewable energy and grid modernization projects and to devote 300 million CAD over five years "to advance the government's commitment to ensure rural, remote and Indigenous communities that currently rely on diesel have the opportunity to be powered by clean, reliable energy by 2030" (Environment and Climate Change Canada, 2020).[13]

As a result, between 2015 and 2020 the number of renewable energy projects in Canada's territories increased significantly (Lovekin et al., 2020; Gignac 2020a). Energy projects in the North have also seen a noteworthy growth of Indigenous participation. This could lay the groundwork for renewing Canada's relationship with Indigenous Peoples and continue the reconciliation process that was one of the most important elements of the political platform of the Trudeau government (Prime Minister of Canada 2016a; Fitzgerald and Lovekin, 2018, 21).

Energy and Climate Change Strategies of the Territories

As previously mentioned, the territories' emissions represent less than 0.4% of Canada's total. However, in 2015–2019, they only decreased marginally (by 0.05 megatons), thanks only to the reduction of the NWT's emissions by 18%. During the same period, Yukon's emissions rose by 30% and Nunavut's by 14% (Government of Canada, 2021).[14] The reason for this is the growing population of the territories (it has grown in the three territories by 11.5% between 2016 and 2020, most notably in Yukon by 17.57%), as well as the way the energy is generated. Although in 2018 electricity from large-scale hydro dams dominated energy grids in Yukon and the Northwest Territories, Nunavut was 100% dependent on diesel which was also the second source of electricity generation in NWT and Yukon (Canada Energy

---

[13] Nevertheless, in terms of diesel reduction, the new climate change strategy lowered expectations with very careful wording that the communities that depend on diesel will "have the opportunity to be powered by clean, reliable energy by 2030" (Environment and Climate Change Canada, 2020; Markusoff, 2021).

[14] In 2019 Yukon's emissions were 0.53, the NWT's 1.7 and Nunavut's 0.64 megatons (Government of Canada, 2021).

Regulator, 2020a). Fossil fuels dominate in space heating in all territories and, paradoxically, the increased energy demand from electric heating resulted in an increase in burning fossil fuels (Thomson, 2019).

Given these facts, providing clean energy while addressing climate change by reducing greenhouse gas emissions has become critical for territorial governments. These two objectives are to be found in all territorial energy strategies. There are, however, additional caveats that need to be considered in the process of transformation of northern communities that rely on diesel to cleaner energy sources. Firstly, the average price of kWh in the territories is from 3 to 12 times higher than Canada's average. This is partially due to the cost of diesel fuel, but also due to the natural circumstances of northern Canada (climate, remoteness and isolation of communities). The same factors make people living in northern Canada an energy-intensive society in terms of electricity and heating but also transportation. It also means that to make energy affordable for residents rates have to be subsidized by the governments, which in turn puts a heavy burden on territorial budgets.[15] Moreover, the subsidies are based on fuel consumption, which discourages moving away from diesel (Poelzer et al., 2016, 17; Thomson, 2019).

Secondly, for a long time, there were not many clean and affordable alternatives to diesel in electricity, transport and heating suitable for northern climates. Only recently has the situation begun to change, accelerated by growing knowledge about the negative effects of fossil fuels. However, significant funding is still needed for new infrastructure (in terms of capital costs) to switch from diesel to other clean sources. Territories have only recently been undergoing changes to meet the challenges of introducing public partnerships in the form of Independent Power Producer (IPP)[16] policies, among others.

Thirdly, while all three territories have begun the transition to clean energy for electricity generation, their plans also include retrofitting homes and businesses and switching to alternative energy sources for individual and district heating systems. One option being considered is the use of biomass in the form of wood pellets or wood chips. However, biomass energy systems are challenging in some parts of the North simply because resources may be limited or non-existent (e.g., in Nunavut) (Fitzgerald and Lovekin, 2018, 16).

Yukon

Yukon has been the most advanced in the energy transformation among the Canadian territories. It is not only in the best position in terms of how energy is produced but

---

[15] Up to 25% of the budgets of public agencies responsible for housing in the North are connected with subsidizing power and fuel costs (Thomson, 2019).

[16] Defined as "a corporation, person, agency, or other legal entity or instrumentality that owns or operates facilities for the generation of electricity for use primarily by the public, and that is not an electric utility" (Poelzer et al., 2016, 35).

also in terms of the policies that the government has put in place to accelerate and facilitate this shift while keeping costs affordable for residents.

Firstly, around 24% of Yukon's energy comes from renewable resources. Over the years, more than 90% of electricity production came from dams. Only four communities are not connected to the Yukon main electricity grid and are served by four microgrids that are powered primarily by diesel generators. However, only 26% of thermal energy comes from renewable sources. The rest is mainly made of diesel fuel (Government of Yukon, 2020, 18, 46).

Secondly, with regard to Yukon's greenhouse gas emissions, they have increased significantly since 2005, the reference year for the Paris Agreement (from 0.57 to 0.69 megatons, an increase of 21%) (Government of Canada, 2021). To mitigate the effects of climate change as well as reduce emissions Yukon introduced several steps from the 2016 Pan-Canadian Framework for Clean Growth and Climate Change. Among them was the federal government's carbon pollution pricing system that came into effect in Yukon in 2019 (Government of Canada, 2019, 52). The same year, the territorial legislature realized the seriousness of the situation by voting unanimously for a motion to declare a climate emergency in the territory (CBC News, 2019). The following year, the Yukon government published an environmental strategy entitled "Our Clean Future." Among its four goals, the most significant is the reduction of GHG emissions by 263 kilotons or 30% by 2030. This goal is to increase the use of clean electricity to the point where, on average, 93% of the electricity on Yukon's grid comes from renewable sources.[17] This includes reducing the use of diesel and other fuels for electricity generation in remote and off-grid communities by 30% by 2030, compared to 2010 (Government of Yukon, 2020, 14–15, 20). The climate change strategy also includes switching to zero emission vehicles—by 2030 there should be nearly 5000 zero emission passenger cars on Yukon roads (Government of Yukon, 2020, 35).

Thirdly, energy rates in Yukon are mandatorily harmonized across all but one municipality, meaning that the higher costs of diesel generating energy are distributed to all Yukon ratepayers (Fitzgerald and Lovekin, 2018, 23). Yukon also implemented the Independent Power Production Policy, as well as the Micro-generation Program which allowed businesses, communities and First Nation governments to generate renewable energy and feed it into the electricity grid to serve local demand (Government of Yukon, 2020, 20, 47–48). Yukon's goal is to have a working independent power production project in all off-grid communities by 2030 (Government of Yukon, 2020, 48). Overall, policies offer stability and transparency for all stakeholders and have helped to increase energy generation from clean sources that are affordable and reliable (Government of Canada, 2019, 8).

Fourthly, the Yukon government has been implementing renewable energy projects in partnership with communities and Indigenous Peoples. All of the goals of the Yukon Climate Change Strategy to 2020 have been defined not only by the

---

[17] Whether clean power comes from solar or other sources will be up to the public utility provider to decide. The strategy also pays attention to the need to upgrade energy storage to make use of seasonal resources.

territorial government but also by participating Yukon Indigenous Nations, transboundary Indigenous groups and Yukon municipalities.[18] Currently, at least two remote communities are engaged in community-scale renewable energy projects: Kluane First Nation Government from Burwash Landing (wind power project) and the Vuntut Gwich'in Government (solar power and battery storage). Additional projects are in the earlier stages of development (Fitzgerald and Lovekin, 2018, 23; Government of Yukon, 2020, 29; Government of Canada, 2019, 56).

Finally, Yukon plans to meet 50% of its heating demand with renewable energy sources. This will be accomplished through a combination of reducing energy demand from more efficient homes (retrofitting homes and buildings) and building local renewable clean heat (i.e., smart electric heating systems, but also biomass) (Government of Yukon, 2020, 21, 44). The largest biomass project in Yukon is located in Whitehorse (Gignac, 2020b). However, the Yukon's biomass energy strategy, which includes using wood and wood waste from forest fires and logging operations for heating,[19] has been criticized by environmentalists who argue that "'clean biofuels can threaten forests while contributing to air pollution and climate change" (Gignac, 2020b; Government of Yukon, 2016) Furthermore, while the Yukon's climate strategy states that the territory will use "local, sustainably harvested biomass," it still leaves questions about where the wood will be sourced from in order to support an increase in wood use for heating (Government of Yukon, 2020, 44).

Northwest Territories

The Northwest Territories are less advanced than Yukon on the path to energy transformation. Energy generation in the NWT is more dependent on fossil fuels, while policies to accelerate and facilitate the transition to clean energy are less innovative and forward-looking.

In terms of the energy mix, the NWT generates more than half its power and heat from diesel and fuel oil and about a third from hydroelectric resources (Canada Energy Regulator, 2017). Electricity is more dependent on hydro (70%), supported by diesel (25%) and natural gas (5%) and other renewables: wind (4%) and solar (less than 1%) (Government of Northwest Territories, 2018, 24; Canada Energy Regulator, 2020b).[20] However, diesel remains the sole or primary source of electricity for all remote communities or industries that are not connected to either of the NWT's two hydroelectric grids (Canada Energy Regulator, 2020b).

---

[18] Moreover, the Council of Yukon First Nations and the Assembly of First Nations-Yukon Region are preparing "a First Nations-led perspective on climate action in Yukon" (Government of Yukon, 2020, 29).

[19] Heating with biomass (cordwood, bulk pellets, or wood chips) can cost 50% less than using fossil fuels or electricity (Government of Yukon, 2016, 11).

[20] Hydroelectricity production in the NWT depends on precipitation. In normal precipitation years, about 75% of electricity comes from hydroelectricity, but in drier years the production is lower and backup power comes from diesel generators (Canada Energy Regulator, 2020b).

As for the NWT's greenhouse gas emissions, in 2016 about half of them were related to the industry, with the rest came from fossil fuel use for transportation (35%), community heating (10%) and electricity generating (4%) (Government of Northwest Territories, 2018, 10). In addition, the Northwest Territories were the only Canada's northern jurisdiction to reduce GHG emissions between 2005 and 2019 (by 16% or by 0.2 megatons to 1.4 megatons) (Government of Canada, 2021). However, the NWT's emissions must be reduced by 30% by 2030, or by an additional 0.4 megatons, to meet its obligations from the Pan-Canadian Framework (Government of Northwest Territories, 2018, 10). To this end, the NWT has introduced several steps contained in two documents: the 2018 energy strategy (Government of Northwest Territories, 2018) and the 2019 climate change strategy (Government of the Northwest Territories, 2019). The government's reduction plans are based on six goals: to reduce GHG emissions from diesel-depended communities by 25% by 2030, to reduce GHG emissions from transportation by 10%, to increase the use of renewable energy for heating to 40% while increasing building efficiency by 15%. In addition, in September 2019 the government introduced the carbon tax in the Northwest Territories (Government of Canada, 2019, 52).

Since most of the NWT's emissions come from industry, the government decided that making cleaner energy available to mines located in the Northern Territories was key to achieving the climate change goals. The most important element of the energy and climate change strategies was the Taltson River Hydroelectric Expansion Project. Its goal is to significantly increase the hydroelectric capacity of the 60-year-old dam and connect the South Slave region with North Slave grid as well as with the North American electricity system. This connection will also serve northern communities and mines located north of Great Slave Lake (Government of Northwest Territories, 2018, 6). Once finalized, the project would reduce greenhouse gas emissions by 224 kilotons or 44% of the emissions needed to be eliminated to reach the NWT target (Government of Northwest Territories, 2019). The Taltson River expansion has been introduced decades ago and the main obstacle is the cost associated with it, estimated at 1 billion CAD. Currently, the NWT government secured federal funds only for the initial phase of the project (Government of Northwest Territories, 2019). It is questionable whether it can be built in time to help meet the 2030 greenhouse gas reduction target. In addition, the project has generated controversy and protests among First Nations and environmental advocates (Gleeson, 2020a; Thomson, 2019).

Among other planned solutions for reducing GHG emissions in the NWT, there is the development of alternative energy sources (including wind, solar, mini-hydro, liquefied natural gas, geothermal, transmission lines, combined heat and power, energy storage or variable speed generators) (Government of Northwest Territories, 2018, 20). Already proven are wind power potential of Inuvik and a few additional communities, for three communities (Fort Providence, Kakisa, and Whatì) only extending existing transmission lines is needed, and several other diesel-powered communities can be served with mini-hydro (run-of-river). Liquefied Natural Gas could also play a role in some communities, as it is already used in Inuvik. Solar panels, especially when paired with variable-speed generators or batteries are also a viable alternative to diesel (Government of Northwest Territories, 2018, 22–23; Government of Canada, 2018, 10).

The NWT's energy strategy also emphasized partnerships with communities and Indigenous governments. This includes "empowerment and capacity-building of Indigenous governments and communities" to participate in energy projects, facilitating the exchange of information as well as the inclusion of "local and traditional knowledge" (Government of Northwest Territories, 2018, 12–13). There have already been several renewable energy projects in the NWT communities, such as the Colville Lake Hybrid Solar-Battery Project, Lutsel K'e Dene First Nations and Fort Simpson Solar Energy Projects as well as a community-owned solar photovoltaic system in Tulita. Other projects are in the preparation stage (Fitzgerald and Lovekin, 2018, 23–24; Government of Northwest Territories, 2018, 11; Government of Canada, 2019, 54, 57).

However, maintaining energy affordability remains a key concern for the NWT government, as the territories have some of the highest electricity rates in Canada. To balance the cost of generating electricity in diesel-dependent communities with places that use cheaper hydroelectricity, the difference is spread across all ratepayers, but not equally, as there are seven territorial energy tariff zones (Fitzgerald and Lovekin, 2018, 23–24). The NWT has also adopted an Independent Power Production Policy in communities (Government of Northwest Territories, 2018, 17). It differs, however, from the IPP model existing in Yukon or in other places in Canada and is less advantageous for community leadership. Moreover, all recent renewable electricity projects in the NWT "have required government subsidies to maintain and not increase electricity rates, even with the high cost of diesel power" (Government of Northwest Territories, 2018, 20).

Finally, as community space heating contributes significantly to the NWT's emissions the territories promote greater use of renewables to maintain affordable and sustainable heating rates. Similar to Yukon's strategy, the government in Yellowknife supports the greater use of biomass for heating, e.g., wood-pellets and encourages switching to wood fuel for heat. In South Slave, thanks to hydroelectricity from Taltson River Project, "electric heat is available to consumers at a reduced rate that is less than the cost to heat with oil" (Government of Northwest Territories, 2018, 30). However, only a limited number of residents took advantage of this opportunity due to technical hurdles related to the rules for joining the program (Gleeson, 2020b).

Nunavut

Nunavut lags behind the other two northern territories in the energy transition. Fossil fuels almost completely dominate its energy mix, yet the territory has the least advanced policies to support a clean energy transition. Moreover, maintaining affordable energy prices is a real challenge for the government.

Nunavut's diesel dependency is estimated at 99%, the highest of any province or territory in Canada. Approximately 54 million liters of diesel are used each year for electricity generation and 145 million liters for heat generation (Lovekin and Quitoras, 2020, 3). There are no territorial or regional electricity grids in Nunavut—in all 25 communities electricity generation is provided within local communities by the utility (Fitzgerald and Lovekin, 2018, 24–25; Canada Energy Regulator 2020c). The use of diesel has high environmental and logistical costs, negatively impacts local air quality, and contributes to black carbon that accelerates snow and ice melt, as well as impacts the region's energy security (World Wildlife Fund Canada, 2019). As a result, Nunavut has the highest electricity rates in Canada, which for residential purposes must be subsidized (up to a certain monthly threshold) and are held to equal rates across all communities (Canada Energy Regulator, 2020c).

Although Nunavut's share of Canada's total emissions is small, the impact of climate change is significant for the environment, economy and daily life of all Nunavut residents. However, Nunavut's greenhouse gas emissions continue to rise.[21] In 2019, they reached 0.64 megatons of carbon dioxide equivalent, 25% higher than in 2005. Even more alarming is the fact that since 2000 emissions have increased 60% (Government of Canada, 2021) (Canada Energy Regulator, 2020c). The territorial government's strategy, entitled "Upagiaqtavut," is, unfortunately, a decade-old document (Government of Nunavut, 2011). Nevertheless, it still serves as a guiding document for mitigation efforts in Nunavut. Among the more recent actions taken by the government in Iqaluit is the introduction of the carbon pricing scheme in 2019 supplemented by the Nunavut Carbon Rebate program to return a portion of the carbon pricing revenues to its residents (Government of Canada, 2019, 52).

Even older is the energy strategy of Nunavut, entitled "Ikummatiit," which was released in 2007 and projected evolution of Nunavut's energy policies only until 2020 (Government of Nunavut, 2007). Its main goals were to make Nunavut's energy system secure (by reducing fossil fuel imports and increasing the use of clean energy), environmentally responsible (by reducing energy-related emissions and increasing energy efficiency), and affordable (by reducing the cost of providing energy). As a result, Nunavut's dependence on fossil fuels was to be reduced (Government of Nunavut, 2007, 5). Although these aims have not been achieved, Nunavut has undergone important changes in the last decade. Most notably, several studies have been undertaken on the availability, feasibility and economics of clean, renewable energy sources in Nunavut (e.g., potential hydropower plants in Akulikutaq, Tungatalik and Qairulituq as well as in Kivalliq and Kitikmeot). Expensive electricity rates make expanding solar power projects promising and economically viable (Canada Energy Regulator, 2020c). Since 2016, several solar pilot projects have begun, mostly in Iqaluit (Government of Canada, 2016, 77). In 2019, Nunavut approved its first hybrid diesel and solar energy power plant (Government of Canada, 2019, 9). Nunavut has also been exploring the technical and financial feasibility of deploying small modular reactors in Canada as well as the possibility of geothermal power (Government of Canada, 2019, 57). Nevertheless, as Lovekin and Quitoras suggest, "with such high

---

[21] Transportation emits the largest amounts of GHG (66%) than electricity and industry. In 2017 Nunavut's power sector emitted 0.143 megatons of carbon dioxide equivalent (Canada Energy Regulator, 2020c).

diesel dependency, renewable energy uptake and diesel reduction efforts in Nunavut require extensive support, including innovative and bold action from QEC [public energy utility—MG] and all levels of government" (Lovekin and Quitoras, 2020, 3).

Nunavut falls behind the other two territories in terms of community renewable energy projects. This is partly due to the fact that until 2018 purchasing electricity by the utility from independent producers was generally prohibited, preventing IPP initiatives (Fitzgerald and Lovekin, 2018, 24–25). It was not until 2018 that Nunavut launched a Net Metering Program for customers who want to produce electricity from small scale renewable energy installations and sell surplus energy to the local grid (Canada Energy Regulator, 2020c; Government of Canada, 2019, 54). Interest in territory-wide community energy planning has also increased due to the availability of federally funded diesel reduction programs. Ottawa recently announced funding for three clean energy projects in Nunavut from the Clean Energy for Rural and Remote Communities Program. Among them are a turbine and battery system in Sanikiluaq that would replace 50% of diesel fuel used for producing electricity in the community. In Arviat, there will be a study for wind, solar and energy storage systems including investigating power-purchase agreements (World Wildlife Fund Canada, 2019; Venn, 2021). However, there are many renewable energy projects in Nunavut that are still waiting for a more robust policy framework that encourages a transition to cleaner energy sources (Lovekin and Quitoras, 2020, 1).

Remote and Indigenous Communities

As previously mentioned, one of the biggest challenges for the three Canadian territories is the transformation of energy production in 80 remote communities (Lovekin, Morales, and Salek, 2020; Natural Resources Canada, 2018b).[22] All are highly dependent on diesel[23] (433 million liters of diesel per year or 63% of consumption in all Canada's remote communities[24]) and Nunavut's dependency rate (99%) makes

---

[22] The definition of a remote community differs in various publications and databases. In this section, I'm using the classification proposed by Moorhouse, et al., which defines it as "a community that is not connected to the North American electricity grid and the North American piped natural gas network and is a permanent or long-term (5 years or more) settlement with at least 10 dwellings" (Moorhouse et al., 2020, 4). According to this definition, there are 238 remote communities in Canada for the heat analysis and 213 remote communities for the electricity analysis. 25 remote communities in the Yukon and NWT are connected to territorial electricity grids that rely on large hydroelectricity hence they are excluded from electricity analyses but their heating systems depend on fossil fuels (Moorhouse et al., 2020, 5).

[23] Yukon with 78% dependency and the NWT with 73% are in fifth and seventh place respectively. Yukon's dependency rate is significantly lower (47%) when including communities using large hydro and those connected to the regional hydro grid. The same is true for the NWT (57%) (Moorhouse et al., 2020, 5).

[24] 78 million liters for electricity generation and additional 355 million liters for heating. Nunavut relies most heavily on diesel (199 million liters) while the Northwest Territories are second (120 million liters), and Yukon third (114 million liters) (Lovekin et al., 2020, 1, 4–5).

the territory the most dependent jurisdiction in Canada (Lovekin et al., 2020, 4–5). Furthermore, diesel consumption in Canada's remote communities has increased since 2015 (from 655 to 682 million liters per year or by 27 million liters). The growth was only partly mitigated (over 12 million liters per year) (Lovekin et al., 2020, 1). Of the various reduction activities and energy efficiency measures, renewable heat and power projects have the greatest impact on reduction. According to a report by the Pembina Institute, the number of these investments in remote communities has increased significantly over the past five years (2015–2020) from 96 to 178[25]; 60% of these (107) were in the three territories, with the largest number in the Northwest Territories (73), Nunavut (18) and Yukon (16) (Lovekin et al., 2020, 3). This was partly due to the falling costs of renewable energy installations and the lack of major technological hurdles to using clean energy sources in remote communities, even above the Arctic Circle (Wilt, 2018; The Canadian Press, 2016).

The growth in the number of renewable energy projects has been significant, yet the cost is considered one of the main obstacles to decarbonizing remote communities. Since 2018, the federal government has introduced several new initiatives to encourage people, businesses and communities to transition from diesel to clean energy sources. The programs, such as the Arctic Energy Fund and funding available through the Canada Infrastructure Bank, are improving the situation, but lack of upfront capital and difficulty in obtaining 100% project financing remain the biggest challenges (Markusoff, 2021; Wilt, 2018).

It is also critical to "choos[e] the right renewable generation source, or a mix of sources, for each community" (Canada Energy Regulator, 2020a). This is because currently only diesel or large hydro can provide stable baseload power generation for remote communities, especially during winter peaks. For space heating, switching to electric heating in winter is beyond the capabilities of not only renewables but also current hydroelectric power. Although emerging technologies such as small nuclear reactors (SMRs) may change the situation in the few next decades. For some communities, the most efficient path to clean energy would be to connect to the North American grid, although the cost is a limiting factor (Canada Energy Regulator, 2020a).

However, switching to renewable energy resources not only contributes to the environment (less noise pollution, fewer emissions from diesel exhausts) but can also provide stability (power outages occur regularly in remote communities) and energy security which in long term can underpin the economic development of northern communities. Building community economic independence (through financial savings and revenue)[26] and creating jobs is particularly important given that nearly nine out of ten remote communities in the Northern Territories are categorized as Indigenous. Furthermore, renewable energy projects can serve precisely as an opportunity to develop self-determination and self-reliance of Indigenous Peoples (Heerema and Lovekin, 2019, 47; Lovekin et al., 2020; Canada Energy Regulator, 2020a). Sustainable energy from wind, solar or water ("the power from

---

[25] Not including wood stoves.

[26] Renewable energy projects could be paid off within a decade (Thomson, 2019).

Mother Earth") is consistent with Indigenous values and Indigenous communities through local sources of energy can not only increase their autonomy but also renew "traditional connections to their natural surroundings" (Markusoff, 2021). Some experts even believe that clean energy may be "the secret story of reconciliation" (McDiarmid, 2017).

Several elements are needed to fulfill this hope. Firstly, renewable energy projects require collaboration between Indigenous communities and external stakeholders. If Indigenous Peoples are to be partners, they must have human capacity and certain skills. These elements are needed to be able to lead a project and not having it forced on a community by outside participants (Poelzer et al., 2016, 21; Wilt, 2018). There are several programs aimed at building the capacity of Indigenous communities, such as the Impact Canada Indigenous Off-Diesel Initiative or the Clean Energy for Rural and Remote Communities (Government of Canada, 2019, 9). Secondly, because there are drawbacks associated with renewable energy development (such as the impact on fragile Arctic environment, possible conflict over land use, potential adverse effects on communities from wind turbine noise or toxic waste from solar cells); it requires a strong social license based on clear communication between stakeholders. Thus, Indigenous participation in renewable projects is a key element for success (Poelzer et al., 2016, 43). However, Dave Lovekin of the Pembina Institute points out that there are still no comprehensive policies that "support Indigenous inclusion in developing these projects", as well as encourage them to solicit local knowledge (Thomson, 2019). This may hinder the federal government's official goal of eliminating diesel for electricity generation in remote communities by 2030.

Yukon

According to the Pembina Institute report, 16 renewable energy projects have taken place in 21 remote Yukon communities: 10 renewable electricity and six renewable heating projects (Lovekin et al., 2020, 3). This is the smallest number among northern territories, yet Yukon's approach to transitioning to clean energy is considered the most comprehensive. Several of its features deserve attention.

Firstly, Yukon has significant and well-developed government policies in many areas, including those dedicated to transitioning communities from diesel to renewable energy sources (Heerema and Lovekin, 2019, 33). As early as 2012, the territory set a goal to reduce emissions from diesel generation in communities connected to the Yukon grid by 20% by 2020. And it met that target two years early (Government of Yukon, 2018). In the new climate and energy strategies adopted in 2020, the territory set another target to reduce diesel use for electricity generation by 30 per cent by 2030 (Government of Yukon, 2020, 48). What is also important among the three territories only Yukon has power procurement policies that valued clean energy in a way that takes into account all costs associated with diesel generation (Heerema and Lovekin, 2019, 35).

Secondly, 11 of Yukon's 14 First Nations have signed self-government agreements that significantly impact their ability to implement energy projects because they have given the Indigenous communities the opportunity to lead and own them. In addition, Yukon has one of the most supportive environments in Canada for clean energy projects in remote Indigenous communities. Not only is the Yukon's goal to have an independent power production project in all off-grid communities by 2030, but the territorial utility policy is to have at least 50% of projects have an Indigenous ownership component (Government of Yukon, 2020, 48; Heerema and Lovekin, 2019, 34–35, 49). The Yukon policies are considered emblematic of changes in the north that allow small-scale local projects to grow and support Indigenous land and resource management (Thomson, 2019; Gignac, 2020b).

Examples of Yukon's community-led projects include two wholly Indigenous-owned ones. The first is a solar panel installation with battery storage microgrid project in Old Crow (Vuntut Gwitchin First Nation) that offsets nearly a quarter of the community's annual diesel consumption and completely shuts down the generator for most of the summer (Government of Yukon, 2020, 30; Thomson, 2019; Lyons, 2018). The second is a wind installation at Burwash Landing (Kluane First Nation), that, when completed, will meet one-fifth of diesel demand by allowing diesel generators in the community to be turned off at certain times of the year (Heerema and Lovekin, 2019, 35; Thomson, 2019). Other projects involve solar panels in Mayo, biomass heating systems in Teslin Tlingit First Nation community buildings. Additional projects are in development, such as a biomass heating system for the Carcross/Tagish First Nation, the largest battery storage site in the North in Whitehorse on Kwanlin Dün First Nation Settlement Land that overlaps with the traditional territory of the Ta'an Kwäch'än Council or a solar farm in Beaver Creek and electric thermal storage heating and biomass energy projects in several communities (Government of Yukon, 2020, 29–30; Gignac, 2020b; Rudyk, 2021).

Northwest Territories

The Northwest Territories hold the record among Canada's northern jurisdictions with 73 remote energy projects (20 renewable electricity and 53 renewable heat developments as of 2020) located in 34 remote communities (Lovekin et al., 2020, 3). A large number of installations contrasts with the weak regulatory framework for reducing diesel generators in remote communities. This is despite having enacted a 25% GHG reduction target for remote communities and a goal to increase the share of renewables used for heating to 40% in 2030. In addition, incentives and financing programs for clean energy and energy efficiency (such as the Residential Renewable Energy Fund and the Energy Efficiency Incentive Program) should also be credited. On the other hand, although the 2030 energy strategy describes a Renewable Electricity Participation Model, it does not provide enough clarity in partnerships with remote communities (Government of Northwest Territories, 2018, 18; Heerema and Lovekin, 2019, 37). According to Heerema and Lovekin much has yet to be done also in IPP projects regulations and power procurement policies, including how clean energy is valued. The experts signal that these elements are blocking greater involvement in community-led projects and, as a result, slow down the off-diesel transition. The introduction of a community-led procurement model could be an important step towards reconciliation with Indigenous peoples, where the NWT government has some catching up to do (Government of Northwest Territories, 2018, 20, 40; Heerema and Lovekin, 2019, 36–37).

Currently, renewable energy projects in remote communities in the Northwest Territories are primarily implemented under a net metering policy and are directed by the territorial public utility rather than communities. Examples include a hybrid solar-diesel system in Colville Lake, a variable-speed generator pilot project combined with solar panels in Aklavik, and a planned wind project in Inuvik. Among a limited number of independent power producers in the NWT is the Lutsel K'e Dene First Nation, which developed solar power in 2015 (Heerema and Lovekin, 2019, 38; Government of Northwest Territories, 2018, 17; Thomson, 2019). Smaller projects include the Deline Got'ine Government solar panels on the government-owned hotel's roof in Deline. The community is looking to expand the system and also switch to biomass for heating (Markusoff, 2021). The community of Tulita is also in the process of developing a solar energy project (Heerema and Lovekin, 2019, 38). Additionally, there are renewable energy projects in several commercial communities. For example, in 2012 wind turbine project was installed Diavik Diamond Mine (Canada Energy Regulator, 2020a).

Nunavut

There are 18 renewable energy projects in Nunavut's 25 remote communities that rely entirely on diesel for electricity and heating (Lovekin et al., 2020, 3). However, progress across the territory has been slow, and community-owned projects are the exception in Nunavut. According to Heerema and Lovekin, this is due to a lack of long-term policies and regulations in Nunavut. For example, the outdated 2007 "Ikummatiit" energy strategy only mentions reducing diesel reliance. The "Upagiaqtavut" climate change strategy, released four years later, did not set targets for transitioning from diesel to clean energy in remote communities (Government of Nunavut, 2007, 2011). There are insufficient incentives and funding programs at the territorial level to support clean energy and energy efficiency (limited to home renovation incentives). There is a lack of direct financial support for clean energy implementation (Heerema and Lovekin, 2019, 40). In addition, there are no clear power procurement policies and regulations in Nunavut that valued clean energy in a way to encourage renewable energy projects in communities (Heerema and Lovekin, 2019, 39–41). Only recently has the territorial utility introduced a Commercial and Institutional Power Producer program that allows to generate electricity using renewable energy systems and sell it to the local grid (Qulliq Energy Corporation, 2021a). However, the program has several shortcomings that pose a threat "it would not unlock opportunities for renewable energy [...], nor would it likely decrease dependency on diesel fuel" (Lovekin and Quitoras, 2020, 4). Nunavut has also begun developing a new IPP policy that could make a difference in community-led diesel reduction projects (Qulliq Energy Corporation, 2021b). However, until the final version is implemented, residential customers in Nunavut use a net metering program that allows to generate their own power and reduce the amount of power they need from the utility. Experts believe that Nunavut needs short-term action to support community-scale projects, because, as of 2019, none of the few clean energy projects in the territory "have been led at the community level" (Rogers, 2018; Heerema and Lovekin, 2019, 40). Furthermore, Nunavut has not fully implemented the UNDRIP and its commitment to reconciliation could be deeper (Heerema and Lovekin, 2019, 39). Paradoxically, even the Commercial and Institutional Power Producer program does not include any incentives or priority for Inuit ownership (Lovekin and Quitoras, 2020, 8).

The real challenge for the Arctic territory is the fact that there are many pressing, competing priorities. Most energy projects in Nunavut currently are connected with replacing aging energy infrastructure with newer diesel power plants. This is a critical issue as many diesel generators reaching the end of their lifespan (Canada Energy Regulator, 2020c). However, although more efficient diesel generators reduce greenhouse gas emissions, this means maintaining the territory's dependence on fossil fuels.

A few examples of renewable energy projects in Nunavut include a farm developed by the community of Rankin Inlet and a private company and Nunavut's first hybrid solar-diesel power plant in Kugluktuk (Infrastructure Canada, 2019; Canada Energy Regulator, 2020c; Thompson, 2018). Micro-hydro and wind microgrid potential studies have been conducted in several Nunavut communities, but the most comprehensive feasibility assessment of renewable energy projects in any Nunavut community was completed in 2019 (Thomson, 2019; Heerema and Lovekin, 2019, 41; World Wildlife Fund Canada, 2019, 36). Additionally, since reducing diesel consumption also applies to the Nunavut mines, the company that owes Meadowbank and Meliadine mines near Baker Lake is planning to install wind turbines, to lower diesel use by 15%. It is also considering a partnership with the local Inuit community that would be an owner of the wind project. If succeeded this may become a breakthrough project for the territory that set an example for other Indigenous communities (Thomson, 2019).

Conclusions

In April 2021 Ottawa announced that Canada's GHG emissions have increased by seven million tones since 2015. And the main source of the growth is the oil and gas industry and transportation (Government of Canada, 2021). In addition, carbon emissions are projected to soar in 2021 (International Energy Agency, 2021). This is nowhere near the target of more than 7% needed to stay under the 1.5-degree goal of the Paris Agreement (United Nations Environment Programme, 2019). Although the situation of the three northern territories seems to look different from the rest of Canada—their emissions decreased between 2015 and 2019—the real picture is more complex. Firstly, it is important to remember that that the territorial actions, various programs, policies, goals and targets resulted in only a marginal change in greenhouse gas emissions. It is not certain that the territories are able to maintain a downward trend with population growth. A cautionary example is a significant increase in emissions in the Yukon. Moreover, Canada is already behind the leaders, especially the Nordic countries, where the implementation of renewable energy development policies is most advanced. Yukon, Nunavut, and the Northwest Territories can certainly do more to increase renewable energy and transition away from fossil fuel-based power generation. Opportunities arising from the several new federal programs started by the Trudeau Liberals after 2015, backed by territorial funding options, appear to be a needed boost as significant uptake of clean energy investments is clearly evident. In addition, technological advancements that lower the costs of renewables, coupled with the development of energy, could have positive implications for the North. However, even communities that have already implemented clean energy projects still cannot completely avoid diesel. Clearly, the energy transition in Canada's three northern territories is not yet complete. Despite its peculiarities, the North, like Canada, needs bold moves. There is a need for continued investment in infrastructure, progressive goal setting, and innovative climate and energy policies. Only through additional actions, such as creating opportunities for Indigenous communities that support Indigenous self-governance, capacity building, or more community-led energy projects, does change in remote northern communities still have a chance of reaching the net zero goal by 2050.

References

Canada Energy Regulator. (2017). *"Market snapshot: Explaining the high cost of power in Northern Canada"*. https://www.cer-rec.gc.ca/en/data-analysis/energy-markets/market-snapshots/2017/market-snapshot-explaining-high-cost-power-in-northern-canada.html

Canada Energy Regulator. (2020b). *"Provincial and territorial energy profiles—Northwest territories"*. https://www.cer-rec.gc.ca/en/data-analysis/energy-markets/provincial-territorial-energy-profiles/provincial-territorial-energy-profiles-northwest-territories.html

Canada Energy Regulator. (2020c). *"Provincial and territorial energy profiles—Nunavut"*. https://www.cer-rec.gc.ca/en/data-analysis/energy-markets/provincial-territorial-energy-profiles/provincial-territorial-energy-profiles-nunavut.html

Canada Energy Regulator. (2020a). *"Canada's energy future towards net-zero"*. https://www.cer-rec.gc.ca/en/data-analysis/canada-energy-future/2020/net-zero/index.html

CBC News. (2019, October 10). "Yukon MLAs unanimous in declaring climate emergency". https://www.cbc.ca/news/canada/north/yukon-government-climate-emergency-1.5317293

Environment and Climate Change Canada. (2020). "*A healthy environment and a healthy economy*". https://www.canada.ca/en/environment-climate-change/news/2020/12/a-healthy-env ironment-and-a-healthy-economy.html

Fitzgerald, E., & Lovekin, D. (2018). "Renewable energy partnerships and project: Economics research supporting indigenous-utility partnerships and power purchase agreements". *Pembina Institute.* https://www.pembina.org/pub/renewable-energy-partnerships-and-project-economics

Gignac, J. (2020a, July 9). "Renewable energy projects in Canada's remote communities have doubled in past five years." *The Narwhal.* https://thenarwhal.ca/renewable-energy-canada-rem ote-communities-pembina

Gignac, J. (2020b, October 23). "Yukon's climate plans rely on biomass. But is it actually good for the environment?" *The Narwhal.* https://thenarwhal.ca/yukon-biomass-climate-change-plan/

Gleeson, R. (2020b, October 2). "N.W.T. Green energy advocate urges using more electricity for heat." *CBC News.* https://www.cbc.ca/news/canada/north/nwt-green-energy-advocate-urges-ele ctrical-heat-1.5747307

Gleeson, R. (2020a, September 9). "There are better options than billion dollar Taltson expansion, say energy leaders." *CBC News.* https://www.cbc.ca/news/canada/north/energy-leaders-say-bet ter-options-than-billion-dollar-taltson-expansion-1.5716653

Government of Nunavut. (2007). "Ikummatiit: The government of Nunavut energy strategy". https:// gov.nu.ca/sites/default/files/ikummatiit_energy_strategy_english.pdf

Government of Nunavut. (2011). "Upagiaqtavut—Setting the course: Climate change impacts and adaptation in Nunavut". https://www.gov.nu.ca/sites/default/files/3154-315_climate_engl ish_sm.pdf

Government of Yukon. (2016). "Yukon biomass energy strategy". https://yukon.ca/sites/yukon.ca/ files/emr/emr-yukon-biomass-energy-strategy.pdf

Government of Canada. (2016). "Pan-Canadian framework on clean growth and climate change". http://publications.gc.ca/site/eng/9.828774/publication.html

Government of Yukon. (2018). "Climate change action plan update: January 2016–June 2018". https://web.archive.org/web/20190126005748/. https://yukon.ca/sites/yukon.ca/files/env/env-cli mate-change-action-plan-update.pdf

Government of Northwest Territories. (2018). "2030 energy strategy of northwest territo-ries". https://www.inf.gov.nt.ca/sites/inf/files/resources/gnwt_inf_7272_energy_strategy_web-eng.pdf

Government of Canada. (2018). "Pan-Canadian framework on clean growth and climate change: Second annual synthesis on the status of implementation". https://www.canada.ca/content/dam/ themes/environment/documents/weather1/20170113-1-en.pdf

Government of the Northwest Territories. (2019). "2030 NWT climate change strategic framework 2019–2023 action plan." 2019. https://www.enr.gov.nt.ca/sites/enr/files/resources/128-climate_c hange_ap_proof.pdf

Government of Northwest Territories. (2019). "Joint release—Canada and Northwest territories announce joint investment in the Taltson hydroelectricity expansion project". https://www.gov. nt.ca/en/newsroom/joint-release-canada-and-northwest-territories-announce-joint-investment-taltson

Government of Canada. (2019). "Pan-Canadian framework on clean growth and climate change: Third annual synthesis on the status of implementation". https://www.canada.ca/content/dam/the mes/environment/documents/weather1/20170113-1-en.pdf

Government of Yukon. (2020). "Our clean future". https://yukon.ca/sites/yukon.ca/files/env/env-our-clean-future-draft.pdf

Government of Canada. (2021). "Greenhouse gas sources and sinks: Executive summary 2021". https://www.canada.ca/en/environment-climate-change/services/climate-change/greenh ouse-gas-emissions/sources-sinks-executive-summary-2021.html

Heerema, D., & Lovekin, D. (2019). "Power shift in remote indigenous communities a cross-Canada scan of diesel reduction and clean energy policies." *Pembina Institute.* https://www.pembina.org/ reports/power-shift-indigenous-communities.pdf

Infrastructure Canada. (2018). "Investing in Canada: Canada's long-term infrastructure plan". https://www.infrastructure.gc.ca/plan/about-invest-apropos-eng.html

Infrastructure Canada. (2019). "Kugluktuk residents to benefit from a cleaner, more energy efficient power plant". https://www.canada.ca/en/office-infrastructure/news/2019/08/kugluktuk-res idents-to-benefit-from-a-cleaner-more-energy-efficient-power-plant.html

International Energy Agency. (2021). "Global energy review 2021." https://www.iea.org/reports/global-energy-review-2021

Lovekin, D., Moorhouse, J., Morales, V., & Salek, B. (2020). "Diesel reduction progress in remote communities: Research summary". *Pembina Institute.* https://www.pembina.org/reports/diesel-reduction-progress-research-summary-pdf.pdf

Lovekin, D., Morales, V., & Salek, B. (2020). "Diesel reduction progress in remote communities. Modelling approach and methodology. Appendix A—Remote communities". *Pembina Institute.* https://www.jstor.org/stable/resrep25475.6

Lovekin, D., & Quitoras, M. (2020). "Recommendations on qulliq energy corporation's CIPP policy application." *Pembina Institute.* https://www.jstor.org/stable/resrep25462

Lyons, K. (2018, June 25). "Vuntut gwitchin first nation plugs in old crow solar power project." *Yukon News.* https://www.yukon-news.com/business/vuntut-gwitchin-first-nation-plugs-in-old-crow-solar-power-project/

Markusoff, J. (2021, March 3). "The long road to clean power for first nations communities." *Maclean's.* https://www.macleans.ca/economy/business/the-long-road-to-clean-power-for-first-nations-communities/

McDiarmid, M. (2017). "Federal budget money earmarked to help indigenous communities get off diesel." *CBC News.* https://www.cbc.ca/news/politics/indigenous-remote-federal-budget-1.397 5022

McKay, J. (2019). "In Iqaluit, Trudeau announces plans to take Arctic communities off diesel but offers few details." *CBC News,* issued 2019. https://www.cbc.ca/news/canada/north/trudeau-nun avut-visit-1.5312588

Moorhouse, J., Lovekin, D., Morales, V., & Salek, B. (2020). "Diesel reduction progress in remote communities. Modelling approach and methodology." *Pembina Institute.* https://www.pembina.org/reports/diesel-reduction-technical-report-final.pdf

Natural Resources Canada. (2018a). "Government of Canada supports clean energy in rural and remote communities". https://www.newswire.ca/news-releases/government-of-canada-supports-clean-energy-in-rural-and-remote-communities-674300013.html

Natural Resources Canada. (2018b). "Remote communities energy database." The atlas of Canada. https://atlas.gc.ca/rced-bdece/en/index.html

Natural Resources Canada. (2019). "Canada launches off-diesel initiative for remote indigenous communities". https://www.canada.ca/en/natural-resources-canada/news/2019/02/canada-launches-off-diesel-initiative-for-remote-indigenous-communities.html

Parliament of Canada. (2020). "Bill C-12". https://www.parl.ca/LegisInfo/BillDetails.aspx?Lan guage=en&Mode=1&billId=10959361

Poelzer, G., Gjorv, G. H., Holdmann, G., Johnson, N., Magnusson, B. M., Sokka, L., Tsyiachin iouk, M., & Yu, S. (2016). *"Developing renewable energy in arctic and sub-arctic regions and communities: Working recommendations of the fulbright arctic initiative energy group."* 2016. https://renewableenergy.usask.ca/documents/FulbrightArcRenewableEnergy.pdf

Pollon, C. (2017). "What will it take to get Canada's arctic off diesel?" Reveal. https://revealnews.org/article/what-will-it-take-to-get-canadas-arctic-off-diesel/

Prime Minister of Canada. (2016a). "Statement by the Prime Minister of Canada on advancing reconciliation with indigenous peoples". https://pm.gc.ca/eng/news/2016/12/15/statement-prime-min ister-canada-advancing-reconciliation-indigenous-peoples

Prime Minister of Canada. (2016b). "U.S.—Canada joint statement on climate, energy, and arctic leadership". https://pm.gc.ca/en/news/statements/2016/03/10/us-canada-joint-statement-climate-energy-and-arctic-leadership

Prime Minister of Canada. (2021). "Prime Minister Trudeau announces increased climate ambition". https://pm.gc.ca/en/news/news-releases/2021/04/22/prime-minister-trudeau-announces-increased-climate-ambition

Qulliq Energy Corporation. (2021b). "Independent power producer program". https://www.qec.nu.ca/customer-care/generating-power/independent-power-producer-program

Qulliq Energy Corporation. (2021a). "Frequently asked questions: Commercial and institutional power producer program". https://www.qec.nu.ca/sites/default/files/cipp_faqs_18feb2021_eng.pdf

"Reference Re Greenhouse Gas Pollution Pricing Act, 2021 SCC 11." (n.d.).

Rogers, S. (2018, January 4). "Nunavut community to expand solar project with new federal funds." *Nunatsiaq News*. https://nunatsiaq.com/stories/article/65674nunavut_community_to_expand_solar_project_with_new_federal_funds/

Rudyk, M. (2021, February 23). "Yukon energy one step closer to having largest battery storage site in the North." *CBC News*. https://www.cbc.ca/news/canada/north/yukon-energy-battery-site-whitehorse-1.5924354

The Canadian Press. (2016, June 1). "Wind, solar wouldn't cost more than diesel power in parts of Nunavut: Study." *CBC News*. https://www.cbc.ca/news/canada/north/nunavut-renewable-energy-possible-1.3610340

Thompson, J. (2018, September 20). "Company testing rankin inlet as site for wind turbines." *Nunatsiaq News*. https://nunatsiaq.com/stories/article/65674company_testing_rankin_inlet_as_site_for_wind_turbines/

Thomson, J. (2019, February 11). "How can Canada's north get off diesel?" *The Narwhal*. https://thenarwhal.ca/how-canadas-north-get-off-diesel/

United Nations Environment Programme. (2019). "Cut global emissions by 7.6% every year for next decade to meet 1.5 °C Paris target—UN report". https://www.unep.org/news-and-stories/press-release/cut-global-emissions-76-percent-every-year-next-decade-meet-15degc

"Vancouver Declaration on Clean Growth and Climate Change." (2016). https://itk.ca/wp-content/uploads/2016/04/Vancouver_Declaration_clean_Growth_Climate_Change.pdf

Venn, D. (2021, April 8). "Feds announce $7.6M for Nunavut clean energy projects". *Nunatsiaq News*. https://nunatsiaq.com/stories/article/feds-announce-7-6m-for-nunavut-clean-energy-projects/

Wilt, J. (2018, March 6). "Canada's commitment of $220 Million to transition remote communities off diesel a mere 'Drop in the bucket'". *The Narwhal*. https://thenarwhal.ca/canada-s-commitment-220-million-transition-remote-communities-diesel-mere-drop-bucket/

World Wildlife Fund Canada. (2019). *"Renewable energy in Nunavut scoping analysis"*. https://wwf.ca/wp-content/uploads/2020/03/POWERING-NUNAVUT'S-FUTURE-with-habitat-friendly-renewable-energy.pdf

WWF International Arctic Programme. (2005). "2° Is too much! Evidence and implications of dangerous climate change in the arctic". http://arcticwwf.org/site/assets/files/1606/2degreesis2much.pdf

Marcin Gabryś holds a Ph.D, in political science from the Jagiellonian University. He works as an Assistant Professor at the Department of Canadian Studies of the Institute of American Studies and Polish Diaspora at the Jagiellonian University. His academic interests concentrate on Canada's politics, in particular Canadian foreign policy and northern regions of Canada. Author, co-author and editor of books and a dozen scientific articles. Former editor-in-chief of "TransCanadiana. Polish Journal of Canadian Studies." He received research grants from, among others, the International Council for Canadian Studies, the Department of Foreign Affairs and International Trade and Polish National Science Centre. Visiting researcher at York University, McGill University and University of Ottawa.

Chapter 7
Resilience to Environmental Challenges and the National Disaster Insurance Program in Kenya

Christophe Dongmo

Abstract Kenya's economy and ecological system are fragile and vulnerable to climate change. The country's key poverty-environment challenges are related to soil degradation, deforestation, loss of biodiversity and ecosystem services, land, air and water pollution, environmental health concerns due to malnutrition, pollution, environmental migrations, vulnerability to natural disasters, lack of secured land, and unreliable access to food and water. At the outset, Kenya's economy is highly dependent on natural resources, whose exploitation may generate large economic benefits. However, their unsustainable use increases environmental degradation and decreases economic growth and livelihood opportunities. Over the last decades, Kenya has put in place a number of laws, strategies, and policy frameworks to support sustainable development and the green economy. In 2006, with the support of donor agencies, the country implemented its first index-based national disaster insurance program. The scheme targeted 5 million transiently food-insecure people, who, due to drought and climate change, faced food insecurity and hunger. This target group threatened to become chronically food-insecure if they did not receive timely support during drought conditions, as they could be forced to resort to negative coping strategies such as forced migrations, violence or the sale of productive assets. These populations were also beneficiaries of the Productive Safety Net Program. Building on the 2006 experience, development stakeholders further expanded the concept in 2007 by designing a comprehensive drought risk management framework that included risk financing. Using theoretical, analytical and quantitative survey methods, this chapter shows that changing climate patterns are undermining Kenya's resilience of poorer communities; and that the lack of functioning safety nets to help the country absorbs loss and recovers from environmental challenges could lead to populations adopting negative coping strategies that aggravate vulnerability to climate risk exposure. The chapter argues that, through the release of adequate funds to vulnerable groups in Kenya, drought index insurance was of great importance and made the Productive Safety Net Program effective and manageable in the country. Referring to prospective policy and strategy measures, the chapter reveals the prevailing gaps between the environmental commitments made and the actual implementation to

C. Dongmo (✉)
Leiden University African Studies Centre, Leiden, Netherlands

© The Author(s), under exclusive license to Springer Nature Switzerland AG 2022   145
D. Kurochkin et al. (eds.), *Energy Policy Advancement*,
https://doi.org/10.1007/978-3-030-84993-1_7

improve development outcomes. Weak capacity in environmental management and enforcement is in striking deficits. Indeed, Kenya's growing population requires more fuelwood and more agricultural production, which increases demands for new farmland, accelerates deforestation, and forest degradation. It is estimated that, unless action is taken to change the traditional development path, an area of 9 million hectares might be deforested between 2010 and 2030. Over the same period, annual fuelwood consumption will rise by 65% with large effects on Kenya's forest degradation. In the end, it is contended that Kenya still faces deficits in terms of corruption, strategic and operational planning, lack of human and financial capacity, green technology, and know-how. Indeed, environmental governance needs to be improved at all levels. Weak capacity in environmental management, insufficient law enforcement and monitoring are shortcomings that need to be addressed in order to meet MDG targets (especially MDG 7 on environmental sustainability) to move the country towards green growth.

Introduction

Changing weather patterns are undermining the resilience of Kenya's poorer communities. The combination of increasing hazard risks and decreasing resilience constitute the major causes of food insecurity and hunger in poorer communities.[1] Over the last decades, Kenya has put in place a number of laws, strategies, and policy frameworks to support sustainable development and the green economy. In 2006, with the support of donor agencies, the country implemented its first index-based national disaster insurance program. The scheme targeted 5 million transiently food-insecure people, who, due to drought and climate change, faced food insecurity and hunger. This target group threatened to become chronically food-insecure if they did not receive timely support during drought conditions, as they could be forced to resort to negative coping strategies such as forced migrations, violence, or the sale of productive assets. These populations were also beneficiaries of the Productive Safety Net Program. Building on the 2006 experience, development stakeholders further expanded the concept in 2007 by designing a comprehensive drought risks management framework that included risk financing.

This chapter shows that changing climate patterns are undermining Kenya's resilience of poorer communities; and that the lack of functioning safety nets to help the country absorbs loss and recovers from environmental challenges could lead to populations adopting negative coping strategies that aggravate vulnerability to climate risk exposure. The chapter argues that, through the release of adequate

---

[1] United Nations Office for Disaster Risk Reduction (UNISDR), *percentages of People Affected by Disasters, 1991–2005* (Brussels: Catholic University of Louvain, EM-DAT: OFDA/CRED International Disaster Database, 2009) Fig. 8.2.

funds to vulnerable groups in Kenya and policy advancement, drought index insurance was of great importance and made the Productive Safety Net Program effective and manageable.

Referring to prospective policy and strategy measures, the chapter reveals the prevailing gaps between the environmental commitments made and the actual implementation to improve development outcomes. Weak capacity in environmental management and enforcement is in striking deficits. Indeed, Kenya's growing population requires more fuelwood and agricultural production, which increases demands for new farmland, accelerates deforestation, and forest degradation. It is estimated that, unless action is taken to change the traditional development path, an area of 9 million hectares might be deforested between 2010 and 2030. Over the same period, annual fuel wood consumption will rise by 65% with large effects on Kenya's forest degradation. In the end, it is contended that Kenya still faces deficits in terms of corruption, strategic and operational planning in the forestry sector, lack of human and financial capacity, green technology, and know-how. Indeed, environmental governance needs to be improved at all levels. Weak capacity in environmental management, insufficient law enforcement and monitoring are shortcomings that need to be addressed in order to meet Millennium Development Goals (MDGs) targets to move the country towards green growth. The chapter is structured in two parts: the political economy of Kenya's deforestation and environmental challenges and the index-based national disaster insurance program.

The Political Economy of Kenya's Deforestation and Environmental Challenges

The most relevant environmental challenges in Kenya include climate change, land degradation, overgrazing, deforestation, indoor air pollution, water pollution, loss of biodiversity and ecosystem services, the spread of invasive alien species, urban outdoor air pollution, toxic household wastes, high urbanization rates, rapid economic growth that is largely driven by agricultural production, infrastructure expansion, and increasing energy demand. Since there are no functioning safety nets to help them absorb the loss and recover from disaster impacts, people adopt negative coping strategies that aggravate climate risk exposure.

According to Kenya's Readiness Preparation Proposal (R-PP) document, closed canopy forest cover by 2010 was conservatively estimated to be just over 1.5%, which includes indigenous forests and plantations. The indigenous closed canopy forest is reported to be at just over one million hectares. However, not all of this can be considered s primary forest characterized by only indigenous trees and a healthy forest ecosystem of the main forests in Kenya. Five large mountain forests exist as water catchment areas: the Mau Forest Complex, Mount Kenya, the Abrades, and Mount Elgon and Charangon, commonly referred to as Kenya's "Water Towers."

Large areas of the country are exposed to the threat of water scarcity in relation to changing precipitation and temperature patterns.[2] Looking back as far as 1968, Kenya suffered a total of 98 natural disasters (droughts, floods, and related epidemics), of which the great majority (69 events) occurred since the turn of the millennium.[3] About 83% of the Kenyan landmass is classified as arid or semi-arid land (ASAL). Since 1964, a total of 101 disasters (droughts, floods, and related epidemics) affected a total of 58.66 million people in the country. The great majority of these events occurred over the past two and a half decades.

Nearly 25% of Kenya's population lives in areas vulnerable to the effects of climate change, water shortages, and land degradation. Most of them are geographically located in the drier north-eastern and northern regions, around 24.5 million hectares of land. Although Kenya has 3.5 million hectares of forest, arid, and semi-arid land characterized by sparser tree cover extend over a much larger area, it should be noted, however, that initial estimates on forest cover are subject to considerable change due to revisions in the definition of a forest and new survey methods. A recent report carried out by Kenya Forest Services (KFS), based on a broader interpretation of forests and improved satellite technology, estimated the country's total forest cover at 6.6%.[4] The revision from less than 2% to nearly 7% is significant given that the Kenyan Constitution provides that the country should ensure a tree cover of 10%. Initial estimates on rates of deforestation are likely to be unreliable and should be seen as indicative of trends only.

Kenyans face market and production risks that make their yearly incomes unstable and unpredictable. Relying on disasters data from 1991 through 2005, the United Nations Office for Disaster Risk Reduction (UNISDR) and the International Disaster Database of the Catholic University of Louvain (Belgium) reveal that 85% of all the people affected by natural disasters recorded in developing countries suffered the effects of drought or flood.[5] Among the population groups with increased vulnerability to droughts and floods, are smallholder farmers and day labourers.

Between 1980 and 2000, Kenya lost nearly 50% of its forest cover. Some 300,000 ha of forest were destroyed due to intensive logging, charcoal production and large-scale clearance of wooded areas for tea plantations. Symbolic of this destruction is the Mau Forest, at 273,000 ha the largest forested area in Kenya with a seven-lake drainage basin covering more than 69,000 km^2, from which one-quarter of its canopy had disappeared, threatening the survival not only of millions of wildebeest and thousands of gazelles and buffaloes migrating through Kenya and Tanzania but also of riparian communities. However, thanks to the implementation of the Green Zones Development Support Project, with US$38.8 million in funding from the

---

[2] UNISDR Emergency Events Database (EM-DAT), op. cit. n. 1.

[3] Ibid.

[4] Ibid., p. 12.

[5] UNISDR Emergency Events Database (EM-DAT), op. cit. n. 1.

African Development Bank, more than 14,000 ha of forest was replanted between 2007 and 2016, in order to stem this deadly trend.[6]

Years of overexploitation of forest resources without respect for ecosystems had left bare the hills. Deforestation had even caused a local river in the Rift Valley to choke up. On these cleared areas around the Mau forest threatened by drought and famine, several inhabitants found themselves up against the wall. This critical situation not only imperiled thousands of animal and plant species and the indigenous population but also aroused concerns about the economic future of Kenya, since vital sectors, including agriculture, tourism, and energy depend on the natural environment.[7] Meanwhile, the Kenya Forest Service is working to prevent illegal logging. Since Kenya is deeply reliant on the natural environment, it is vital for policymakers to ensure that the country protects the forest cover to secure social and economic development.

Farmers in Kenya also face the risk of catastrophes: crops may be destroyed by drought or pest outbreaks; product prices may plummet because of adjustments in local or world markets; and assets and lives may be lost to hurricanes, fires, and floods. The types and severity of the risks confronting farmers vary by farming system, agro-climatic region, and policy and institutional setting, and they are particularly burdensome to small-scale farmers in the developing world. When not adequately managed, agricultural risks slow economic development and poverty reduction, thereby contributing to humanitarian crises.

There are prevailing humanitarian challenges associated with weather extremes in Kenya. More frequent and severe extreme droughts and related losses of soil fertility are the most important consequences. From 2008 through 2011, consecutive droughts affected an average of 4 million people. In 2013, about 170,000 people were displaced due to floods.[8] Moreover, the latter contributed to desertification and other forms of land loss such as landslides, which in the future might be compounded by sea-level rise along the coast that may affect major destination areas of migrants, particularly Mombasa city.[9] The impact of these natural environmental changes on migration is not always clear. In 2009, Cecilia Cinthia—Njenga (UN-Habitat) and Paola Kim Blanco (Columbia University) carried out a survey in Nairobi among migrants on behalf of the World Bank. The study reveals that 44% of the respondents considered environmental change as a major reason for their migration to the city.[10]

Kenya is experiencing climate change and its impacts on the environment and natural resources. Released in May 2003, the country's environment and climate

---

[6] African Development Bank, "Kenya Forests: Over 14,000 ha Reforested under 10 years, thanks to African Development Bank," December 10, 2018, accessed January 7, 2019, https://www.afdb.org/en/news-and-events/kenya-forests-over-14-000-hectares-reforested-under-10-years-thanks-to-african-development-bank-18832/.

[7] Ibid.

[8] Internal Displacement Monitoring Centre (IDMC, 2014).

[9] International Office for Migration (IOM), "Migration, Environment and Climate Change" *Policy Brief Series* Issue 1, Vol. 2, (January 2016).

[10] Cecilia and Blanco (2009).

change policy brief presents key environmental sustainability challenges and opportunities, their linkages to poverty reduction and socio-economic development.[11] There have been 12 serious droughts since 1990, with each one affecting some 4.8 million people. The average annual costs of the damage caused are estimated at some US$1.25 billion—with each drought reducing the country's Gross Domestic Product by an average of 3.3%.[12] Existing estimates of forest cover in Kenya are complex and to some extent contested. The population of Kenya is severely affected by floods due to the climatic conditions. Some parts of the arid or semi-arid land areas, and other parts of the country, are also prone to the risk of floods, particularly riverine floods, such as in Tana River county and Garissa county.[13]

Climate change is already having an impact in Kenya. The country's continued climate change is expected to bring greater variability, and extreme weather events, such as droughts, which will further drive degradation of Kenya's ecosystems. The impact of climate change in Kenya is already apparent in the increasing temperature and declining rainfall, particularly in northern parts which are exceptionally vulnerable to drought. The likely impacts of increased climate variability and change include[14]: increased food insecurity; outbreaks of diseases such as malaria, dengue fever and water-borne diseases such as cholera and dysentery due to floods; respiratory diseases associated with droughts; and heavy rainfalls which tend to accelerate land degradation and damage the communication infrastructure.

Land degradation is one of the most serious problems in Kenya. Natural factors such as rainfall and erodible soils, population pressure, overgrazing, unsustainable land use, and expansion of farming cause severe land degradation which affects agricultural productivity. Agriculture is the source of livelihood to an overwhelming majority of the Kenyan population, as it employs more than 80% of the labour force and is the basis of the national economy. A decrease in seasonal rainfall has devastating implications on agricultural production, leading to food insecurity, malnutrition, and famine. The frequency and intensity of drought are likely to increase over the coming decades, which will present a serious threat to biodiversity, ecosystems, water, agriculture, and healthcare. Furthermore, land degradation leads to loss of vegetation cover and loss of biodiversity and ecosystem services. The estimated annual costs of land degradation in Kenya range from 2 to 6.75% of agricultural gross domestic product.

---

[11] The Environmental and Climate Change Policy Brief was written, at the request of Sweden International Development Agency (SIDA), by Emelie César and Anders Ekbom at SIDA's Helpdesk for Environment and Climate Change.

[12] The Republic of Kenya, "Kenya Post-Disaster Needs Assessment (PDNA) 2008–2011 Drought," accessed January 29, 2019, http://www.gfdrr.org/sites/gfdrr/files/Kenya_PDNA_Final.pdf.

[13] International Office for Migrations (IOM), "Assessing the Evidence: Migration, Environment and Climate Change in Kenya," Evidence for Policy (MECLEP), Prepared for IOM by Dulo Nyaoro, Jeanett Schade and Kersti Schmid, accessed January 29, 2019, https://publications.iom.int/system/files/assessing_the_evidence_kenya.pdf, 12.

[14] Sweden International Development Agency (SIDA), "Helpdesk for Environment and Climate Change," accessed November 6, 2019, https://www.sidaenvironmenthelpdesk.se/.

Deforestation is widespread in the country.[15] Forests cover 12.3% of Kenya. However, official estimates on forest cover are subject to considerable change due to revisions in the definition of a forest and new survey methods. In a recent report by Kenya Forest Service, based on a broader interpretation of forests and improved satellite technology, the total forest cover in the country was estimated at 6.6%. The revision from less than 2% to nearly 7% is significant since the Kenyan Constitution states that the country should ensure a tree cover of 10%. Final estimates on rates of deforestation are also likely to be unreliable and should be seen as indicative of trends only. However, according to the Food and Agriculture Organization (FAO), Kenya is likely to lose some 12,000 ha of closed canopy forest each year.[16] A 2012 United Nations Environment Program reports that deforestation in only the *Water Towers* was about 50,000 ha between 2000 and 2010, or 5000 ha per year. The cash value of trees felled during this time is roughly estimated at Kenyan shillings 1362 million per year.[17] Overall, the average annual deforestation rate of 1% is high compared to other Sub-Saharan African countries, set at 0.6%.

Indeed, Kenya's growing population requires more fuelwood and more agricultural production which increases the need for new farmland, accelerates deforestation, and forest degradation. Unless action is taken to change the traditional development path, an area of 9 million hectares might be deforested between 2010 and 2030. Over the same period, annual fuelwood consumption will rise by 65% with large effects on Kenya's forest degradation.

Kenya has been hit hard by illegal settlement, logging, and charcoal production, reducing forest cover to 7% of its landmass. Charcoal and timber production, unregulated logging, and urbanization have further eroded Kenya's savannas, coastal mangroves, and mountainous woodlands. In the 1960s, forest-covered about 10% of Kenya's land. That figure has since fallen to 6%.[18] As much as 10% of Kenya's population relies on forest resources to make a living, according to the Kenyan ministry of environment and the United Nations. Woods around Mount Kenya, the Aberdares mountain range, and other water towers store and feed rainwater throughout the year to the rivers and lakes that account for most of Kenya's water resources.

Local Kenyan farmers and foresters change tack to end dependence on the forest. In 2005, determined to reverse the trend, Kenyan authorities approached the African Development Bank and secured a US$38.8 million loan to implement a green zone development project. This was the biggest contribution of a financial partner in this sector. It did so with two aims in mind: to promote regeneration and conservation of the forest, in order to protect the environment; and to improve livelihoods in rural areas and the incomes of communities living adjacent to forest areas. Two years later in 2007, the Kenya Forest Service was formed, to work closely with the country's

---

[15] IOM, op. cit. n.13, p. 12.

[16] Wandago (2002).

[17] United Nations Environment Programme (UNEP) (2012).

[18] Lily (2016).

farmers. The first task assigned to both parties was to rebuild the national vegetation over an area of 7000 km^2 located at the edge or in the heart of 21 classified forests.[19]

To meet this colossal challenge, training was delivered in beekeeping and fish farming, especially to farmers and foresters to help them develop a completely different activity that ended their economic dependence on the forest.[20] In less than 10 years, the results have been spectacular: working hand in hand, farmers and loggers have rewooded 14,300 ha of degraded forests. To better protect the 'green lung' of the country, buffer zones have been created through the planting of 1500 ha of tea and 5700 ha of fuelwood, supported by the improvement of 342 km of rural roads. The project also has positive economic benefits, with the creation of 3000 sustainable jobs in communities bordering the forests. A total of some 17,100 households, 40% headed by women, have seen their incomes increase.[21]

In a bold initiative to combat climate change, poverty, and hunger, Kenya announced, in September 1996, a plan to restore 5.1 million hectares of deforested land, an area that constitutes 9% of the country. The goal is part of a global campaign called the *Bonn Challenge*, which aims to have 350 million hectares of forest planted worldwide by 2030.[22] On September 8, Judy Wakhungu, Minister of Environment Water and Natural Resources announced that the plan would provide Kenyans "with the opportunity to reduce poverty, to improve food security, to address climate change and to conserve our valued biodiversity."[23] In other words, the program provides the most coherent and systematic effort to restore degraded forests and other landscapes, thereby proving the country "with the opportunity to reduce poverty, to improve food security, to address climate change and to conserve its valued biodiversity."[24]

Kenya's reforestation pledge is an update of a promise the country made in 2009 to replenish deforested areas over the next 20 years. Those efforts were hampered by illegal logging, land, and political disputes. The government is promising a coherent and systematic effort based on a series of assessment maps to determine where and what types of reforestation efforts should be made. Kenya set the 5.1 million hectares goal by creating maps detailing all of its landscape restoration opportunities. These include reforestation of degraded natural forests, planting trees on farms and ranchlands, and planting vegetation as buffers along waterways and roads. Trees, which store carbon, help to prevent soil erosion, retain soil fertility and regulate water flows, and provide habitats for wildlife.

---

[19] African Development Bank, op. cit. n. 6.

[20] Ibid.

[21] Ibid.

[22] The Bonn Challenge is a global effort to bring 150 million hectares of the world's deforested and degraded land into restoration by 2020, and 350 million hectares by 2030. Underlying the Bonn Challenge is the Forest Landscape Restoration approach, which aims to restore ecological integrity at the same time as improving human well-being through multifunctional landscapes.

[23] World Resources Institute (WRI), "Kenya Commits to Restore 5.1 Million Hectares of Land Based on New National Opportunity Maps," WRI, accessed October 29, 2019, https://www.wri.org/news/2016/09/release-kenya-commits-restore-51-million-hectares-land-based-new-national-opportunity.

[24] Ibid.

Landslide losses and other forms of ground failure are increasing in Kenya as development expands under the pressures of increasing populations.[25] They affect communities nationwide. At the outset, the concept "landslide" describes many types of downhill earth movements, ranging from rapidly moving catastrophic rock avalanches and debris flows in mountainous regions to more slowly moving earth slides and other ground failures. In addition to the different types of landslides, the broader scope of ground failure includes subsidence, permafrost, and shrinking soils.

Despite advances in science and technology, landslides continue to result in human suffering, billions of dollars in property losses, and environmental degradation. In a major study on landslides, the most critical ground-failure problem facing Kenyan's regions, Maina-Gichaba Charles (University of Nairobi), Kipseba Enoch K. (Kenya Ministry of Environment and Mineral Resources) and Masibo Moses (Kenya Ministry of Mining) show that as the population increases and the society becomes ever more complex, the economic and societal costs of landslides and other mass-wasting processes will continue to rise[26]; and that the resulting encroachment of developments into hazardous areas, expansion of transportation infrastructure, deforestation of landslide-prone areas, and changing climate patterns may lead to continually increasing landslide losses.[27] They argue that a significant, sustained, long-term effort to reduce losses from landslides and other ground failures in Kenya will require a national commitment among all levels of government and the private sector. Otherwise stated, the government must provide leadership, coordination, research support, incentives, and resources to encourage communities, businesses, and individuals to undertake mitigation to minimize potential losses and to employ mitigation in the recovery following landslides and other natural hazard events.[28]

Land sliding has social, economic, and environmental impacts. These include loss of life, agricultural land, and destruction of infrastructure. Landslides tend to bury all that is their way, resulting in the destruction of life and property. They may bury or sink buildings, rubble and boulders moved to block roads, railways, and lines of communication or waterways. They may destroy all property along their way and render agricultural land unproductive. In Kenya, the majority of landslides are caused or triggered by water and/or human activities. Slope saturation by water is a primary cause of landslides. This effect can occur in the form of intense rainfall, changes in groundwater levels, and water-level changes along coastlines, earth dams, and the banks of lakes, reservoirs, canals, and rivers.[29]

Indoor air pollution is another serious environmental problem causing acute respiratory illness. It hits the poorest the most, particularly women and children. These problems are mainly caused by poor households' use of traditional polluting stoves. Other major drivers behind Kenya's environmental degradation include high population growth, high urbanization rates, and rapid economic growth that is largely

---

[25] Kenvironews (2007). See, SIDA's Helpdesk, op. cit., n.14.

[26] Charles et al. (2013).

[27] Ibid.

[28] Ibid.

[29] Ibid.

driven by agricultural production, infrastructure expansion, and increasing energy demand. Furthermore, institutions have insufficient capacity to prevent and manage the major environmental issues, and there are gaps between political environmental commitments and actual implementation to improve environmental outcomes.

Irregular excisions of forests, mismanagement of state plantations, and corruption escalated in Kenya's Forest Department in the 1990s and early 2000s. Indeed, development stakeholders supporting the implementation of REDD+ activities recognize that corruption in the forestry sector is a barrier to achieving the goals of reducing deforestation and forest degradation. When corruption acts as an indirect driver of deforestation and degradation, it is appropriate for the implementation of REDD+ activities to be embedded in wider efforts to better understand the nature and impacts of corruption in the forestry sector, as well as contribute to reforms that may reduce these problems. Otherwise stated, countries embarking on implementing REDD+ but failing to address wider governance and corruption issues are more likely to see diminished funding for preparation activities and partnerships, which are critical for their success and program redeliveries.

In 2013, Kenya carried out a major study on the Corruption Risk Assessment for REED+ in the country.[30] Commissioned by the National REDD+ Coordination in the Ministry of Environment, Water and Natural Resources and the UN-REDD Program, in collaboration with the U4 Anti-Corruption Resource Centre, the report provides an analysis of how corruption may influence the ability of REDD+ activities to have successful economic, environmental, and social outcomes.[31] It also provides recommendations by a variety of national stakeholders to respond to these risks. Substantively, the report considers the historical context, describing how past policy and institutional failures—including corruption—, are an important factor in understanding the history of deforestation, forest degradation, and the failure of the state to regulate and sustainably manage and conserve forests for the benefit of all.[32] In the 1990s and early 2000s, irregular excisions of forests, mismanagement of state plantations, and corruption in the then Forest Department escalated.

Corruption led to a loss of government credibility to manage forests responsibly. The Corruption Risk Assessment for REED+ study yielded positive impacts for Kenya. This culminated in the Presidential moratorium on harvesting timber from state plantations. These developments influenced significant governance changes in the mid-2000s, with the enactment of new forest legislation and the establishment of a new semi-autonomous forest agency, Kenya Forest Service. The Forest Act 2005 provided among others, for stakeholder participation in forest management.

---

[30] Kenya Ministry of Environment (2013).

[31] The UN-REDD Programme is the United Nations collaborative initiative on Reducing Emissions from Deforestation and Forest Degradation (REDD+) in developing countries. Launched in 2008, the Programme builds on the convening role and technical expertise of FAO, UNDP, and UNEP. It supports nationally-led REDD+ processes and promotes the informed and meaningful involvement of all stakeholders, including indigenous peoples and other forest-dependents communities on national and international REDD+ implementation.

[32] Kenya Ministry of Environment, Water and Natural Resources and UN-REDD Programme, op. cit. n. 30.

The nature of forestry governance continues to evolve through the emergence of the outsourcing of conservation of public forests to the private sector, the lifting of the moratorium for harvesting timber, the regularization of charcoal production, as well as through the process of devolution established in the Constitution. Though capacity is still limited, the Kenyan government has shown considerable political will regarding its environmental problems, by establishing environmental protection agencies at the federal level and in all regional states, formulating various environmental proclamations, ratifying important environmental Conventions, and promoting environmental investments.

The forestry sector plays an important economic, social, and cultural role in Kenya. Some 10% of the population lives within five kilometers of forests and relies on forest resources for their livelihoods. In 2007, it was estimated that direct revenue from the exploitation of forests contributed 1% to Kenya's GDP though this figure is likely to be a considerable underestimate given the large informal economy that relies on forests and forest-based products. Likewise, 90% of all Kenya's harvested wood is thought to be for fuel, with over half of this being for subsistence and non-commercial use, while the commercial charcoal sector is substantial, estimated at 135 billion Kenyan Shillings.

Economic Returns of the Index-Based National Disaster Insurance Program

In most in low-income economies, there is a continuing expansion of credit activities. As a result, the poorest setting schemes are usually group-based, allowing aligned incentives and cheap monitoring in a way that economizes on information and transaction costs. Improved basic safety nets are also being developed for the poor, although protection is usually limited to large scale disasters. Nowadays, support is being extended through targeted conditional cash transfers payable, provided households meet specific criteria, such as committing to sending children to school. Finally, in most communities, people have long organized themselves to provide some forms of informal mutual support for each other.[33] A key issue for any further insurance provision is how it should relate to safety nets, credit schemes, and existing informal insurance schemes. In this chapter, this concern is central to our analysis.

There exists a multitude of interventions and innovations in credit and insurance markets that are changing the policy environment. In "Insurance, Credit, and Safety Nets for the Poor in a World of Risk," Daniel Clarke and Stefan Dercon discuss the key interactions between private and public mechanisms dealing with risk, and their implications for poverty.[34] How could insurance be more effectively delivered to the poor, and what should its role be relative to other microfinance programs, safety nets, and informal insurance systems? The two Oxford scholars focus on

---

[33] Marcel (1992), Townsend (1995).

[34] Daniel and Stefan (2009).

the various interactions, including how insurance may crowd out credit and informal insurance, and implications for the design of insurance schemes. Using the Ethiopian Rural Household Survey, a panel data survey covering about 1450 households across the country, the prevalence of earlier different types of risks and detailed data on a variety of (self-reported) shocks that affected people during the period between 1999 and 2004, they argue that well-designed insurance schemes, building on existing informal systems, and focusing on catastrophic and serious covariate risks, could offer protection against risk and contribute to poverty reduction beyond the combined impact of microcredit programs, safety nets and existing informal mutual support systems.[35]

In 2006, with the support of the World Food Program and the World Bank, Kenya implemented its first index-based national disaster insurance program. The scheme targeted 5 million transiently food-insecure people, who, due to drought and climate change, faced food insecurity and were unable to meet their livelihoods under normal weather conditions. The seasonally food-insecurity risk threatened to become chronically food-insecure if they did not receive timely support during drought conditions, as they could be forced to resort to negative coping strategies, such as violence and the sale of productive assets. These project beneficiaries were also beneficiaries of the Productive Safety Net Program (PSNP). Kenyan farmers are set to benefit from the launch of a new innovative, index insurance scheme that utilizes advanced technology and satellite data to assist agricultural workers in the face of flooding and drought conditions.

The Public–Private Partnerships have resulted in the launch of important Government-backed insurance schemes in Kenya, namely the Kenya National Agricultural Insurance Program and the Kenya Livestock Insurance Program (KLIP). These schemes help to protect the livelihoods of some of the region's poorest against the negative impacts of natural disasters and severe weather. For Olivier Mahul, World Bank Program Manager of the Disaster Risk Financing and Insurance Program, "this partnership between government and the private sector for the benefit of vulnerable farmers builds on international good practice and is innovative."[36] One aspect of the new scheme will focus on livestock insurance, while another will be dedicated to protecting maize and wheat production. Likewise, the program has been designed and built on experiences of comparable experiences in Mexico, India, and China. Interestingly, both schemes utilize the advanced technology to establish an index that will be used to determine when a policy is triggered, essentially using satellite data to assess the impact adverse weather events have had on livestock and crop conditions.[37]

Drought index insurance is of great importance and may make the Productive Safety Net Program (PSNP) effective and manageable.[38] Olivier Mahul, the World Bank Program Manager, further expands on this point: "The programme introduces

---

[35] Ibid.

[36] Ibid.

[37] Agro Insurance (2016).

[38] Niels and Ulrich (2010).

a state-of-the-art method of collecting crop yield data, using statistical sampling methods, GPS-tracking devices, and mobile phones.[39] This offers the promise of greater accuracy and transparency." Otherwise stated, it "could pave the way for other large-scale agricultural insurance programmes in Africa."[40]

The Kenyan Livestock Insurance Program (KLIP), a public–private partnership developed by the government of Kenya and reinsured by Swiss Re, is a good example of insurance and technology coming together to deliver financial protection where it is needed most. The World Bank mentions that the KLIP initiative was first introduced for 5000 farmers throughout Turkana and Weir, with plans to significantly broaden its reach by 2017.[41] The Program announced the payout of $2 million insurance to thousands of livestock owners in Kenya hit by drought, by February 2017, which averaged around $170 per household. In this case, the $2 million payouts will help save 70,000 tropical livestock—primarily cows, goats, and camels—that in turn sustain approximately 100,000 people across six regions.

The livestock insurance program uses satellite technology to measure vegetation available to livestock. Payment is triggered for feed, veterinary medicines, and water trucks when the satellite data shows drought is so bad that animal lives are at risk. This scheme aims at improving farmers' financial resilience to these shocks, thereby enabling them to adopt improved production processes to help break the poverty cycle of low investment and low returns. It will obtain data from satellites to estimate the availability of pasture on the ground and will trigger a payout to participating farmers when pasture availability falls below a predetermined threshold. It's a smart and innovative approach. While the two schemes do not carry payout based on the actual flood or drought event, the data received from satellites, GPS, and other devices take into account the weather event and determines if a payout will be triggered from the resulting impact on pasture, and crop production.

Programs such as the livestock insurance scheme will alleviate some of the financial burdens the government is facing with catastrophes, meaning both greater post-event financial stability and faster recovery. During the six-year period of 2005–2011, the Kenyan Government estimated that it spent more than $69 million a year on disaster relief. The work of the World Bank in these schemes demonstrates how index insurance technology and structures can be utilized to provide insurance to the very poorest and create parameterized pools of risk which can provide an opportunity to reinsurance and insurance-linked securities (ILS capital). These initiatives demonstrate the future of insurance for weather and certain catastrophe risks, in regions where indemnity coverage remains impossible. They may demonstrate that their efficiency suggests that the coverage should always remain index or parametric based, while technology provides the trigger data.

In any event, the national disaster insurance scheme could be replicated and launched in other countries and regions that are susceptible to natural disasters and have a strong reliance on the agricultural sector. At scale, similar programs could

---

[39] Cited by Clarke and Dercon, op. cit. n.34.

[40] Ibid.

[41] Ibid., n. 32.

require reinsurance protection, which given the parametric nature of the underlying insurance, may result in opportunities for insurance-linked securities (ILS) players as well as traditional reinsurance firms. The innovative use of satellites, mobile phones, and other advanced technology underlines the potential for this type of scheme to be replicated and put to good use in other emerging, underserved, and underinsured regions. The large majority of the poor in Kenya are farmers, so this initiative has the potential to have a significant impact on economic development.

Concluding Thoughts

The key poverty-environment linkages in Kenya are related to environmental health concerns related to malnutrition, polluted water, and indoor air pollution, vulnerability to natural disasters and climate change, lack of secure tenure to land and other natural resources, and unreliable access to food and water. Weather-related disasters threaten food security. Gains in development are at increasing risk from a variety of threats, including climate change-induced disasters, which can exacerbate poverty.[42] For example, the intensity, amount, frequency, and type of precipitation are tending to result in more frequent catastrophic events such as droughts, floods, and tropical storms. Ecosystem degradation, chronic poverty, and unplanned urbanization underpin this growing risk of devastating disasters. By 2030, these looming risks are forecast to cause average losses of about 12% of developing countries' gross domestic products, but cost-effective risk reduction measures could reduce this figure by more than 50%.[43]

Environment and climate change are costly for the country and may affect the delivery of the Kenya Vision 2030 plans and the Sustainable Development Goals. Over the last decades, the Kenyan government has put in place a number of policies, strategies, and laws designed to support sustainable development and the country is set to move towards a greener economy. However, there are gaps between the environmental commitments made and the actual implementation to improve environmental outcomes. Weak capacity in environmental management and enforcement are key challenges. It is estimated that environment and climate change, including adaptation and mitigation strategies, will cost Kenya around 3% of the GDP or USD 2 billion every year. Although Kenya contributes to only a small share of the global greenhouse gas (GHG) emissions—which is the major cause of climate change—the country is equally exposed to its impacts.[44]

For many decades, risk transfer mechanisms such as insurance schemes have been used to manage risk by transferring it to third parties with more stable financial bases. Historically, this has enabled economic growth, and it is now also being considered as a tool for risk management and risk reduction in developing countries. The *Hyogo*

---

[42] Stefan (2004).

[43] Ibid.

[44] IOM, op. cit. n.13, at 12–13.

Framework for Action 3 and the *Bali Action Plan 4* clearly spell out that "risk sharing and transfer mechanisms such as insurance" are an important element in "disaster reduction strategies and means to address loss and damage associated with climate change impacts in the developing countries that are particularly vulnerable to the adverse effects of climate change."[45] The Hyogo Framework for Action (HFA) is a global blueprint for disaster risk reduction efforts over the next decade. During the World Conference on Disaster Reduction, held in Kobe, Hyogo (Japan) in January 2005, 168 governments adopted a ten-year plan to make the world safer from natural hazards. The HFA's goal is to reduce substantially disaster losses—in the lives and the social, economic, and environmental assets of communities and countries—by 2015.

In the same vein, the Bali (Indonesia) 13th Conference of the Parties (COP13, December 2007) to the United Nations Framework Convention on Climate Change (UNFCCC) drew up an action plan identifying negotiation elements for an agreement to be reached at COP15 in Copenhagen (Denmark), in 2009. The *Bali Road Map* includes the Bali Action Plan, which launched a "new, comprehensive process to enable the full, effective and sustained implementation of the Convention through long-term cooperative action, now, up to and beyond 2012," with the aim of reaching an agreed outcome and adopting a decision at COP15 in Copenhagen. Governments divided the plan into five main categories: shared vision, mitigation, adaptation, technology, and financing. Other elements in the Bali Road Map included: a decision on deforestation and forest management; a decision on technology for developing countries; the establishment of the Adaptation Fund Board; and the review of the financial mechanism, going beyond the existing Global Environmental Facility.

Kenya has, recently, achieved notable progress towards many of the Sustainable Development Goals (SDG), including those for poverty, access to education, and health. The country has had a remarkable economic growth (an average of 10% per year). Improvements have also been made in basic infrastructure and in strengthening both regional and national policies and governance capacity.[46] Kenya's high ambitions and efforts to promote sustainable development are also manifested by the establishment of the national strategy Climate Resilient Green Economy (CRGE), a particularly promising and important initiative to promote resource-efficient, low-polluting alternatives to business-as-usual economic growth, which entails significant environmental risks such as continued reliance on, and use of, polluting sources of energy, erosive agriculture, non-sustainable forestry, and depletion of natural capital in sectors like mining and construction.

The country faces many challenges in terms of lack of human and financial capacity, green technology know-how, and proliferation. Environmental governance needs to be improved at all levels. Weak capacity in environmental management, and insufficient law enforcement and monitoring mechanisms are key challenges that need to be addressed in order to meet MDGs targets, in particular, SDG 13 and

---

[45] Niels and Ulrich (2010).

[46] UN-REDD (2013).

11 on climate action, sustainable cities and communities, and move towards a greener economy.

Indeed, Kenya should create a common platform for inter-agency and interministerial coordination. This initiative will enhance coherent policymaking for migration as adaptation and the prevention of forced migrations in the context of climate and environmental change. In this respect, the focus should be put on disaster, adaptation, migration, land-use, and urban policies, combined with do-no-harm approaches in the context of the wider development efforts undertaken in the country. Planning should build on existing knowledge and exchange with experts and civil society. The technical working group of the Migration, Environment and Climate Change: Evidence for Policy (MECLEP) project, composed of relevant private and governmental stakeholders, provides a useful starting point in this respect.[47]

References

Agro Insurance, Kenya—World Bank Backs Index Insurance Scheme to Assist Farmers, 18 March 2016. http://agroinsurance.com/en/kenya-world-bank-backs-index-insurance-scheme-to-assist-farmers/.

African Development Bank, Kenya Forests: Over 14,000 ha Reforested under 10 years, thanks to African Development Bank, December 10, 2018, https://www.afdb.org/en/news-and-events/kenya-forests-over-14-000-hectares-reforested-under-10-years-thanks-to-african-development-bank-18832/.

Ben, W. Country paper: Kenya tropical secondary forest management in Africa. In *Workshop on tropical secondary forest management in Africa*, Nairobi, Kenya, 9–13 December 2002, FAO. http://www.fao.org/3/j0628e/J0628E54.htm.

Cecilia, K.-N., & Paola, K. B. (2009, May). *Migration in Nairobi: Environmental migration and its urban manifestation at the local scale*. Washington D.C.: The World Bank.

Charles, M.-G., Kipseba Enoch, K., & Moses, M. (2013). Overview of landslide occurrences in Kenya causes, mitigation, and challenges. In *Developments in Earth Surface Processes* (vol. 16, Chapter 20, pp. 293–314).

Daniel, C., & Stefan, D. (2009, October). Insurance, credit, and safety nets for the poor in a world of risk. DESA Working Paper No. 81, ST/ESA/2009/DWP/81.

International Office for Migration. (2016, January). Migration, environment and climate change. *Policy Brief Series, 2*(1).

International Office for Migrations. (IOM). Assessing the evidence: Migration, environment and climate change in Kenya, Evidence for Policy (MECLEP), Prepared for IOM by Dulo Nyaoro, Jeanett Schade and Kersti Schmid, 12. https://publications.iom.int/system/files/assessing_the_evidence_kenya.pdf.

Kenvironews. (2007). Landslides in Kenya—How do we preserve life and property? Google, http://www.Kenvironews, Wordpress.com.

Kenya Ministry of Environment, Water and Natural Resources and UN-REDD Programme, A corruption risk assessment for REDD+ in Kenya (Nairobi, 2013).

Lily, K. (2016, September). Kenya is planting a forest the size of Costa Rica. *QUARTZ AFRICA*.

Marcel, F. (1992). Solidarity networks in preindustrial societies: Rational peasants with a moral economy. *Economic Development and Cultural Change, 41*(1), 147–174.

---

[47] IOM, op. cit. n.13.

Niels, B., & Ulrich, H. (2010). WFP revolution from food aid to food assistance. In O. Steven, G. Ugo, & S. Susanna (Eds.), *World food programme, revolution: From food aid to food assistance* (pp. 107–108). Rome: World Food Programme.

Republic of Kenya, Kenya post-disaster needs assessment (PDNA) 2008–2011 drought, http://www.gfdrr.org/sites/gfdrr/files/Kenya_PDNA_Final.pdf.

Stefan, D. (2004). Growth and shocks: Evidence from rural Ethiopia. *Journal of Development Economics, 74*(2), 309–329.

Sweden International Development Agency (SIDA). Helpdesk for environment and climate change. Retrieved on November 6, 2019, from https://www.sidaenvironmenthelpdesk.se/.

Townsend, R. M. (1995). Consumption insurance: An evaluation of risk-bearing systems in low-income economies. *The Journal of Economic Perspectives, 9*(3), 83–102.

United Nations Office for Disaster Risk Reduction (UNISDR). (2009). *Percentages of people affected by disasters, 1991–2005.* Brussels: Catholic University of Louvain, EM-DAT: OFDA/CRED International Disaster Database.

United Nations Environment Programme (UNEP). (2012). Kenya integrated forest ecosystem services. Technical Report.

UN-REDD Programme and Kenya Ministry of Environment. Water and natural resources-REDD programme a corruption risk assessment for REDD+ in Kenya (Nairobi, 2013).

World Resources Institute (WRI). Kenya commits to restore 5.1 million hectares of land based on new national opportunity maps. WRI. https://www.wri.org/news/2016/09/release-kenya-commits-restore-51-million-hectares-land-based-new-national-opportunity.

Christophe Dongmo is Community and Youth Advocacy Director at Water, Energy and Environment (EEE) and Associate Fellow of the Leiden University African Studies Centre in the Netherlands. In the past, he served as Senior Regional Communication Officer at the International Committee of the Red Cross (ICRC); Country Representative of Denis and Lenora Foretia Foundation; Associate Research Fellow at The Hague Academy of International Law (The Netherlands), Chief-Editor of *Cameroon Journal on Democracy and Human Rights* (CJDHR), and Editorial Assistant of The *South African Law Journal* (SALJ). Christophe's major fields of interest are Political Economy of the Developing World, Development Economics, International and Comparative Law of Human Rights, African—American History and Diplomatic History. His track record indicates about fifty combined peer reviewed journal articles, international conference papers and academic research papers. A law graduate of the University of Yaoundé (Cameroon), he holds postgraduate Master's degrees in Human Rights Law, International Economics, Economic History, and Political Science from the University of the Witwatersrand (South Africa), School of Advanced International Studies (SAIS—Italy), Vanderbilt University (USA), and the Johns Hopkins University (USA).

Chapter 8
Ethiopia's Climate Change Policies in Retrospect: From Conservationism to Green Economy

Mathias N. Bimir

Abstract Low-income countries have been severely affected by climate change for several decades due to their limited capacity for adaptation. Ethiopia is among the low-income countries where climate change severely affected its socio-economic development processes. This chapter reviewed the ways Ethiopia has been responding to environmental and climate change problems in the last few decades. The chapter focuses on the evolution of policies and the discursive and institutional aspects that shape them. The review indicates that environmental interventions were introduced since the 1970s with the top-down planned conservation campaigns. This state conservationism evolved in the 1990s with the emergence of new actors and new forms of environmental governance guided by the sustainable development paradigm. The climate policy discourses further shifted towards low-carbon transformation in the post-Copenhagen period with the introduction of a green economy strategy based on the natural resources endowments to develop renewable energy alternatives.

Introduction

The Intergovernmental Panel on Climate Change (IPCC) concludes that countries in Sub-Saharan Africa are likely to face a steeper increase in mean temperatures and greater variability in rainfall patterns, than other regions this century.[1] Ethiopia is among these countries that have been increasingly facing the devastating impacts of climate change. Geographically, Ethiopia is in the Eastern part of Africa, a region usually noted for volatile climatic conditions and climate-led economic and social crises. The presence of the Indian Ocean to the east, regional lakes, as well

---

[1] IPCC is a joint institution of World Meteorological Organization and the United Nations Environment Program that provide an authoritative international statement of scientific understanding of climate change.

M. N. Bimir (✉)
Hong Kong University of Science and Technology, Hong Kong, China
e-mail: mnbimir@connect.ust.hk

© The Author(s), under exclusive license to Springer Nature Switzerland AG 2022
D. Kurochkin et al. (eds.), *Energy Policy Advancement*,
https://doi.org/10.1007/978-3-030-84993-1_8

as high mountains, induce localized climatic patterns in this region (Alemu and Mengistu, 2019) which elevates temperature and precipitation variability in this region (Adhikari et al., 2015). Ethiopia remains highly affected by climate change because, among others, the economy largely depends on climate-sensitive agricultural production (Alemu and Mengistu, 2019). Ethiopia's vulnerability to climate change is further heightened by the country's high poverty levels. A large proportion of Ethiopia's population depends on natural resources, so the depletion and deterioration of these resources result in reduced agricultural productivity, diminishing quality of life (Tedla & Lemma, 1998). The growing population increases the demand for agricultural land, that aggravated deforestation in many areas for decades (Table 8.1).

The mean annual temperature in Ethiopia has risen by about 1.3 °C, an average rate of 0.28 °C per decade since 1960, with increasing rainfall variability (Simane et al., 2016; Zegeye, 2018). The occurrence of droughts has also increased since the 1970s resulting in intensified desertification in many areas (Motuma, 2017). The country has experienced 16 major national droughts since the 1980s, along with dozens of other local droughts (Alemu and Mengistu, 2019), with yearly mean rainfall variation from 25 to 50% in some regions (Gonzalo et al., 2017). Notably, the impact of climate change on Gross Domestic Product (GDP) in Ethiopia is predicted to be between 0.5 and 2.5% each year (Simane et al., 2016). The 2015 El Niño alone increased the surface temperature in the central and eastern equatorial Pacific Ocean causing food shortages for millions of people. Consequently, both temporary and permanent internal migration are among common coping mechanisms in communities that are the most severely affected, due to factors such as varying agricultural productivity. Predictions show that droughts and floods are likely to become more severe in the coming decades. The government of Ethiopia acknowledged

Table 8.1 Climate change trend in Ethiopia[2]

	Temperature	Rainfall	Extreme events
Trend	Mean temperature rises by 1.3 °C from 1960, more hot days and nights, fewer cold days and nights	High temporal variability	Regular severe flood and drought events
2020	+1.2 °C (0.7–2.3 °C)	+0.4%	Greater increase in rainfall in Oct-Dec, mainly in the south and east
2050	+2.2 °C (1.4–2.9 °C)	+1.1%	Heavy rainfall events El Niño led uncertainties
2090	+3.3 °C (1.5–5.1 °C)	Wetter conditions	Rising flood and drought Heatwaves and higher evaporation

[2] Data from Conway and Schipper (2011). On Adaptation to climate change in Africa.

the alarming climate change concern and incrementally ameliorated its policies and institutions. Climate change was not understood in its present form during the 1970s and 1980s. Consequently, soil and forest degradation were the central concerns on which the conservation campaign was based, from the 1970s. This narrow perception of climate impacts has led to the narrow framing of interventions, due to the lack of a well-founded policy narrative. The regime change in 1991, together with the prevailing sustainable development paradigm, pushed for a discursive and institutional shift in in Ethiopia. This chapter has systematically reviewed the evolution of climate discourses, actions, and institutions to capture how climate policy shifts and what affects it.

Early Environmental Discourses, Institutions, and Actions

Hajer (1995) wrote that policies involve redefining a given trend in a way that one can be easily discerned. Policy discourses define the options and operate as resources that empower certain actors and prohibit others (Hajer, 1995; Hovden & Lindseth, 2004). Actions emerge from discursive struggles, through agents promoting certain discourses, struggling over, or identifying with them (Litfin, 1994). Hovden and Lindseth (2004) also add that actors act within the framework of discourses, which exist independently of the intentions and motives of these actors. Thus, understanding climate actions requires one to discern the ideas and discourses they are built on, the actors involved, and the institutions carrying them. Hajer pointed out two important accounts of discourse: discourse structuration, the ways ideas are referred to convey legitimacy on actors, and discourse institutionalization, in which practices become routinized in practices and institutions. Therefore, conducting policy analysis, including environmental policy, seeks to uncover the evolving discourses (Leipold et al., 2019).

Environmental actions in Ethiopia have been guided by discourses based on perceived experiences because of massive degradation of the environment. Hoben (1995) notes much of northern Ethiopia is a dissected, sloping terrain, with fragile soils, subject to highly erosive rainstorms. Efforts to address environmental problems began with conservation actions as early as the 1950s. But what does the conservation discourse entail? The term conservation is interpreted in different but related ways. Conservation, according to the Cambridge dictionary, involves: (1) the protection of plants and animals, nature, as well as interesting and important structures and buildings, from damaging human activities, and (2) carefully using valuable natural substances that exist in limited amounts to make certain they will be available for as long time as possible. These two dictionary definitions can be interpreted in different ways, depending on the perspectives one can have. The interpretation entails the preservation and recovery of resources if it is framed from the direction of saving or protecting resources. In the second definition, the focus is on using finite resources as wisely as possible, to sustain their availability in the long run. This is just one example to understand how discourses can be framed to direct policy actions. Ethiopia's conservation programs are explained below.

State Conservationism (1974–1991)

The Marxist revolution of 1974 brought a highly centralized, top-down approach to devise solutions to public problems. Food insecurity and environmental degradation were at the top of the government agenda. One of the narratives postulates that the growing population accelerates resource depletion so that agricultural production declines and food deficits escalate which resulted in increased poverty. The regime pressed an ambitious reform on rural social economic and political institutions, to spur agricultural development tackling environmental problems (Hoben, 1995). Keeley and Scoones (2000) mention that two approaches came to dominate the policy discourse that guides the aggressive move to address food insecurity i.e., the Green Revolution and Environmental Rehabilitation. The green revolution, derived from experiences in Asia, emphasized the need for boosting food production through mechanization and technology transfer. This narrative has been put forward by the technical-scientific elite in research institutions and laboratories, including economists from the World Bank.

Environmental thinking in Ethiopia has not been inherent in the national policy processes (Ruffeis et al., 2010). The environmental debate in Ethiopia by the time targeted soil and forest degradation in pursuit of food security. The debates established environmental conservation as a defended discourse, guiding actions of the Marxist regime. Before the 1974 revolution, conservation had a focus on the preservation of wildlife sanctuaries and heritages, mainly for tourist attraction. Policies in the 1970s grounded in the socialist ideology, the state became the owner of resources and institutions (Bekele, 2008). At the local level, peasant associations were established to implement the top-down conservation and afforestation programs (Hurni, 1988) on large plots of land forcefully taken from communities (Cheever et al., 2011). This state-run conservation campaign came to be equated with the construction of physical structures on land deemed to be at risk, backed by donors and non-government organizations (Hoben, 1995; Rahmato, 2001). The scientific base when the program commences was limited as the revolution aggressively pushed conservationism. Conservation studies became inevitable later to support interventions through research and partly to legitimize the campaign.

Hoben (1995) notes that environmental paradigms pass to aid recipient countries through training, institution building, and investment. Western donors, that had a limited chance to enter the country due to antagonistic relations with the regime, were actively engaged in environmental programs. Donor agencies and expatriate advisors advocate the narratives supporting conservation, together with the humanitarian components, as entry loopholes to Marxist Ethiopia. For instance, Hans Hurni's (a Swiss advisor at the Ministry of Agriculture) influence was strictly in favor of soil conservation, instead of systemic intervention to environmental degradation (Keeley & Scoones, 2000). Hans Hurni led the soil conservation research project, while the Food and Agricultural Organization (FAO) experts managed the Ethiopian Highland Reclamation Study (EHRS) (Ruffeis et al., 2010; Constable and Belshaw, 1986). A series of projects were carried out under EHRS with food-for-work incentives for communities (Maxwell & Belshaw, 1990). The formation of scientific knowledge through these studies enhanced rural development strategy, that anticipates higher food productivity (Ruffeis et al., 2010).

The conservation studies led to the formulation of the Conservation Strategy of Ethiopia (CSE) supported by the World Conservation Union (IUCN) (Motuma, 2017; Ruffeis et al., 2010). CSE was not as such a broad policy with clear policy instruments but served as a foundation for conservation actions (Held et al., 2012; Rahmato, 2001) and advance rural development programs (Hoben, 1996). While addressing the complexities of the environmental problems requires a systemic intervention, CSE was narrowly framed, neglecting the socio-cultural and economic drivers of degradation. For a society that had a long history of ancestral land ownership and communal knowledge, planned environmental intervention face defiance from local communities. The failure to consider the long-established local institutions and the cultural context of the society led to its ineffectiveness (Hoben, 1995). Structurally, the top-down approach and donor-framed discourses undermined the participation of local actors, such as farmers and schools. Environmental problems and solutions are embedded in the local contexts. The expatriate advisors undervalued indigenous practices and local knowledge, which rebounded to the program eventually. The difference in agro-ecological and socio-economic settings should have been recognized before the adoption of conservation measures (Bekele & Drake, 2003). For instance, the delineation of national parks in areas traditionally used by pastoralists; development of large fuelwood plantations in areas of mixed small-holder agriculture, and large irrigation schemes in dry season grazing areas were notable gaps (Tedla & Lemma, 1998). Finally, the planned and indigenous institutions evolved into a negative institutional interaction leading to the ineffectiveness of CSE. Rahmato (2001) points out that most of the assets created by the conservation program were either demolished or subject to disuse following the collapse of the Marxist regime, what he called a colossal wastage of resources and a stinging rebuff to state environmentalism. Incorporation of benefit-sharing and considering the interests of rural communities in the design of conservation programs would have increased the acceptance of interventions.

The Regime Change and Emergence of New Policy Spaces

There is a dominant view that environmental issues in developing countries lack institutional, political, and financial resources to environmental problems (De Oliveira, 2002). The 1991 regime change was accompanied by an ideological shift in environmental management, manifested by new institutional structures and the emergence of new actors (Cheever et al., 2011). Environmental civil society groups emerged from within and outside of Ethiopia, with new space to steer and enforce programs. The new government introduced the development strategy of the country, Agricultural Development Led Industrialization (ADLI), to develop the economy and reduce poverty. The formation of the short-lived Ministry for Natural Resources and Environmental Protection (MoNREP) in 1993 was the first attempt to independently institutionalize environmental affairs. MoNREP was formed by separating the environmental department from the Agricultural Ministry to increase environmental institutions which did not last long. Assele et al. (2019) remarks on the antagonistic views from the old bureaucracy from MoA which led to the remerging back. The limitation on policy capacity from lack of experts and finance hampered the development of a separate environmental ministry.

The environmental reforms in the early 1990s were connected to the dynamics in the international arena. At the outset, the Earth Summit of 1992 urged nations to establish institutions entirely dedicated to sustainable development and environmental protection (Held et al., 2012). Ethiopia's participation in this summit introduced it to the sustainable development paradigm mainly through Agenda 21 implementation and impact assessment process (Worku, 2017; Ruffeis et al., 2010; Damtie & Bayou, 2008). Agenda 21 implementation triggered the transitional government that was desperately looking for development aid to new forms of foreign aid and partnerships. One of the prominent outcomes of this condition was the emergence of a raft of environmental and non-government organizations (ENGOs). Ayana et al., (2018) note that ENGOs in the forest and environmental governance were enabled by changes in socio-political trends at both the national and international levels. They were involved, among others, in promoting participatory management, which appeared paradoxical to the portrayal of Ethiopia as a semi-authoritarian state (Mulugeta, 2013). ENGOs became involved in environmental steering, both directly and indirectly, depending on available spaces. Implementing pilot projects, documenting, and communicating field evidence, networking with like-minded actors, and investing human and financial resources were among the actions of ENGOs (Ayana et al., 2018).

Institutionalization of Environmental Initiatives

The 1995 constitution incorporated environmental concerns, marking the political will of the new government to environmental actions. One aspect is that the environment is framed from a human rights perspective in the constitution, offering impetus for subsequent policies. The section about the environment states that *"Every person has the right to live in a healthy and clean environment"*[3] indicating protection of the environment is a universal interest for all citizens. The human rights perspective on the environment was recognized in the international arena several decades

---

[3] Art. 44 of the 1995 Federal Democratic Republic of Ethiopia Constitution.

ago. The United Nations recognized that technological changes could threaten the fundamental rights of human beings and ratified a declaration on the interdependence between the protection of the environment and human rights in the late 1960s (Thorme, 1990). The rights perspective was a new narrative in Ethiopia, introduced by the 1995 constitution. Following the constitutional remarks about the environment, Ethiopia established the Environmental Protection Agency (EPA) and formulated the Environmental Policy, marking a new horizon in the environmental politics of Ethiopia. Every project which falls in any category listed and, in any directive, issued pursuant to this Proclamation shall be subject to environmental impact assessment.[4]

The primary intent of EPA was particularly to foster a system of Environmental Impact Assessment (EIA) on development projects and other programs (Damtie & Bayou, 2008). There were two important specific missions pertinent to the EPA's establishment. The first involves negotiating and undertaking capacity building in relevant agencies, to ensure environmental policy integration. This entails advancing environmental communication and training experts both at the federal and local levels. The second focused on the regulation, prediction, and management of environmental impacts from proposed development projects to proactively respond to adverse effects. The latter was challenged mainly by a lack of clear instruments to regulate environmental affairs in other sectoral policies and projects. Therefore, regulatory instruments were perceived inevitably late, for which the Impact Assessment Proclamation and the pollution control proclamations were ratified in 2002 (Mulugeta, 2013; Ruffeis et al., 2010); regulatory instruments sought to enforce the polluter pays principle (Fig. 8.1).

The environmental policy was the first key document that captured environmental issues and sustainable development principles (César & Ekbom, 2013), deriving the essential aspects from the conservation strategies (Held et al., 2012). The policy reiterates environmental degradation as a key problem guiding the narrative. However,

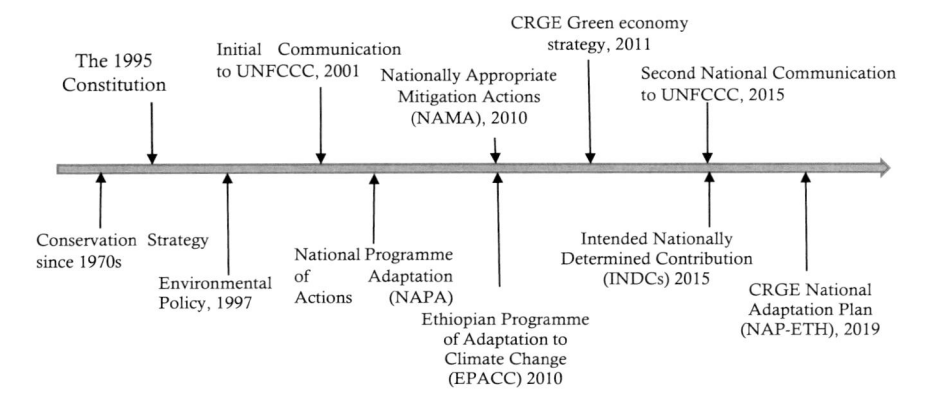

Fig. 8.1 Major climate change related policies in Ethiopia (*Source* The writer's compilation)

---

[4] Art. 5 of the Environmental assessment proclamation 299/2002.

several valuable insights distinguish it from the conservation strategies of earlier times. The first is that the environment is taken as a human right based on the constitution, hence, the rights-based approach was enmeshed in the policy goal and implementation mechanisms. Environmental goals are detailed across several sectors, including cross-sectoral issues such as gender. The rights-based element also entailed the promotion of public participation in environmental governance, which necessitates deviating state environmentalism and creating public awareness. Secondly, beyond the issue of natural resources, the policy includes man-made resources, such as cultural and social values. This shift brought institutions previously not within the environmental domain into the environmental policy framework. Thirdly, the inter-generational equity concern is incorporated in conserving the utilization of non-renewable resources. This entails matching with the sustainable development paradigm. Fourthly, the policy recognizes the importance of a multi-level and participatory framework to foster implementation through what it stated as an 'integrated and cross-sectoral principle'. According to this principle, inclusiveness was a foreseeable pathway to legitimize the policy and convince donors who were at the back and forth of the environmental policy.

... policy goal is to improve and enhance the health and quality of life of all Ethiopians and to promote sustainable social and economic development through the sound management and use of natural, human-made, and cultural resources and the environment as a whole to meet the needs of the present generation without compromising the ability of future generations to meet their own needs.[5]

De Oliveira (2002) explains that environmental issues may appear in government discourses but are hardly a priority in action. One reason is the fight for a share of the scant public budget, leading to dissociation with economic development programs. A rigorous environmental policy is considered detrimental to economies, while the pressure from the international arena usually promotes sustainability considerations. In Ethiopia, poverty eradication is the main development goal, given a significant share of the population remains below the poverty line. The mechanisms followed to achieve this goal have had an overriding focus on agriculture, while strengthening industrial development (Cheever et al., 2011) through the Agricultural Development Led Industrialisation (ADLI) strategy. The state pursued developmentalism as a guiding ideology to realize state-led initiatives, calling poverty the ultimate enemy that needs aggressive state economic intervention. Under the political economy of the developmental state model, policies are implemented to maintain the strategy over a sustained period, without interruptions by electoral cycles or by interest groups (Dejene & Cochrane, 2019). The environmental policy and associated discourses have been grappling with this dominant political and economic hegemony over policy processes in Ethiopia's developmental state realm.

Notwithstanding the promotion of environmental actions, EPA had limitations in implementing the policy. The lack of essential authoritative power (Gubena, 2016) and scarcity of policy expertise (Damtie & Bayou, 2008) hampered policy

---

[5] From the 1997 environmental policy of Ethiopia.

capacity and integration. The EPA's lower rank created difficulty to enforce environmental goals in other policy sectors and levels of government (Held et al., 2012). The Ethiopian Panel on Climate Change (2015) also wrote about the unclear diffusion of responsibilities across sectoral departments which impede environmental policy integration. The absence of sectoral environmental units (Damtie & Bayou, 2008), coupled with a lack of instruments such as impact assessment lowered compliance with environmental protection (Mulugeta, 2013). For instance, hydroelectric power projects, such as Melka Wakena were undertaken without impact assessment (Worku, 2017). This jeopardized the very basis on which agenda 21 implementations were depended in Ethiopia. At the local level, Zinabu et al. (2018) notice the Kombolcha industrial zone where disintegration between the environment and investment in industrial waste disposal noticed. It implies that awareness of or the political commitment to environmental problems has been delimited to the policy level. The environmental policy plans remained confined to one agency until recently (Assele et al., 2019; Held et al., 2012). Role ambiguity and overlaps create coordination problems as it is still observed. For instance, forest governance intersects among five different institutions with their respective sectoral motives and goals—agriculture, tourism, wildlife conservation, biodiversity, environment, and forestry.

Rethinking the Subnational Level

The subnational scale has become an increasingly valuable tier in a multi-level environmental governance structure. Jörgensen et al. (2015) point out that subnational governments are no longer mere observers in international climate policies, but also influential actors. Earlier, the subnational role was conceived as part of decentralization (vertical) in policymaking and implementation, a concept that has been at the core of the development and governance debates in developing countries (De Oliveira, 2002). The need for a participatory development process, difficulty to govern complex society and non-state actors pushing for greater accountability and transparency triggered decentralization (Cheema & Rondinelli, 1983). The presumption for administrative and fiscal decentralization aimed at promoting more participatory, responsive, government structures that extend improved environmental management (Cheever et al., 2011). Concerning environment and climate change, the role of subnational actors in domestic policy processes mainly in multi-tiered systems has become an important arena, including in policy initiation and implementation (Jörgensen et al., 2015). Yet, central governments in developing countries tend to have more financial and human resources, compared with local governments, which hamper the institutional capacity of the latter (De Oliveira, 2002).

Ethiopia decentralized under a federal system which was carried out in two phases. The first round in the early 1990s devolved power to regions with partial autonomy in policy decisions on most development issues. The constitution bestowed substantial decision-making autonomy to the sub-national units, including managing resources under their jurisdiction (Ayenew et al., 2007). The second wave of decentralization introduced in 2002 empowered district governments as the center of socioeconomic development, bringing the government closer to the people (Cheever et al., 2011; Wamai, 2008). This political reform brought the formation of regional environmental authorities, to deal with environmental management at the subnational level (Cheever et al., 2011). Regions establish environmental agencies and related institutions in line with the national environmental council and EPA's direction (Assele et al., 2019). The regional environmental protection agencies have the discretion to make policy decisions in line with the national policy. The decentralized system ultimately increased the participation of lower-level actors, increasing the legitimacy of policies derived from central government.

Keeley and Scoones (2000) observe an increasingly significant relationship between national and subnational policy actors, the federal becoming less important in many policy areas. Particularly for climate adaptation, which is operationalized at the local level, the decentralized structure fostered policy actions. The dissolution of power offered more opportunity for engaging various actors at the subnational level, through coordinated but differentiated responsibilities (Damtie & Bayou, 2008). The subnational scale has got more room for policy maneuver, and the opportunity to reinterpret and transform policies coming from the center. The previously neglected local and indigenous climate practices obtain the opportunity to be sources of policy learning and increase the legitimacy of actions. For instance, new perspectives on watershed management were observed in the Tigray region that advances more integrated conservation farming in non-irrigated areas (Damtie & Bayou, 2008). The roles of the subnational arena are not confined to domestic policy matters in recent years. A noteworthy example is the engagement of the city of Addis Ababa in the C40s[6] global network of urban sustainability informs the changing role of subnational actors beyond the national arena. Transnational networks play a key role in transferring policy ideas, knowledge, and governing mechanisms from which subnational actors obtain a policy capacity. Notwithstanding those positive headways, there are perceived shortcomings in enforcing environmental actions at subnational and local levels. Lack of consistency in regulatory mandates of regional EPAs, coupled with blending environmental departments into other sectors, is one of the observed gaps (Damtie & Bayou, 2008) and local tiers suffered from confusion, lack of clarity, and support (Damtie & Kabada, 2012). Such institutional disparity among regions causes inconsistency in the implementation of the national environmental policy.

Disparities among the federal regions were also typical observations in terms of policy formulation, implementation with the central government. Keeley and Scoones (2000) note that policies were embedded in local settings i.e., the political histories, cultures of regional bureaucracies and administrations, the histories of educational advantage and disadvantage, as well as in ideologies and practices of governance and participation. Virtanen et al., (2011) also note that authentic grassroots consultations were lacking, as the NAPA document was more a product of the federal authorities than of climate change realities felt on the ground. Yet, effective implementation of planned actions in Ethiopia demands local environmental controlling institutions,

---

[6] C40 is a network of the world's megacities committed to addressing climate change.

with necessary instruments and mechanisms for law enforcement (Zinabu et al., 2018). Another limiting factor is the heavy reliance on the federal government for resources as there is no subnational government, except the capital Addis Ababa, that has budgetary self-sufficiency in Ethiopia.

Participation in International Climate Regimes

Global climate governance is a polycentric system and different actors act with different means and ends. Never (2013) connects the participation of countries in global climate regimes to their power in the international arena. The instrumental, structural, and discursive powers shape participations. The first two explain the power of developed and emerging economies like China, that directly influence the negotiation processes. The discursive power explains indirectly influencing the identity, perceptions, and preferences of other actors. Developing countries use a discursive moral power to seek support by raising the alarming vulnerability to climate change for which they did not cause global GHG emissions. Climate policy in Ethiopia occurred within the evolving international governance dynamics that shaped domestic policy. From the outset, the country signed many of the international conventions, including the UNFCCC, the Convention to Combat Desertification, the Cartagena Protocol on Biosafety to the Convention on Biological Diversity, the Kyoto Protocol and the Paris Agreement. Following the UNFCCC ratification, Ethiopia began capacity-building work at the National Meteorological Agency (NMA) organizing a climate change and air pollution research team. Since the ratification of the UNFCCC framework, NMA served even if it was initially formed to monitor the weather and provide a forecast.

Ethiopia's rise to prominence in climate change policy was late but rapid (Held et al., 2013). Ethiopia became more internationally visible in the 2000s, with the 2001 initial communication to UNFCCC and the National Adaptation Program of Action (NAPA) in 2007. The initial communication was the first international document that conceived climate change as a distinct issue of concern. The initial communication acknowledged climate change as a global problem, that requires global action, and states that Ethiopia can contribute to the efforts to slash GHG emissions.[7] Jordan et al. (2018) argue that climate policies are prone to diffusion since the subject requires coordinated action by many, or ideally even all jurisdictions.

The IPCC guideline was adopted in estimating the GHG emissions which indicate the transfer of a new and scientific approach to climate change measurement. However, integrating climate action in Ethiopia's domestic national planning process was less attention. Held et al., (2012) mentioned that the 5-year national development strategy of 2005–2009 hardly mentioned planned climate actions. Donor agencies criticize the government of Ethiopia for not integrating well climate actions in its development planning. Amidst this criticism, the Ministry of Water Resources and

---

[7] Initial National Communication of Ethiopia to the UNFCCC (2001).

NMA developed the NAPA document as per the articles of the UNFCCC, which requires parties to prepare a national adaptation plan. NAPA intended to gain immediate climate finance and technology transfer, substantiated by the low adaptive capacity of the country. NAPA projects were of low priority within the government and have been practically shelved (Virtanen et al., 2011). The lack of political interest in climate actions was one of the main reasons for not implementing NAPA. The period of 2007/2008 global financial crisis also affected access to climate finance as it was in many developing countries. Let us see how some of the global climate regimes shape domestic climate actions here below.

The Clean Development Mechanism and REDD+

The Parties to the UNFCCC in 1997 adopted the Kyoto Protocol to operationalize emissions reductions through, among others, two important mechanisms. These were the Clean Development Mechanism (CDM) and Reducing Emissions from Deforestation and Degradation (REDD+). Both programs intend to address market failure through financially rewarding emission reductions via a carbon market (Mustalahti et al., 2012; Parker et al., 2008). CDM was deemed as the most innovative tool of the Kyoto Protocol (Dechezleprêtre et al., 2008), which witnessed remarkable participation from the developing world (Wara, 2007). Firstly, it attracted more participation, mainly due to its voluntariness to attain measurable mitigation of emissions. Secondly, CDM was found to be low-cost, replicable, and providing benefits in a short time (Brown et al., 2011), backed by the Clean Development Fund (CDF) and the joint implementation framework (Sutter & Parreño, 2007). The strong anticipation of technology transfer, attached to the designing and implementing of CDM projects, made it more attractive to host nations. With these anticipations, Africa alone registered 44 projects in a few years for an anticipated reduction of 55 million tons of CO_2 up to the end of 2012 (Okubo & Michaelowa, 2010).

The population rise in Ethiopia resulted in land-use changes, conversion of forests to farmlands and the high density of livestock also increased GHG emissions. As Watson et al., (2013) state that the benefits of ecosystem services are often overlooked while deforestation and forest degradation are driven largely by private incentives. The focus in Ethiopia is on agricultural intensification, policy on the forest sector stagnated from the mid-1990s undermining institutional structure and resource allocations (Ayana et al., 2013). Amidst this condition, the CDM and REDD+ mechanisms brought climate finance opportunities and EPA prepared to host projects. International Non-Governmental Organisations took the pioneering role in CDM and REDD+ initiatives. CDM started with the Humbo assisted forest regeneration project, led by World Vision backed by the World Bank's Bio-Carbon Fund (Brown et al., 2011). World Vision's prior experience since the time of the conservation program in Ethiopia enabled it to take the lead in CDM projects. EPA's role was confined to support activities, such as defining forests for UNFCCC and issuing acceptance of CDM implementing entities, considering the development role of projects (Bekele et al., 2015). Yet, the uncertainties in the CDM framework caused the regulations developed for licensing carbon finance-related activities to remain shelved (Hoch, 2012). There is consensus that the achievements in CDM in Ethiopia are far less, compared to the potentials and anticipations in Ethiopia. Only two projects obtained certifications for emission reductions.

Many energy sector projects prevailed under the NAMA framework but none of them entered the CDM framework. Around 97% of Ethiopia's electricity generated is produced by hydropower plants whose grid emission factor is very low. This structural condition limits the potential to generate CERs under the current baseline rules of CDM. Domestic and international factors account for the limited achievements in this market mechanism. Okubo and Michaelowa (2010) note that CDM subsidies were also mostly spent on capacity building and project development so that the support could not mobilize a significant number of projects. The decline in the global emission certification prices discouraged certifications, as is the case in many low-income countries. Held et al. (2013) mention the extremely onerous requirements for registering land-use and forestry projects, and their exclusion from the European Emissions Trading System. Hoch (2012) notes that the case in Ethiopia has been strongly driven by the global regime level shaping the regulatory mechanisms. For example, most of the communication about the Jumbo CDM project was through World Vision, other national actors had only a marginal role.

The REDD+ process also had a stronger connection with non-state actors in Ethiopia. Pioneer REDD+ projects began soon after the endorsement of the Kyoto Protocol. Norway was the financer for the Bale REDD+ project, initiated by FARM Africa/SOS Sahel and the Oromia region Forest and Wildlife Enterprise (Gonzalo et al., 2017). FARM Africa, and SOS Sahel had a strong presence in Participatory Forest Management (PFM) in Ethiopia which helped in endorsing projects and the governance architecture. The REDD+ evolved through different policies from the government forest plan in the PASDEP 2005/5–2009/10 to tax incentives for farmers who plant trees on their land as stipulated in the 2007 forest policy. At this stage emissions reduction was not a prescribed goal by the government. The 2010 NAMA plan stressed reducing deforestation and securing carbon sequestration through reforestation and sustainable management of existing forests. This REDD+ policy became integrated into the Climate Resilient Green Economy (CRGE) Strategy that underscored forest carbon sequestration as one of its four pillars. Several REDD+ institutions emerged such as the national REDD+ Secretariate, REDD+ Steering Committee (RSC), and REDD+ Technical Working Group (RTWG). The global regimes such as the Warsaw Framework contributed to framing the REDD+ goals within CRGE. These institutional arrangements are also cascaded down and vertically integrated to the sub-national level in pursuit of preparedness for funding from the Forest Carbon Partnership Facility (FCPF) and other sources. Developing safeguarding instruments is an essential aspect to ensure social and environmental risks during the implementation of REDD+ projects. Although Ethiopia has the EIA proclamation, its scope was not enough for REDD+, thus it developed four instruments. These instruments include the Strategic Environmental and Social Assessment, Environmental and Social Management Framework, Resettlement Policy Framework, and Process

Framework (Gonzalo et al., 2017). Finally, both the CDM and REDD+ processes inform that the frameworks pass through a complex governance arrangement, from global regimes to the local level. As Newell et al. (2009) note, a plurality of actors, dispersed authority, and network-oriented initiatives reshuffle institutions in host countries.

Ethiopia and the Copenhagen Negotiation

The period after COP12 in Nairobi in 2006 manifests growing African efforts to take part in global climate negotiations. Two initiatives were observed in the regional climate change deals: the Nairobi Work Programme on Impacts, Vulnerability, and Adaptation on one hand and the Nairobi Framework on the other (Held et al., 2013). The first focuses on assessing vulnerability to climate change and craft adaptation measures, while the latter is aimed at helping sub-Saharan Africa countries participate in the Clean Development Mechanism (CDM). As Roger and Belliethathan (2016) mention, the number of submissions to the UNFCCC by African states and the Africa Group of Negotiators (AGN) increased substantially. The goal of AGN was seizing opportunities, especially funding for climate actions in the continent. The regional momentum and the subsequent preparation for the Copenhagen summit elevated Ethiopia's international visibility. The Conference of African states on Climate Change in 2009 convened leaders from eight states, including Ethiopia, and the platform promoted the climate change policy agenda in Ethiopia (Held et al., 2013). The conference nominated the Prime Minister of Ethiopia, Meles Zenawi, to represent Africa which shaped the negotiations on climate finance at Copenhagen considerably. Vidal (2009) writes that Prime Minister Meles Zenawi played a more pronounced role in Copenhagen, dominating the conversation around African nations' calling for robust financial packages for climate actions. The call for climate finance sought to secure $30 billion in "new and additional" funding for 2010–2012 and $100 billion by 2020. The event marked Africa's voice in history as a unified whole claiming a compensatory financial package for climate actions. Mr. Zenawi also negotiated to give developing countries control over the disbursal of funds and asked for an intergovernmental panel that would monitor and address issues related to the financial pledges. The creation of the High-Level Advisory Group on Climate Change Financing, in which Mr. Zenawi became the Co-Chair was the result of the negotiation (Roger & Belliethathan, 2016). This momentum transformed Africa's and Ethiopia's position from marginal participant to key player at the UNFCCC through a claimed policy space in the global climate governance. Consequently, the size of Ethiopia's delegation increased from three persons at COP12 in 2006 in Nairobi to forty-seven at Copenhagen three years later (Held et al., 2013).

Ethiopia obtained a renewed leadership role in the African Union until COP17 in Durban and became the chair of the High-Level Advisory Group on Climate Change Financing that studies various alternatives for monitoring and delivering the financial pledges made at Copenhagen. These regional and international engagements have led to a raft of new initiatives and institutional structures domestically. It includes, among others, the development of Nationally Appropriate Mitigation Actions (NAMA), a voluntary emission reduction submitted to the UNFCCC, and the Ethiopian Programme of Action on Climate Change (EPACC). NAMA aimed to unleash the huge potential of renewable energy resources but was criticized for not including essential actions in land use planning and energy efficiency policy measures. While EPACC replaced the 2007 NAPA with a more programmatic approach to adaptation, NAMA included various sectors through projects and has been registered by UNFCCC. Ethiopia's continued involvement, such as in chairing of the Least Developed Countries (LDC) Group at UN climate change negotiations, has bestowed it with new partnership opportunities. For instance, the strategic partnership with Norway and the UK that focused on forestry, agriculture, energy, MRV, and biodiversity prevailed, following the conference in Cancún.

Towards Green Economy Strategy

The post-Copenhagen period marked the introduction of a new horizon in the environmental politics of Ethiopia. The country endorsed a green economy policy that was publicized at the Durban conference in 2011, signalling a shift away from antagonizing environmental actions and economic development. The essence of the green economy was first coined in the book *Blueprint for a Green Economy* by Pearce et al., (1989) in response to the undervaluation of environmental and social costs. The intent was to correct the pricing system to produce a more favourable environmental outcome (Le Blanc, 2011). The post-2008 financial crisis reinvigorated the green economy discourse, major international organizations also redefined it in their global interventions. The United Nations Environmental Programme (UNEP) described it as a low-carbon, resource-efficient, and socially inclusive economic development (UNEP, 2011). The Organization for Economic Cooperation and Development (OECD) alternatively used green growth to reveal development that ensures the continuation of environmental resources and services (OECD, 2011), while the World Bank added cleanliness through reducing pollution, environmental damages, and building resilience to natural hazards (World Bank, 2012). Death (2015) extends the narrative of the green economy in four dimensions: resilience, growth, transformation, and revolution. While resilience and green growth do not deviate from the above conceptions, the transformational and revolutionary lenses entail a fundamental shift in the development process, the scope of visibility goes up to planetary and civilizational.

At the core of the development goal of Ethiopia is poverty reduction. The country looks at boosting agricultural productivity, strengthening industrial production, and boosting export (Medhin & Mekonnen, 2019; Okereke et al., 2019). Ethiopia's green economy policy intends to achieve a low carbon and fast-growth economy goal while building resilience for the present and anticipated climate shocks. This ideational shift reveals that the conventional development path is perceived to result in a higher rate of GHG emissions and the degradation of natural resources. Freire (2017) argues that a green economy is a superior policy approach for African countries to advance sustainable and inclusive growth. Development partners like the World Bank also integrated the idea of a green economy into the development assistance packages that inspired countries like Ethiopia to go for it. The strategy in Ethiopia anticipates a low carbon transition in key economic sectors that are more prone to climate change or yield a potential to reduce emissions. Although the environmental policy of Ethiopia aspired to consider long-term environmental protection over economic gains, incorporating environmental and social costs into development planning was not evident until the adoption of the green strategy. The anticipation regarding the green economy is not because the country is of high emission, but because economic opportunities are foreseen through emission reduction initiatives. The latest five-year national development plans, the Growth and Transformation Plans (GTPs) of 2010–2020 were devised with the underlying green development paradigm. For instance, GTP I (2011–2015) envisaged a Gross Domestic Product growth rate of 11% in pursuit of middle-income status (Lavinia, 2017), while building 8000 MW of energy including from the Grand Ethiopia Renaissance Dam (GERD) (Fig. 8.2).

The discursive shift towards green economy is rooted in the paradigm of ecological modernization which conceive environmental issues as positive-sum games of economic growth and environmental solutions (Hajer, 1995). Climate change is still a barrier to development, but it is also considered as an opportunity, through harnessing Ethiopia's vast renewable resources mainly hydropower (Okereke et al., 2019). The resource endowments are envisaged to tackle some of the economic risks, identifying

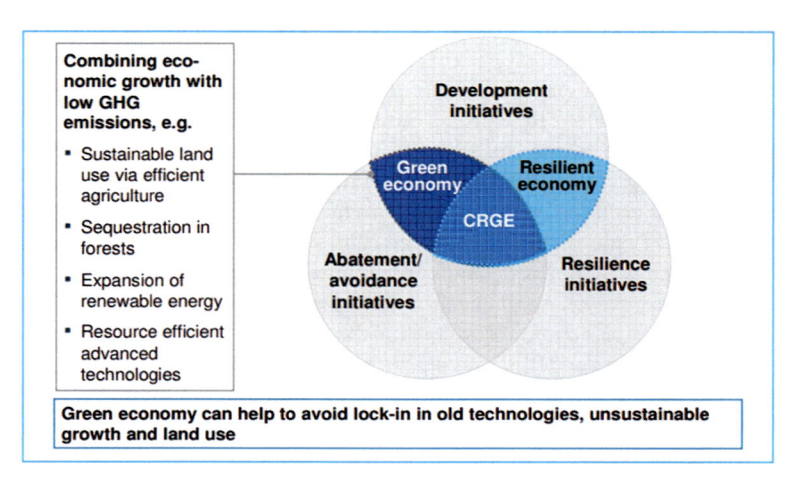

Fig. 8.2 The green economy pathway and its components[8]

---

[8] The Climate-Resilient Green Economy strategy of Ethiopia. 2011 p. 21.

the lowest-cost GHG abatement options, and attracting international finance (Medhin & Mekonnen, 2019). There is a strong indication that green growth leads to poverty reduction, reduced vulnerability to climate change, greater energy security, and more secure livelihoods (World Bank, 2012). Notwithstanding the promises of the green economy strategy, there are implementation challenges in a low-income country that wrestles with complex socio-economic problems. Le Blanc (2011) notes that the efficacy and appropriateness of the green economy to transition is still unclear, despite the recognition bestowed in any of the above narratives. Implementing a green development strategy requires passing, above all, through the stress of advancing rapid economic development to halt chronic poverty. It needs significant investment over a long period, taking advantage of technology innovations to avoid locking in inefficient and costly technology and infrastructure (OECD, 2011). The efforts to switch to cleaner sources of energy are tougher ambitions for Ethiopia that require, among others, a large amount of capital and technology. The latest political instabilities and reshuffling of the institutions, including the downgrading of the Ministry of Environment from its cabinet status, also hamper the institutional capacity to enforce the green economy policy.

Conclusion

Climate change is perceived to remain as one of the top challenges to development and social stability in Ethiopia. The discourses and institutions underlying climate actions have witnessed incremental amelioration from narrow state conservation programs in the 1970s to participatory and broader frameworks including the late green economy strategy. The conservation campaigns of early times were focusing on ensuring food security in drought-prone areas. So that the actions were attached to food aid in these communities as an incentive to develop degraded areas. The ineffective state conservationism of early times served as a learning exercise from which participatory approach became a vital component of environmental policy in the 1990s. The 1990s political reforms played a paramount role in unveiling the formation of environmental institutions, both at the federal and subnational levels. Although it lacks specific policy instruments, the Environmental Policy adopted in 1997 remains the main policy regarding the environment and the management of natural resources in general. While administrative reforms led to the federal and local level dissolution of power, the international momentum towards sustainable development paradigm motivated new forms of environmental governance in Ethiopia. The attachment of aid to the inclusion of sustainable development issues in development planning was manifested in some of the national programs, influencing the discursive framing of policies and institutions. For instance, the introduction of the Kyoto Protocol through the CDM and the REDD+ programs shaped the mitigation dimension of the climate interventions as a learning platform. Learning from these regimes, together with the participation in other climate change regimes in the 2000s led to the adoption of the green economy paradigm. Ethiopia's endowment in the abundance of water resources enables to push for green development by shifting to renewable energy from hydropower. The green transformation realm can ensure resilience and emissions reduction if successfully backed by the anticipated energy transition and systemic interventions across scales. However, accessing sufficient climate finance for the major projects that would shift the energy sector can be a major hurdle. The absence of a national emissions trading scheme, a carbon tax, or carbon capture and storage systems remains a gap in advancing climate policy, although efforts to establish are underway. Nonetheless, the 64% carbon emissions reduction goal by 2030 can be considered as one of the most determined plans ever presented from low-income countries. Particularly the renewable energy access to the wider rural population has huge potential to reduce deforestation which is a major source of carbon emission. In addition to the 70% of the population that does not access electricity in the rural areas, the national electricity demand will exceed the supply of installed hydropower capacity at present. The green economy pathway which is significantly based on hydropower offers a promising policy direction to clean energy access and low carbon transition. In addition to promoting domestic institutional capability, Ethiopia needs to strengthen its climate diplomacy to access further climate finance in the next decade to reach the transition goal.

References

Adhikari, U., Nejadhashemi, A. P., & Woznicki, S. A. (2015). "Climate change and Eastern Africa: A review of impact on major crops." *Food and Energy Security, 4*(2), 110–32, https://doi.org/10.1002/fes3.61

Alemu, T., & Mengistu, A. (2019). "Impacts of climate change on food security in Ethiopia: Adaptation and mitigation options: A review." *Climate Change Management*, 397–412. https://doi.org/10.1007/978-3-319-75004-0_23

Assele, A. A., Aberra, Y., & Diriba, D. (2019). "Trends and regulatory challenges of environmental institutions: Evidence from federal and selected regions of Ethiopia." *Environmental Management and Sustainable Development*, 8(2), 42. https://doi.org/10.5296/emsd.v8i2.14603

Ayana, A. N., Arts, B., & Wiersum, K. F. (2013). Historical development of forest policy in Ethiopia: Trends of institutionalization and deinstitutionalization. *Land Use Policy, 32*, 186–196. https://doi.org/10.1016/j.landusepol.2012.10.008

Ayana, A. N., Arts, B., & Wiersum, K. F. (2018). How environmental NGOs have influenced decision making in a 'Semi-Authoritarian' state: The case of forest policy in Ethiopia. *World Development, 109*, 313–322. https://doi.org/10.1016/j.worlddev.2018.05.010

Ayenew, M., Assefa, T., & Gebre-Egziabher, T. (2007). A rapid assessment of wereda decentralization in Ethiopia. *Decentralization in Ethiopia*, 69–101.

Bekele, M. (2008). "Ethiopia's environmental policies, strategies and programs." *Digest of Ethiopia's national policies, strategies, and programs*, (pp. 337–69).

Bekele, M., Yemiru T., Zerihun M., Solomon Z., Yibeltal T., Maria B., & Habtemariam, K. (2015). The context of REDD+ in Ethiopia: Drivers, agents and institutions. Vol. 127. CIFOR.

Bekele, W., & Drake, L. (2003). Soil and water conservation decision behaviour of subsistence farmers in the eastern highlands of Ethiopia: A case study of the Hunde-Lafto area. *Ecological Economics, 46*(3), 437–451. https://doi.org/10.1016/s0921-8009(03)00166-6

Brown, D. R., Dettmann, P., Rinaudo, T., Tefera, H., & Tofu, A. (2011). Poverty alleviation and environmental restoration using the clean development mechanism: A case study from

Humbo, Ethiopia. *Environmental Management, 48*(2), 322–333. https://doi.org/10.1007/s00267-010-9590-3

César, E., & Anders, E. (2013). Ethiopia environmental and climate change policy brief. Sida's helpdesk for environment and climate change.

Cheever, M., Graichen, K., Homeier, D., Howell, J., Kefauver, O., & Kimball, T. (2011). *"Environmental policy review: Key issues in Ethiopia 2011"*. Colby College Environmental Studies Program.

Conway, D., & Schipper, E. L. (2011). Adaptation to climate change in Africa: Challenges and opportunities identified from Ethiopia. *Global Environmental Change, 21*(1), 227–237. https://doi.org/10.1016/j.gloenvcha.2010.07.013

Damtie, M., & Bayou, M. (2008). Overview of environmental impact assessment in Ethiopia: Gaps and challenges. MELCA.

Death, C. (2015). Four discourses of the green economy in the global South. *Third World Quarterly, 36*(12), 2207–2224. https://doi.org/10.1080/01436597.2015.1068110

Dejene, M., & Cochrane, L. (2019). Ethiopia's developmental state: A building stability framework assessment. *Development Policy Review, 37*, 161–178. https://doi.org/10.1111/dpr.12414

Freire, M. E. (2017). *"Urbanization and green growth in Africa."* Growth dialogue.

Gonzalo, J., Zewdie, S., Tenkir, E., & Moges, Y. (2017). "REDD+ and carbon markets: The Ethiopian process." *Managing Forest Ecosystems: The Challenge of Climate Change*, 151–83. https://doi.org/10.1007/978-3-319-28250-3_8

Gubena, A. F. (2016). Environmental impact assessment in Ethiopia: A general review of history, transformation and challenges hindering full implementation. *Journal of Environment and Earth Science, 6*(1), 1–9.

Hajer, M. A. (1995). *The politics of environmental discourse: Ecological modernization and the policy process.* Clarendon Press.

Held, D., Nag, E.-M., & Roger, C. (2012). *The governance of climate change in developing countries: A report on international and domestic climate change politics in China, Brazil, Ethiopia, and Tuvalu.* Agence française de développement.

Held, D., Roger, C., & Nag, E.-M. (2013). "Ethiopia's path to a climate-resilient green economy." *Climate Governance in the Developing World*, 218–37.

Hoben, A. (1995). Paradigms and politics: The cultural construction of environmental policy in Ethiopia. *World Development, 23*(6), 1007–1021. https://doi.org/10.1016/0305-750X(95)00019-9

Hoben, A. (1996). "The cultural construction of environmental policy: Paradigms and politics in Ethiopia." *The lie of the land: Challenging received wisdom on the African environment*, (186–208). James Currey Ltd.

Hoch, S. (2012). *Governing clean development in LDCs: Do CDM rules promote renewable energy in Ethiopia?* Albert-Ludwigs-Universitat Freiburg.

Hovden, E., & Lindseth, G. (2004). Discourses in norwegian climate policy: National action or thinking globally? *Political Studies, 52*(1), 63–81. https://doi.org/10.1111/j.1467-9248.2004.00464.x

Hurni, H. (1988). Degradation and conservation of the resources in the Ethiopian highlands. *Mountain Research and Development, 8*(2/3), 123. https://doi.org/10.2307/3673438

Jordan, A., Huitema, D., Van Asselt, H., & Forster, J. (2018). *Governing climate change: Polycentricity in action?* University Press.

Jörgensen, K., Jogesh, A., & Mishra, A. (2015). Multi-level climate governance and the role of the subnational level. *Journal of Integrative Environmental Sciences, 12*(4), 235–245. https://doi.org/10.1080/1943815x.2015.1096797

Keeley, J., & Scoones, I. (2000). Knowledge, power and politics: The environmental policy-making process in Ethiopia. *The Journal of Modern African Studies, 38*(1), 89–120. https://doi.org/10.1017/s0022278x99003262

Lavinia, R. (2017). *"Towards the decarbonization of the economy: A comparative study between Sweden, China, and Ethiopia."* Master's Thesis. Lund University.

Le Blanc, D. (2011). "Special issue on green economy and sustainable development." In *Natural resources forum*, (Vol. 35(3), pp. 151–154). Blackwell Publishing Ltd.

Leipold, S., Feindt, P. H., Winkel, G., & Keller, R. (2019). Discourse analysis of environmental policy revisited: Traditions, trends, perspectives. *Journal of Environmental Policy Planning, 21*(5), 445–463. https://doi.org/10.1080/1523908x.2019.1660462

Litfin, K. (1994). *Ozone discourses: Science and politics in global environmental cooperation.* University Press.

Maxwell, S., & Belshaw, D. (1990). *"Food-for-development: New roles for food aid in Ethiopia."* World food programme food-for-development mission, World Food Programme.

Medhin, H., & Mekonnen, A. (2019). *Green and climate-resilient transformation in Ethiopia.* Oxford University Press.

Mellese, D., & Salamon, K. (2012). *The need for redesigning and redefining institutional roles for environmental governance in Ethiopia.* MELCA-Ethiopia.

Michael, C., & Belshaw, D. (1986). The Ethiopian highlands reclamation study: Major findings and recommendations. In *ONCCP (Office of the national committee for central planning). Towards a food and nutrition strategy for Ethiopia: Proceedings of the national workshop on food strategies for Ethiopia,* (pp. 8–12).

Motuma, F. Y. (2017). "A review on policy change for climate change in Ethiopia." *Journal of Resources Development and Management, 2*(2), 1.2.

Mulugeta, G. (2013). Defiance of environmental governance: Environmental impact assessment in Ethiopian floriculture industry. *Journal of Environmental Research and Management, 4*(4), 219–229.

Mustalahti, I., Bolin, A., Boyd, E., & Paavola, J. (2012). "Can REDD+ reconcile local priorities and needs with global mitigation benefits? Lessons from Angai forest, Tanzania." *Ecology and Society, 17*(1). https://doi.org/10.5751/es-04498-170116

Newell, P., Jenner, N., & Baker, L. (2009). Governing clean development: A framework for analysis. *Development Policy Review, 27*(6), 717–739. https://doi.org/10.1111/j.1467-7679.2009.00467.x

Okereke, C., Coke, A., Geebreyesus, M., Ginbo, T., Wakeford, J. J., & Mulugetta, Y. (2019). Governing green industrialisation in Africa: Assessing key parameters for a sustainable socio-technical transition in the context of Ethiopia. *World Development, 115,* 279–290. https://doi.org/10.1016/j.worlddev.2018.11.019

Okubo, Y., & Michaelowa, A. (2010). Effectiveness of subsidies for the clean development mechanism: Past experiences with capacity building in Africa and LDCs. *Climate and Development, 2*(1), 30–49. https://doi.org/10.3763/cdev.2010.0032

De Oliveira, J. A. P. (2002). "Implementing environmental policies in developing countries through decentralization: The case of protected areas in Bahia, Brazil". *World Development, 30*(10), 1713–36. https://doi.org/10.1016/S0305-750X(02)00067-0

Organization for economic cooperation and development. (2011). Towards green growth: Monitoring progress. *OECD Publishing.* https://doi.org/10.1787/22229523

Parker, C., Mitchell, A., Trivedi, M., & Mardas, N. (2008). *"The little REDD book: A guide to governmental and non-governmental proposals for reducing emissions from deforestation and degradation."* Global Canopy Program.

Pearce, D. W., Markandya, A., & Barbier, E. (1989). *EB, 1989. Blueprint for a green economy.* Earth scan Publication.

Rahmato, D. (2001). Environmental change and state policy in Ethiopia: Lessons from past experience. *Forum for Social Studies Monograph Series, 2,* 10–108.

Roger, C., & Belliethathan, S. (2016). Africa in the global climate change negotiations. *International Environmental Agreements: Politics, Law and Economics, 16*(1), 91–108.

Rondinelli, D. A., Nellis, J. R., & Cheema, G. S. (1983). Decentralization in developing countries. *World bank staff working paper, 581.*

Simane, B., Beyene, H., Deressa, W., Kumie, A., Berhane, K., & Samet, J. (2016). Review of climate change and health in Ethiopia: Status and gap analysis. *Ethiopian Journal of Health Development, 30*(1), 28–41.

Sutter, C., & Parreño, J. C. (2007). "Does the current clean development mechanism (CDM) deliver its sustainable development claim? An analysis of officially registered CDM projects." *Climatic Change, 84*(1), 75–90. https://doi.org/10.1007/s10584-007-9269-9

Tedla, S., & Lemma, K. (1998). Environmental management in Ethiopia: Have the national conservation plans worked? *OSSREA*.

Thorme, M. (1990). "Establishing environment as a human right". *The Denver Journal of International Law & Policy, 19*(2).

United Nations Environmental Program. (2011). *"Towards a green economy: Pathways to sustainable development and poverty eradication.* UNEP.

Vidal, J. (2009). "Copenhagen climate summit in disarray after 'Danish text leak". *The Guardian, 8.*

Virtanen, P., Palmujoki, E., & Gemechu, D. T. (2011). "Global climate policies, local institutions and food security in a pastoral society in Ethiopia". *Consilience,* (5), 96–118.

Wamai, R. G. (2008). *Reforming health systems: The role of NGOs in decentralization-lessons from Kenya and Ethiopia.* International Society for Third Sector Research.

Wara, M. (2007). *Measuring the clean development mechanism's performance and potential.* Stanford University.

Watson, C., Mourato, S., & Milner-Gulland, E. J. (2013). "Uncertain emission reductions from forest conservation: REDD in the Bale mountains, Ethiopia". *Ecology and Society, 18*(3). https://doi.org/10.5751/es-05670-180306

Worku, H. (2017). Mainstreaming environmental impact assessment as a tool for environmental management in Ethiopia: Current challenges and directions for future improvements. *Environmental Quality Management, 26*(4), 75–95. https://doi.org/10.1002/tqem.21506

World Bank. (2012). *Inclusive green growth: The pathway to sustainable development.* World Bank Publications. The World Bank.

Zegeye, H. (2018). Climate change in Ethiopia: Impacts, mitigation and adaptation. *International Journal of Research in Environmental Studies, 5*(1), 18–35.

Zinabu, E., Kelderman, P., van der Kwast, J., & Irvine, K. (2018). Impacts and policy implications of metals effluent discharge into rivers within industrial zones: A Sub-Saharan perspective from Ethiopia. *Environmental Management, 61*(4), 700–715. https://doi.org/10.1007/s00267-017-0970-9

Mathias N. Bimir is a research student at the division of environment and sustainability, the Hong Kong University of Science and Technology. A former lecturer in public policy and development management in Ethiopia, his work now focuses on climate policy processes and sustainability transitions in developing countries. He is currently working on his thesis on climate policy processes, policy integration, and policy networks in the context of Ethiopia.

Chapter 9
Emerging Frontiers of Energy Transition in Sri Lanka

Gz. MeeNilankco Theiventhran

Abstract Energy transitions in the global South have evolved over time and space. Climate emergency has pushed countries towards renewables, and energy transitions have been part of the international political discourse coupled with climate commitments. Exploring the complex and diverse interactions between energy transitions and climate change mitigation is essential, especially to the global South, where on the one hand, it is seen as part of the development discourse and on the other as honouring the international climate commitments. There is a growing need to identify and analyse potential social and economic disruption arising from energy transition, taking into account policies and strategies to ensure equitable energy systems and minimise if not pre-empt disruption. Examining the patterns of the energy transition, dynamics of transition from a justice perspective in the overall socio-political and economic contexts will outline the emerging frontiers of the energy transition. This chapter looks at the challenges of escaping the carbon lock-in using an analytical framework where the interplay between agents and the nexus—climate commitments, energy security and justice—is analysed with the socio-politico-economic considerations to understand the trajectories of energy transitions. The framework brings fresh insights into understanding the carbon lock-out pathways in the global South context through the case study from Sri Lanka. It is argued that a holistic policy framework for energy transitions must incorporate democratic concerns from below to create pathways for just energy transition.

Introduction

Climate change is widely seen as a crisis, and governments worldwide have acknowledged it and have formulated international treaties and climate commitments. There is ample academic scholarship to prove that climatic changes have created existential threats to human societies in the age of anthropogenic global warming. Research has

Gz. M. Theiventhran (✉)
Department of Computer Science, Electrical Engineering and Mathematical Science, Western Norway University of Applied Science, Bergen, Norway
e-mail: Gnaalazcirthy.Meenilankco.Theiventhran@hvl.no

shown that climate change affects more in the global South than in the global North due not least to population, economic vulnerability and governance issues (Aiken et al., 2017; Blicharska et al., 2017; Udin, 2017). In the fight to save the planet, energy has become one of the critical areas where drastic changes are required. Forging transitions towards green energy solutions in the global South is thus a key concern for mitigating climate change, reducing societal vulnerability and fostering development.

Energy transitions refer to profound changes in energy systems. They involve many interconnected elements: political will, regional and global political interests, policy instruments, energy providers, delivery systems, technology, innovation, and end-users (Hoggett, 2014; Westphal, 2011). The climate emergency has brought decarbonisation and energy transition to the forefront. The Paris Accord of 2015 seeks to limit average global temperature rise to "well below 2 °C" in the present century; to achieve this the global energy transition has to aim for near total decarbonisation of the world energy system by 2050 (IRENA, 2018).

Developing countries increasingly foresee energy transitions as part of their development strategy. Energy security—ensuring enough energy for all—is a significant concern for any developing nation. The UN Paris Climate Change Conference and the ensuing Paris Agreement require every country in the world to make plans for and commit to reducing emissions. This has created considerable policy challenges. The shift in energy systems has predominantly focused on technology and finance, seeking to address the challenge of climate change through strategies for ecological modernisation that involve multiple stakeholders (Newell, 2018). Over the past decade, renewable energy diffusion has thus been pursued through private investments, multilateral and bilateral assistance and the help of novel technologies. There has been less focus on user-oriented strategies or social issues such as climate justice.

Energy transitions are now also viewed from a socio-technical perspective, and the emergence of just transitions literature has given more emphasis on issues of justice in energy transitions (Geels & Schot, 2007; Kern & Smith, 2008). It has been argued that the failure to address the justice issues in energy transitions can create new or reinforce old inequalities (Jenkins et al., 2017). The broader term socio-technical transitions refers to profound structural changes in systems such as energy and transport, which involve long-term and complex reconfigurations of technology, policy, infrastructure, scientific knowledge and social and cultural practices towards sustainable ends (Geels, 2011). The UN Sustainable Development Goal seven calls for access to affordable, sustainable and modern energy for all. It states that a just transition should incorporate social and economic considerations, with equity and 'leaving no one behind' as guiding principles (UN, 2017).

In the recent academic literature, innovation has received much attention, especially regarding sustainability transitions. Innovations act in multiple ways as both 'push' and 'pull' factors driving the energy transition. Advances in technology, improved efficiency, and cost reduction have made renewable energy a competitive alternative and central to the energy transition discourse. There is, however, a widespread concern that the renewable energy sector has yet to make emerging new clean energy technologies such as solar and wind accessible to low-income communities, both rural and urban. Clean energy companies continue to market their products primarily to commercial customers, financially capable of adopting new technologies for economic gain. Those less well-off still await their turn, as they have done in the past. Investment and innovation remain a major challenge for developing countries to induce renewable energy systems into the policy mix.

For policymakers in developing countries, ensuring energy security while adhering to climate commitments and guaranteeing energy justice is a challenge. Various drivers and barriers influence the energy transition pathways. The dialectical relationship between energy justice, energy security and climate commitment shapes policy. While the current climate commitments of states are geared towards achieving the envisioned 2050 target, IRENA (2021, 9) and others note that the transition speed is far from what is needed to be in line with the Paris Agreement. In order to achieve the 2050 target, the commitments need to reflect in policies. IRENA (2021, 9) also points out that if these policies are not fully implemented, emissions could potentially rise by 27% over the coming three decades. This encapsulates the importance of policy advancement and its challenges in energy transitions.

There is growing literature on the policy challenges in energy transitions in developing countries (Saculsan & Mori, 2020; Murshed, 2021). However, there has been little research that describes and explains the energy transitions in the light of climate commitments and justice. This chapter tries to address this knowledge gap by looking at how entanglements between climate commitments, energy security, and justice shape policy advancement and how the interlinkages between government, private sector, and the public shape energy transition. Against this backdrop and through a case study of Sri Lanka, the chapter addresses the following question: How has Sri Lanka progressed on a decarbonised development path through energy transitions? The chapter uses agency theory to understand the situated actors' and agentic processes in the energy transition in the case of Sri Lanka.

Building on existing literature, the next section outlines an analytical framework that centres on notions of carbon lock-in. Section "Methods" introduces the case study by contextualising Sri Lanka's energy landscape. The research methods are presented in Section "Sri Lanka's Energy Landscape" and followed by the framework's operationalisation through the Sri Lankan case study in Section "Analysis and Discussion". Finally, the analytical conclusions in Section "Conclusions" argue that the energy transition pathways are determined and regularised by national priorities rather than international climate commitments and the question of justice remains peripheral and detached from the state's energy transition discourse.

Analytical Framework: Unlocking the Carbon Lock-in

There is a tendency of carbon-intensive systems to persist over time and delay low carbon alternatives, which has come to be known as the "carbon lock-in." It happens due to single or multiple factors—economic, technical, political and institutional—and has a large impact, influencing the decisions that characterize our lives (Erickson et al., 2015). The social and institutional connection between fossil fuels and the ways in which we use energy has tenacious powers that are extremely resistant to change. Despite the climate impacts being known and the availability of cost-effective alternatives, the inertia of high carbon systems poses challenges for policymakers that are very hard to overcome. Carbon-intensive development trajectories are sustained and reinforced through path-dependent processes (Berkhout, 2002; Unruh, 2000). This section develops an analytical framework for understanding the role of agency in carbon lock-in and identifies the possible pathways to "loosen" the carbon lock-in.

The framework contains two triads (Fig. 9.1). The energy transition is taking place as an outcome of the contended appositeness of these two triads. Firstly, energy transition does not occur in an automatic and mechanistic way in a vacuum; agency plays a key role as policy, finance, politics, and society need to be in line to achieve the transition. In any energy transition, three key agents shape the transition and its pathways, namely, government, private sector, and the public. This is represented in the left-hand triad. These agents influence and are influenced by a second triad: a nexus of climate commitments, energy security and justice concerns.

The latter triad delineates a state's energy transition pathways. For every government, energy security is a primary concern in energy transition; hence energy is deeply embedded in other sectoral and policy contexts (Goldthau & Sovacool, 2012). Apart from energy being a national security concern, it is also a global concern where governments have committed to decarbonisation, and these climate commitments have a role in charting pathways to energy transition (Kern & Rogge, 2016; Meckling & Hughes, 2018). At the local level, energy justice forms the core of energy transition discourse, and people at the lowest level of the power structure and in the peripheries face justice issues (Healy & Barry, 2017; Kumar, 2018; Mulvaney, 2013). They try to make their voices heard through different avenues and methods.

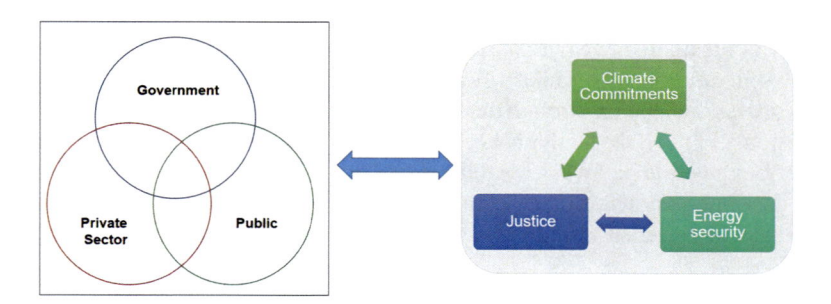

Interplay between triads

Fig. 9.1 Analytical framework of two interlinked triads of energy transitions

Climate Commitments—Energy Security—Justice

The climate commitments of a nation are underlined by its Nationally Determined Contributions (NDCs). One of the vital components for executing the global response to climate change under the UNFCCC Paris Agreement are voluntary commitments to emission reductions called NDCs. NDCs presented to the United Nations Framework Convention on Climate Change (UNFCCC) outline the nation's process to decrease emissions.

Energy security is at the present firmly snared with other energy strategy issues, for example, giving sufficient attention to existing energy structures and relieving environmental impacts (Goldthau, 2011). It is a common perception that energy security implies various things in various circumstances and to various individuals. In 2007 the Asia Pacific Energy Research Centre introduced the "Four As of energy security": availability, accessibility, affordability and acceptability (APERC, 2007). Over the years, indicators for defining energy security have varied. Hippel et al. (2011) presented a 'comprehensive energy security paradigm' with six indicators, whilst a generic framework for the description and analysis of energy security by Hughes (2012) contained three. Sovacool (2011) proposed 20 indicators for energy security. Chester (2010) argues that the concept of energy security has indeed become both 'slippery' and 'multi-dimensional'. The meaning of energy security has varied over the years and in accordance with the needs of the specific sector focus. Through a comprehensive literature review, Christian Winzer (2012) concludes that the common concept driving all energy security definitions is the shortfall of insurance from or versatility in the face of risks brought about by or affecting the energy supply chain.

Energy justice has arisen as another crosscutting research field that tries to apply justice standards to energy strategy, energy creation and frameworks, energy utilisation, energy activism, energy security and environmental change. Energy justice aims to give all people, across all regions, protected, affordable, and manageable energy. It is defined in three subsets. The first fundamental of energy equity is distributional justice. This is an inherently spatial idea that addresses both the inconsistent allocation of ecological advantages and impacts and the lopsided appropriation of related duties (Walker, 2009). The second fundamental is procedural justice, which aims for fair strategies that involve all partners in a non-prejudicial manner (Bullard, 2005; Walker, 2009). All parties ought to have the option to participate and their choices ought to be considered continually. This requires cooperation, fair-mindedness and transparency by government and industry (Davies, 2006) as well as the fitting and thoughtful commitment systems (Todd & Zografos, 2005). The third fundamental of energy justice is recognition justice. Recognition is not equivalent to cooperation; recognition justice is more than resilience and asserts that people should be genuinely addressed, that they should be safeguarded from risks and be offered concrete political rights (Schlosberg, 2013). Fraser (1998) identifies three main categories of misrecognition; cultural domination, non-recognition, and disrespect. This is a very important aspect of environmental justice where the rights of ethnic minorities, underprivileged and marginalized comes into the forefront.

The interconnections between climate commitments, energy justice and energy security pose the following core questions:

1. How might a low-carbon energy transition influence energy security and vice versa?
2. How do climate commitments endanger and empower energy justice?
3. How can energy security challenge and ensure energy justice?

To understand this interplay, it is important to understand the role of agency. The agency plays a role in shaping energy transition pathways. The relationship between government, private sector, the public and resulting dynamics influences energy policymaking and affects the outcomes. Onyx and Bullen (2000, 29) define agency as 'the capacity of the individual to plan and initiate action' and the capacity to react to issues outside of one's immediate range of authority to create an ideal impact. Harvey (2002, 173) defines agency as 'the capacity of persons to transform existing states of affairs'. Bhaskar (2010) describes it as the deliberate causality that achieves a novel situation that would not have happened otherwise. Agency is essential for citizens to be able to influence their social context, and all the more critically to react and rise above misfortune and emergency. It cultivates social activity that enables residents to obtain rights and assets (Horvath, 1998); citizens should know that they have agency. The private sector also has agency based largely on technology/innovation and investment/finance. The public sphere has agency through its institutions, policymaking, governance, and administration.

Interlinkages between these triads and the role of the agency are explored in the energy transition pathways with the related drivers and barriers. The Sri Lankan case study outlines the emerging frontiers in Sri Lanka's energy transitions against the backdrop of the 'climate commitments-energy security-justice' nexus.

Government/State: Indifference and Inertia Towards Sustainability Transitions

Governments play a crucial role in energy transition, where a distinction can be made between top-down and bottom-up approaches. The top-down approach means that state actors engage at the global level in international negotiations on climate mitigation. The other is the bottom-up approach, where local needs and political interests receive priority. Policymaking is determined by the government's balancing act to fulfill these obligations at once local and international. Sustainable energy transitions include a shift of assets between the contending private sector and political electorates. Actors in this process have fluctuating levels of political and financial power. As regards government, the transition literature has looked at the development of socio-technical aspects (Baker et al., 2014; Geels & Schot, 2007; Goldthau & Sovacool, 2012; Smith et al., 2005), political structures and political economy factors (Voß & Bornemann, 2011; Meadowcroft, 2009, 2011; Fouquet, 2016).

Given the importance of energy for economic development and growth, energy security has most often been the priority in energy policymaking. Reduction of greenhouse gases and combating climate change has been identified as a public good with its complex externality problems (Burck et al., 2011). The recent focus on climate change and environmental protection has also been incorporated even though governments have varying opinions on the matter. Since the ratification of the Kyoto protocol in 1998 and the subsequent climate conference in Copenhagen in 2009, many countries could not deliver on their commitments (Löschel et al., 2010; Nordensvärd & Urban, 2011; Ekins & Speck, 2014).

Dolsak (2001) argues that contention between the public and private sector about policies has led to conflicts between national and global priorities. This has made some countries continue their existing energy setups without transitioning due to political risk. Some countries are prepared to act only if global monetary assistance is provided. The third category of developing countries is openly dedicated to combating climate change, even using their limited resources.

Private Sector: New Avenues

In a developing country context, the private sector plays a crucial role in the energy transition. The private sector is important in two key ways. First, new technologies and innovations need to be introduced into the developing countries by the private sector. Second, investments and finance are crucial for any energy transition where states are too poor to support the transition. Energy technologies are central to both the problem and the solution. For Sri Lanka to become a low-carbon society, there is a need to unlock the technological efficiency potential and lower emissions of both energy-supply and end-user applications (Acemoglu et al., 2012; Gillingham et al., 2008; IPCC, 2014). Technologies to reduce energy consumption have been recognised as cost-effective measures to spur a sustainable energy system and attract much attention.

The commercialisation of clean energy technology is inhibited by two externalities associated with 'clean' innovation (Jaffe et al., 2005; Rennings, 2000). Firstly, environmental costs are not reflected in conventional energy generation, to the disadvantage of clean technologies. Secondly, knowledge spillover is often a disincentive to innovation since developers capture only a fraction of the benefits from the knowledge and technological learning they create while incurring almost all costs. Negative market features such as asymmetric information, institutional or regulatory failures, and bounded rationality add to policy intervention's rationale (Gillingham & Sweeney, 2012). Besides, substituting conventional energy is complicated by the "initial installed base advantage" of conventional energy (Veugelers, 2012), which implies a technological lock-in stemming from high returns to scale, network effects and industry standards (Arthur, 1989). These are among key considerations that demand policy measures to encourage clean energy investment (Acemoglu et al., 2012).

Scaling up renewables to meet energy security and environmental goals requires an altogether more significant investment than estimated. While the central part of investment might come from the private sector, public capital suppliers have a significant task to incentivize these private sources. IRENA (2015) report points out that most of the investment needed for renewable energy transition must come from the private sector, and historically it has covered a large share of renewable energy investment, accounting for over 85%. It serves as a critical project implementer and will in the future continue to act as a central driving force of renewable energy deployment (IRENA, 2016). Over the past decade, international organisations have promoted a market-based approach that puts energy, historically a public good, into the private sector's realm and continue to push this to make energy a private commodity. The state's inability to finance the renewable transition and the push from bilateral and multilateral donors to involve the private sector has led the private sector to dominate the energy sector. It is argued that the global energy transition will depend on the ability to develop countries to attract massive levels of investment for the renewable energy markets (IRENA & CPI, 2020; IEA, 2020).

Public: Quest for Justice

Providing clean, safe, reliable, and affordable energy for all is a key challenge that most of the developing world is facing. People are at the centre of the energy transition as prosumers. The choices, preferences, and behaviours of individuals and households are essential to energy transitions. This behavioural factor, along with acceptability and affordability, is essential to a just energy transition. Energy transitions will struggle without sufficient public support (Perlaviciute & Steg, 2015). Investment in specific energy efficiency technologies such as light bulbs and electric vehicles, the adaptation of rooftop solar, construction of windmills or solar parks and energy consumption are all contingent on the public's acceptance and actions. It is also important to communicate that a just energy transition also offers possibilities for inclusive and progressive development. Civil society and social movements can be viewed as a key to problem-solving, including both affirmation and contestation related to market and state activities (Grin et al., 2011).

Methods

The empirical analysis is drawn from a dataset assembled over two years, from September 2018 to January 2021. Primary data was obtained through 36 semi-structured interviews, of which eight were conducted digitally. Secondary data was collected from government policy documents, Cabinet papers, Gazettes, reports, websites, presentation materials and academic literature. Data collection occurred in five phases, out of which two were direct fieldwork, another two were desk research, and one was virtual fieldwork due to the Covid-19 pandemic.

The first phase, conducted between September 2018 and November 2018, focused on understanding the fundamentals of Sri Lanka's energy transition. It mainly contained secondary data. The second phase was the first field visit to Sri Lanka from November to December 2018, when interviews were conducted with government officials, politicians, local level administrators, civil society organizations, private sector and ordinary citizens. Altogether 12 interviews were conducted. The third phase took place between January to October 2019 in the form of desk reviews and email communications. The fourth was fieldwork in Sri Lanka from November 2019 to January 2020, where 16 more interviews were conducted. The final phase of the data collection comprised virtual fieldwork (Skype and Zoom interviews, WhatsApp and Viber chats and email correspondence) and data analysis of the secondary data.

Interviews were conducted in the local languages (Tamil and Sinhala) and were transcribed into English, the coding was done manually and the quotations were categorized into government, private sector and public. They were also coded with reference to energy security, climate commitments and justice. Integration of primary and secondary data produced a dataset that was used to analyze the actors and agency in the energy transition in Sri Lanka.

Sri Lanka's Energy Landscape

Sri Lanka has agreed to make electricity generation 100 per cent renewable as rapidly as possible and by 2050 at the latest (UNDP & ADB, 2017; ADB, 2019). Sri Lanka pledged at the 22nd UNFCCC Conference of Parties in Marrakech, Morocco, as part of the Climate Vulnerable Forum, to use only renewable energy for electricity generation by 2050. At that time—in 2016—52% of Sri Lanka's electricity was generated through fossil fuels (ADB, 2019; World Bank, 2019). Indigenous fossil fuel resources are scarce, so fossil fuels are imported, which amounts to a significant part of Sri Lanka's annual import expenditure. According to the available reports, Sri Lanka's annual electricity consumption growth rate is 2.6%, and electricity sales have an annual increase of 4.9% (CEB, 2019). Sri Lanka has a high energy intensity in the economy, indicating a comparatively high economic output per unit of energy used (CEB, 2019; Central Bank, 2020). Fossil fuels dominate Sri Lanka's primary energy supply sources (see Fig. 9.2).

The share of renewable energy in the primary energy mix is about 46% in 2017, showing a 5.8% reduction compared with 2015 (ADB, 2019). Sri Lanka has almost achieved 100% electrification by 2018; but the areas affected by the civil war in the Northern Province were left behind even though the war ended almost a decade ago (see Fig. 9.3). By 2017, the industrial sector accounted for 24.3%; the transport sector 36.2%; households, commerce, and others accounted for 39.6% of the total energy use (CEB, 2019).

Fig. 9.2 Sri Lanka's energy mix. *Source* SEA 2019

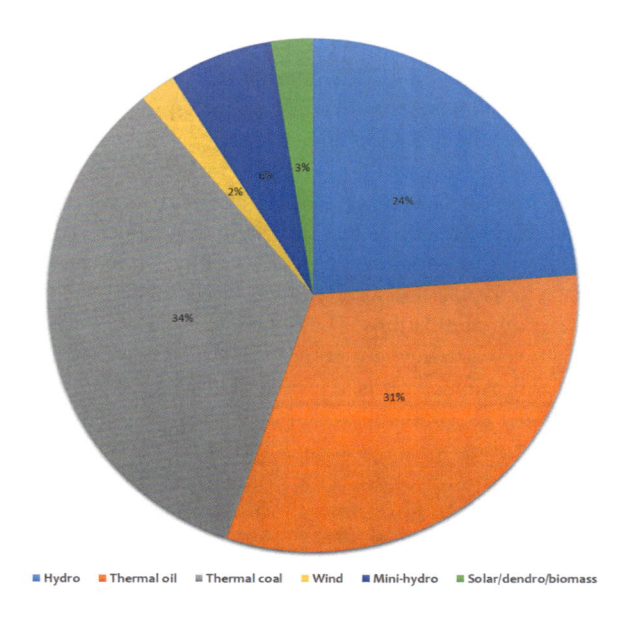

Fig. 9.3 Access to electricity in different provinces breakdown, *Source* CEB annual report 2018

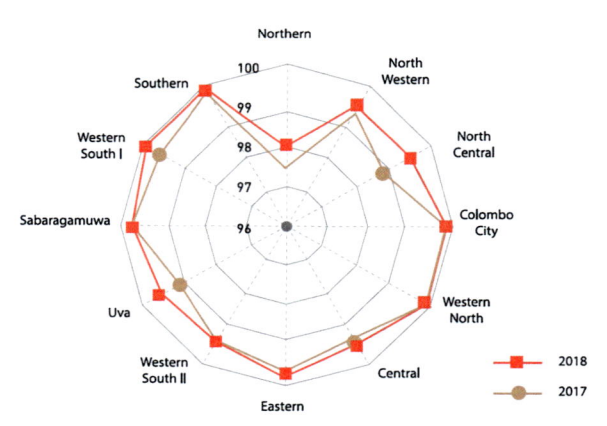

Sri Lanka has ample renewable energy sources (UNDP and ADB 2017, World Bank, 2019). Electricity generation in Sri Lanka was almost 100% from hydropower until mid-1995 (World Bank, 2019). Almost all the economic potential has already been developed for hydropower generation in large-scale power plants, and possible small-scale hydro projects are underway. Due to the increase in electricity demand during the last 25 years, its power generation mix has shifted to a mixed hydro and thermal system. Solar power is abundantly available in Sri Lanka as the country lies within the equatorial belt. There is also good wind energy potential, and it is estimated that Sri Lanka can gain a utilizable wind power potential of 5600 MW, of which only 228 MW has been utilized up to now (CEB, 2020).

In 2006 when the new government took office, it produced the overall development plan 'Mahinda Chintana: Vision for a New Sri Lanka, a ten-year development framework (2006–2016)'. For the energy sector, the framework reads: "*sustainable development of energy resources, conversion facilities and delivery systems to enable access to and use of energy services by the entire population, and the safe, reliable delivery of such energy services at a regionally competitive price, through commercially viable institution subjected to independent regulation.*"

As a follow-up, in June 2008 the Sri Lankan government published National Energy Policy and Strategies, which contained vital policy guidelines that included: providing basic energy needs, ensuring energy security, promoting indigenous resources and protecting the community from the adverse environmental impacts of energy facilities. In March 2015, the Sri Lanka Energy Sector Development Plan for a Knowledge-based Economy 2015–2025 outlined specific targets, and two of them were crucial for increasing renewables in the energy mix: (1) to make Sri Lanka an energy self-sufficient nation by 2030; (2) increase the share of electricity generation from renewable energy sources from 50% in 2014 to 60% by 2020, and finally (3) meet the total demand from renewable and other indigenous energy resources by 2030. In line with this, Sri Lanka submitted its NDCs in September 2016 to UNFCCC.

In 2017, the United Nations Development Programme and Asian Development Bank produced a report on the possible scenarios for achieving '100% electricity through renewable energy in 2050'. In its findings, the report identified the plausible electricity generation mix and financial interventions required for Sri Lanka to achieve its goal, while also highlighting the numerous technical and economic challenges the country is likely to face on its road to 100% renewable energy in the power sector. It also pointed out a fundamental challenge for the policymakers: it estimated that investments around USD 55 billion would be necessary for the power sector to achieve the 100% renewable energy scenario by 2050, while this achievement would save the government USD 19 billion by avoiding the use of imported fossil fuels (UNDP & ADB, 2017).

Analysis and Discussion

The analytical framework described in Section "Analytical Framework: Unlocking the Carbon Lock-in" will be applied to the Sri Lankan case study to analyse the role of agency in the climate commitments-energy security-justice nexus. Special attention is given to how institutional inertia in the government sector contributes to carbon lock-in. Further, the private sector and the public's role in reinforcing carbon lock-in and negated justice will also be discussed.

Agency in Play

The analytical framework's application to the Sri Lankan case is illustrated in an actor centric diagram that outlines the key Sri Lankan actors involved in the energy transitions and climate change (Fig. 9.4). The analysis shows that the modes of the agency are not external to institutions and space; instead, they are tied with institutional resources and processes. This mode of the agency is explained through human-centric accounts of agency, where the qualitative interview data will be used and the analysis will be conceptualized through the framework.

The Sri Lanka government has four ministries that are central within climate and energy. Ministry of Power is tasked with 'Catering to the power requirement of all urban and rural communities based on the long-term power generation plan and providing power supply that establishes the market competitiveness of Sri Lankan businesses and establishing energy security. Ceylon Electricity Board (CEB), which controls electricity generation, transmission, distribution and retailing, is assigned under the ministry. Under this ministry, there is a State Ministry for Solar, Wind and Hydro Power Generation Projects Development, which is tasked with assisting in the formulation of renewable energy projects with the goal of "assuring of obtaining low-cost power." Sri Lanka Sustainable Energy Authority (SLSEA), created through a Parliament Act tasked to facilitate renewable resources and energy efficiency, is under the State ministry's purview. The Ministry of Energy is tasked to focus on petroleum and natural gas, but it also has the broader responsibility to 'formulating policies in the subject of energy' and ensuring the obtainment of low-cost energy. Ceylon Petroleum Corporation, an institution under the Ministry of Energy, provides petroleum to CEB to produce electricity.

The Public Utilities Commission of Sri Lanka (PUCSL) is the economic, technical and safety regulator of the electricity industry. The commission regulates the industry

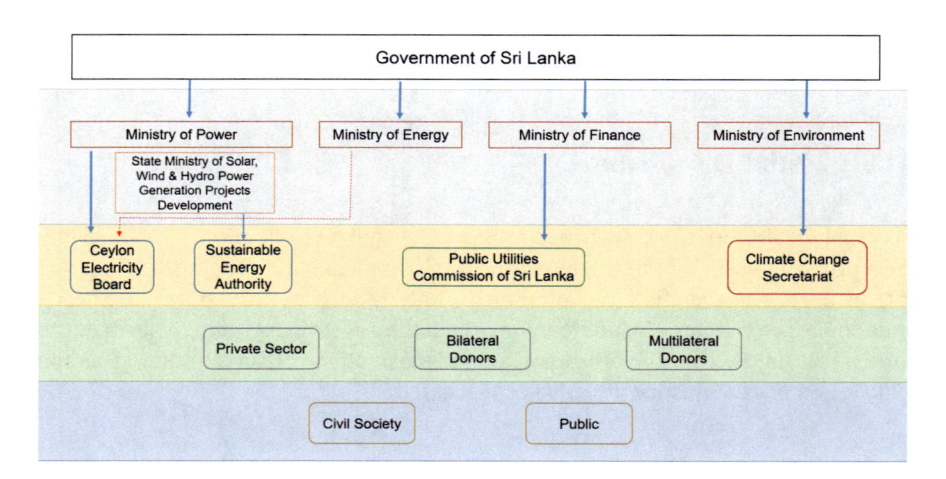

Fig. 9.4 Energy sector actor diagram

through licenses, regulations, rules and methodologies, and is an independent body under the Ministry of Finance. The Climate Change Secretariat (CCS) is the foremost institution in Sri Lanka that coordinates climate change-related matters and was established in 2008 under the Ministry of Environment. It is the national focal point on climate change-related matters and leading the process of mainstreaming climate change into other development areas.

These four institutions—CEB, SLSEA, PUCSL, CCS—and their ministries play a crucial role in shaping the policy pathways on Sri Lanka's energy transition. Interestingly these institutions have non-compatible goals that are outlined in their mandates. It creates an interesting paradox for the institutions to cooperate. The recent developments in the Sri Lankan energy sector illustrate this paradox. The new government coming into power in 2019 announced in early 2020 that the renewable energy contribution to the national grid should be 80% by 2030 (Sirimane, 2020). At the end of 2019, 40% of power generation is from coal, 40% from oil and 15% is from hydro. Less than 3% is from wind and solar (CEB, 2020). Coal and oil are essential, and the plan foresees the transformation of energy sources from 70% imported fuel to 80% indigenous sources (CEB, 2020). This paradigm shift is foreseen in a very short period of ten years that is challenging and needs policy consistency.

Nevertheless, in January 2021, the Cabinet approved two coal power plants and two LNG plants 300 MW, each totalling 1200 MW (Andree, 2020). As a follow-up in September 2020 the President said Sri Lanka would focus on achieving 70% electricity from renewables by 2030 instead of 80% (Daily News, 2020). Sri Lanka's latest Long Term Generation Expansion Plan (LTGEP) for the period 2020–2039, foresees 55% new coal and oil additions (CEB 2019).

A Sri Lankan energy expert, who has worked in the government sector, explained the thought process of the government institutions and their internal conflicts:

> The government institutions work in silos. They are very much focused on achieving what has been assigned to them. Institutions do not work holistically; they fail to see the bigger picture and the possible synergies. There is always a tug-of-war between institutions over superiority. The independent institutions – in this case, PUCSL – suffer the most. (Interview, 28-09-2020)

The interviews with the officials in these institutions at the local and national level showed the disconnect between competing narratives that each organisation pushes forward. Officials working for the SLSEA position themselves closer to CEB rather than PUCSL, which is advocating for renewables. The SLSEA, even though is mandated to look for a sustainable energy future, feels that Sri Lanka needs more coal power plants and argues that the vision of the SLSEA is "an Energy Secure Sri Lanka" while acknowledging that Sri Lanka has its NDCs to achieve.

To illustrate the above, the coded qualitative data was used to produce a sector prioritisation matrix, that is, an indication of which of the overarching energy issues are prioritized among the principal actors. The primary and secondary data were classified into three sectors, and then each of them was coded according to their priority. For example, if interview data suggest high priority for energy security and the next priority to justice and the least priority to climate commitments, it was

Table 9.1 Sector prioritisation matrix

Sector	Subsector	Energy security	Climate commitments	Justice
Government	CEB	1	3	2
	SLSEA	1	2	3
	PUCSL	3	2	1
	CCS	2	1	3
Private sector	Solar and wind	2	1	3
	Fossil fuel	1	3	2
	Bilateral/multilateral	1	2	3
Public	Public (war zones)	2	3	1
	Public (general)	1	3	2
	Civil society	2	3	1

1, High; 2, Medium; 3, Low

coded accordingly, giving 1 to high priority and 2 to medium priority and 3 to low priority (see Table 9.1). After coding, specific patterns started to emerge within the sectors. For example, the people living in the former war zones gave priority to the justice aspect of energy, while others prioritised energy security. Likewise, the different institutions within the government had varying priorities and preferences. Subsectors of sectors emerged after the coding process, and it is reflected in the table above.

This table gives an overall view of the agencies in play and their priority in the nexus. In the table, the government is comprised of four key organisations, namely Ceylon Electricity Board (CEB), Sri Lanka Sustainable energy authority (SLSEA), Public Utilities Commission of Sri Lanka (PUCSL), and Climate Change Secretariat (CCS). Likewise, the private sector is sub-categorised into three: Companies that work on solar and wind energy, companies that produce electricity through fossil fuels and the bilateral and multilateral agencies like World Bank, Asian Development Bank and Japan International Cooperation Agency (JICA). While coding, the priority among the people living in the former war zones and the other regions differ, and the people's priority order is different to the civil society. Here the civil society encapsulates the broader meaning, including NGOs, civil society and grassroot organisations. In line with the analytical framework, this matrix shows the complicated nature of energy policymaking. The foremost actors in government prioritise energy security and align with the fossil fuel sector. This contrasts with climate commitments, which are only championed by the institutions working on renewable energy, but they stand alone and are relatively powerless.

Finally, energy justice is also a marginalised concern, championed by civil society and the public. In contrast to the institutions, there is a lack of strong agency at the bottom. In short, there is a powerful alliance for energy security, and it is understood as sustaining fossil fuel and the foremost driver of business-as-usual, or 'lock-in' in energy provisioning. The following sections will analyse the agencies' preferences through the framework to demonstrate the emerging energy transition pathways.

Institutional Inertia

In the Sri Lankan setting, the climate commitments-energy security-justice nexus can be understood through the institutions. Resistance to change is referred to as institutional inertia. Over the years politicization of institutions for public administration has made them weak and subservient to politicians (Uyangoda & Törnquist, 2013). This politicization and weakening have given the institutions a considerable loss of leeway, where they are rigid, unresponsive, leaving little room for policy change and adaptation.

Based on the collected data, three main mechanisms of institutional inertia can be identified in the case of Sri Lanka: (1) uncertainty, (2) path dependence, and (3) power. The following section will recapitulate how these mechanisms generate inertia and act as barriers to achieving just energy transitions and climate commitments.

Uncertainty

Government officials at the different levels pointed out during the fieldwork that the state institutions are weak and they experience policy changes, political influence and interference in decision making. It was evident during the conversations with the local level administrators; they explained the difficulties of being co-governed by different ministries, which take contrasting stances to each other, causing a lot of uncertainty. Local institutions, even though have the authority to act, avoid it and it has been their easiest and safest option. Unavailability of coherent and policy informed decisions and instructions creates uncertainty in the state institutions and institutional inertia. It was striking to find that even within one institution there are divergent opinions and policy stances that are contrary to each other. It happens at the national level where institutional incongruences and contradictions add to the uncertainty of the institutions expected to cooperate and deliver policy outcomes.

During the interviews, almost all acknowledged that uncertainty influences their way of working. At the local level, uncertainty is a sense of fear, where local officials are cautious that they do not do anything that upsets their superiors. Therefore, they are hesitant to initiate or explore, and instead prefer to stay dormant. At the top level, it is about dejection towards the system that is politicised. One official from a critical institution said:

> For us, uncertainty is not an exception but a norm. Our political decision-makers focus on political outcomes, which are short-sighted and not policy-driven. In most cases, these political decisions pave the way for policymaking. Eventually, we know it will change with the change of government in the next five or ten years. (Interview 09-01-2020)

Politicization in policymaking was very evident with Sri Lanka's changing renewable energy targets. At the outset it was planning for 100% renewables by 2050, then it became very ambitious and stated 80% renewables by 2030 as an election promise. Later it came down to 70% and then the cabinet approved the building of coal and LNG plants. At the present rate, Sri Lanka will end up with 45% renewables by 2030 according to estimates. The constant changes are attributed to decisions that are not in line with the policies. The data affirm that uncertainty appears at the institutions' different levels due to politicization and has promoted inertia. It has been a significant drawback in achieving just energy transitions politically and policy-wise.

Path Dependence

Path dependence refers to the outcomes of 'self-reinforcing or positive feedback processes' in a social system (Pierson, 2004, 10). Mahoney (2000) argues that path dependence generates a historically embedded inertia. This can be explained as the inability to change development paths due to past choices and decisions. For instance, this is the case in a 'carbon lock-in', where the possibility for just transitions is curtailed by the historical precedence and domination of the carbon-based energy sector. The outcome is that there is a lack of support politically and socially for lock-out. Path dependence relates to both formal and informal institutions. Assemblages of technologies, bureaucracies, and worldviews also influence the institutions' path dependencies (Burch, 2011). Institutional inertia is embedded in social structures, power relations and daily practices that help to sustain the incumbent practices and resist change (Hoffman & Ventresca, 1999).

Electricity generation in Sri Lanka was almost 100% from hydropower until mid-1995. With globalisation taking its shape and influence in South Asia in the late 1990s, Sri Lanka witnessed a rapid electricity demand growth. Sri Lanka's limited potential to develop new hydropower facilities allowed the shift to a mixed hydro-thermal system in electricity generation. Initially, the state-owned CEB was the only entity allowed to engage in electricity generation, transmission, and distribution. After 1996, Sri Lanka allowed the private sector to develop power plants to sell electricity to CEB. This had a drastic impact on the Sri Lanka's energy mix. (see Fig. 9.5).

Even though Sri Lanka had the option to invest more in renewables, the CEB and the private sector preferred to take oil and later coal as additional electricity generation sources. "Least-cost option" was the credo of successive Sri Lankan governments. CEB, as well as private companies, were resistant to change. One retired CEB official echoed this and explained how path dependence influences policy decisions.

When Sri Lankan energy mix became mixed with oil and coal, it perfectly fitted our demand-side management, especially to handle our peak load. Adding thermal into the system did not hamper our existing systems, which were dominated by hydro. So that change was smooth, and over the years, we were convinced that thermal power generation along with hydro is the best-case option for least cost power generation. When Sri Lanka came up with its climate commitments in 2016, it was just a fancy idea. There was no buy-in from CEB, but we agreed

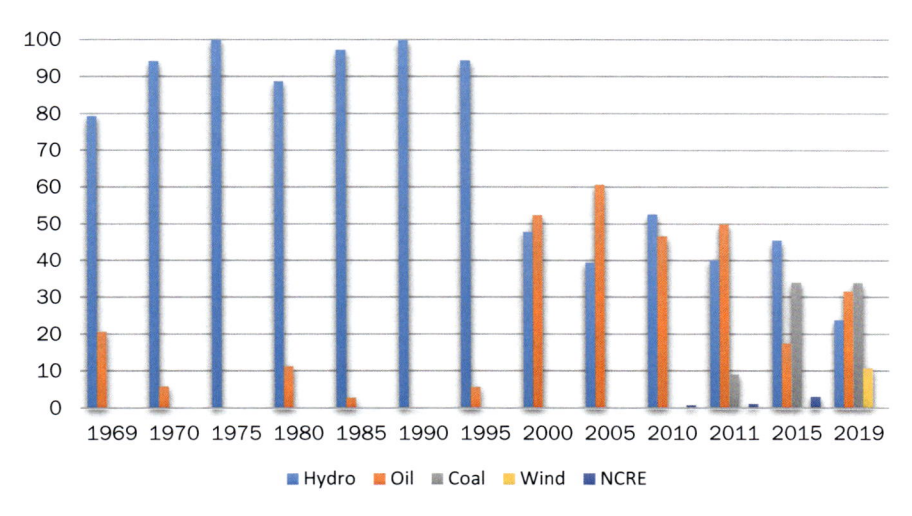

Fig. 9.5 Electricity generation mix 1969–2019, *Source* CEB, 2019

that Solar PV could act as standalone without being connected to the grid since it will create instability to the grid." (Interview, 16-12-2019)

Sri Lanka has drafted several possible pathways to achieve 100% renewables by 2050. CEB is in favour of the continued use of fossil fuel since it will not distress the present energy infrastructure. It also argues that it is the cheapest option (CEB, 2019). It has been estimated that the government needs around US$54–US$56 billion in total in the power sector to achieve a 100 per cent renewable scenario (UNDP & ADB, 2017). Hence even though there are frameworks, policies, and vision to decarbonize and achieve climate commitments, the carbon lock-in strengthened by path dependence continues.

Power

During an interview with a very senior government official who has worked over four decades in ministries and institutions, I asked the following question: "*Have you ever asked the policymakers what was their basis for any new policymaking or the reasons for the change in the existing policy?*" This question captured the essence of institutional inertia in Sri Lanka. Several interviews pointed out directly and distinctly the role of power in their institutional functioning. It was evident through the fieldwork that in several institutions that are working in the realm of energy transitions and climate change, the role of power and the hierarchical attitude are embodied within the DNA of those institutions. Power is an actor's capacity to influence the relationship between that actor and those being influenced (Orjuela, 2008). Power is also produced or legitimized by those who obey (Lilja & Vinthagen, 2009). In this sense, in the Sri Lankan institutional context, power is understood as consensual with common interests between those with much power and those with less and gives the legitimacy to wield power over someone (Hydén & Mmuyo, 2008; Orjuela, 2008).

The senior government official had this to say when asked his take on this question.

> If you go and ask the officials in these institutions who formulate the policies, what was the primacy for policymaking, you will find out that people are not their main concern. It is all about politics and power. Sri Lanka is adding renewables not because it sees it as a future, but they see some profit out of it, and it helps to tick off some boxes in international fora.

Sri Lanka presents a critical disjuncture in the experience of the energy transition, as seen in many other societies in the developing world; with a fundamental dichotomy between the multiple interests of the society and the state power.

It is evident that institutional inertia has its mechanisms and that these mechanisms are interconnected and reinforce each other. The complexity of a negotiated compromise among the institutions has repeatedly demonstrated that collectively and individually, agency undermines climate commitments by pursuing sectoral agendas or inaction. The case data demonstrate a close relationship between government institutions and energy security. Many institutions put energy security first, but others put affordability and availability highest.

Private Sector in Energy Finance

Sri Lanka's renewable energy uptake is mainly taken care of by private sector investments or through donor assistance—as loan or grant—and both mainly in the form of solar and wind projects. Over the past decade, Sri Lanka has witnessed renewable projects that have caused justice and equity questions (Theiventhran, 2021). On the one hand, there is protest and resistance from the public for renewable energy projects; and on the other, there is an uneasiness about renewable energy uptake among CEB, which is founded on three fundamental premises.

1. Wind and solar power output are subject to resource intermittency that affects grid stability.
2. Lower production factors with wind and solar power require a larger quantum of capacity to be installed to match an equivalent thermal power plant's energy yield.
3. The costs incurred in building renewable plant capacity plus backup generation to combat intermittency results in higher electricity prices.

Over the past year, there has been a slowdown in approvals for renewable energy projects and several reasons have been cited. It is noteworthy that Sri Lanka purchases emergency power from private sector companies, which have been operating since they were allowed into the energy sector in 2006.

There are two competing narratives in relation to private sector finance in renewable energy in Sri Lanka. One argues that private sector finance is decisive to achieve global climate commitments, where renewable uptake is instrumental in bringing the desired changes to the energy system (during the interviews private sector entities working on renewables argued strongly on this). The other argues that incorporating renewables will create instability in the energy system and make electricity generation expensive (This was outlined in the interviews with the CEB and few energy experts). Sri Lankan private sector in energy is diverse and has competing and complementing interests that make policymaking strenuous. The Sri Lankan private sector in renewables is emerging and yet to find its full potential of the agency. By contrast, the private sector which is working with fossil fuels is well established including its relationship with the state and policymakers.

The role of the bilateral and multilateral donors in renewable uptake is mixed. China and India have provided grants to build solar and wind parks in Sri Lanka. Asian Development Bank (ADB) has financed a 100 MW Wind Park. On the other hand, China has built Sri Lanka's first coal power plant, India and China are bidding for coal plants in Sri Lanka. India, Japan and China are involved in LNG projects. World Bank has recommended LNG and argues LNG is the best way to meet the growing energy demand in Sri Lanka (World Bank, 2019). Both bilateral and multilateral donors argue that their support is to ensure Sri Lanka attains energy security.

The Sri Lankan case shows that the private sector as an agency induces energy policymaking through its attractive financial capabilities. Nevertheless, it is not linear, on the one hand, companies working on renewables are pushing for more renewables so that Sri Lanka meets its climate commitments; whilst the bilateral and multilateral actors with their focus on energy security support the continuation of and even new facilities for fossil fuels. Energy finance both private and from donors has thus overpowered concerns about issues such as energy justice.

Is this putting the cart before the horse? Clearly, both private and public sectors have vital roles to play: but as we have seen, the private sector has increasing agency, which in some cases is pulling outcomes in the direction of fossil fuels and path dependency, as well as lacking focus on the social justice issues of the energy transition. One might add that they also appear to prioritise supply side over demand side energy efficiency and energy conservation, topics that do not explore in detail here but which are equally vital for sustainable energy transitions.

Public

Sri Lanka's public discourse on energy is mixed. Sri Lanka has a history of regular blackouts, and the environmental impact of Sri Lanka's first coal power plant has created some awareness. The public has remained largely silent with very little agency, but it has had a significant impact on the national discourse when they act. The PUCSL officials detailed that the cataclysmic failure of the first power plant and its environmental disasters prompted the public to react to the proposed second coal power plant in Sampoor, the Eastern part of Sri Lanka. Environmental activists pointed out that public protest and subsequent halting of the power plant have proved the public's power and created awareness over coal plants. Environmental organizations and social movements stood in solidarity with the public and created a form of social capital that evolved as an agency, taking advantage of Sri Lanka's climate commitments in order to also harness a fight for justice.

This resistance also promoted a discourse about renewables as the better way forward and created an atmosphere for policymaking in favour of renewables as noted by a senior official at the ministry of environment. However, a few years down the line solar and wind facilities have also come under criticism and have faced resistance. Loss of land, livelihood and environmental concerns, lack of consultation and awareness are some of the reasons for these protests. The interviews with the protesters and civil society activists revealed that there are questions of justice in multiple ways. People feel that these energy projects are being imposed upon them. Interviewees at the grassroots level stressed the importance of openness and answerability of the state and the importance of procedural justice. Further, they said that their social and political capital is weak and they can only have a minimal impact, whereas private capital and the state's institutions have a powerful agency that dominates the energy transition discourse and undermines justice.

These social issues are compounded by the lack of clear policy frameworks, the private sector's economic motives, and the state institutions' institutional inertia. This had an impact in shaping the climate commitment-energy security-justice nexus, where energy security became the primary concern and affordability and cost are higher priorities too, the energy justice became the least concern.

Conclusions

In this chapter, the case of Sri Lanka's ongoing energy transition was explored from an agency perspective. The analysis brought together the dynamics of different actors and how different formations influence or have little influence on Sri Lanka's energy transition discourse. Agency in different forms creates critical frontiers both spatially and temporally. Understanding how these processes constituted these agencies and contrariwise could empower the policymakers to design interventions that accommodate competing narratives and achieve acceptability and sustainability. This chapter investigated how the 'climate commitments-energy security-justice nexus has influenced the energy transition pathways in Sri Lanka. The analysis explained the agency's role and how the carbon lock-ins are reinforced through institutional inertia, and how justice issues are neglected or undermined. Hence, the Sri Lankan case study points to some essential paradoxes and possibilities regarding clean and just energy transitions in developing country contexts. A holistic policy framework for energy transitions must incorporate democratic concerns from below. To do this calls for, at the very outset, a firm political commitment for renewables and sustainable solutions to be designed and implemented in ways that are acceptable by all.

The problem of path dependency is that it has provided the basis for energy security while it has failed to address the climate question. However, path dependency provides options to conceptualize energy transitions in an energy security perspective that has taken the central role in de-carbonization discourse and has reinforced carbon lock-in. A key challenge in any new type of transition is to confront and negotiate unknown challenges and concerns, in this case, new energy systems with renewables and accommodating the gradual phase-out of fossil fuels as well as social justice. In this process, inertia among actors could reinforce the path dependency, undermine the path creation, and fortify carbon lock-in. In the case of Sri Lanka's energy transition, there are three emerging frontiers. These can help to understand how climate commitments influence energy transitions in developing countries and what space does justice has in this relationship.

First, Sri Lanka's climate action process has been a relatively subdued, painless process not conducive to decisive actions, with weak institutions, where policies and frameworks were made without incorporating them into the more comprehensive national policy. Quite paradoxically, international organizations and multilateral partners have pushed for better alignment between climate action and energy transition, yet supporting fossil fuels. Later the private sector joined in on the action. Inertia adds to this lack of effectiveness.

Second, the 'reconstitution' of state-private sector relations. The relationship between private finance for renewables and energy justice is complicated. The emergence of a post-liberalized political economy and the decline of state control in private capital, weak state institutions and limited public finance has reconfigured Sri Lanka's state-private sector relations. This 'reconstitution' of state-private sector relations has paved the way for the re-politicization of Sri Lanka's energy landscape favouring the non-renewable future—the opposite direction from the country's goals.

Third, Sri Lankan policymakers, like its citizens, have taken energy transition for granted based mainly on affordability and availability. Clean energy has not been a critical part of the energy security discourse, and the call for climate action is detached from the energy transition. Nor has energy justice been in focus. Sri Lanka has not experienced a significant climate calamity even though it experiences severe droughts and floods annually. Climate action was an outcome of Sri Lanka's international engagements, especially with the United Nations. Sri Lanka's NDCs and its commitment were not born from a public or social movement. Sri Lanka's climate commitment was not grassroots-driven and was not based on local needs. Sri Lankans feel the impact of climate change in many ways, but there was no sensitization about climate action.

All the above can lead to a new condition of hollowed-out energy transitions, detaching de-carbonization from energy security, impeding social and justice issues, and confining the action to a relatively minimal and in part undesirable energy transition. In summary, responding to the climate commitments while ensuring equitable energy necessitates an inclusion and recognition of the different capabilities, and the agency approach offers a valuable framework for exploring the emerging frontiers of the energy transition.

It is surely fair to say that whilst issues of carbon lock-in, path dependency and inertia are found in many countries, both rich and poor, their impact particularly impedes increased attention to "newer" aspects of energy transitioning such as social justice. Energy is still often seen as mainly a technical-economic field, with little attention to the cultural and social sciences aspects and approaches. Such considerations depend on the entire socio-political context. They are still relatively little in focus internationally and are naturally both complex and sensitive. Social justice issues highlight the uneven distribution of agency in Sri Lankan society. In a post-conflict context such as Sri Lanka, this may further hinder or raise opposition to positive energy transitions.

References

Acemoglu, D., Aghion, P., Bursztyn, L., & Hemous, D. (2012). The environment and directed technical change. *American Economic Review, 102*(1), 131–166. https://doi.org/10.1257/aer.102. 1.131

ADB. (2019). Sri Lanka: Energy sector assessment, strategy, and road map. Asian Development Bank.

Aiken, G. T., Middlemiss, L., Sallu, S., & Hauxwell-Baldwin, R. (2017). Researching climate change and community in neoliberal contexts: An emerging critical approach. *Wiley Interdisciplinary Reviews: Climate Change, 8*(4). https://doi.org/10.1002/wcc.463

Andree, M. (2020, January 24). Cabinet approves setting up power plants: Two 300 MW coal plants, Two 300 MW LNG approved. *Ceylon Today*.

APERC. (2007). Asia Pacific energy research centre. *A quest for energy security in the 21st century: Resources and constraints*. Tokyo: Institute of Energy Economics.

Arthur, W. B. (1989). Competing technologies, increasing returns, and lock-in by historical events. *The Economic Journal, 99*(394), 116. https://doi.org/10.2307/2234208

Baker, L., Newell, P., & Phillips, J. (2014). The political economy of energy transitions: The case of South Africa. *New Political Economy, 19*(6), 791–818. https://doi.org/10.1080/13563467.2013. 849674

Berkhout, F. (2002). Technological regimes, path dependency and the environment. *Global Environmental Change, 12*(1), 1–4. https://doi.org/10.1016/s0959-3780(01)00025-5

Bhaskar, R. (2010). *Plato etcetera: The Problems of philosophy and their resolution*. Routledge.

Blicharska, M., Smithers, R. J., Kuchler, M., Agrawal, G. K., Gutiérrez, J. M., Hassanali, A., & Huq, S., et al. (2017). Steps to overcome the north–south divide in research relevant to climate change policy and practice. *Nature Climate Change, 7*(1), 21–27. https://doi.org/10.1038/nclima te3163

Bullard, R. (2005). Environmental justice in the 21st century. Essay. In J. S. Dryzek, & D. Schlosberg (Eds.), *Debating the earth: The environmental politics reader* (pp. 322–356). Oxford University Press.

Burch, S. (2011). Sustainable development paths: Investigating the roots of local policy responses to climate change. *Sustainable Development, 19*(3), 176–188. https://doi.org/10.1002/sd.435

Burck, J., Bals, C., & Rossow, V. (2011). *The Climate Change Performance Index 2010*. Bonn: Germanwatch.

CEB. (2019). *Long term generation expansion plan 2020-2039 (DRAFT)*. Colombo: Ceylon Electricity Board.

CEB. (2019). *Annual Report 2018*. Ceylon Electricity Board.

CEB. (2020). *Statistical Digest 2019*. Ceylon Electricity Board.

Central Bank. (2020). *Recent economic developments 2020*. Colombo: Central Bank of Sri Lanka.

Chester, L. (2010). Conceptualising energy security and making explicit its polysemic nature. *Energy Policy, 38*(2), 887–895. https://doi.org/10.1016/j.enpol.2009.10.039

Daily News. (2020, September 14). *Country must generate 70% renewable energy by 2030—President.*

Davies, A. R. (2006). Environmental justice as subtext or omission: Examining discourses of anti-incineration campaigning in Ireland. *Geoforum, 37*(5), 708–724. https://doi.org/10.1016/j.geoforum.2005.06.005

Dolsak, N. (2001). Mitigating global climate change: Why are some countries more committed than others? *Policy Studies Journal, 29*(3), 414–436. https://doi.org/10.1111/j.1541-0072.2001.tb02102.x

Ekins, P., & Speck, S. (2014). The fiscal implications of climate change and policy responses. *Mitigation and Adaptation Strategies for Global Change, 19*(3), 355–374. https://doi.org/10.1007/s11027-013-9533-4

Erickson, P., Kartha, S., Lazarus, M., & Tempest, K. (2015). Assessing carbon lock-in. *Environmental Research Letters, 10*(8). https://doi.org/10.1088/1748-9326/10/8/084023

Fouquet, R. (2016). Historical energy transitions: Speed, prices and system transformation. *Energy Research & Social Science, 22*, 7–12. https://doi.org/10.1016/j.erss.2016.08.014

Fraser, N. (1998). Essay. In *Social justice in the age of identity politics: Redistribution, recognition, participation.* Berlin.

Geels, F. W. (2011). The multi-level perspective on sustainability transitions: Responses to seven criticisms. *Environmental Innovation and Societal Transitions, 1*(1), 24–40. https://doi.org/10.1016/j.eist.2011.02.002

Geels, F. W., & Schot, J. (2007). Typology of sociotechnical transition pathways. *Research Policy, 36*(3), 399–417. https://doi.org/10.1016/j.respol.2007.01.003

Gillingham, K., & Sweeney, J. (2012). Barriers to implementing low-carbon technologies. *Climate Change Economics, 03*(04), 1250019. https://doi.org/10.1142/s2010007812500194

Gillingham, K., Newell, R. G., & Pizer, W. A. (2008). Modeling endogenous technological change for climate policy analysis. *Energy Economics, 30*(6), 2734–2753. https://doi.org/10.1016/j.eneco.2008.03.001

Goldthau, A. (2011). Governing global energy: Existing approaches and discourses. *Current Opinion in Environmental Sustainability, 3*(4), 213–217. https://doi.org/10.1016/j.cosust.2011.06.003

Goldthau, A., & Sovacool, B. K. (2012). The uniqueness of the energy security, justice, and governance problem. *Energy Policy, 41*, 232–240. https://doi.org/10.1016/j.enpol.2011.10.042

Grin, J., Rotmans, J., & Schot, J. (2011). *Transitions to sustainable development; new directions in the study of long term transformative change.* Taylor & Francis Group.

Harvey, D. L. (2002). Agency and community: A critical realist paradigm. *Journal for the Theory of Social Behaviour, 32*(2), 163–194. https://doi.org/10.1111/1468-5914.00182

Healy, N., & Barry, J. (2017). Politicizing energy justice and energy system transitions: Fossil fuel divestment and a 'just transition.' *Energy Policy, 108*, 451–459. https://doi.org/10.1016/j.enpol.2017.06.014

Hippel, D., von., Suzuki, T., Williams, J. H., Savage, T., & Hayes, P. (2011). Energy security and sustainability in Northeast Asia. *Energy Policy, 39*(11), 6719–6730. https://doi.org/10.1016/j.enpol.2009.07.001

Hoffman, A. J., & Ventresca, M. J. (1999). The institutional framing of policy debates. *American Behavioral Scientist, 42*(8), 1368–1392. https://doi.org/10.1177/00027649921954903

Hoggett, R. (2014). Technology scale and supply chains in a secure, affordable and low carbon energy transition. *Applied Energy, 123*, 296–306. https://doi.org/10.1016/j.apenergy.2013.12.006

Horvath, P. (1998). Agency and social adaptation. *Applied Behavioral Science Review, 6*(2), 137–154. https://doi.org/10.1016/s1068-8595(99)80008-7

Hughes, L. (2012). A generic framework for the description and analysis of energy security in an energy system. *Energy Policy, 42*, 221–231. https://doi.org/10.1016/j.enpol.2011.11.079

Hydén, G., & Mmuya, M. (2008). *Power and policy slippage in Tanzania: Discussing national ownership of development.* Swedish International Development Co-operation Agency.

IEA. (2020). *Renewable market update: Outlook for 2020 and 2021*. Paris: International Energy Agency.

IPCC. (2014). *Climate change 2014. Impacts, adaptation and vulnerability: Part A, Volume 1: Global and sectoral aspects. Working Group II contribution to the IPCC fifth assessment report*. Cambridge: Cambridge University Press.

IRENA. (2015). *Renewable energy benefits: Measuring the economics*. Abu Dhabi: International Renewable Energy Agency.

IRENA. (2016). *Unlocking renewable energy investment: The role of risk mitigation and structured Finance*. Abu Dhabi: International Renewable Energy Agency.

IRENA. (2018). *Global energy transformation: A roadmap to 2050*. Abu Dhabi: International Renewable Energy Agency.

IRENA. (2021). *World energy transitions outlook: 1.5°C Pathway*. Abu Dhabi: International Renewable Energy Agency.

IRENA & CPI. (2020). *Global landscape of renewable energy finance 2020*. International Renewable Energy Agency.

Jaffe, A. B., Newell, R. G., & Stavins, R. N. (2005). A tale of two market failures: Technology and environmental policy. *Ecological Economics, 54*(2–3), 164–174. https://doi.org/10.1016/j.ecolecon.2004.12.027

Jenkins, K., McCauley, D., & Forman, A. (2017). Energy justice: A policy approach. *Energy Policy, 105*, 631–634. https://doi.org/10.1016/j.enpol.2017.01.052

Kern, F., & Rogge, K. S. (2016). The pace of governed energy transitions: Agency, international dynamics and the global paris agreement accelerating decarbonisation processes? *Energy Research & Social Science, 22*, 13–17. https://doi.org/10.1016/j.erss.2016.08.016

Kern, F., & Smith, A. (2008). Restructuring energy systems for sustainability? Energy transition policy in the Netherlands. *Energy Policy, 36*(11), 4093–4103. https://doi.org/10.1016/j.enpol.2008.06.018

Kumar, A. (2018). Justice and politics in energy access for education, livelihoods and health: How socio-cultural processes mediate the winners and losers. *Energy Research & Social Science, 40*, 3–13. https://doi.org/10.1016/j.erss.2017.11.029

Lilja, M., & Vinthagen, S. (2014). Sovereign power, disciplinary power and biopower: Resisting what power with what resistance? *Journal of Political Power, 7*(1), 107–126. https://doi.org/10.1080/2158379X.2014.889403.

Löschel, A., Sturm, B., & Vogt, C. (2010). The demand for climate protection: An empirical assessment for Germany. Mannheim: Zentrum für Europäische Wirtschaftsforschung.

Mahoney, J. (2000). Path dependence in historical sociology. *Theory and Society, 29*(4), 507–548. https://doi.org/10.1023/A:1007113830879

Meadowcroft, J. (2009). What about the politics? sustainable development, transition management, and long term energy transitions. *Policy Sciences, 42*(4), 323–340. https://doi.org/10.1007/s11077-009-9097-z

Meadowcroft, J. (2011). Engaging with the politics of sustainability transitions. *Environmental Innovation and Societal Transitions, 1*(1), 70–75. https://doi.org/10.1016/j.eist.2011.02.003

Meckling, J., & Hughes, L. (2018). Global interdependence in clean energy transitions. *Business and Politics, 20*(4), 467–491. https://doi.org/10.1017/bap.2018.25

Mulvaney, D. (2013). Opening the black box of solar energy technologies: Exploring tensions between innovation and environmental justice. *Science as Culture, 22*(2), 230–237. https://doi.org/10.1080/09505431.2013.786995

Murshed, M. (2021). Can regional trade integration facilitate renewable energy transition to ensure energy sustainability in South Asia? *Energy Reports, 7*, 808–821. https://doi.org/10.1016/j.egyr.2021.01.038

Newell, P. (2018). Trasformismo or transformation? The global political economy of energy transitions. *Review of International Political Economy, 26*(1), 25–48. https://doi.org/10.1080/09692290.2018.1511448

Nordensvärd, J., & Urban, F. (2011). The ambiguous role of corporations in climate change mitigation: An explorative appraisal of corporations in China, Malaysia and the US. Brighton: Institute of Development Studies.

Onyx, J., & Bullen, P. (2000). Measuring social capital in five communities. *The Journal of Applied Behavioral Science, 36*(1), 23–42. https://doi.org/10.1177/0021886300361002

Orjuela, C. (2008). *The identity politics of peacebuilding: Civil society in war-torn Sri Lanka.* Sage.

Perlaviciute, G., & Steg, L. (2015). The influence of values on evaluations of energy alternatives. *Renewable Energy, 77*, 259–267. https://doi.org/10.1016/j.renene.2014.12.020

Pierson, P. (2004). *Politics in time history, institutions, and social analysis.* Princeton University Press.

Rennings, K. (2000). Redefining innovation—Eco-innovation research and the contribution from ecological economics. *Ecological Economics, 32*(2), 319–332. https://doi.org/10.1016/s0921-8009(99)00112-3

Saculsan, P. G., & Mori, A. (2020). Why developing countries go through an unsustainable energy transition pathway? The case of the Philippines from a political economic perspective. *Journal of Sustainability Research, 2*(2). https://doi.org/10.20900/jsr20200012

Schlosberg, D. (2013). Theorising environmental justice: The expanding sphere of a discourse. *Environmental Politics, 22*(1), 37–55. https://doi.org/10.1080/09644016.2013.755387

Sirimane, S. (2020, February 14). Renewable energy sources set to power Lanka by 2030. *Daily News.* https://www.dailynews.lk/2020/02/14/finance/211412/renewable-energy-sources-set-power-lanka-2030

Smith, A., Stirling, A., & Berkhout, F. (2005). The governance of sustainable socio-technical transitions. *Research Policy, 34*(10), 1491–1510. https://doi.org/10.1016/j.respol.2005.07.005

Sovacool, B. K. (2011). Evaluating energy security in the Asia Pacific: Towards a more comprehensive approach. *Energy Policy, 39*(11), 7472–7479. https://doi.org/10.1016/j.enpol.2010.10.008

Theiventhran, G. M. N. (2021). Energy transitions in a post-war setting: Questions of equity, justice and democracy in Sri Lanka." Chap. 6 In Johanna H. A. Kumar, A. Pols (Eds.), *Dilemmas of energy transitions in the global south: Balancing urgency and justice* (pp. 94–110). New York Routledge.

Todd, H., & Zografos, C. (2005). Justice for the environment: Developing a set of indicators of environmental justice for Scotland. *Environmental Values, 14*(4), 483–501. https://doi.org/10.3197/096327105774462692

Uddin, K. (2017). Climate change and global environmental politics: North-South divide. *Environmental Policy and Law, 47*(3–4), 106–114. https://doi.org/10.3233/epl-170022

UN. (2017). *Leaving no one behind: Equality and non-discrimination at the heart of sustainable development.* New York: United Nations.

UNDP & ADB. (2017). *100% electricity generation through renewable energy by 2050: Assessment of Sri Lanka's power sector.* Colombo: United Nations Development Programme & Asian Development Bank.

Unruh, G. C. (2000). Understanding carbon lock-in. *Energy Policy, 28*(12), 817–830. https://doi.org/10.1016/s0301-4215(00)00070-7

Uyangoda, J., & Törnquist, O. (2013). Re-Politicizing local government for politics of transformation: Arguments from Sri Lanka. Essay. In K. Stokke (Ed.), *Democratization in the Global South: The Importance of Transformative Politics* (pp. 277–301). Palgrave Macmillan.

Veugelers, R. (2012). Which policy instruments to induce clean innovating? *Research Policy, 41*(10), 1770–1778. https://doi.org/10.1016/j.respol.2012.06.012

Voß, J.-P., & Bornemann, B. (2011). The politics of reflexive governance: Challenges for designing adaptive management and transition management. *Ecology and Society, 16*(2). https://doi.org/10.5751/es-04051-160209

Walker, G. (2009). Environmental Justice and normative thinking. *Antipode, 41*(1), 203–205. https://doi.org/10.1111/j.1467-8330.2008.00663.x

Westphal, K. (2011). "Energy in an era of unprecedented uncertainty: International energy governance in the face of macroeconomic, geopolitical, and systemic challenges." Essay. In D. D. Koranyi (Ed.), *Transatlantic energy futures: Strategic perspectives on energy security, climate change and new technologies in Europe and the United States* (pp. 1–26). Center for Transatlantic Relations.

Winzer, C. (2012). Conceptualizing energy security. *Energy Policy, 46,* 36–48. https://doi.org/10.1016/j.enpol.2012.02.067

World Bank. (2019). *Sri Lanka Energy InfraSAP.* The World Bank.

Gz. MeeNilankco Theiventhran is a Research Fellow at the Department of Computer science, Electrical engineering and Mathematical sciences at Western Norway University of Applied Sciences, where he is pursuing his research interests in energy, politics, and society in the global South. His work focuses on geopolitical dynamics and policy challenges confronting developing countries in achieving clean energy transitions. He has an interdisciplinary background comprising political science, geography and engineering, and 15 years of work experience involving teaching, project management, public policy, and international development. He is a lecturer at the International Summer School, University of Oslo, where he also coordinates the International Development Studies Master programme.

Chapter 10
Environmental Policy Development in Nigeria

Edidiong Samuel Akpabio

Abstract It is glaring that the earth is getting warmer and the blame lies primarily on human beings (Spore, 2008). Man's activities have continued to directly or indirectly affect the climatic conditions of the world today, hence the bulk of the blame lies with humans rather than on natural causes. Granted that the consequences of climate change are multifaceted and manifest in the political, social and economic dimensions, it is important to state that the earth has warmed an average of 0.6 °C over the past 100 years (Environment Canada, 2008). While the phenomena of climate change has diverse consequences ranging from food scarcity, disease conditions, strife and conflicts amongst others, human lives are being changed with the occurrence of climate change, while global warming has continued to produce devastating and untoward consequences in the recent past. Take for instance, the flooding in Bangkok, India and Australia coupled with the heat waves in Europe amongst others. Hence, having recognized the dangers inherent in climate change, several mechanisms have been put in place to tackle the challenges of climate change with the most prominent of them being the United Nations Framework Convention on Climate Change and the Kyoto protocol. It is clear without any iota of doubt that the climate deserves to be reinvigorated and this can only happen if there is a tenacious adherence to the spirit and letters of this agreement. Overtime humanity has harmed the environment so much so that the environment requires healing. Man harmed his environment through carrying out actions that are inimical to the sustainability of the environment and harmful to the climate. It is sad to state that Nigeria has been labeled the second largest most gas-flared nation in the world and Africa's second largest emitter of greenhouse gases after South Africa (German Development Institute, 2012). To further underscore the importance of climate change, an Intergovernmental Panel on Climate Change (IPCC) was established at the global level to focus its attention on the climate change conundrum. It is equally important to state that proper management of the climate is key to the sustenance of today's world as the entire globe can cease to exist if the climate is not well catered for. One key challenge of climate change is the polarized views of stakeholders on the causative factors and remedies to this conundrum as researchers have continued to maintain divergent opinions on

E. S. Akpabio (✉)
Department of Political Science, Trinity University, Yaba, Lagos, Nigeria
e-mail: edidiong.akpabio@trinityuniversity.edu.ng

the causal factors responsible for climate change. This in itself is a challenge as confusion is likely to erupt with this plethora of views hence the tendency for the accentuation of the climate change conundrum. Also important to note is the fact that these diversity in viewpoints is not limited to researchers alone, as policymakers have also caught the bug. While some advocate the adoption of adaptation strategies, others are okay with the use of mitigation strategies. This lack of policy cohesion and coordination has continued to impair the efforts made towards defeating the climate change conundrum.

Introduction

It is glaring that the earth is getting warmer and the blame lies primarily on human beings (Spore, 2008). Man's activities have continued to directly or indirectly affect the climatic conditions of our world today, hence the bulk of the blame lies with humans rather than on natural causes. Granted that the consequences of climate change are multifaceted and manifest in the political, social and economic dimensions, it is important to state that the earth has warmed an average of 0.6 degrees centigrade over the past 100 years (Environment Canada, 2008). While the phenomena of climate change has diverse consequences ranging from food scarcity, disease conditions, strife and conflicts amongst others and human lives are being changed with the occurrence of climate change, global warming has continued to produce devastating and untoward consequences in the recent past. Take, for instance, the flooding in Bangkok, India and Australia coupled with the heat waves in Europe amongst others. Hence, having recognized the dangers inherent in climate change, several mechanisms have been put in place to tackle the challenges of climate change with the most prominent of them being the United Nations Framework Convention on Climate Change and the Kyoto protocol. It is clear without any iota of doubt that the climate deserves to be reinvigorated and this can only happen if there is a tenacious adherence to the spirit and letters of this agreement. Overtime humanity has harmed the environment so much so that the environment requires healing. Man harmed his environment through carrying out actions that are inimical to the sustainability of the environment and harmful to the climate. Nigeria has been labeled the second largest most gas-flared nation in the world and Africa's second largest emitter of greenhouse gases after South Africa (German Development Institute, 2012). To further underscore the importance of climate change, an Intergovernmental Panel on Climate Change (IPCC) was established at the global level to focus its attention on the climate change conundrum. It is equally important to state that proper management of the climate is key to the sustenance of today's world as the entire globe can cease to exist if the climate is not well catered for. One key challenge of climate change is the polarized views of stakeholders on the causative factors and remedies to the climate change conundrum as researchers have continued to maintain divergent opinions on the causal factors of climate change. This in itself is a challenge as confusion is likely to erupt with this plethora of views hence the tendency for the accentuation of the climate change conundrum. Also important to note is the fact that these his diversity in viewpoints is not limited to researchers alone, as policymakers have also caught the bug. While some advocate the adoption of adaptation strategies others are okay with the use of mitigation strategies. This lack of policy cohesion and coordination has continued to impair the efforts made towards defeating the climate change conundrum.

It is a misplaced priority that while Africa is busy chasing after the attainment of the sustainable development goals, she is neglecting a key catalyst for her attainment of these goals which is the environment, this is undisputably so as proper management of the climate remains a key catalyst for the attainment of the Sustainable Development Goals (SDGs). In 1987, the Brundtland commission had stated that for development to be sustainable it must meet the needs of the present without compromising the ability of the future generations to meet their needs. As plausible and laudable as this may seem, it is quite unfortunate that climate change is already compromising the ability of the future generation to meet their needs. This is because the environment is a major resource for man's needs to be met. This throws up a question; If the environment is distorted, how can man meet his needs? Climate change has affected humanity very significantly because of its effects on the environment which man depends on for survival hence, the need to develop mitigation and adaptation strategies towards the climate change conundrum cannot be overemphasized. At the onset of this problem (climate change), mitigation was essentially accepted but times have changed as adaptation is now accepted as the best approach towards this climate change conundrum. Aside the contention over what to accept; be it mitigative or adaptative in nature, several bilateral and multilateral strategies have been deployed with the sole objective of attaining victory over the climate change debacle. This aside, while we allude to the position that the effects of climate change are global, research has shown that although developed countries are adversely affected by the consequences of climate change, developing countries are more prone to its effects as they lack adequate adaptive capacities and are often victims of a poor, porous and clumsy policy framework.

Coming down to Nigeria, it is obvious that climate change has adversely affected millions of the populace as a huge percentage of the workforce are employed in the agricultural sector, hence, climate change will affect agricultural activities and lead to huge job losses. It is, therefore, in order to state that climate change is man's greatest enemy. Hence, it behooves on Man to collectively join forces to defeat this malaise. Especially as it pertains to Nigeria, it is important to state that there is a nexus between climate change and violent conflicts and the consequences of climate change have led to migration challenges in the Nigerian nation. What is therefore the way forward for Nigeria in this conundrum of climate change? How can Nigeria mitigate the effects of climatic dysfunction on its populace? The answers to these questions are not farfetched as this work provides feasible solutions that can lead the Nigerian state out of this quagmire.

Conceptual Definition's

Public policy is whatever the government chooses to do or not to do (Dye, 1972). This definition by Dye emphasizes that public policy is the government's sole decision to embark on. However, for Rose (1969), public policy is not a decision, it is a course or pattern of activity, this implies that the pattern of activities a particular government carries out is the sum total of her policies. Irrespective of the definition adopted, it is important to note that public policies are key structures for governance and administration.

It is important to state that although climate change and global warming are often misconstrued to refer to the same thing, they are quite differentas global warming is a component of climate change. Climate change is an adverse change as it leads to irregular and unpredictable rainfall and sunshine, which negatively affects farming activities. Mitigation and adaptation, are two frontline measures necessary for confronting the climate change conundrum. What then is climate change? climate change refers to any change in climate overtime whether due to natural variability or as a result of human activity (McCarthy, 2001). McCarthy's definition of climate change implies that the occurrence of climate change is beyond Man's activity hence the need for a properly articulated and implementable adaptation policy as man's actions have a limited role to play in the occurrence of climate change.

Batie (2008), tagged climate change as a wicked problem by this he meant that the challenge of climate change was a burden on the human race and required concerted efforts to overcome. It is also defined as a change of climate which is attributed directly or indirectly to human activity that alters the composition of the global atmosphere and which is in addition to natural climate variability observed over comparable time periods (Parry, 2007). Studies have shown that human activity has played a great role in the climate change conundrum. Although there are natural causes of climate change, human activities continue to accentuate the impacts of climate change on the globe. Aside from affecting negatively on rainfall patterns climate change affects the natural ecosystems, biodiversity and human health (Zoellick & Robert, 2009), with these negative impacts on the natural ecosystem, man's existence is threatened. Looking at the impact of climate change on rainfall and the importance of adequate and timely rainfall for crop cultivation there is a necessity to give climate change issues adequate governmental attention as choosing to neglect issues associated with climate change is to willingly beckon on food scarcity and the implications of food scarcity are manifold and catastrophic.

Globalization and the Climate Change Debacle

Climate change has become an international issue so much so that several world leaders continue to converge at diverse fora to seek practicable, feasible and workable solutions to its menace. Nigeria has played a significant role in ending this global challenge through her active participation at diverse levels of engagement. To further butress the concerted efforts made by Nigeria, at a summit on climate change attended by several world leaders, Nigeria's current president stated thus…

> Nigeria will continue to champion the core principles and goals of the new sustainable development agenda and hopes that the next conference of parties will eventually become a global milestone to combat and cushion the dire impacts of climate change… (President Buhari, 2015)

The history of climate change has been traced by some scholars to the industrial revolution which took place in Europe in the eighteenth century. This revolution which led to the invention of machines with the intent to simplify man's activities, brought about the use of combustible machines which required fossil fuels to run. It is however, worrisome to state that these fossil fuels ran machines have continued to negatively affect the ozone layer and contribute fundamentally to the climate change conundrum. Also important to state is the increase in globalization which has worsened the climate change debacleas industrialization has made the world more prone to climate change as the effects of climate change are international in nature and do not respect national boundaries. In Nigerian, government policies have been largely affected by environmental considerations which explains her active engagements in several climate change agreements, pacts and protocols which she has either initiated or entered into. It is sad to note that with the quantum of such pacts globally the challenges of climate change continue to bestride the globe like a colossus of sorts and despite the signing of the Kyoto agreements to reduce carbon emission rates, climate change continues to devastate our world.

Nigeria and the Dilemma of Climate Change

The present state of truncated development on the African continent can be traceable to climate change. This is largely because climate change leads to disasters and such disasters could be diversionary to the government with the likelihood of consuming a large chunk of the nation's budget meant for development. More importantly is the fact that the rise in disasters irrespective of the propensity could be a threat to development gains and hinder the implementation of the Millennium Development Goals (ISDR, 2008). Also worthy of note is the fact that the Nigerian state is in a dilemma, although this is not restricted to Nigeria alone, the focus of this paper is on the Nigerian state hence the emphasis. The economic losses to the Nigerian nation due to climate change are huge and monumental and with such magnitude of losses, it can deplete her national treasury and stall developmental efforts. Hence, the rationale for allocating funds to implement mitigative policies on the climate. Climate change does not only dim the prospects of national development but also threatens the sustainability of the environment. It has been stated that although climate change is a global challenge its effects are likely to be more for developing states (Jagtap, 2007), hence, Nigeria being a developing state is invariably confronted with this anomaly referred to as climate change. This underscores therefore the need for the development of effective policy measures to save the country from the impending crisis of climate change as Nigeria was identified as a climate change hot spot likely to see a major shift in weather conditions in the twenty-first century by the intergovernmental panel on climate change (Boko et al., 2007). This shows that Nigeria is a state that can be endangered if steps are not taken to mitigate the effects of climate change, hence, the need for policymakers to put in place sustainable climate policies. Rather than continue to initiate policies that would end up in office cabinets, the requisite government parastatals must have policy implementation plans in place to ensure that the policies see the light of the day.

There is a relationship between poverty and climatic dysfunctions. Take for instance the issue of deforestation, which is mostly prevalent amongst the low-income earners who rely on firewood to prepare their meals and throw caution to the wind all in a bid to fulfill this desire. The impact of climate change is varied and multifarious on all facets of society because climate change affects national economic life, food security and even the state of physical infrastructure. While there is a drastic shift from fossil fuels globally, Nigeria's economy can be negatively impacted if this happens as her national budget is nearly 100% dependent on crude oil. To buttress the import of climate change on her national life it has been discovered that it is key to poverty eradication as Nigeria is gradually sliding back into the list of the poorest states on the globe and important to her attainment of the SDGs. Little wonder that the Nigerian vision 2020 has the promotion of renewable energy sources and investment in low carbon fuels as one of its objectives.

Nigeria seems to be one of the nations on the earth worst hit by the climate change conundrum as her near mono-produce economy has made it very vulnerable to climatic dysfunction. She is the most populated state on the African continent, home to diverse nationals and having so many economic activities, she requires a holistic, feasible and workable policy on climate change. One area that climate change has affected Nigeria negatively is in the area of health. To further exemplify this,due to climate change, she recorded mortalities from heat and experienced the spread of infectious diseases and damage to public health infrastructures. Physical environmentalists (notably meteorologists and climatologists) argue that there is an interwoven relationship between the character of the physical environment and climate change (Amobi & Onyishi, 2015). This viewpoint is very lucid as the physical environment can be negatively impacted if the atmosphere is affected negatively too. The involvement of Man in several anti-climate practices can turn out to be his greatest undoing as the impacts of these anti-climactic practices might take a long while to materialize. Hence, man must have the consciousness that how he treats the environment goes a long way to determine the type of environment he will have in the end. One dangerous dimension to the challenge of climate change in Nigeria is the threat of food shortages, this is rightly so as considering the importance of food to the overall wellbeing of humanity, it is a pity that this has not been taken too seriously by the government. Adejuwon (2004) had stated that global warming negatively impacted crop growth, availability of soil water, caused floods amongst others. Nigeria like other states of the globe depends largely on rain-fed agriculture and the pathetic thing about Nigeria's situation is that her northern region has been plagued for a very long time by the scourge of deforestation hence she needs to make rapid progress in climate change governance if she is serious of attaining sustainable development.

This climate-induced deforestation has come with several untoward consequences as rather than enrich the forest reserves, they are gradually being depleted with a vast number of forest species facing extinction and becoming endangered species. According to the Program manager National LPG Expansion Implementation Plan in Nigeria, 19 states in Northern Nigeria suffer from deforestation and desertification (Sanyaolu, 2017). In a bid to promote the use of clean fuels for cooking and discourage the use of firewood, both corporate organizations and the government have introduced several schemes. These schemes have oftentimes come with subsidy on LPG cooking stoves to enable the indigent members of society discard firewood and discourage the feeling of trees. Almost everyone is negatively impacted by climate change in Nigeri from farmers, multi-national corporations, Non-Governmental Organizations, the government and several others. The Niger-Delta region of Nigeria which is home to Nigeria's black gold (crude oil) which has continued to remain Nigeria's 'cash cow' is gradually becoming a sorry sight as the pollution that has continually resulted from oil spills is having a negative influence on the climate. Streams and rivers have been polluted and this contamination of rivers is likely to endanger the lifespan of the occupants of such communities as they depend on the rivers for their water supplies. Everyone irrespective of social status collectively feels the impacts of climate change, with wind and rainstorms destroying economic assets worth 720 million USD in twelve states of Nigeria between 1992 and 2007 (Akpodiogaga et al., 2009), the magnitude of damage and cost has shown that climate change consequences are very disastrous and highly significant.

One of the major challenges of climate change in Nigeria is illiteracy; this is because of the high rate of uneducated people especially in rural communities. The lack of basic education by these people has led to them not knowing that their actions have continued to worsen the state of the climate. Inadequate national funding for climate-related programs have also stalled the programs from making quick headway. This is evident as a vast number of funding for these climate-related programs come from outside the country, for instance, the UNDP, The World Bank, The British council amongst other international non-governmental organizations. This in itself is a bad signal for people ready to combat the climate change conundrum. The unbundling of the power holding company of Nigeria and the privatization of the distribution arm of the Nigerian state-owned electricity corporations seems to be the albatross of the energy segment as the private companies who are now in charge of electricity distribution have performed dismally low to a point that the small and medium scale enterprises have had to rely on power generating sets or risk being thrown out of business. The continuous utilization of these generating sets comes at a very high cost to the environment as the rate of pollution continues to heighten.

It has been discovered that there is a linkage between climate change and conflictual relations. This is a truism in all respects as the effects of climate change continue to promote conflictual relations and intra-state violence. According to Smith

& Vivekananda, there are 46 countries which are home to 2.7 billion people in which the effects of climate change interacting with economic, social and political problems will create a high risk of violent conflict (Smith & Vivekananda, 2008). Distortions in the ecosystem have often translated to conflicts, for example, chief amongst the causal factors for violent confrontations between cattle herders and sedentary farmers is climate change as Nigeria is on the verge of disintegration if she does not check these farmers-herders uprisings occasioned by climate change. It is equally pertinent to state that the effects of climate change are all-encompassing as climate change has continued to endanger Nigeria's human and national security structures. Another significant contributor to Nigeria's dilemma of climate change is the inefficient and ineffective management of her environment. In spite of the fact that there are waste disposal agencies, they have been unable to effectively manage waste disposal. This is obvious as drains are littered with water sachets, disposable plastic bottles amongst other waste items. The blockage of these water ways has caused significant damage to the environment and continues to aggravate the precarious climatic condition.

Information dissemination is a key explanation for the climate change conundrum in Nigeria because the specialized agencies of government such as the National Orientation Agency and Federal Ministry of Information have done very little or nothing in the area of sensitization and information dissemination. It is worrisome to state that a vast number of the Nigerian populace especially those in the rural areas do not know what climate change is neither do they know its consequences or preventive measures they can apply to mitigate it. Ignorance as we all know has never been accepted as an excuse for misdemeanor. Nigerian citizens need to be properly educated on the dos and don'ts of environmental protection and conservation. They must be friendly to their environment by not harming it. Both the federal ministry of information and the national orientation agency ought to enlighten the public by carrying out sensitization workshops in all the 774 local government areas of Nigeria using their local dialects to achieve effective communication. There is also the problem of lack of quality and sophisticated equipment's at the agency as most of their weather forecast equipment's cannot match with the latest technology in vogue hence the challenge of sending wrong weather forecast which could be hugely misleading and defeat the government's desire to mitigate the challenges associated with climate change. Equally worthy of note is the fact that most National Emergency Management Agency officials are not committed to their duties as they are lukewarm and highly lethargic, hence, quite a number of employees do not discharge their duties with the expected level of zeal and commitment to duties hence the lapses recorded in the agency. The Nigerian Meteorological Agency whose primary responsibility is to forecast weather conditions seems to be resting on its oars as the nation is yet to maximally benefit from its forecast services which can be attributed to an avalanche of factors.

It is alarming to note that the environmental impact assessment carried out by the ministry of environment seems to be producing little or no results as the environment is continually being degraded and exposed to more harm. The ministry of environment, a government ministry set up with the mandate of protecting the environment has continued to renege on its responsibility. This is a sad development as the ministry was supposed to be a watchdog and environmental police for the Nigerian people. The ministry of petroleum resources on the other hand, despite the numerous sensitization campaigns carried out with the sole objective of putting an end to gas flaring due to its very grave effects on the climate change situation has turned out with limited success. This is quite surprising as one would have expected a high degree of compliance as it pertains to gas flaring. This situation of gas flaring calls for concern as most oil-producing companies continue to flare gas with reckless abandon. Hence, rather than convert this gas to other advantageous uses they are flared to continue to negatively impact the atmosphere and in the end worsen the climate change dilemma.

Impacts of Climate Change on Nigeria

- **Agricultural Sector**: The effects of climate change have negatively influenced this sector, which is segmented into crop cultivation and livestock farming, this is evident in the distortion in rainfall patterns which has affected farming seasons while droughts have made pasture for livestock unavailable. These untoward occurrences have led to the death of crops and livestock.
- **Distortion of the Eco-system**: Climate change distorts the ecosysteming which the citizenry depend on hence leading to the endangering of lives depending on the ecosystem for survival.
- **Power Sector**: The power sector of Nigeria's economy is on the verge of suffering the consequences of climate change. This is obvious as most power generating stations depend on hydro sources for electricity generation; hence, there is the risk of loss in generation capacity if sea levels are distorted.
- **Internal Migration**: Climate change leads to a surge in the rate of internal migration within Nigeria. This is because most people are likely to leave areas worst-affected to less affected areas.
- **High Rate of Poverty**: Climate change will continue to increase the rate of poverty in Nigeria if it remains unchecked. This is because most low-income earners often have their livelihood threatened by variations in climatic conditions.
- **Intra-State Conflicts**: Climate-induced conflicts continue to be the leading cause of internal insurrections in the Nigerian state. The ongoing herders-farmers confrontation that has led to the death of thousands of Nigerians and rendered many others homeless is a case in point.
- **Decline in National Earnings and Dearth of Commercial Sectors**: Nigeria's national earnings continue to nosedive and suffer sharp decline as many sectors of the economy suffer the ripple effects of climate change. Sectors of the economy that are directly impacted by the consequences of climate change are on the verge of closing up while a few others have long exited the market. Examples of such firms are thermal power generation companies that use sea water as their major resource and food processing companies that rely on farm produce for processing into finished products.

Climate Change, Impacts and Consequences for Food Systems

Climate change impact systems	Direct consequences for food
Increased frequency and severity of extreme Weather events	Crop failure or reduced yields
	Loss of livestock
	Damage to fisheries and forests
	Destruction of agricultural inputs such as seeds tools
	Either an excess or shortage of water
	Increased land degradation and desertification
	Destruction of food supply chains
	Increased costs for marketing and distributing food
Rising temperatures	Increased evapotranspiration resulting in reduced soil moisture
	Greater destruction of crops and trees by pests
	Greater threats to human health (e.g. disease and heat stress) that reduce the productivity and availability of agricultural labor
	Greater threats to livestock health
	Reduced quality and reliability of agricultural yields
	Greater need for cooling/refrigeration to maintain food quality and safety
	Greater threats of wildfires
Shifting agricultural seasons and erratic rainfall	Reduced quantity and quality of agricultural yields and forests products
	Either an excess or shortage of water
	Greater need for irrigation
Sea level rise	Damage to coastal fisheries
	Direct loss of cultivable land due to inundation and salinization of soil
	Salinisation of water resources

Source Care Int' (2011)

X-raying Public Policies in Nigeria

Public policies dictate the direction of government and governance, they provide a road map or blueprint for the government and its agencies. Public policy can be described as the overall framework with which government activities are undertaken to achieve public goals (Malone & Cochran, 2014). Public policy has also been defined as the heart, soul and identity of governments everywhere (Public Administration, 2012). Public policymaking is intricate, dynamic and majorly formulated by the government through its organs and often directed at the future through the needs of the present. There are different variants of public policy which includes regulatory, substantive, distributive, redistributive policies amongst others. There is often the temptation of mistaking policies and decisions to mean the same thing, this is erroneous as they mean different things. The decision is the process of making choices out of alternatives; they are part of policies as groups of decisions that make up a policy.

Policies are the blueprint that determines the tempo of governance, It remains a principal function of government to make public policies that would save the citizenry from certain specific challenges, hence it will be apt to refer to public policies as part of every government globally. Irrespective of the form of government, be it monarchy, tyranny, aristocracy, democracy et al. governance which is majorly preoccupied with taking care of members of the society requires public policies to enable it carry out its responsibilities. Viana (1996), had segmented the policy-making process into four which are agenda-setting, formulation, implementation and evaluation. It is imperative to adopt his approach to the policy-making process as these steps as outlined go a long way in making sustainable public policies. One key part of Viana's policymaking steps is evaluation. When policies are evaluated post-implementation, it aids the policymakers to know how effective the policies have been. In the case of Nigeria, the onus lies on the national assembly to pass bills into laws that eventually translate into public policies. Quite unfortunately, there have been instances where bills sent to the national assembly are unduly delayed legislative attention. It will do her (Nigeria) more better than harm if as a nation bills sent to the national assembly are given expeditious action as undue delays at the national assembly could lead to avertable situations. In Nigeria, there are various agencies charged with the responsibility of public policy execution and implementation. The Federal Ministry of the environment is chiefly responsible for all environmental issues in the Nigerian state. Also embedded in the federal ministry of environment is the special climate change unit which coordinates Nigeria's communication with the UNFCCC. The paucity of adequate human and technical capacities including periodic training has also hampered the smooth functioning of the SCCU. We must reiterate that these agencies carry out their duties within the ambit of the law enacted by the national assembly. In the national assembly, there are specific committees that carry out oversight functions over these agencies, for instance, the national assembly committee on environment and energy is responsible for issues pertaining to climate change. Public policy plays a very significant role in national life, for Nigeria's climate change policies have unfortunately recorded limited successes because of the lack of an all-encompassing database for effective planning.

It is instructive to state that while public policy formulation is important, the proper implementation of those policies is more important. In Nigeria, it is unfortunate to note that one factor that has continued to stall the effectiveness of laudable public policies initiated is the challenge of implementation. While so much energy, time, resources et al. is put into public policy formulation very little can be said for policy implementation. This is a major explanation for the myriad of ineffective public policies in the Nigerian political space. However, considering the dangers that the climate change conundrum poses to her national existence there is an urgent need to strengthen public policies in Nigeria that are environmentally related, because, a strengthened policy implementation framework will greatly aid the nation in its drive to preserve the climate and save it from deterioration and dysfunction. The war against climate variation must be urgent and total without half measures if the state is desirous of winning the war.

Nigerian Government, Climate Change and Policy Response Mechanism

Emissions from Africa are accentuating (Canadell et al., 2009). Unlike in other climes where climate change is still regarded as a myth, in Africa, climate change and its negative impacts are already here. It is surprising that although African countries are not the countries with the highest emission of greenhouse gases they tend to suffer climate change disorders more than other countries with higher emission rates. It has been observed that in most African countries-Nigeria inclusive public policies abound, what is lacking most times is the capacity to see these policies through. In other words, most African governments lack the political will to execute policies made. Take for instance a parastatal in Nigeria referred to as the National Emergency Management Agency (NEMA), whose response to emergencies is always reactive rather than proactive. This is a faulty response attitude, as NEMA should develop a pre-emptive and proactive mechanism that can help to forestall the occurrence of disasters. While its intelligence unit must carry out periodic checks to stop environmental disasters occasioned by climate change from occurring, NEMA has become known for late response and always trying to salvage already sore situations. This negates the reason for its establishment in the first instance.

Lack of adequate technical workforce continues to militate against the government's desire to stop gas flaring in oil production fields in Nigeria. Another dimension to this climate change conundrum is that the health of a significant number of Nigeria's populace is being threatened by the consequences of climate change and her natural resources could also experience same level of threats if the citizenry do not collectively fight the climate change conundrum. One common trend in Nigeria is the penchant for organizing symposiums, seminars et al. that are not specifically targeted to the vulnerable class. These programs are often organized with the sole objective of fulfilling all righteousness rather than being targeted to those in dire need of it. Over the last few years, public power supply and distribution in Nigeria have continued to dwindle, consequent upon this, inadequate power supply has led households and businesses to alternative power sources, which has contributed significantly to household and industrial pollution (Akinyemi et al., 2014), which has left small-scale business owners with no alternative but to provide other sources of energy for themselves and this situation has made them use gasoline power generating sets for long hours daily. These generating sets have further compounded the issues of pollution Nigeria is grappling with and continues to worsen the climate change conundrum. Mideksa and Kallbekken (2010), carried out a research to ascertain the impacts of climate change on the electricity market by looking at prevalent knowledge on the likely effects on demand and supply of electricity. It was on the strength of this that Akinbami (2009), after assessing the implication of the climate change vis-à-vis energy systems and its likely effects on sustainable development in Nigeria admonished the government to be more proactive. By this, he implied putting in place mitigation technologies to forestall the impacts of climate change on the sector.

As a response to climate change, the Nigerian government has reformed the energy sector by putting in place renewable energy policies through the federal ministry of power in a bid to reduce dependency on fossil fuels for power generation in the country. With the awareness that the energy sector will be vulnerable to the impacts of climate change, quite a number of coping strategies are being introduced by the relevant government parastatals. Considering the strategic importance of the energy sector to our collectivity and the fact that access to energy is a crucial enabling condition for achieving sustainable development (Oyedepo, 2012), the federal government is encouraging the use of renewable energy sources for power generation hence the signing of power purchase agreements by the Nigerian bulk electricity trading plc. This PPA's are signed at rates slightly higher than the ones with thermal power sources. The intention is to encourage foreign-based power generation companies to invest in Nigeria's power sector by deploying renewable energy technologies. The energy industry is a strategic component of national life and can desecrate the environment and compound the impacts of climate change if not handled properly. The National Adaptation Strategy and Plan of Action on Climate Change for Nigeria came into existence in December 2011. Since its inception to date, it has continued to take the issues of climate change very seriously. NAPSA-CCN continually continues to strategize and embark on a policy overhaul to identify gaps and effectively plug them. NAPSA-CCN strategies are multifarious and aninteresting feature of the NAPSA-CCN is the fact that it has an avalanche of strategies ranging from energy, education, livelihoods, vulnerable groups, health and sanitation, disaster, migration and security. NASPA-CCN, a climate response policy has been developed by the government and has amongst others the integration of climate change adaptation with sustainable development. The reduction of vulnerabilities of Nigerian citizens to the adverse impacts of climate change and taking full advantage of the emergent opportunities embedded in the challenge. NASPA-CCN vision has revealed that beyond challenges and envisaged problems there are hidden benefits that can be unearthed and discovered from climatic changes. A pertinent question props up, what are the opportunities and how can national policy responses help the citizens especially the entrepreneurial class take full advantage of the embedded benefits in the climate change dilemma?

Vulnerabilities to the consequences of climate change are on an upward trend hence the necessity for periodic vulnerabilities assessment by officials from the ministry of environment. These periodic assessments will aid planning to prevent the occurrence of climate change consequences. It is important to note that issues of the climate must not be treated with levity as their implications are far-reaching and continuous decline could spell grave danger of unimaginable magnitude. Hence, most communities in Nigeria having being impacted negatively by the effects of climate change have put in place coping strategies to enable them surmount the challenges that come with climate change.

Recommendations

The current wave of development currently experienced on the African continent is making her vulnerable to the climate change conundrum, hence, the urgent need for all and sundry to up their game and tackle this menace headlong. Looking at the nation Nigeria, despite the fact that she is making efforts to confront the adverse development of climate change more needs to be done hence the recommendations proffered below.

- **Inter-ministerial composition of climate change unit**: The newly established unit for climate change should be made up of officials from the ministry of finance, trade, commerce and industries and ministry of employment. The reason for incorporating other ministries into this unit is not farfetchedas their various inputs will greatly aid the smooth running of the unit and impact its overall efficiency.
- **Increased sensitizations and heightened public enlightenment**: There is a need to increase sensitization campaigns to the populace on the effects of climate change. The national orientation agency must step up its game by carrying out sensitizations in all the 774 local governments of Nigeria, as there are so many Nigerians that have never heard of the word climate change how much more knowing its effects and the things they can do to avert its occurrence.
- **Effective monitoring of power distribution companies**: It is recommended that the federal ministry of power through its various parastatals charged with the monitoring of the distribution companies rise to the occasion by ensuring that consumers have access to uninterrupted power supply for 24 h daily. If this is achieved, power-generating sets will disappear from homes and business premises while the pollution emanating from them will become outmoded.
- **Partnerships and linkages with universities**: There is a need for expertise in handling environmental considerations. Hence, it is important for the ministry of science and technology to collaborate with the universities and other institutes to conduct researches with a view to overcoming the climate change conundrum. There is also the need for more climate change specific research endeavors by academics and research institutes. It is recommended that there should be centers for climate change research in all universities, polytechnics and monotechnics in Nigeria as the findings from this climate-focused researches will greatly help the most populated African country and save her from being a victim of the

negative consequences of climate change while leading to the introduction of new technologies to aid adaptation in the nation Nigeria.

- **Discovery of opportunities in climate change**: We recommend that a unit be established in the federal ministry of environment with the sole responsibility of discovering the opportunities that the business community can harness as this would greatly aid the national economy. For instance, it has been discovered that flared gas can be used for several profitable purposes while waste materials can be recycled to new items. This recycling in itself can boost national revenues, create employment and save the environment from the crisis of climatic disorderliness and dysfunctionalities.

Concluding Remarks

Climate change requires sound adaptation policies if man must cope with its negative effects. Wigley (1998), had stated that implementing current greenhouse emissions pacts would still not stabilize atmospheric concentrations of GHG emissions and climate. In the case of Nigeria, the government has adopted a response mechanism to the challenges of the climatic disorder through the national climate change policy and putting in place a nationally-appropriate mitigation action. Hence, having carried out such actions in line with the current global action plan on climatic dysfunction-alitites, it is safe to posit that there is a ray of hope for Nigeria as regards climate change. This ray of hope has further gathered currency with the upsurge in power generation plants utilizing renewable energy sources such as solar, wind and waste to electricity sources.

This chapter has therefore identified weak policies as the bane of Nigerian society and revealed that although the government has put in place policy frameworks to address the challenges of climate change, there is a need for such to be strengthened and overhauled for the overall efficiency and sustainability of the environment as a sustainable environment translates to a sustainable society.

References

Adejuwon, S. A. (2004). *Impacts of climate variability and climate change on crop yield in Nigeria.* 'Paper presented at the stakeholders' workshop on assessment of impacts and adaptation to climate change (AIACC), Conference Centre, Obafemi Awolowo University, Ile-Ife, pp. 271–279.

Akinbami, J. F. K. (2009). *Climate change and energy: Issues, prospects and challenges for sustainable development in Nigeria.* Paper presented at capacity building workshop for house of representatives committee on climate change and the media, Kaduna.

Akinyemi, O., Ogundipe, A., & Alege P. (2014). Energy supply and climate change in Nigeria. *Journal of Environment and Earth Science, 4*(14).

Akpodiogaga, P., et al. (2009). Quantifying the cost of climate change in Nigeria, emphasis on "Wind and Rainstorms." *Journal of Human Ecology, 28*(2), 93–101.

Amobi, D., & Onyishi, T. (2015). Governance and climate change in Nigeria: A public policy perspective. *Journal of Policy and Development Studies*, 9(2).

Batie, S. S. (2008). Greatest contributions to our profession by agricultural and resource economists. In *2008 Annual Meeting*, July 27–29, Orlando Florida: Agricultural and Applied Economics Association.

Boko, M., et al. (2007). *Climate change 2007: Impacts, adaptation and vulnerability*. Cambridge University Press.

Care Int'l (2011, April), Adaptation and food security, climate change brief, p. 2 as cited in Odock, C. N. (2012). The political economy of climate change in Nigeria's South-South Zone. *American International Journal of Contemporary Research, 21*(12).

Dye, T. (1972). *Understanding public policy*. Prentice-Hall.

Environment Canada (2008). *What is climate change?* Accessed from https://www.ec.gc.ca/climate/overview-trendse.html on 03/05/2021.

Federal Government of Nigeria (n.d.). *First National Communication on Climate Change*.

German Development Institute (2012). African developments: Competing institutional arrangements for climate policy, the Case of Nigeria. Policy briefing paper no 7.

Houghton, R. A., Raupach, M. R., & Canadell, J. G. (2009). Anthropogenic CO_2 emissions in Africa. *Biogeosciences, 6*(3), 463–468.

International Strategy for Disaster Reduction (2008). *Disaster risk reduction strategies and risk management practices: Critical elements for adaptation to climate change*. Submission to the UN-FCCC Adhoc Working Group on Long-Term Cooperative Action retrieved from www.unisdr.org

Jagtap, S. (2007). Managing vulnerability to extreme weather and climate events: Implications for agriculture and food security in Africa. *Proceedings of the international conference on climate change and economic sustainability*. Nnamdi Azikiwe University, Enugu, Nigeria, June12–14.

Malone, F. E., & Cochran, C. L. (2014). *Public policy: Perspectives and choices* (5th ed.). Lynne Rienner Publishers.

McCarthy, J. J. (Ed.). (2001). *Climate change 2001: Impacts, adaptation and vulnerability: Contribution of working group 11 to the third assessment report of the intergovernmental panel on climate change*. Cambridge University Press.

Mideksa, T., & Kallbekken, S. (2010). The Impact of climate change on the electricity market: A review. *Energy Policy, 38*(7), 3579–3585.

Oyedepo, S. A. (2012). On Energy for sustainable development in Nigeria. *Renewable and Sustainable Energy Reviews, 16*, 2583–2598.

Parry, M. C., et al. (2007) (Eds.). Climate change 2007: Impacts, adaptations and vulnerability: Contribution of working group 11 to the fourth assessment report of the intergovernmental panel on climate change, Cambridge: Cambridge University Press.

Rose, R (1969) (Ed.). *Policy Making in Great Britain*, Macmillian Press.

Sanyaolu, A. (2017). How NLPGA, investors plan to grow $10bn cooking gas market, accessed from https://www.sunnewsonline.com on 8/30/202.

Smith, D., & Vivekananda (2008). *A climate of conflict*. Policy Paper, International Alert, Sida.

Spore. (2008). *Climate change, A bi-monthly magazine of the technical centre for agricultural and rural cooperation*. CTA, Wageningen.

Statement by: HE Muhammadu Buhari, President of the Federal Republic of Nigeria at Summit on Climate Change in New York, 27th September 2015.

Viana, A. L. (1996). Abordagens Metodológicas em Políticas Públicas. *Revista Da Administracao Publica, 20*(2), 5–43.

Wigley, T. M. L. (1998). The Kyoto Protocol: CO2, CH4 and climate implications. *Geophysical Research Letters, 25*(13), 2285–2288.

Zoellick, S., & Robert, B. A. (2009). *Climate smart future* (p. 18). The Nation Newspapers, Vintage Press Limited, Lagos.

Edidiong Samuel Akpabio is a lecturer in the Department of Political Science, Trinity University, Yaba Nigeria. His research interests span food security, social problems in Africa, and a plethora of other topics in African security and development; Edidiong teaches courses in African Politics at his current university. He contributed to the *Encyclopedia of the UN Sustainable Development Goals* and is the author of the work "Attaining SDGs in Africa through Bilateral and Multilateral Partnerships." and also recently co-authored "Food Security and Social Protection in Africa: Re-establishing the Nexus" —all published by Springer.

Chapter 11
Covid-19 Transition Turbulence: Structural Violence in a Time of Economic Paradigm Change

Małgorzata Zachara-Szymańska◉

Abstract This chapter uses Johan Galtung's typology of violence as an interpretative framework for contemporary shifts within the international economic system brought about by the dynamic of the transition towards more sustainable growth. The concept of sustainability is used here not only as a signifier of the direction of economic development, but also as a factor of resilience understood as the capacity of socio-ecological systems to withstand and respond to changes (Folke et al., Ecol Soc 15(4):555–520, 2010). The process of transformation towards sustainability, therefore, is seen as an essential factor in the maintenance of resilience, especially in the conditions of great acceleration of human activities and rising uncertainty. The operational layer of forces shaping the structural level of the global economic order is illustrated by the impact of the Covid-19 pandemic and responses to this threat, analyzed in the context of the transition towards sustainability. The moment of this major global crisis, revealing profound, longstanding vulnerabilities in the global system, can either open policy windows for a more effective transformation, or signify a major shock that fragile systems may be not able to absorb. It is argued that adaptation to changing external drivers and capacity to navigate transitions of different scale and nature is becoming part of the sustainability concept in its more general sense.

Introduction

The Coronavirus pandemic presents not only an immediate public health risk at the global scale, but also a long-term threat to both global stability and sustainable development. Its projected run-on effects exacerbate tensions and uncertainties across societies and produce challenges in other systems, undermining global well-being and amplifying risks associated with the structural conditions of economic and social life. The emergence of the pandemic directly influences the spheres of

M. Zachara-Szymańska (✉)
Faculty of International Topolowa 6/13 and Political Studies, Jagiellonian University, 31-512 Krakow, Poland
e-mail: malgorzata.zachara@uj.edu.pl

economy and environment, bringing new findings related to the concept and practices of sustainability. In consequence of the economic lockdown, global emissions were reduced to record low levels, biodiversity was enhanced, forest and maritime regenerative capacities improved (IEA, 2019).

Coal-fired power generation is reported to have declined by 50% in China, whereas oil consumption declined by 20–30% (Carbon Brief, 2020). Such confirmation of the critical interrelationship between economic activities and environmental conditions doesn't, however, indicate a solution that might be an effective response to the challenges posed by unsustainable growth. Radical responses to pandemics sufficient to result in the improvement of the environment—at high social and economic cost—can only be imposed in the context of an extraordinary crisis.

The appearance and unprecedented intensity of the pandemic presents a factor seriously influencing the structural level of economic systems that is likely to leave a permanent imprint on the sustainability/peace nexus and inspire new perspectives on sustainable development. The scale of the crisis exposed mechanisms via which the structural violence permeates all of the spheres of social and economic relations (Galtung, 1985), and how they are legitimized by the cultural constructs (Galtung, 1990). The scale of the disruption caused, underlying structural conditions and the types of response present a framework for analyzing the present resilience of the socio-economic models and perspective for maintaining the transformative course towards sustainability.

The chapter examines the question of how the pandemic may influence the transition to sustainability and discusses resilience as a primary feature of the economic models currently being mooted. The concept of resilience encompasses all the structural imbalances that weaken the ability of countries, communities and individuals to effectively and efficiently cope with the challenges we are facing. Resilience has long been present in the sustainability debate (Adger, 2000; Brown, 2015; Walker & Cooper, 2011), but its importance has now been elevated by the systemic vulnerabilities exposed by the pandemic. The UN resolution adopting Sustainable Development Goals indicates that "…sustainable development recognizes that eradicating poverty in all its forms and dimensions, combating inequality within and among countries, preserving the planet, creating sustained, inclusive and sustainable economic growth and fostering social inclusion are linked to each other and are interdependent" (UN, 2015: 5). Yet the recasting of sustainability as a complex, multidisciplinary and, indeed, 'wicked' problem has also been a way to excuse the slow transition to the new models. Before the pandemic, progress in attaining sustainable growth as reflected in all the Sustainable Development Goals had been mixed (Moyer & Hedden, 2020). By analysing the impact of the pandemic this article asks how the approach to the complexities of the transition to sustainability might change, and how this change can be reflected in post-pandemic policy design. It focuses on two questions in particular:

- How does the pandemic influence the way in which sustainability is conceptualized and reflected in social practices? Sustainability provides here a conceptual and normative framework oriented at the direct interventions needed to reduce the potential negative impact of climate variability on the economic well-being of the societies. The chapter's hypothesis assumes that the concept of sustainability is being transformed, as pandemics may result in a re-negotiation of the importance of inclusive growth as a part of systemic resilience, alongside efficiency and profitability.

- How have forms of structural violence existing in economic systems been exacerbated by the pandemic, and how will they influence views on social design in the post-pandemic world? The article uses Galtung's typology of violence (Galtung, 1969) as an interpretative framework for contemporary shifts within the international economic system caused by the dynamic of the transition towards more sustainable growth. The forces shaping the structural level of the economic order are illustrated by the impact of Covid-19 and responses to the pandemic examined in the context of the sustainability transition. Structure-oriented analysis reveals the mechanisms of economic reasoning that stand behind certain moves and the policies of individual and group actors. Within this framework, the roots of violence are traced to the way in which society is organized, how resources are distributed and what kind of opportunities are created.

The aim of this chapter is to understand the interplay between the forces building sustainability and driving responses to economic consequences of the pandemic. The point of departure for this text is the assumption that, due to magnitude of changes brought by Covid-19, the hierarchy of the factors shaping the socio-economic environment is being rescheduled. As governments consider public health and economic strategies responsive to the crisis, they also create the grounds on which the structural weaknesses of systems that inhibited their ability to respond comprehensively to the pandemic could be addressed in the future.

Coronavirus pandemic—The Turbulence of the Transition

The original concept of positive peace was built upon a reference to the human health system, in which health was understood not only as an absence of disease but also an ability to develop a strong immune system able to prevent and resist health hazards (Galtung, 1985). So not only the effectiveness of the global economic system in its actual (non-sustainable) and potential (sustainable) forms is taken into consideration, but also the system's resilience. Global economic changes are perceived here as factors influencing the systemic ability to resist causes of violence and develop more synergies that could reduce structural vulnerabilities. The framework conditions that increasingly challenge sustainable development and undermine systemic resilience are described by the VUCA (volatility, uncertainty, complexity, and ambiguity) concept, which identifies the high frequency and magnitude of change in the contemporary socio-economic arena (Bennett & Lemoine, 2014; Shambach, 2004).

Such an outlook has also influenced the conceptualization of social realities in the context of sustainability, giving prominence to the non-linear trends in both natural and cultural systems (Folke et al., 2010; Lovejoy, 2005). The first usage of the concept coincided with the emerging field of complexity and chaos theory, and later the approach was widely adopted following the financial crisis of 2008–2009, when societies suddenly found themselves faced with similar conditions while addressing global economic turmoil. Another vivid example of complex system dynamic has been provided by the most recent global crisis, triggered by the Coronavirus pandemic.

A novel type of coronavirus (Covid-19) first appeared in Wuhan in China, in December 2019/January 2020. From here, this highly infectious virus caused a cataclysmic course resulting in over 2.6 million deaths worldwide by March 2021 (WHO, 2020). The real total number of cases remains unknown as testing is limited in most countries.

The appearance and spread of the virus prove the prominence of the VUCA factors of uncertainty, indeterministic tendencies, and non-linear relationships and feedback processes in defining a threat and response formulation. The pandemic not only confirms the diagnosis of the unprecedented level of threat that the global order needs to contend with, but also presents a major phase of turbulence in the evolution of the global economic system that may either accelerate or block the transition to sustainability. This is due to the nature of pandemics that have the features of the 'black swan'—a single, highly transformative factor that shapes social realities on a large scale (Taleb, 2007). While the nature of such pandemics is still open to debate, this outbreak matches the description of the three attributes typical for a 'black swan' event:

- It is an outlier, being outside the realm of regular expectations. The possibility of the pandemic has been long predicted, as disease outbreaks such as SARS, Ebola, Marburg, hantavirus, Zika and avian influenza are all considered to be outcomes of anthropogenic impacts on ecosystems (World Bank, 2012). Analysts of the US National Intelligence Council, in a report released in 2012, suggested that 'An easily transmissible novel respiratory pathogen that kills or incapacitates more than one percent of its victims is among the most disruptive events possible' (NIC, 2012). The timing of its appearance and exact nature of this specific SARS-CoV-2 coronavirus had not been predicted, but the probability of a global pandemic involving a highly infectious respiratory virus was considered a plausible scenario. This does not mean, however, that protective systems were in place when the outbreak occurred. So the effect of the shock and 'strategic surprise' that multiply the consequences of pandemics puts the Covid-19 in the category of being outside the realm of regular expectations.
- Explanations for the occurrence are concocted after the fact, making it explainable and predictable. The mechanism of cross-species transmission of viruses is already fairly well researched, providing an explanatory platform for the new mutation's appearance. The potential impact of the pandemic and the pace of its reproduction could also be assessed on the basis of global mobility and increased urbanization.
- It carries an extreme impact. A pandemic bearing a threat to the survival of a substantial part of the global population has triggered unprecedented responses that have impacted all levels of social interaction. At the initial stage, with a limited

medical capacity to treat the disease, nonpharmaceutical interventions (NPI) were the main strategy for containing the social risk. In consequence, one-half of the world's population was asked to stay home (Baker et al., 2020). The most popular measures varied from lockdown (home isolation, voluntary/required quarantine), to different forms of social distancing affecting vulnerable groups or entire populations. This framework of action included the closure of schools/universities and non-essential businesses/workplaces, and the cancelling or postponing events (i.e., major conferences and tradeshows, concerts and festivals, political debates and elections, sports seasons, including the Summer Olympics 2020). With international travel bans affecting over 90% of the world population within just two months, the framing of the global tourism system moved from over-tourism to 'nontourism' (Gössling et al., 2020).

The capacity of individuals, societies and systems to respond to and influence change has been tested, bringing a reorientation in hierarchies of policy objectives and shared beliefs. Governments around the world have been forced to impose a suite of extraordinary public policies, limiting the public health crisis but also producing long-term impacts in expectations of the role of government, national debt and general economic model.

The importance of resilience has grown drastically, both in the context of economic sustainability and recognition of the need to redesign social models so that they can better absorb and adapt to the crisis, as well as better address change and uncertainty more generally. The fragility of the international and national systems has been exposed, fueling changes in alliances, institutions and the global economy. Dealing with the immediate health crisis has accelerated adaptive mechanisms ranging from the rapid loosening of regulations regarding the manufacture of medical devices such as masks and ventilators, or eliminating barriers to the employment of medical professionals, to massive public increases in public welfare spending and in public debt. The extraordinary situation of the pandemic has revealed, however, an urgent need to build such adaptive mechanisms into the regular economic framework so as to ensure the rapid transformation of complex economic systems when local and structural circumstances change.

Covid-19 and the Global Economic Order

The global economy presents a complex, ever-evolving structure in which actors operate according the scripts driven by markets, technology, global value chain orchestration, open innovation and a whole variety of other factors. While economic activities are undertaken by actors, structural conditions provide the spectrum of options that they have at their disposal. In 2020 the pandemic has marked a deep change in the operational structures of the global and local economies. Limitations on international, regional and local imposed by governments immediately affected national economies, resulting in the most severe disruption since World War II. The interconnectedness of economic relations caused a cascade effect in all sectors, even those only loosely related to the ones most impacted by the lockdown. Global supply chains have been interrupted and production in China dropped, which led to a negative supply shock. A direct impact on income and economic growth was noted due to premature deaths, workplace absenteeism, and decreased productivity. An estimated 81% of the global workforce has been hit by full or partial lockdown measures (ILO, 2020).

The situation was particularly pressing for informally employed workers: in India, 90% of street vendors have not been able to work; in Africa 35 million informal service sector jobs, as well as 15 million in the manufacturing and construction sectors, are vulnerable (Jayaram et al., 2020). Job market uncertainty decreased income and the inability of households and companies to make long-term budgeting plans have modified consumers' spending behaviors, undermining market confidence (OECD, 2020). Many economic actors have adopted a 'wait and see' approach, minimizing their market activities. Substantial detrimental effects on tourism, air transport, public transport, accommodation, cafes and restaurants, conferences, tourism and services have been reported. Travel restrictions have cost the tourism industry alone over $200 billion globally, excluding other loss of revenue for tourism and travel, and were forecast to cost the aviation industry a total loss of US 113 billion (Peterson & Thankom, 2020). Constraints on production and supply chains resulted in obstacles to food production and transport, eroding the food security of millions of people. The World Bank estimates that 40–60 million more people will find themselves in the condition of extreme poverty due to the Covid-19 pandemic (Pangestu, 2020).

According to the International Monetary Fund, the global economy is expected to shrink by 3% in 2020 with 'the worst economic fallout since the Great Depression,' while global debt increased this year by 19% relative to gross domestic product (IMF, 2020).

The world financial and oil markets significantly declined as well. Since the start of 2020, leading U.S. and European stock market indices (the S&P 500, FTSE 100, CAC 40, and DAX) have lost a quarter of their value, with oil prices declining by more than 65% as of April 24, 2020 (Pak et al., 2020).

The economic impact of the Covid-19 pandemic can be measured also by the scale of the recovery plans designed by governments all around the world to prevent the crisis from having devastating long-terms effects. The stimulus packages in the leading world economies were the highest ever recorded, reflecting the premise that the economic damage has to be stopped at any cost for the sake of minimizing the escalation of the human tragedy. Provisions of the Coronavirus Aid, Relief, and Economic Security Act, or CARES Act, signed in March 2020 secured US 2.7 trillion in March and April (about 13% of the gross domestic product) to provide economic relief to individuals, firms and states. It was the largest economic stimulus in American history. The European Commission agreed to dedicate a US 2.1 trillion budget and coronavirus relief package, which is the biggest in European history, far outstripping the post-World War II Marshall Plan (Hepburn et al., 2020).

The pandemic has tested the resilience of national economies, their structural conditions indicated by the level of income inequality, the dynamism of ecosystem for entrepreneurship, degree of the precariousness of employees, amongst other factors that will shape the long-term consequences of this disruption.

In some countries, economic turmoil is likely to reverse positive trends in socio-economic progress, which means pushing a significant number of people into unemployment and poverty while increasing inequality. The level of health inequalities is directly combined with the fluctuations in income distribution in the aftermath of Covid-19, which is especially striking in systems without universal healthcare coverage. The market inequalities deepened by the pandemic are likely to shape the structural features of highly developed economies. The impact of the pandemic on different economic sectors and occupations has been related to their digital maturity. Firms at the technological frontier strengthened their dominance in increasingly concentrated markets. The growing level of automation of low- to semi-skilled tasks has resulted in a demand for higher-level skills, negatively impacting wages and jobs at the lower end of the skill spectrum (Rose, 2020). While technology has become a core enabler in responding to the challenges of the pandemic, it is probable that the benefits of technological transformation will continue to be shared highly unequally. The 'winner takes it all' principle, reinforced during the pandemic, is likely to provide transformative opportunities to those with access to infrastructure, capital and knowledge, leaving those without further behind (Quresh, 2020).

The extreme situation of the pandemics revealed that economics has been the major point of reference in both imposing responsive strategies and balancing mitigation efforts with the potential social harm connected to the severe limitation of economic activity. Resources were needed to prevent the spread of the virus on the one hand, and have to be invested in systems that have been seriously weakened by the massive consequences of the 'lockdown' on the other.

While the general impact and full consequences of the pandemic 'black swan' cannot yet be estimated, its appearance undoubtedly carries the transformative potential for both. Further, its magnitude and scale may carry the transformational potential for the structural order of the global economy. This is the essence of major crises—unexpected events of high magnitude redesign realities and reframe cognitive references, transforming the way people think about their social environments and behave in shaping them.

Covid-19 and Structural Violence

The emergence of the major security and economic threat in the form of pandemics, reinforced the need for renewed attention to structural violence. Global data provide evidence that the unprecedented public health crisis has exacerbated income inequality, the long-run distribution of resources, and inequality of opportunity on several dimensions (Stiglitz, 2020). Even in the wealthiest countries, Covid-19 disproportionately affects certain demographics; the limits of public health responses are visible in the experiences of poor and ethnic communities. In many aspects these circumstances can be directly related to Johan Galtung's observation about the structural elements in which the asymmetries and patterns of domination, present in social and economic relations are rooted. Galtung describes structural violence as 'avoidable impairment of fundamental human needs or…the impairment of human life, which lowers the actual degree to which someone is able to meet their needs below that which would otherwise be possible' (Galtung, 1993: 106). The concept was further elaborated in "Typologies of Violence" (1981), leading to the conclusion that both direct and structural violence undermine the need for bodily and psychological integrity, basic material needs and human rights. Economic exploitation and deprivation are frequently linked with sexism, racism, xenophobia and other forms of social pathology. All these circumstances, therefore, create "a broad rubric that includes a host of offenses against human dignity… ranging from racism to gender inequality…[to] extreme and relative poverty" (Farmer, 2005: 8).

The pandemic sheds new light on social and economic inequalities throughout the world, as the systems considered the most economically resilient—the United States and Western Europe—proved to be strongly harmed. The blows struck by the pandemic have not, however, operated as a great equalizer. The distribution of harm has been unequal, disproportionately affecting the most marginalized and vulnerable groups. As Public Health England's report confirms, "the impact of COVID-19 has replicated existing health inequalities and, in some cases, has increased them" (PHE, 2020: 4). Biocultural research also suggests that in most of the states where the data is gathered (mostly in the UK and the USA) inter-population variation in vulnerability to coronavirus isn't located in genes, but mostly in social and structural differences between groups (Bhala et al., 2020).

Health disparities, including inadequate access to healthy food, housing and financial insecurity, discrimination, and uncertain legal status have all played role in differentiating individual and group responses to the pandemic. These are rooted in historical, political, and social injustices which hamper effective prevention, detection, and treatment in outbreaks of communicable diseases (Devakumar et al., 2020).

The United States provides a striking example, as Covid-19 mortality rates are double the average in poor communities, and the impact of the pandemic has been considered equally defined by economic circumstances as by the biological characteristics of victims (Patterson & Clark, 2020). The US Centers for Disease Control and Prevention indicated that 33% of hospitalized patients in March 2020 were Black, compared to 18% in the general population (Garg, 2020). The moment of crisis amplified the consequences of existing health disparities. Black Americans are 1.5 times more likely to be underinsured or lack health insurance than Whites (Artiga et al., 2019), which has determined the timing and quality reactions to Covid-19: "In Los Angeles county low-income zip-codes have triple the Covid-19 mortality rates of wealthy ones" (Shamsher et al., 2020). In Louisiana, 70% of deaths have occurred among African Americans (Cabral, 2020). In Milwaukee County, 81% of the deaths from Covid-19 were among Black residents, despite their comprising only 26% of that county's population (Johnson & Buford, 2020).

The connection between the economic and public health consequences of the pandemic creates a vicious circle of disparity: the rising unemployment rate and the increasing number of individuals lacking health insurance coverage exacerbate the prevailing social breakdown, thereby exacerbating health inequalities. An additional burden has been imposed on vulnerable populations (including those in nursing facilities, prisons and the homeless) that already face barriers predisposing them to worse health and economic outcomes. The correlation between poverty and resilience to shock seems straightforward, indicating a further dynamic in the struggle to cope with Covid-19 and future risks.

The features of the job market make the members of certain groups more compelled to risk exposure to COVID-19 (Laster Pirtle, 2020), and social factors such as resource allocation, geographic location, and public-versus-private hospital systems have heavily influenced access to necessary supplies and COVID-19 testing. The circumstances of the pandemic, where protective measures have been linked to certain behaviours or access to the resources, have revealed the effects of the unequal distribution of these resources on health risks. Black and Latino individuals in the US are overrepresented in the low-paying jobs considered essential for the condition of the economy during lockdown (Laster Pirtle, 2020). Many of them can least afford to comply with stay-at-home or work-at-home mandates, as they depend on daily wages and losing one or two paychecks may lead them into homelessness. In the US only 9.2% of workers in the lowest quartile of wage distribution can telework, compared with 61.5% of workers in the highest quartile (Blow, 2020). Low-wage workers neither have the power or resources to change their high exposure jobs, nor demand workplace protections. In comparison, White workers in high-status, high-wage jobs (like physicians) and easy access to protective equipment have infection rates similar to the general public despite high levels of exposure (McClure et al., 2020).

Structural violence existed long before the emergence of Covid-19, but the psychological conditions of the pandemic—growing anxiety, fears connected to economic and health insecurity, and stress, have amplified its impact on social tensions, rising levels of xenophobia and racial proliferation. Many historical health crises have resulted in the stigmatization of certain ethnic and social groups, as mechanisms of fear and frustration associated with crisis produce cognitive bias. As a result, certain ethnic groups have faced accusations of spreading germs, as others have perceived them to be "dirty" or "sickly" (Taylor, 2019).

An FBI investigation of hate crimes against Asian and Asian-Americans reported an increase in anti-Asian hate crimes during the pandemic, due to the belief that people of Asian descent are solely responsible for causing it. The president's introduction of the terms of "Chinese virus" or "China virus" to the public debate reproduced existing patterns of anti-Asian violence and served as a legitimization of their manifestations (Chiu, 2020).

The extreme situation of the pandemic has not only revealed the scale of oppression mediated by political and information power centers, but also the pace of its reproduction in the aftermath of the significant socio-economic disruption it caused.

The historical context, cycles, systems, and structures exposed minority and under-privileged communities to disproportionate risk, undermining the effective pandemic response and leaving a permanent imprint on people's lives and livelihoods.

Covid-19 Implications for the Transition Towards Sustainability

The global medical emergency caused by Covid-19 has created a major challenge in maintaining the momentum of environmentally responsible practices and frameworks. The risks created by the pandemic triggered a radical response focused on saving lives and preserving livelihoods, thereby tackling the essence of sustainability logic. Although the concept of sustainability is problematic (Caprar & Neville, 2012; Faber et al., 2005), it unquestionably focuses on the natural limits to human survival. Sustainability emerges in the form of sustainable development, defined by the Brundtland World Commission in 1987 as "development that meets the needs of the present without compromising the ability of future generations to meet their own needs" (Brundtland Report, 1987: 43). The seminal Club of Rome report "Limits to Growth" defines sustainability as a "condition of ecological and economic stability that is sustainable far into the future" (Meadows, 1972: 24, 158).

Sustainability, especially in the context of development, is inextricably linked to the postulate of strengthening both social equity and economic growth in the way human societies are organized. The conceptual underpinnings of sustainable development have been clearly linked to economic optimization in the reality of scarce natural resources. In effect, the sustainability-peace nexus cannot be analysed without taking into account the effects on a society's welfare spread through a number of transmission channels, which have recently been modified by the pandemic.

Covid-19 has directly influenced the economic conditions of societies for years to come and may lead to a redefinition of policies related to sustainable growth. The scale of the pandemic's consequences has transformed not only markets, but also the hierarchies of social needs, the definition of safety, and the financial policies of states. It is symptomatic that the pandemic crisis has been called a sustainability crisis, and a direct resemblance between Covid-19 and climate change has been recognized by many authors (Hepburn et al., 2020; Klenert et al., 2020; Manzanedo & Manning, 2020). Both phenomena cause unprecedented, large-scale changes around the world, becoming directly translated into security and economic terms.

"The climate emergency is like the COVID-19 emergency, just in slow motion and much graver. Both involve market failures, externalities, international cooperation, complex science, questions of system resilience, political leadership, and action that hinges on public support." (Hepburn et al., 2020).

There are two kinds of possible strategies that may be derived from the resemblance and collaterality between these two crises, bearing fundamental consequences for the sustainable development in the years to come. On the one hand, post-pandemic trauma may reinforce discourses and policies in favor of the sustainable models of growth that address climate change and environmental concerns (EC, 2020). On the other, the momentum could be just temporary, as the global system faces a difficult path to recovery and on the way economic effectiveness may gain priority over environmental sustainability. The emergency track may either negatively influence the prospect of investing substantial resources in environmental policies, or raise the profile of sustainability concerns in the hierarchies of social needs and political agendas.

There are some strong voices in the debate, arguing that the pandemic marked a turning point in sustainability performance. CO_2 emissions have fallen sharply due to the shut-down of economic activities, while the trend in recent years has been towards rising emissions, as growth in energy-use from fossil fuel sources outpaced the rise of low-carbon sources and activities, especially in developing countries (Peters et al., 2020). The various containment measures and mobility restrictions created unique circumstances for a large-scale socio-environmental experiment, providing data unquestionably demonstrating the unsustainability of the dominant economic model.

Therefore, the introduction of economic recovery efforts has been widely seen as an opportunity to enhance key societal objectives, connected to the transition towards sustainability, understood as a way of improving the structural resilience of the current economic model. The socio-economic experiment of guiding the world through the pandemic can be useful in projecting more sustainable solutions, as emergency preparedness and sustainability strategies share similarities in terms of modelling human behavior and systemic changes in economic scenarios.

The Covid-19 outbreak also brought with it more securitization of climate policies, as cognitive frames of the notions of prosperity and well-being have been renegotiated, making sustainability issues more prominent. If security is "defined by actors who respond to cultural factors" (Katzenstien, 1996), the pandemic has definitely been perceived as a grave global security threat, causing chaos, conflict and a destabilization of the global order. It could therefore become a turning point in the sustainability transition triggered by passing a critical threshold that tips the current socio-economic system out of this stability domain (Rockström et al., 2009).

Such a scenario, originating in Joseph Schumpeter's notion of 'creative destruction' (1942), sees the crisis as an opportunity to destroy over-accumulated and inefficient capital, by reducing overcapacity and creating openings for new market players. The scale and reach of the crisis present an opportunity for reducing structural deficiencies by introducing more sustainable patterns of economic activity and redesigning current market relations. 'Green technologies', the priorities of the European Green Deal, structural leverages for private investments in smart electricity grids or electric car charging infrastructure can become a new engine of capitalist growth (Bina, 2013).

The logic of this process assumes that the accumulation of new ideas, technologies and concepts will increase to reach the point of overcoming 'the green growth

paradox', occurring when the effects of emissions reduction are not a direct consequence of renewable energy expansion, but are connected to a reduction in aggregate
demand and production due to increased unemployment (D'Alessandro et al., 2020).

A 'creative destruction' scenario for a global post-Covid-19 economy seems
tangible, given the scale of the harm experienced by societies due to lack of structural
resilience, as well as the amount of investment dedicated to the economic recovery.
Such a prospect is not, however, directly embedded in the policies guiding the stimulus investments, which in May 2020 accounted for about US 7 trillion in spending
for the G20 economies (Segal & Gerstel, 2020). It has been estimated that 4% of the
policies guiding these investments have the potential to support the development of
the green economy, but the beneficial effect is likely to be balanced by the equivalent
of 4% of policies likely to cause further climate disruption (Hepburn et al., 2020:
6). Estimates from climate change researchers suggest that the US package does not
include any direct green or climate commitments, except for USD 900 million for the
Low Income Home Energy Assistance Program (LIHEAP) (Smith, 2020). Furthermore, the UN Department of Economic and Social Affairs (2020) expects that the
pandemic is likely to undermine efforts to achieve the 2030 Sustainable Development
Goals, with highly differentiated impacts on lower-income countries.

On this basis, it does not seem that the shock of the pandemic will contribute to
establishing the models of development that could increase structural resilience. As
the scale of global threats concerning the peace/sustainability nexus expanded due
to pandemic 'transition turbulence', economic unsustainability is likely to manifest
itself in increased vulnerability to future risks (Burke et al., 2020).

Conclusion

This chapter has aimed to investigate the impact of the pandemic on approaches
to the complexities of the transition to sustainability. Empirical data on the structural conditions of the global economic order, and interlinkages between structural
violence and sustainability principles have been presented. The Covid-19 pandemic
crisis was seen as having introduced major turbulence into the introduction of sustainability standards, as well as representing a possible turning point in approaches to
social and economic design. Increased recognition of the importance of the systematic consideration of the complex adaptive nature of social systems has been built
here, especially in relation to two areas of analysis:

- Conceptualization of sustainability in policies and social practices: the coronavirus pandemic has influenced economic relationships and preferences, altering
  the way people think about social and economic relations. The scale of the
  pandemic's consequences further undermined the established economic model,
  so economic growth per capita cannot be linked automatically with human well-
  being and social cohesion. The usual, immediate gains in economic welfare are
  increasingly seen as directly derived from actions that generate environmental

and social harms, weakening the resilience of the system. The focus in sustainability practices may shift from the trade-off between climate damages and lost opportunities for consumption to the ability of human systems to anticipate, cope, and adapt.

- The role of structural violence in social design: analysis of the Covid-19 pandemic in the context of the notion of structural violence provides an overview of the weaknesses of the economic system that limit states' and people's ability to protect themselves against the major disruption. The pandemic itself does not fit into Galtung's original definition of violence, as it bears the features of a random accident and could not have been be prevented by infrastructural improvements or better standards of nutrition. Rich and poor states have been equally hit by the disease. The consequences of the crisis, however, appear to be differentiated and dependent on socio-economic structures and the ways in which societies are organized. Structural conditions rooted in the long-term accumulation of socioeconomic advantage and disadvantage along the lines of race, class, and other factors determine the unequal impact of COVID-19 on people's health, ability to protect themselves from infection, and economic wellbeing.

A crisis of this scale, revealing profound, longstanding vulnerabilities in the global system, can play a role of a 'focusing event', rescheduling conceptual frameworks and widening a policy window. Its repercussions have touched citizens of the developed and developing world alike, creating a unique situation in which a common goal can be recognized. It has become apparent that material abundance does not have equal protection and structural resilience, so the rich, Western world must more intensively implement positive peace-building measures strengthening social relationships within the framework of more just and equal models of society. The pursuit of the new sustainable economy and sustainable human development leads through efforts to manage and resolve conflict—between different groups competing over resources, and between clashing ideologies, values and interests. The essence of the ongoing transformation lies not only in arguments about the need to adjust the existing economic practices so as to reflect higher environmental standards, but more in a redefinition of the logic of growth and ability to implement these new principles in very diverse social landscapes.

The pandemic has been a dramatic 'signifier of sustainability threat', having arisen as a consequence of the neglect of the issues of environmental and social justice in the shaping of the economic realm. But if the transformation towards greater resilience is insufficiently decisive, this multilayered shock may not be absorbed by too-fragile systems. The latter scenario allows mechanisms of power imbalances that perpetuate structural violence and unequal experiences of citizenship, as in the process of Covid-19 crisis management "the insight and resources are channeled away from constructive efforts to bring the actual closer to the potential" (Galtung, 1969: 169).

Funding The research leading to these results received funding from Jagiellonian University, Future Society POB.

Conflicts of Interest The author has no financial or proprietary interests in any material discussed in this article.

References

Adger, W. N. (2000). Social and ecological resilience: Are they related? *Progress in Human Geography, 24,* 347–364.

Artiga, S., Orgera, K., & Damico, A. (2019). Kaiser Family Foundation, Issue Brief Changes in Health Coverage by Race and Ethnicity since Implementation of the ACA, 2013–2017. Retrieved January 12, 2020, from https://www.kff.org/racial-equity-and-health-policy/issue-brief/changes-in-health-coverage-by-race-and-ethnicity-since-the-aca-2010-2018/.

Baker, S. R., Bloom, N., Davis, S. J., & Terry, S. J. (2020). COVID-induced economic uncertainty (No. 26983). National Bureau of Economic Research.

Bennett, N., & Lemoine, G. J. (2014). What a difference a word makes: Understanding threats to performance in a VUCA world. *Business Horizons, 57*(3), 311–317.

Bhala, N., Curry, G., Martineau, A. R., Agyeman, C., & Bhopal, R. (2020). Sharpening the global focus on ethnicity and race in the time of COVID-19. *The Lancet, 395.* Retrieved March 03, 2021, from https://www.thelancet.com/journals/lancet/article/PIIS0140-6736(20)31102-8/abstract.

Bina, O. (2013). The green economy and sustainable development: An uneasy balance? *Environment and Planning c: Government and Policy, 31*(6), 1023–1047.

Blow, C. (2020). Social distancing is a privilege. *The New York Times: Opinion.* Retrieved March 08, 2021, from https://www.nytimes.com/2020/04/05/opinion/coronavirus-social-distancing.html.

Brown, K. (2015). *Resilience, development and global change.* Routledge.

Brundtland, G. (1987). Report of The World Commission on Environment and Development: Our Common Future. Retrieved January 22, 2020, from http://www.un-documents.net/our-common-future.pdf.

Burke, J., Fankhauser, S., & Bowen, A. (2020). Pricing carbon during the economic recovery from the COVID-19 Pandemic. Grantham Research Institute on Climate Change and the Environment Policy Brief.

Cabral, J., & Cuevas, A. G. (2020). Health inequities among latinos/hispanics: Documentation status as a determinant of health. *Journal of Racial Ethnic Health Disparities.* Retrieved February, 2021, from https://pubmed.ncbi.nlm.nih.gov/32026286/.

Carbon Brief. (2020). Analysis: The global coal fleet shrank for first time on record in 2020. Retrieved August 30, 2021 from https://www.carbonbrief.org/analysis-the-global-coal-fleet-shrank-for-first-time-on-record-in-2020.

Chiu, A. (2020). Trump has no qualms about calling the coronavirus the "Chinese Virus." That's a dangerous attitude, experts say. The Washington Post. Retrieved August 30, 2021 from https://www.washingtonpost.com/nation/2020/03/20/coronavirus-trump-chinese-virus/.

D'Alessandro, S., Cieplinski, A., Distefano, T., & Dittmer, K. (2020). Feasible alternatives to green growth. *Nature Sustainability, 3,* 329–335.

Devakumar, D., Shannon, G., Bhopal, S. S., & Abubakar, I. (2020). Racism and Discrimination in COVID-19 Responses. *Lancet, 395,* 1194–1194.

European Commission. (2020). Europe's Moment: Repair and Prepare for the Next Generation. Communication from The Commission to The European Parliament. COM (2020) 456 final. Retrieved February 02, 2021, from https://eur-lex.europa.eu/legal-content/EN/TXT/?uri=COM: 2020:456:FIN.

Faber, N., Jorna, R., & van Engelen, J. (2005). The sustainability of "sustainability": A study into the conceptual foundations of the notion of "sustainability." *Journal of Environmental Assessment Policy and Management, 7,* 1–33.

Farmer, P. (2005). *Pathologies of power: Health, human rights, and the new war on the poor.* University of California Press.

Folke, C., Carpenter, S. R., Walker, B., Scheffer, M., Chapin, T., & Rockstrom, J. (2010). Resilience thinking: Integrating resilience, adaptability and transformability. *Ecology and Society, 15*(4), 555–520.

Galtung, J. (1969). Violence, peace, and peace research. *Journal of Peace Research, 6*(3), 167–191.

Galtung, J. (1985). Twenty-five years of peace research: Ten challenges and some responses. *Journal of Peace Research 22*(2), 141–158.

Galtung, J. (1990). Cultural violence. *Journal of Peace Research, 560* 27(3), 291–305.

Galtung, J. (1993). Kultuerlle Gewalt. *Der Burger Im Staat, 43,* 106.

Garg, S. (2020). Hospitalization rates and characteristics of patients hospitalized with laboratory confirmed coronavirus disease 2019—COVID-NET, 14 States", March 1–30, 2020, MMWR. *Morbidity and Mortality Weekly Report, 2020*(69), 458–464.

Gössling, S., Scott, D., & Hall, M. C. (2020). Pandemics, tourism and global change: A rapid assessment of COVID-19. *Journal of Sustainable Tourism.* Advance online publication. https://doi.org/10.1080/09669582.2020.1758708.

Hepburn, C., O'Callaghan, B., Stern, N., Stiglitz, J., & Zenghelis, D. (2020). Will COVID-19 fiscal recovery packages accelerate or retard progress on climate change? *Oxford Review of Economic Policy, 36*(S1).

IEA. (2019). CO_2 Emissions Statistics. Retrieved February 06, 2021, from https://www.iea.org/articles/global-co2-emissions-in-2019.

ILO. (2020). ILO monitor 2nd edition: COVID-19 and the world of work. *International Labour Organization.*

IMF. (2020). Global Financial Stability Report (April 2020), 118. Retrieved February 06, 2021, from https://www.imf.org/en/Publications/GFSR/Issues/2020/04/14/global-financial-stability-report-april-2020.

Jayaram, K., Leke, A., Ooko-Ombaka, A., & Sun, Y. S. (2020). Finding Africa's path: Shaping bold solutions to save lives and livelihoods in the COVID-19 Crisis. McKinsey Institute.

Johnson, A., & Buford, T. (2020). Early data shows African Americans have contracted and died of coronavirus at an alarming rate. Retrieved February 12, 2021, from https://www.propublica.org/article/early-data-shows-african-americans-have-contracted-and-died-of-coronavirus-at-an-alarming-rate.

Katzenstein, P. J. (1996). Introduction: Alternative perspectives on national security. In P. J. Katzenstein (Ed.), *The culture of national security: Norms and identity in world politics* (pp. 1–32). Columbia University Press.

Klenert, D., Funke, F., Mattauch, L., & O'Callaghan, B. (2020). Five Lessons from COVID-19 for advancing climate change mitigation. *Environmental and Resource Economics, 76,* 751–778.

Laster Pirtle, W. N. (2020). Racial capitalism: A fundamental cause of novel coronavirus (COVID-19) pandemic inequities in the United States. *Health Education Behaviour, 47*(4), 504–508.

Lovejoy, T. E. (2005). Conservation with a changing climate. In T. E. Lovejoy & L. Hannah (Eds.), *Climate change and biodiversity* (pp. 325–328). Yale University Press.

Manzanedo, R. D., & Manning, P. (2020). COVID-19: Lessons for the climate change emergency. *The Science of the Total Environment, 742,* 140563. Advance online publication. https://doi.org/10.1016/j.scitotenv.2020.140563.

McClure, E. S., Vasudevan, P., Bailey, Z., Patel, S., & Robinson, W. R. (2020). Racial capitalism within public health—How occupational settings drive COVID-19 disparities. *American Journal of Epidemiology, 189*(11), 1244–1253.

Meadows, D. H. (1972). *The limits to growth: A report of the club of rome's project on the predicament of mankind.* Universe Books.

Moyer, J. S., & Hedden, S. (2020). Are we on the right path to achieve the sustainable development goals. *World Development, 127,* 1047–1049.

National Intelligence Council (NIC). (2012). *Global trends 2030: Alternative worlds.* United States National Intelligence Council.

Organization for Economic Cooperation and Development (OECD). (2020). *Consumer confidence index*, Organization for Economic Cooperation and Development (OECD).

Pak, A., Adegboye, O. A., Adekunle, A. I., Rahman, K. M., McBryde, E. S., & Eisen, D. P. (2020). Economic consequences of the COVID-19 outbreak: The need for epidemic preparedness. Frontiers. *Public Health 8*, 241.

Pangestu, M. E. (2020). Hunger amid plenty: How to reduce the impact of COVID-19 on the world's most vulnerable people. Retrieved March 03, 2021, from https://blogs.worldbank.org/voices/hunger-amid-plenty-how-reduce-impact-covid-19-worlds-most-vulnerable-people.

Patterson, A., & Clark, M. A. (2020). COVID-19 and power in global health. *International Journal of Health and Policy Management, 9*(10), 429–431.

Peters, G. P., Andrew, R. M., Canadell, J. G., Friedlingstein, P., Jackson, R. B., & Korsbakken, J. I. (2020). Carbon dioxide emissions continue to grow amidst slowly emerging climate policies. *Nature Climate Change, 10*(2), 10.

Peterson, O., & Thankom, A. (2020). Spillover of COVID-19: Impact on the Global Economy. Retrieved August 30, 2021 from https://www.researchgate.net/publication/340236487.

Public Health England (PHE). (2020). Disparities in the Risk and Outcomes of COVID-19. PHE Report June 2020.

Qureshi, Z. (2020). *Inequality in the digital era in work in the age of data*. BBVA.

Rockström, J., Steffen, W., Noone, K., Persson, Å., Chapin, F. S., III., Lambin, E. F., Lenton, T. M., Scheffer, M., Folke, C., Schellnhuber, H. J., Nykvist, B., de Wit, C. A., Hughes, T., van der Leeuw, S., Rodhe, H., Sörlin, S., Snyder, P. K., Costanza, R., Svedin, U., … Foley, J. A. (2009). A safe operating space for humanity. *Nature, 461*, 472–475.

Rose, N. L. (2020). Will competition be another COVID-19 casualty? The Hamilton Project, Brookings.

Schumpeter, J. A. (1942). *Capitalism, socialism, and democracy*. Harper.

Segal, S., & Gerstel, D. (2020). Breaking down the G20 Covid-19 fiscal response: May 2020 Update, CSIS. Retrieved March 03, 2021, from https://www.csis.org/analysis/breaking-down-g20-covid-19-fiscal635 response-may-2020-update.

Shambach, C. S. A. (2004). Strategic leadership primer. United States Army War College, Department of Command, Leadership, and Management.

Shamsher, S., Schneberk, T., Hsieh, D., & Bourgois, P. (2020). Interpersonal and structural violence in the wake of COVID-19. *American Journal of Public Health, 11*(11), 1659–1661.

Smith, D. C. (2020). 'Green responses' to COVID-19: Europe and the United States diverge yet again. *Journal of Energy and Natural Resources Law, 3*(38), 209–212.

Stiglitz, J. (2020). Conquering the great divide. *IMF Finance & Development, 57*(3), 17–19.

Taleb, N. N. (2007). *The black swan: The impact of the highly improbable*. Random House.

Taylor, S. (2019). *The psychology of pandemics: Preparing for the next global outbreak of infectious disease*. Cambridge Scholars Publishing.

United Nations. (2015). *Transforming our world: the 2030 agenda for sustainable development*.

Walker, J., & Cooper, M. (2011). Genealogies of resilience: From systems ecology to the political economy of crisis adaptation. *Security Dialogue, 42*, 143–160.

WHO. (2020). Coronavirus disease (COVID-19) situation reports. Retrieved March 03, 2021, from https://www.who.int/emergencies/diseases/novel-coronavirus-2019/situation-reports.

World Bank. (2012). People, pathogens and our planet. *The Economics of One Health*. World Bank.

Małgorzata Zachara-Szymańska Ph.D. is an associate professor at the Faculty of International and Political Studies, Jagiellonian University in Poland, working on social change, environmental sustainability, governance of global processes, and political leadership, with emphasis on individual empowerment.

Chapter 12
Conclusion

Elena V. Shabliy

Abstract The question of justice is central to many disciplines. First and foremost, it is an important philosophical question that was addressed and discussed by major philosophers and thinkers. Justice is one of the main problems in jurisprudence as well; recent global energy law development addresses the issues of (in)justice. Environmental justice, for example, focuses on important ideas of *procedural* justice, *distributive* justice, *restorative* justice, *corrective* justice, *inter-generational* justice, *social* justice, and last but not least—*recognition* justice. Energy justice and policy advancements are closely interrelated; the COVID-19 crisis, however, may have an impact in the realization of policy-making process in the nearest future. The Biden-Harris Administration Administration issued Executive Orders to address both— the pandemics and environmental crisis. This book offers global insights in the policy development and advancement in the developed and developing economies. It also focuses on such issues as international environmental justice and global energy justice. Most country parties acknowledge the importance and urgency of climate change mitigation and adaptation. The U.S. agenda is to concentrate on environmental justice. The Unites States joined the Agreement in 2016 and withdrew four years later. The United States officially rejoined the Paris Agreement in 2021, following a sustainable climate pathway and supporting international environmental systems. When we change environmental system, it has a significant impact on global health outcomes. Sea level rise, global rising temperature, extreme floods and droughts have a direct impact on our health dimensions and various Earth systems. Environmental allergies, nutritional diseases, cardiovascular diseases, newborn outcomes are those few health issues that may be caused by climatic changes.

This volume presents a critical assessment of climate change mitigation and adaptation strategies across various regions. It scrutinizes the concept of international environmental justice that is central to this book. Climate change constitutes the tragedy

E. V. Shabliy (✉)
Cambridge, USA
e-mail: shabliy@fas.harvard.edu

of the commons problem and affects the existing biosphere. We may acknowledge or disagree with the tragedy of the commons ideas; however, the problem of changing climate is persisting, and it is already visible globally. Garret Hardin stresses out that the population is growing exponentially; the tragedy of the commons, as Hardin explains, reappears in problems of pollution.[1] He convincingly argues: "… the air and waters surrounding us cannot readily be fenced, and so the tragedy of the commons as a cesspool must be prevented by different means, by coercive laws or taxing devices that make it cheaper for the polluters to treat his pollutants than to discharge them untreated."[2] Climate change causes mass population migration; in Bangladesh, for example, the sea rising level causes community displacement; limited access to clean water in the area may also add to this problem.

There is evidence that our planet is getting warmer: "2020 was one of the hottest years in recorded history."[3] Keeping temperature rise well below 2 degrees Celsius is one of the most important goals that was featured by the Paris Agreement and put in the epicenter of the discussion. This volume demonstrates that there are significant climate change mitigation and adaptation policy advancements. However, GHG emissions are growing globally: "The evidence from hundreds of new mitigation scenarios suggests that stabilizing temperature increase within the twenty-first century requires a fundamental departure from business-as-usual."[4] It is important to note that fossil fuel air pollution causes millions of deaths[5] (Fig. 12.1).

The question of justice is central to many disciplines; first and foremost, it is a fundamental philosophical question that was addressed and discussed by major philosophers and thinkers. Justice is also one of the main problems in jurisprudence; recent global energy law development addresses the issues of (in)justice. Environmental justice, for example, focuses on important ideas of *procedural* justice, *distributive* justice, *restorative* justice, *corrective* justice, *inter-generational* justice, *social* justice, *performative* justice, and last but not least—*recognition* justice.[7] Energy justice and policy advancements are closely interrelated; the COVID-19 crisis, however, may have an impact on the realization of the policy-making process in the nearest future.

---

[1] Garret Hardin, "The Tragedy of Commons," *Science*, Dec. 13, Volume 162, No. 3859, 1968, 1245.

[2] Ibid.

[3] "NASA Says 2020 Tied for Hottest Year on Record," https://www.scientificamerican.com/art icle/2020-will-rival-2016-for-hottest-year-on-record/#:~:text=The%20results%20are%20finally% 20in,in%20the%20number%2Dtwo%20spot. *Scientific American.* Last accessed 5/19/2021.

[4] Climate Change 2014 Mitigation of Climate Change, Intergovernmental Panel on Climate Change, https://www.ipcc.ch/site/assets/uploads/2018/02/ipcc_wg3_ar5_full.pdf, vii. (last accessed 5/19/2021).

[5] "Fossil Fuel Air Pollution Responsible for 1 in 5 Deaths," https://www.hsph.harvard.edu/c-cha nge/news/fossil-fuel-air-pollution-responsible-for-1-in-5-deaths-worldwide/#:~:text=New%20r esearch%20from%20Harvard%20University,meaning%20that%20air%20pollution%20 from (last accessed 5/24/2021).

[6] Temperatures are expected to rise in the future.

[7] .

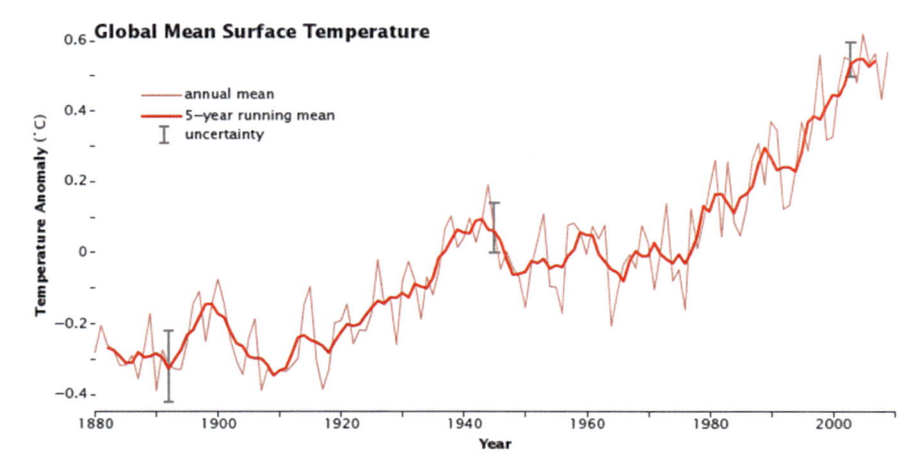

Fig. 12.1 Global mean surface temperature.[6] (*Source* https://earthobservatory.nasa.gov/features/ GlobalWarming/page2.php. NASA figure from Goddard Institute for Space Studies Surface Temperature Analysis)

The Biden-Harris Administration issued Executive Orders to address both—the pandemics and environmental crisis. Biden plans to secure environmental justice and equitable economic opportunity structure.[8] President Biden invited 40 world leaders to *Leaders Summit on Climate* that was held on April 22 and 23, 2021.[9] He signed the Executive Order to rejoin the Paris Agreement; the United States officially became a Party of the Paris Accord.[10] In Session 1— "Raising Our Climate Ambition"—all participating countries acknowledged the importance of the GHG emissions reduction: Japan is expected to cut emissions 46–50% below 2013 levels by 2030; Canada plans to reduce its NDCs (National Determined Contributions) to 40–45% by 2030; India plans to develop renewables by 2030 and launch the "U.S.-India 2030 Climate and Clean Energy Agenda 2030 Partnership;" Argentina aims to support renewable energy and end illegal deforestation in the country; the United Kingdom will advance climate change policy; the European Union will reduce net GHGs by at least 55% by 2030 and "a net zero target by 2050;"[11] the Republic of Korea is planning to combat climate change; China is planning to reduce the GHGs; Brazil plans to achieve net zero by 2050; Russia called for international collaboration

---

[8] "The Biden Plan to Secure Environmental Justice and Equitable Economic Opportunity," https:// joebiden.com/environmental-justice-plan/ (last accessed 5/19/2021).

[9] Ibid.

[10] The United States Officially Rejoins the Paris Agreement, https://www.state.gov/the-united-sta tes-officially-rejoins-the-paris-agreement/#:~:text=On%20January%2020%2C%20on%20his,unp recedented%20framework%20for%20global%20action. (last accessed 5/20/2021).

[11] "Raising our Climate Ambition," https://www.state.gov/leaders-summit-on-climate/day-1/ (5/20/2021).

to address powerful GHGs.[12] In Session—2 "Investing in Climate Solutions"—President Biden underlined the importance of developed countries to support developing countries; "[t]he participants also recognized the need for governments to embrace key policies, including meaningful carbon pricing, enhanced disclosure of climate-related risks, and phasing out fossil fuel subsidies."[13] The U.S. banks are committed to investing $4.16 trillion in climate-related issues over the next ten years.[14]

This book offers global insights into policy development and advancement in developed and developing economies. It also focuses on such important issues as international environmental justice and global energy justice. Most country parties acknowledge the importance and urgency of climate change mitigation and adaptation. The U.S. agenda is to concentrate on environmental justice. When we change the environmental system, it has a significant impact on global health outcomes. Sea level rise, global rising temperature, extreme floods, and droughts have a direct impact on our health dimensions and various Earth systems. Environmental allergies, nutritional diseases, cardiovascular diseases, newborn outcomes are those few health issues that may be caused by climatic changes. Rising temperatures may cause respiratory and heart-related diseases as well as brain function deterioration.

Futhermore, the Arctic is melting, and this alone will cause multiple problems, including health dimensions and sea-level rise. Rising temperatures are problematic since in some geographic areas people will not be able to survive. This volume opens with the discussion of climate change mitigation approaches within universities and a changing paradigm in the academic settings. Then, a discussion of environmental disasters once again proves the importance of the climate change dialogue. Further, the concept of international environmental justice is emphasized. Energy justice and energy equity are integral parts of the environmental justice movement. Income inequality negatively impacts climate change mitigation and adaptation strategies as well as the environment.

This volume also discusses the energy transformation in Canada. The book provides an international perspective on environmental and energy justice, public and social policy development worldwide—Africa, Turkey, the U.S., Canada, the Caribbean region, and Sri Lanka. Kenya, Ethiopia, Nigeria, to name a few—are especially experiencing climate change and its impacts on the environment and natural resources. Climate change is already having a ubiquitous impact, and it will remain one of the top challenges and priorities for humanity. Higher economic equality may increase renewable energy generation and consumption. The last chapter highlights the process of transformation towards sustainability; it presents a current pandemic crisis as a signifier for further global policy development and sees it as an opportunity.

---

[12] Ibid.

[13] Ibid.

[14] Ibid.

References

Climate Change 2014 Mitigation of Climate Change. (2021). Intergovernmental Panel on Climate Change, https://www.ipcc.ch/site/assets/uploads/2018/02/ipcc_wg3_ar5_full.pdf, vii. (last accessed 19 May 2021).

del Guayo, I., Godden, L., Zillman, D. D., Montoya, M. F., & González, J. J. (2020). *Energy justice and energy law*. Oxford University Press.

Fossil Fuel Air Pollution Responsible for 1 in 5 Deaths. (2021). https://www.hsph.harvard.edu/c-change/news/fossil-fuel-air-pollution-responsible-for-1-in-5-deaths-worldwide/#:~:text=New%20research%20from%20Harvard%20University,meaning%20that%20air%20pollution%20from (last accessed 24 May 2021).

Hardin, G. (1968, December 13). "The tragedy of commons." *Science, 162*(3859), 1243–1248.

NASA Says 2020 Tied for Hottest Year on Record. (2021). https://www.scientificamerican.com/article/2020-will-rival-2016-for-hottest-year-on-record/#:~:text=The%20results%20are%20finally%20in,in%20the%20number%2Dtwo%20spot. *Scientific American*. Last accessed 19 May 2021.

Raising our Climate Ambition. (2021). https://www.state.gov/leaders-summit-on-climate/day-1/ (20 May 2021).

The Biden Plan to Secure Environmental Justice and Equitable Economic Opportunity. (2021). https://joebiden.com/environmental-justice-plan/ (last accessed 19 May 2021).

The United States Officially Rejoins the Paris Agreement. (2021). https://www.state.gov/the-united-states-officially-rejoins-the-paris-agreement/#:~:text=On%20January%2020%2C%20on%20his,unprecedented%20framework%20for%20global%20action. (Accessed 20 May 2021).

Wang, X. (2019). "Reflections on the relationship of energy justice and environmental justice." *SSRN Electronic Journal*, SSRN Electronic Journal.

Elena V. Shabliy is a Visiting Scholar at Columbia University; she was a Visiting Scholar at Harvard University in 2015–2017, NYU in 2020, and Boston University in 2020–2021. She is the editor of *Representations of the Blessed Virgin Mary in World Literature and Art* (Lexington, Rowman and Littlefield, 2017) and co-editor of *Emancipation Women's Writing at Fin de Siècle* (Routledge, 2018), *Renewable Energy: International Perspectives* (Palgrave Macmillan, 2019), *Global Perspectives on Women's Leadership and Gender (In)Equality* (Palgrave Macmillan, 2020), *Discourses on Sustainability: Climate Change, Clean Energy, and Justice* (Palgrave Macmillan, 2020), and *Women's Human Rights in Nineteenth-Century Literature and Culture* (Lexington, Rowman and Littlefield, 2020). She studied at Lomonosov Moscow State University; in 2018, Dr. Shabliy was a Postdoctoral Fellow at Harvard University.